Fodor's

UTAH

WELCOME TO UTAH

From mountain-biking on slickrock to hiking past dinosaur fossils, Utah has thrilling adventures for everyone. The world-class ski resorts of the Wasatch Mountains are a haven for those seeking perfect powder, and national parks such as Arches and Zion offer colorful geology lessons with natural arches, hoodoos, and mesas in brilliant ocher and red. History lovers can ponder petroglyphs made by the earliest inhabitants or explore the Mormons' pioneer past in Salt Lake City. At the end of the day's activities, a hot tub and plush bed await.

TOP REASONS TO GO

★ **National Parks:** Spectacular Zion, Bryce Canyon, Arches, Capitol Reef, and Canyonlands.

★ **Outdoor Fun:** Rafting the Colorado River, fishing at Flaming Gorge, and more.

★ **Sundance:** The resort is an artist's dream, the indie film festival a must-do.

★ **Skiing:** Superb snow, varied runs, and swanky resorts like Deer Valley and Snowbird.

★ **Frontier History:** The Pony Express Trail, Wild West towns, and the Golden Spike.

★ **Salt Lake City:** Remarkable Temple Square, plus renowned museums and gorgeous vistas.

12
TOP EXPERIENCES
Utah offers terrific experiences that should be on every traveler's list. Here are Fodor's top picks for a memorable trip.

1 Winter Sports

The "greatest snow on Earth," plentiful sunshine, and beautiful panoramas make Utah a fabulous winter playground. Deer Valley Resort *(above)* in Park City draws crowds with its groomed ski trails for families as well as experts. *(Ch. 2, 3, 4)*

2 Scenic Drives

Mirror Lake Scenic Byway *(above)* through the Uinta Mountains is one of the state's unforgettable drives. Highway 12 is another stunner. *(Ch. 5, 6, 7, 8, 9, 10, 11)*

3 Bryce Canyon National Park

Drive the main park road for breathtaking views into the canyon. For a closer look, accessible hikes take you into the amphitheater to see limestone spires, called hoodoos. *(Ch. 8)*

4 Sundance

A ski resort and year-round artistic retreat, Sundance is best known for the annual independent film festival founded by Robert Redford and based in nearby Park City. *(Ch. 3)*

5 Dinosaur Tracking

Utah is a treasure chest of dinosaur remains. See tantalizing footprints at several museums, including the Natural History Museum of Utah *(above)* in Salt Lake City. *(Ch. 2, 5, 9, 12)*

6 Delicate Arch

Recognize this arch? Utah's calling card is this well-known rock formation in Arches National Park. Get up close on a moderate 3-mile hike and marvel at its scale. *(Ch. 10)*

7 Water Sports

Skiing grabs the headlines but fly fishing, boating, and river rafting, especially on the mighty Colorado River *(above)*, make this a year-round destination. *(Ch. 5, 12)*

8 Salt Lake City

At the foot of the Wasatch Mountains, Utah's capital has a stunning setting, Mormon culture, cosmopolitan dining, and easy access to outdoor activities. *(Ch. 2)*

9 Zion National Park

Angels Landing Trail *(below)*, with its exhilarating overlooks, and the Narrows Trail, set in a river between dramatic 2,000-foot cliffs, make Zion one of America's top parks. *(Ch. 7)*

10 Moab

This countercultural frontier town is a hub of artsy activity and a great base for Arches National Park. It's a must for biking, rock-climbing, and rafting as well. *(Ch. 12)*

11 Great Salt Lake

The best place to explore one of the earth's saltiest locales is Antelope Island, home to scores of bison *(above)* and a pit stop for migrating birds. *(Ch. 2)*

12 Two-wheeled Fun

Mountain-bike trails, such as the world-famous Slickrock Trail near Moab and the White Rim Trail *(above)*, are unparalleled. *(Ch. 5, 11, 12)*

CONTENTS

1 EXPERIENCE UTAH **13**
What's Where 14
Utah Planner 18
Utah Outdoor Adventures 19
If You Like 24
Great Itineraries 26
Utah with Kids 30

2 SALT LAKE CITY **31**
Orientation and Planning 34
Exploring 39
Sports and the Outdoors 49
Where to Eat 52
Where to Stay 60
Nightlife and Performing Arts 64
Shopping 67
Side Trips from Salt Lake City 69

**3 PARK CITY AND
THE SOUTHERN WASATCH** **81**
Orientation and Planning 82
Park City and the Wasatch Back . . . 86
South of Salt Lake City 108

4 NORTH OF SALT LAKE CITY . . **113**
Orientation and Planning 114
Ogden City and Valley 118
The Golden Spike Empire 127
Bear Lake Country 129

**5 DINOSAURLAND AND
EASTERN UTAH** **133**
Orientation and Planning 135
Northeast–Central Utah
(Castle Country) 137
The Uinta Basin 142

**6 CAPITOL REEF
NATIONAL PARK** **151**
Welcome To
Capitol Reef National Park 152
Exploring 158
Sports and the Outdoors 159
What's Nearby 162
Where to Eat 165
Where to Stay 166

7 ZION NATIONAL PARK **167**
Welcome To Zion National Park . . 168
Exploring 174
Sports and the Outdoors 176
What's Nearby 180
Where to Eat 181
Where to Stay 182

**8 BRYCE CANYON
NATIONAL PARK** **183**
Welcome To
Bryce Canyon National Park 184
Exploring 191
Sports and the Outdoors 193
Shopping 196
What's Nearby 197
Where to Eat 199
Where to Stay 201

9 SOUTHWESTERN UTAH **203**
Orientation and Planning 204
Utah's Dixie 208
Grand Staircase–
Escalante National Monument 220

10 ARCHES NATIONAL PARK . . . **225**
Welcome To
Arches National Park 226

CONTENTS

Exploring 233
Sports and the Outdoors 235
What's Nearby.................... 242
Where to Eat 244
Where to Stay 246

**11 CANYONLANDS
NATIONAL PARK 249**

Welcome To
Canyonlands National Park....... 250
Exploring 256
Sports and the Outdoors 258
What's Nearby.................... 266
Where to Stay 268

**12 MOAB AND
SOUTHEASTERN UTAH 269**

Orientation and Planning......... 270
Moab 273
Southeastern Utah............... 286

TRAVEL SMART UTAH 293

INDEX 305

ABOUT OUR WRITERS....... 312

MAPS

Exploring Salt Lake City........ 36–37
Downtown Salt Lake City.......... 42
Capitol Hill and the Avenues 44
East Side and
the University of Utah 46
Where to Eat and
Stay in Salt Lake City 56–57
Park City and
the Southern Wasatch............. 84
Park City and Environs............. 88
Park City.......................... 90
South of Salt Lake City 108
North of Salt Lake City 116
Northern Utah.................... 128
Dinosaurland and Eastern Utah... 138
Central Bryce Canyon 194
Southwestern Utah 206
Utah's Dixie...................... 209
St. George 216
U.S. 89 and
Grand Staircase–Escalante........ 220
Devils Garden Trail............... 240
Island in the Sky................. 262
Needles........................... 264
Moab and Southeastern Utah..... 272
Moab 275
Southeastern Utah............... 288

ABOUT THIS GUIDE

Fodor's Recommendations

Everything in this guide is worth doing—we don't cover what isn't—but exceptional sights, hotels, and restaurants are recognized with additional accolades. **Fodor's Choice★** indicates our top recommendations. Care to nominate a new place? Visit Fodors.com/contact-us.

Trip Costs

We list prices wherever possible to help you budget well. Hotel and restaurant price categories from $ to $$$$ are noted alongside each recommendation. For hotels, we include the lowest cost of a standard double room in high season. For restaurants, we cite the average price of a main course at dinner or, if dinner isn't served, at lunch. For attractions, we always list adult admission fees; discounts are usually available for children, students, and senior citizens.

Hotels

Our local writers vet every hotel to recommend the best overnights in each price category, from budget to expensive. Unless otherwise specified, you can expect private bath, phone, and TV in your room. For expanded hotel reviews visit Fodors.com.

Top Picks	Hotels &
★ **Fodor's**Choice	**Restaurants**
	🏨 Hotel
Listings	↘ Number of
✉ Address	rooms
✉ Branch address	¶◎¶ Meal plans
☎ Telephone	✕ Restaurant
🖷 Fax	⌐ Reservations
⊕ Website	🏛 Dress code
✍ E-mail	▭ No credit cards
✇ Admission fee	Ⓢ Price
☉ Open/closed	
times	**Other**
Ⓜ Subway	⇨ See also
✛ Directions or	☞ Take note
Map coordinates	🏌 Golf facilities

Restaurants

Unless we state otherwise, restaurants are open for lunch and dinner daily. We mention dress code only when there's a specific requirement and reservations only when they're essential or not accepted.

Credit Cards

The hotels and restaurants in this guide typically accept credit cards. If not, we'll say so.

EUGENE FODOR

Hungarian-born Eugene Fodor (1905–91) began his travel career as an interpreter on a French cruise ship. The experience inspired him to write *On the Continent* (1936), the first guidebook to receive annual updates and discuss a country's way of life as well as its sights. Fodor later joined the U.S. Army and worked for the OSS in World War II. After the war, he kept up his intelligence work while expanding his guidebook series. During the Cold War, many guides were written by fellow agents who understood the value of insider information. Today's guides continue Fodor's legacy by providing travelers with timely coverage, insider tips, and cultural context.

EXPERIENCE UTAH

WHAT'S WHERE

1 **Salt Lake City.** Though it is the home of the Mormon Church, Utah's capital city is surprisingly progressive, and an ideal launch pad for your Utah adventure. The region played host to the 2002 Winter Olympics, but has more to offer than religious and sporting sights. Don't miss the new museums, walkable downtown shopping at Gateway and City Creek, and an emerging dining scene.

2 **Park City and the Southern Wasatch.** Miners tunneled throughout the beautiful Wasatch Range to build the local economy, but modern-day prospectors look skyward to winter snow and summer sunshine to drive the economy in this primo spot. Three world-class resorts, historic Main Street, and the Sundance Film Festival are just a few reasons to escape to the mountains less than an hour from Salt Lake City Airport. The bucolic college town of Provo, home to America's "driest" university (Brigham Young University), lies at the other end of the excitement spectrum.

3 **North of Salt Lake City.** Much of northern Utah is within the boundaries of the Wasatch-Cache National Forest, with breathtaking landscapes, miles of trails, and the turquoise waters of

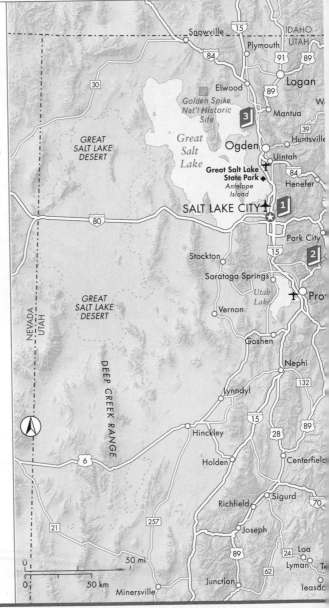

1

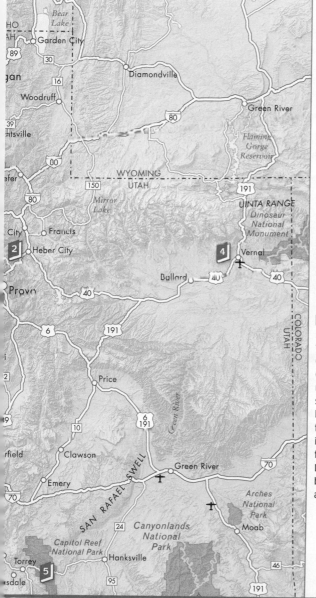

Bear Lake. Busy tourists invariably skip this region for the national parks in the south, so come here to escape crowds. Ogden and Logan offer services, restaurants, ski resorts, and universities.

4 **Dinosaurland and Eastern Utah.** Imagine high Western skies and an endless range, and you have a vision of eastern Utah. The Uinta Range of the Rocky Mountains is a land of craggy peaks and remote ranches, where fertile farms and grazing lands mingle with red-rock deserts. Mirror Lake, Flaming Gorge, and the Dinosaurland National Monument deliver entirely unique experiences.

5 **Capitol Reef National Park.** Formed by cataclysmic forces that have pushed and compressed the earth, this otherworldly landscape is marked by oversize, unique sandstone formations, some layered with plant and animal fossils. It is best known for its 100-mile long geological feature, the Waterpocket Fold. Loa, Teasdale, and Torrey have become hot spots for artists and wanderers.

WHAT'S WHERE

6 Zion National Park.
Known for its sheer 2,000-foot cliffs and river-carved canyons, Zion deserves to be on every Las Vegas and/or Grand Canyon agenda. There is no match for the soaring perspective on trails like Angels Landing and the Narrows, but you don't have to hike to see why the park is so special: the roadways leading through Zion provide ample viewing opportunities.

7 Bryce Canyon National Park. The bizarrely shaped, bright red-orange rocks that are this park's signature formation are known as hoodoos. If you can hit the trails at sunrise or sunset, your reward will be amazing colors; the sun's light at either end of the day intensifies the rocks' deep orange and crimson hues. See every vista in the park from the 18-mile Main Road, then retreat to the historic Lodge at Bryce Canyon for dinner or a ranger talk.

8 Southwestern Utah.
You can play golf year-round in the retirement community of St. George, but the region's best attractions are not man-made. Venture onto trails, view an active dinosaur excavation site, or lose yourself in the mostly road-free, expansive Grand Staircase–Escalante National Monument.

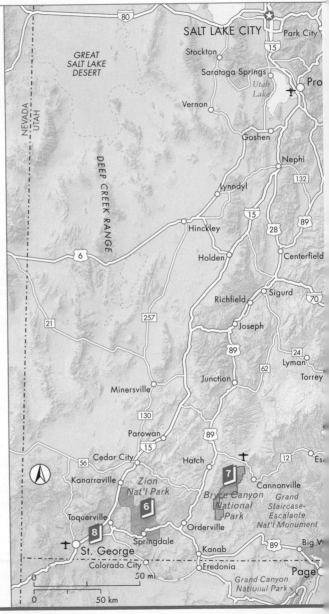

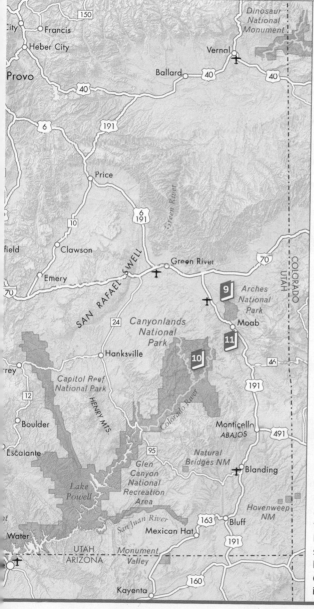

9 Arches National Park.
The largest collection of
natural sandstone arches in
the world—more than 2,000—
are within this park, but the
landscapes framed by the
graceful structures leave just
as lasting an impression. The
desert here is a rich tapestry
of red, purple, and chocolate
hues. Look carefully for hardy
wildlife and desert flowers—
true survivor tales under year-
round sunshine

**10 Canyonlands National
Park.** This might be the most
difficult park to truly fathom
without putting on your hiking
boots. Canyonlands is best
enjoyed on a hike, mountain
bike, or raft. You'll wish you
were a high-flying bald eagle
or red-tail hawk to appreciate the precipice of adjacent
Dead Horse Point and the
wishbone canyons carved by
the Colorado and Green rivers.

**11 Moab and Southeastern
Utah.** Home to the world-
famous Slick Rock mountain
bike trail—and some of America's best river rafting—Moab
is a countercultural retreat
with quirky and original
boutiques, restaurants, bars,
and locals. The perfect base
for Arches and Canyonlands
National Parks, this area's
sagebrush flats, slot canyons,
broad mesas, and snow-
capped peaks leave a lasting
impression.

UTAH PLANNER

When to Go

Home to both inhospitable desert and mountains renowned for their powdery snow, Utah is a breathtakingly bipolar state. You can bike, fish, and swim year-round in St. George, or ski from November to July 4 at Snowbird ski resort. Visit national parks in spring and fall to avoid millions of visitors, but be prepared for shoulder season rain or snow. Fall color can be found in nearly every canyon in the state. In July and August, secure lodging in advance as even RV parks and campgrounds fill to capacity.

DRIVING TIMES		
FROM–TO	MILES	HOURS
Las Vegas–St. George	120	2
Salt Lake City–St. George	300	4
St. George–Zion	40	1
Yellowstone–Salt Lake City	320	5
Salt Lake City–Moab	235	4
Las Vegas–Zion	160	2½
Zion–Bryce	85	1½
Canyonlands–Salt Lake City	240	4

Getting Around

Utah's pristine beauty requires a car, motorcycle, or RV for access. In summer, winding mountain roads and long dry basins are either a boon (convertibles, motorcycles) or bane (some roads were not built with RVs in mind). In winter, high elevations and serious storms make a sturdy car the best option. Storms occasionally shut down highway passes and/or resort access.

The only places in Utah where you can get around without a car are Salt Lake City and Park City. You can enjoy two world-class ski resorts in Park City (grab a taxi or shuttle from the airport and ride the town's public transportation), though it's harder to get to resorts like Alta, Snowbasin, or Snowbird.

The Predominant Religion

The population of Utah was estimated to be 3 million in 2016.

Mormons generally don't use or consume tobacco, caffeinated drinks, or liquor, but these products are widely available in stores. Members of the LDS faith generally observe Sunday as a day of rest, so many stores (including liquor stores), restaurants, and other services may be closed.

Mark Your Calendar

Utah has a few annual events that are worth planning your trip around.

■ **Sundance Film Festival** takes place annually over 11 days at the end of January (January 18–January 28, 2018).

■ Utah's **Pioneer Day** celebrations mark Brigham Young's arrival on July 24, 1847. Statewide, you will find fireworks, rodeos, parades, and fairs.

■ **Ski season** traditionally begins Thanksgiving week at many resorts. Plan to ski in late November, March, or April to avoid the biggest crowds. Prices spike and accommodations fill around major holidays like President's Day.

UTAH OUTDOOR ADVENTURES

BICYCLING

Utah's open roads are frequented by Tour de France stars, including locals Levi Leipheimer and David Zabriskie, and since 2010 the Larry H. Miller Tour of Utah has been one of America's premier multiday stage races. Add to that Moab's Slick Rock, Porcupine, and White Rim trails for mountain bikers, and Utah is one of the top destinations for cycling in the United States.

Rules of the Road

On the road, stay as close as possible to the right side, in single file. If you're nervous about cars, hop on the **Legacy Parkway Trail** near Salt Lake City Airport and ride 15 miles north on a perfectly flat, paved trail that skirts Great Salt Lake. If you're downstate, the rural roads outside St. George, Cedar City, and Moab offer miles of varied topography with relatively little traffic to affect the experience.

Best Rides

Antelope Island State Park. It's cheaper to enter Antelope on two wheels, and much more enjoyable, but only strong riders should brave the 7-mile causeway, especially in the heat of summer. Once you reach the island, however, there are miles of rolling and empty trails.

Bonneville Shoreline Trail. Partway up and along the Wasatch Front on the northeast side of Salt Lake City, this hiking and mountain biking trail offers expansive views of the entire Salt Lake Valley, plus points west and south. Its level of difficulty is easy to moderate, with challenging stretches near the University of Utah Hospital.

Flaming Gorge National Recreation Area. Because it mixes high-desert vegetation—blooming sage, rabbit brush, cactus, and wildflowers—and red-rock terrain with a cool climate, Flaming Gorge is an ideal destination for road and trail biking. The 3-mile round-trip Bear Canyon–Bootleg ride begins south of the dam off U.S. 191 at the Firefighters' Memorial Campground and runs west to an overlook of the reservoir.

Klondike Bluffs Trail. This trail offers the less-experienced mountain biker a relatively easy introduction to the sport. The climb to Klondike Bluffs is not difficult, and the reward is a fantastic view into Arches National Park. Access is off U.S. 191, 15 miles north of Moab—not the main park entrance.

Slickrock Trail. America's most famous mountain-biking trail is a 12-mile loop through sagebrush and sand, over slick granite rock and across undulations that can only be described as moonlike. It's well marked, popular, and incredibly challenging. Not recommended for kids under 12.

Wasatch Over Wasatch Trail. Known as the "W.o.W. Trail," this new single-track winds through Pine Canyon and definitely has the coveted wow-factor, with 12 miles of breathtaking views. Be prepared for a lot of climbing and a quick descent at the end. Expansion plans will connect the trail to the Park City-area trail system—almost 400 miles of trail and the first-ever trail system to be designated by the **International Mountain Biking Association** as a "Gold Level Ride Center."

FISHING

Here, blue-ribbon trout streams remain much as they were when Native American tribes, French fur trappers, and a few thousand miners, muleskinners, and sodbusters first placed a muddy footprint along their banks.

What to Bring

Bring or rent a rod and reel, waders, vest, hat, sunglasses, net, tackle, hemostats, and sunscreen. Always buy a fishing license.

When to Go

The season is always a concern when fishing. Spring run-offs can cloud the waters. Summer droughts may reduce stream flows. Fall weather can be unpredictable in the west.

Best Fishing

Flaming Gorge. For some of the finest river fishing, try the Green River below Flaming Gorge Dam, where rainbow and brown trout are plentiful and big. Fed by cold water from the bottom of the lake, this stretch has been identified as one of the best trout fisheries in the world.

Lake Powell. Formed by the construction of Glen Canyon Dam, this popular recreational attraction in southern Utah is home to a wide variety of fish, including bass—striped, smallmouth, and largemouth—as well as bluegill and channel catfish. Ask the locals about night fishing for stripers.

Provo River. One of Utah's world-class fly-fishing rivers, the Provo is divided into three sections, starting in the High Uintas Wilderness about 90 minutes east of Salt Lake City and ending in Utah Lake in Provo. Brown and rainbow trout are the big draw here.

HIKING

Don sturdy boots, pack water, lean on the hardworking park rangers for guidance, and head out for a few hours. Your heart, lungs, and soul will thank you. Trailheads depart from most cities, too, including worthy treks from downtown Salt Lake City, Ogden, Park City, and Moab.

Safety

Know your limits, and make sure the terrain you are about to embark on does not exceed your abilities. It's a good idea to check the elevation change on a trail before you set out, and be careful not to get caught on exposed trails at elevation during afternoon storms (rain or snow) any time of year. Dress appropriately, bringing layers to address changing weather conditions, and always carry enough water. Also, make sure someone knows where you're going and when to expect your return. Also be advised that much of rural Utah is a black hole for cellular coverage.

When to Go

Spring in Utah brings an explosion of wildflowers and color (Alta Ski Area and Mirror Lake are two destinations near Salt Lake City to walk in May or June). Fall brings a turning of cottonwood and cypress leaves that rivals autumn in the Shenandoah mountains. Summer's heat makes many desert locales unbearable, but the shade and breeze of Utah's canyons have offered respite for centuries. The hardiest outdoor types will even gear up in the dead of winter with snowshoes.

Best Hikes

Angels Landing Trail, Zion National Park. A 5-mile round-trip hike, with 1,500 feet of elevation gain, including a series of steps known as "Walter's Wiggles," this is the one trail in Zion no healthy hiker should miss. If you're afraid of heights, stop short at Scout's Lookout for the breathtaking view and head back down the trail.

Fiery Furnace Walk, Arches National Park. This two- to three-hour walk through narrow sandstone canyons is only offered via ranger-led tour (daily from mid-March to October). The landscape is an unforgettable, physically demanding maze, and the rangers illuminate the geologic history and reassure nervous hikers.

Grandeur Peak. For views of the Salt Lake Valley and Parley's Canyon, start at the trailhead at Church Fork Picnic Area in Mill Creek Canyon. This wide trail follows a stream and tops out at almost 8,300 feet. With quick and easy access from downtown, this 6-mile round-trip hike is a great way to get a bird's-eye view of the capital city.

Hickman Bridge Trail, Capitol Reef National Park. Just 2 miles long, this trail is a perfect introduction to Capitol Reef. You'll walk past a great natural bridge as well as Fremont culture ruins.

Mount Timpanogas. An hour-and-a-half southeast of Salt Lake City, "Timp" is one of the tallest and most striking of the Wasatch Mountains. Access to Timpanogas Cave is via a 3-mile round-trip hike led by park rangers daily in summer. Be aware that outside temperatures can reach triple digits, even at 6,700 feet—but inside the caves it's 45°F year-round.

The Narrows Trail, Zion National Park. Experience the thrill of walking in the Virgin River, peering up at millennia-old rock canyons, hanging gardens, and sandstone grottoes. To see the Narrows you must wade—and occasionally swim—upstream through chilly water and over uneven, slippery rocks, but the views are breathtaking.

HORSEBACK RIDING

Horseback-riding options in Utah run the gamut from hour-long rides on a well-worn trail to multiday excursions out into the wilderness. June through August is the peak period for horse-packing trips; before signing up with an outfitter, inquire about the skills they expect. ■ TIP→ Most horseback-riding outfitters have a weight limit of 250 pounds, and children must be at least seven years old.

Best Horseback Rides

Bryce Canyon National Park. Sign up for a guided tour at Ruby's Horseback Adventures near the park entrance. Let the animals do the work as you descend and emerge hundreds of feet into the Bryce Amphitheatre to see the unrivaled orange-pink spires and hoodoos.

Capitol Reef National Park. Much of this park is accessible only on foot or horseback, which promises an experience of wide-open Western spaces that hark back to the time of cowboys. Indeed, some of the trails may have been used by herdsmen and Native Americans. Sandstone, canyons, mesa, buttes—they're all here. Check at the visitor center for details of horseback-riding outfitters and opportunities for an unforgettable experience.

Zion Ponderosa Ranch Resort. Just east of Zion National Park at the site of a former pioneer logging camp, this multipursuit resort offers plenty of things to do after time spent in the saddle meandering along the multitude of pioneer-era trails. When you're not in the saddle you can drive an ATV, ride a zip line or mountain bike, or learn how to rappel and rock climb on the resort's 40-foot climbing wall. At the end of a long day, relax in a cabin, glamp in a deluxe tent, or hunker down in your own private covered wagon.

RAFTING

Dozens of tour companies throughout the West offer relatively tame floats—starting at around $70 for one day. Others cater more to thrill-seeking tourists.

How to Choose a Trip

Beginners and novices are encouraged to use guides, and many offer luxurious multiday trips in which they do everything, including searing your steak in a beach barbecue, setting up your tent, and rolling out your sleeping bag.

The International Scale of River Difficulty is a widely accepted rating system that ranges from Class I (the easiest) to Class VI (the most difficult—think Niagara Falls). When in doubt, ask your guide about the rating on your route before you book. Ratings can vary greatly throughout the season due to run-off and weather events. Midsummer is ideal for rafting in the West, although many outfitters will stretch the season, particularly on calmer routes.

Best River Runs

Cataract Canyon. It begins below Moab and takes three to five days as you wind your way to Lake Powell. Expect a smooth ride for the first day or two, before you dive into the rapids. This multiday adventure offers broad beaches, Native American ruins, deep-color canyon walls, and waves as high as 20 feet.

Colorado River, Moab. The Grand Poobah of river rafting in Utah. There are numerous outfitters in the Moab area with a wide assortment of half, full, and multiday trips on the river. Even though it is

the same river, it meanders in parts and rages in others.

Green River. Before it meets up with the Colorado River, the Green River offers plenty of stunning scenery and fast water through canyons such as Desolation and Gray. Desolation Canyon is a favorite family trip, with wildlife sightings, hikes, and beaches. Sign on with an outfitter in the town of Green River.

Weber River. You may see more kayakers than rafters on the Weber, but there are stretches that offer Class II rapids that are commercially run. For a one-day excursion, this is a great side trip from Salt Lake City or Park City.

Westwater Canyon. This short stretch of river can be negotiated in two to three hours, but with notable rapids like Funnel, Sock-it-to-me, and Skull Rapid, it's an action-packed ride.

SKIING AND SNOWBOARDING

Utah's "greatest snow on Earth" can be a revelation for skiers and snowboarders familiar only with the slopes of other regions. In Utah the snow builds up quickly, leaving a solid base at each resort that hangs tough all season, only to be layered with thick, fluffy powder that holds an edge, ready to be groomed into rippling corduroy or left in giddy stashes along the sides and through the trees. Off-piste skiing and half-pipe-studded terrain parks are the norm, not the special attractions, here. The added bonus of Utah terrain is that it has something for everyone, often within the same resort.

Best Slopes

Alta and Snowbird resorts. These Little Cottonwood Canyon neighbors, within 40 minutes of downtown Salt Lake City, are regularly ranked the top ski resorts in the United States. Seasons with 500 to 600 and more inches of Utah's famous powder are at the root of the accolades. A joint pass lets you ski both mountains on one ticket, but snowboarders are still not allowed at Alta. Snowbird has the longest season in the nation, occasionally staying open through July 4.

Brian Head Resort. The closest Utah ski resort to the Las Vegas airport, Brian Head is worth checking out for the novelty of skiing in southern Utah. The red-orange rocks of Cedar Breaks National Monument form a backdrop to many trails, which tend to focus on beginner and intermediate skiers and snowboarders. Experts can ski off the 11,000-foot summit.

Deer Valley and Park City resorts. The two Park City resorts are known for their great groomed trails, fine dining, and accommodations. Deer Valley is one of two resorts in America that doesn't allow snowboarders, but Park City Mountain Resort, which now encompasses Park City and the resort area formerly known as Canyons, caters to both skiers and riders. The skiing is excellent, but for many it's the whole experience—including the midday feast at Silver Lake Lodge and farm-to-table dining at The Farm—that keeps them coming back.

Snowbasin and Powder Mountain resorts. An hour north of Salt Lake City, Ogden-area residents will tell you the best skiing is at this pair of resorts. Powder Mountain has more skiable terrain than any resort in North America, and Snowbasin was good enough to host the Olympic downhill and slalom during the 2002 Winter Games. These two are often cheaper and less crowded than the Salt Lake City and Park City resorts.

Utah Olympic Park. At the site of the 2002 Olympic bobsled, luge, and ski-jumping events in Park City, you can take recreational ski-jumping lessons or strap in behind a professional driver for a bobsled ride down the actual Olympic course.

IF YOU LIKE

Dinosaur Fossils

The context of dinosaur skeletons in urban museums never quite fits, but when you see giant rib fossils protruding from the ground in central Utah, your lessons in Jurassic history will snap into focus.

Cleveland-Lloyd Dinosaur Quarry. On the way to Moab (via 30 miles of dirt road), lies a dense concentration of at least 46 allosaurus remains. It's a mystery to scientists why so many bones, but not intact skeletons, are clustered here.

Dinosaur National Monument. Near the Wyoming and Colorado borders, you will find an exposed hillside with 65-million-year-old fossils, plus hiking trails and campsites.

Natural History Museum of Utah. The stunning copper-clad exterior of this museum blends into the mountains east of Salt Lake City. Inside, find a massive gallery with more than 30 reconstructions of dinosaur skeletons. You can also watch paleontologists working on fossils in a glassed-in lab.

St. George Dinosaur Discovery Site at Johnson Farm. At the very southern end of the state, a local optometrist found dozens of dinosaur tracks in 2000 and turned his family farm into a museum.

Scenic Drives

Cowboy poets and country artists sing the praises of the wide-open spaces of the West, but Utah's size can create challenges for time-pressed visitors. Take these routes and the miles will fly by—except for all the times you'll want to stop to take photographs.

Highway 89. If you've had enough of Interstate 15, Highway 89 is a 502-mile scenic alternative from Bear Lake on the Idaho border to Glen Canyon on the Arizona line. Other bodies of water that are accessible from Highway 89 include Great Salt Lake and Utah Lake. Take Highway 89 not to save time, but to see historic sites like the Pony Express and Oregon trails, charming old downtowns, and Utah's agricultural heart including orchards, farms, and ranches.

Provo River Canyon. The gateway to Robert Redford's Sundance Resort, this drive from Provo to Park City parallels rushing rapids during snow melt and soothing gurgles the rest of the year. Parley's, Emigration, Big and Little Cottonwood, Mill Creek, Ogden, and Logan are seven other canyons from the Wasatch front equally worth driving. Because of their proximity to Utah's population base, all have trailheads, services, and restaurants.

Scenic Byway 12. Grand Staircase-Escalante covers 2 million acres of southern Utah, much of it linked to this All-American road between Torrey (Capitol Reef National Park) and Bryce Canyon National Park. Pause to see red rock, slickrock, canyons, forest, waterfalls, and an abundance of desert wildlife including deer, elk, and birds of prey.

Trail of the Ancients. The heart of country once home to the Anasazi people, Hovenweep, Natural Bridges, and Four Corners National Monuments are your landmarks in this most remote corner of southeast Utah. Expect very little traffic and burning heat as you pass miles and miles of rock formations, petroglyphs, and mountain ranges. Fill up on gas, water, and food when you can—services are spread pretty thin here.

Exceptional Eats

Predominantly Mormon Utah liberalized its liquor laws when it welcomed the world for the 2002 Winter Olympic

Games, and when restaurateurs realized they could profit, the dining scene exploded. Although many small towns offer little more than diners, with a little assistance you can find award-winning food and drink.

Canyon cuisine. Not every canyon has a great restaurant, but Emigration (Ruth's Diner), Mill Creek (Log Haven), Provo (Tree Room at Sundance Resort), and Big Cottonwood (Silver Fork Lodge) have outposts for a delicious meal before or after you hit a trailhead. All offer respite from the summer heat, but may close during big snowstorms in winter.

Park City. It figures that the wealthy playground of Park City would attract buzzworthy chefs, but this is much more than a ski town—it's also heaven on earth in the summer. Time your trip to hit the summer Savor the Summit, when more than 30 restaurants set up a mile-long table on Main Street (which isn't flat, by the way) or the Food and Wine Classic.

Rural kitchens. What is perhaps the most nationally recognized restaurant in Utah lies far from the state capital in red rock country. Hell's Backbone Grill & Farm in Boulder (population 220) was a semifinalist for a James Beard Award in 2017. The Southwestern cuisine features local, organic ingredients, many of which are grown on the restaurant's 6-acre farm.

Salt Lake City. Utah is now home to world-class chefs and mixologists. Table X and HSL earn high marks for their new American cuisine. You'll also find great restaurants from across the global spectrum, including Mexican (Red Iguana and Alamexo), Japanese (Takashi), Indian (Bombay House), Middle Eastern (Mazza), and Greek (Aristo's and Manoli's), and several microbreweries.

Small Towns

Leave behind the more densely populated Wasatch front and discover a plethora of small towns with Main Street diners, well-maintained museums, and plentiful parks.

Go North, Young Man. Logan is a post-card-quality college town in the gorgeous Cache Valley. Straddling the Idaho border, Bear Lake's waters are stunningly blue, and its raspberry milk shakes are famous across the state. East of Ogden in the Ogden Valley, the tiny pioneer town of Huntsville abuts a picturesque reservoir minutes from world-class skiing. Any of these lesser-known locales could serve as a peaceful basecamp for a great deal of outdoor adventure.

Highway Detours. On your way to the southern parks, don't miss the frontier capital of the Utah territory, Fillmore. Also on Interstate 15, Cedar City is home to Southern Utah University. St. George is a booming retirement community with golf courses, resorts, and shopping.

Mountain Hideaways. Park City's legacy as a silver mining town pervades an authentic, steep-sloped Main Street that would thrive even without the ski resorts and the Sundance Film Festival. Nearby communities Heber and Midway offer mountain-fed, trout-filled streams amidst ranches and farms.

National Park Gateways. Zion National Park's gateway town is Springdale, an artsy community with traditional bed-and-breakfasts, eateries, and the incomparable backdrop of the canyon. Moab fuels visitors to Arches and Canyonlands with granola and outfits them with gear shops galore, but it also offers arts and theater by a community of out-of-state transplants who never left.

GREAT ITINERARIES

UTAH'S FIVE GLORIOUS NATIONAL PARKS, 7 DAYS

It takes considerable gumption and resources to fly and drive from much of the United States to reach the iconic desert of southern Utah. This itinerary will help you see the highlights and navigate the considerable ground you'll cover by car and foot.

Days 1 and 2: Zion National Park
(3 hours from McCarran Airport in Las Vegas)

Start early from Las Vegas, and within three hours you'll be across the most barren stretches of desert and marveling at the bends in the Virgin River gorge. Just past St. George, Utah, on I–15, take the Route 9 exit to **Zion National Park.** Spend your afternoon in the park—if it's mid-March to mid-November, the National Park Service bus system does the driving for you on Zion Canyon Scenic Drive (in fact, when the bus is running, cars are not allowed to enter the canyon).

For a nice introductory walk, try the short and easy **Weeping Rock Trail.** Follow it along the **Emerald Pools Trail** in Zion Canyon itself, where you might come across wild turkeys and ravens. Before leaving the park, ask the rangers to decide which of Zion's two iconic hikes is right for you the next day—the 1,488-foot elevation gain to **Angel's Landing** or river wading along the improbably steep canyon called the **Narrows.** Overnight at **Zion Lodge** inside the park (book well in advance or call for last-minute cancellations), but venture into the bustling gateway town of **Springdale** for dinner and a peak into an art gallery or boutique. Try the **Switchback Grille** or **Bit & Spur** for tasty Southwestern food.

Start at dawn the next day to beat the crowds and heat if you're ascending Angel's Landing (allow three to four hours). If you're headed up the Narrows, you'll be walking in the river, so you might want to wait an extra hour or two for the sun. Either way, pack a lunch and take your time—there's no sense rushing one of the highlights of the U.S. National Park system. Work your way back to your hotel and set a date with your hot tub.

Day 3: Bryce Canyon National Park
(2 hours from Zion)

It's a long 85 miles from Zion to Bryce via Route 9 (the scenic Zion-Mount Carmel Highway), particularly as traffic must be escorted through a 1.1-mile-long tunnel. Canyon Overlook is a great stopping point, providing views of massive rock formations such as East and West Temples. When you emerge, you are in slickrock country, where huge petrified sandstone dunes have been etched by ancient waters. Stay on Route 9 for 23 miles and then turn north onto U.S. 89 and follow the signs to the entrance of **Bryce Canyon National Park.**

Unless you fall in love with the hoodoos, Bryce Canyon can be enjoyed in one day. Central to your tour is the 18-mile main park road, from which numerous scenic turnouts provide vistas of bright red-orange rock (we recommend starting with the view at **Sunrise Point**). You'll notice that the air is a little cooler here than it was at Zion, so get out and enjoy it. Trails most worth checking out include the **Bristlecone Loop Trail** and the **Navajo Loop Trail,** both of which you can easily fit into a day trip and will get you into the heart of the park. Listen for peregrine falcons deep in the side canyons, and keep an eye out for a species of prairie dog that only lives in

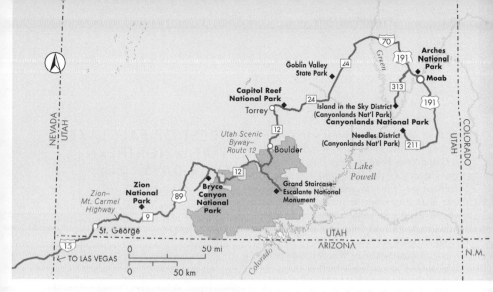

these parts. If you can't stay in the park (camping or the **Lodge at Bryce Canyon** are your options), overnight at **Ruby's Inn**, near the junction of Routes 12 and 63.

Day 4: Capitol Reef
(2½ hours from Bryce Canyon)

If you can, get up early to see sunrise paint Bryce's hoodoos, then head out on the spectacular Utah Scenic Byway–Route 12. If the views don't take your breath away, the narrow, winding road with little margin for error will. Route 12 winds over and through **Grand Staircase–Escalante National Monument**. The views from the narrow hogback are nothing short of incredible. Remember that Capitol Reef is your goal, but Calf Creek Recreation Area, Boulder, Torrey, and Fruita each offer opportunities to stretch your legs, take a walk, and find an off-the-beaten-path gem. Boulder's **Hell's Backbone Grill**, for example, may be the best remote restaurant you'll find in the West, and you don't want to bypass **Fruita's** petroglyphs and bountiful orchards in the late summer and fall.

At the intersection of Routes 12 and 24, turn east onto Route 24 toward **Capitol Reef National Park**. The crowds are smaller here than at other national parks in the state, and the scenery is stunning. Assuming

it's still daylight when you arrive, hike the 1-mile **Hickman Bridge Trail**, stop in at the visitor center, open until 4:30 (later in the summer), and view pioneer and Native American exhibits, talk with rangers about geography or geology, or watch a film. Nearby **Torrey** is your best bet for lodging, and be sure to eat at the seasonal **Cafe Diablo**, serving some of Utah's finest Southwestern cuisine from mid-April to mid-October.

Days 5–7: Moab, Arches, and Canyonlands National Parks
(2½ hours from Capitol Reef to Canyonlands)

Explore Capitol Reef more the next morning. An easy way to do this is to drive the 10-mile **Capitol Reef Scenic Drive**, which starts at the park Visitor Center. When you leave, travel east and north for 75 miles on Route 24. If you want a break after about an hour, stop at the small **Goblin Valley State Park**. Youngsters love to run around the sandstone formations known as "goblins." Continue on Route 24 to I-70 and turn east toward Colorado.

Take Exit 182 south onto U.S. 191, proceeding about 19 miles to Island in the Sky Road. Make sure you have water, food, and gas, as **Canyonlands National Park** offers no services, with the exception of water at The Needles visitor center year-round. Be sure to follow the drive out to **Grand View Point** to look down on the convergence of the Colorado and Green rivers. Along the way, **Mesa Arch** is a half-mile walk and offers a sneak preview of what to expect at Arches. More ambitious individuals should hike the mysterious crater at **Upheaval Dome,** which is a steeper 1-mile round-trip hike. Whether you plan to explore Canyonlands further the next day or move onto **Arches National Park,** backtrack to U.S. 191 and turn right for the final 12-mile drive into **Moab,** a good basecamp for both parks. Along the way, you'll pass the entrance to Arches, which holds the world's largest concentration of natural rock windows.

Build your Arches itinerary around hikes to **Delicate Arch** (best seen at sunrise to avoid the crowds) and **Landscape Arch.** The guided hike in the **Fiery Furnace,** a maze of sandstone canyons and fins, is considered one of the park's most spectacular hikes. Make a reservation for a ranger-led hike in advance if you can, or in person if the park service isn't accepting reservations.

Adventurous types, note that you can raft the Colorado River from Moab or bike the **Slickrock Trail.** Either is well worth a half-day or daylong excursion. Other options include exploring the **Needles District** of Canyonlands (about 90 minutes south), viewing petroglyphs on Route 279 (Potash Road), and driving along the Colorado River north of town to **Fisher Towers.**

You've now enjoyed five national parks and hundreds of miles of scenic drives in southern Utah. It's 4½ hours back to Salt Lake City or about two hours to Grand Junction, Colorado; if Las Vegas is your hub, it's a 6½-hour drive from Moab.

THE BEST OF SALT LAKE CITY AND NORTHERN UTAH, 4 DAYS

Day 1: Salt Lake City

Many people begin their explorations of northern Utah from the comfortable hospitality of downtown **Salt Lake City.** Grab the TRAX light rail (accessible from Terminal 1 at Salt Lake City Airport) to **Temple Square** and begin a walking tour of the city. The temple itself is off-limits unless you belong to the LDS Church, but its grounds and the rest of the complex make for interesting wandering. Immediately south is **City Creek Center,** the city's first upscale shopping district. To the west are **Gateway Mall** and the entertainment district, where you can have lunch on one of the outdoor plazas. The **Discovery Gateway** children's museum and **Clark Planetarium** are best bets here, as well as the **Olympic Legacy Plaza.** Complete your walk by crossing Pioneer Park, heading east through Gallivan Plaza (you may catch live music midday or evenings) as far as **Salt Lake City Main Library**—a modern architectural gem that includes a soaring roof that you can ascend for one of the best views of the city. **Salt Lake Roasting Co.,** in the library promenade, is a good place for a drink or snack. There's ample downtown lodging to choose from. Pamper yourself at the **Grand America Hotel** or ask for a goldfish for your room at **Kimpton Hotel Monaco.** Dining and drinking options are varied. Sample the microbrews from **Squatters Pub Brewery,** then fill up on America's best Mexican food at **Red Iguana** or check out **The Copper Onion** for Continental cuisine.

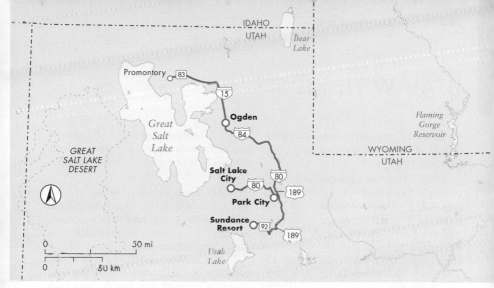

Days 2 and 3: Park City
(40 minute drive from Salt Lake City)

Salt Lake's majesty lies in the hills surrounding it, so tackle them today. **Park City** is 25 miles to the east along I–80 and you can easily spend the entire day wandering its historic Main Street, where the discovery of silver in 1868 led to a boom era of prospectors, mine workers, and schemers. You can still see in the storefronts that dozens of saloons and a red-light district once flourished here in defiance of the Mormon Church. The **Park City Museum** is the perfect place to discover the town's colorful history, and the **Park Silly Sunday Market** (June to September) portrays its modern-day fun side. For lunch or dinner, **Wasatch Brew Pub** is at the top of Main Street, and **Handle** and **High West Distillery** are just off Main on Heber Avenue and Park Avenue, respectively. You can't go wrong with any of them for a meal. If it's winter, hit the slopes; if it's summer hit the trails, where you might just encounter a moose. Either season, stop at **Utah Olympic Park** where you will often glimpse America's next gold-medal hopefuls training in any of a half-dozen disciplines including ski jumping, bobsled, or luge. If you have time and love roller coaster thrills, ride the bobsled course from top to bottom with a trained driver. Indulge in the spa, lounge, or restaurant at Deer Valley's **Stein Eriksen Lodge,** or opt for the equally refined (but no less expensive) **Waldorf Astoria Park City.** The **Newpark Resort** is a more affordable option near the outlet mall.

Day 4: Sundance Resort or Ogden
(45-minute drive from Park City to Sundance; or 1 hour 10 minute drive to Ogden)

You can easily spend several more days in Park City, but its environs are beckoning. There's fly-fishing and rafting on the Provo River, balloon rides, and hot springs. Robert Redford's **Sundance Resort** is a year-round destination for artists, filmmakers, and musicians—not just tourists and skiers. It's about 45 minutes south of Park City through the gorgeous Provo River canyon. Dine at the **Foundry Grill** or **Tree Room** and keep your eyes open for Mr. Redford. Railroad buffs may prefer to make the hour drive north to **Ogden,** where **Union Station** has welcomed trains on the transcontinental route since it opened in 1924. Historic 25th Street has a multitude of restaurants. From there, head west to **Promontory,** Utah, to see where the golden spike was hammered in to connect East and West in 1869.

UTAH WITH KIDS

Virtually no site, restaurant, or destination is off-limits to kids.

City Diversions

In and around **Salt Lake City,** start with two very kid-friendly museums in **Gateway Mall.** The **Discovery Gateway** children's museum has a Life Flight helicopter, pinewood derby racing, a story factory, a construction site, and much more—best suited to children under the age of 11. The **Clark Planetarium** opens kids' eyes to the universe and natural phenomena through its interactive exhibits and 3-D and IMAX theaters. The **Leonardo,** an inspirational museum combining science, art, and technology, is on its own a good reason to bring kids to Utah, and the **Natural History Museum of Utah, Red Butte Garden, Tracy Aviary,** and **Hogle Zoo** are also year-round destinations within the city limits—bundle up in the winter and have any one of them virtually to yourself. See bison in a natural setting on **Antelope Island** (if visiting in October, don't miss the annual bison roundup).

In **Ogden,** you can fly like a bird in the wind tunnel, learn to surf, or rock-climb indoors at the state-of-the-art **Salomon Center.** Young children will enjoy the models and playground at the **George S. Eccles Dinosaur Park.** Older kids can catch the Raptors who are, along with Salt Lake's Bees and Orem's Owlz, a fun, inexpensive, entertaining minor-league baseball team.

Natural Wonders

Utah's outdoor attractions provide plenty of outlets for kids' energies. Hikes offer larger-than-life rewards that can even lure kids away from their iPads. Each of Utah's five national parks has special youth-oriented programming and a **Junior Ranger program** that provides them with an interactive booklet of activities and tasks to complete so that they have fun while learning about environmental responsibility.

In **Arches,** hardy kids over the age of 6 can likely make the 3-mile round-trip hike to **Delicate Arch.** Make **Sand Arch** a destination for littler ones—it's right off the road and offers a massive "sandbox" of soft red sand. In **Zion** kids 10 and up can trek up the Virgin River toward the **Narrows.** At **Bryce** or Zion you can go **horseback riding** to places that might be tough for little legs.

There are **dinosaur excavation** sites near **Vernal, St. George,** and **Price.** Moonlit hikes and telescope tours are nighttime programs offered by park rangers at **Goblin Valley State Park. Moab** has kid-friendly bike trails, and you might find that your BMX-riding teen is more comfortable on the **Slickrock Trail** than you are.

Finally, if you have swimmers, great places to cool off in hot summers include **Lake Powell, Bear Lake,** and glacier-fed rivers and creeks that fill national forest land across the eastern half of the state. And floating in the buoyant waters of the **Great Salt Lake** should be on every kid's bucket list.

SALT LAKE CITY

Updated
by Kwynn
Gonzalez-Pons

Nestled at the foot of the rugged Wasatch Mountains and extending to the south shore of the Great Salt Lake, Salt Lake City is a small, navigable city at the heart of a metropolitan area with more than 1 million residents. The Salt Lake valley has something for everyone, offering striking landscapes and accessible outdoor adventures that lure residents and visitors alike. Canyon breezes turn hot summer afternoons into enjoyable evenings, and snowy winter days are moderated with temperatures warmer than those at most ski destinations, making Salt Lake City an ideal destination year-round.

Salt Lake City's history was built on the shoulders of its Mormon founders, but today its culture equally draws from more modern events and influences, such as hosting the 2002 Winter Olympics, and becoming the preeminent destination for technological or innovative pursuits, earning it the nickname "Silicon Slopes." The city has emerged as the economic and cultural center of the vast Great Basin, between the Rocky Mountains and California's Sierra Nevada.

Since Brigham Young led his first party of pioneers here in 1847, Salt Lake City has been synonymous with the Mormon Church, formally called the Church of Jesus Christ of Latter-day Saints (LDS).

The valley appealed to Young because, at the time, it was under the control of Mexico rather than the U.S. government, which the Mormons believe was responsible for much of their persecution.

Within days, Young drew up plans for Salt Lake City, which was to be the hub of the Mormons' promised land, a vast empire stretching from the Rockies to the Southern California coast. Although the area that eventually became the state of Utah was smaller than Young planned, Salt Lake City quickly outstripped his original vision. Missionaries throughout Scandinavia and the British Isles converted thousands, who flocked to the city to live near their church president—a living prophet, according to Mormon doctrine—and worship in the newly built temple.

In the 1860s, income from railroads and mines created a class of industrialists who built mansions near downtown and whose businesses brought thousands of workers—mainly from Europe and few of whom were Mormon—to Utah Territory. By the time Utah became a state in 1896, Salt Lake was a thriving city. Although the majority of the city was Mormon, it claimed a healthy mix of Protestant, Catholic, and Jewish citizens.

Today the city is an important center for business, medicine, education, and technology. The LDS Church's presence is still evident, as both its

2

TOP REASONS TO GO

Downtown: The Mormon Church is centered here in a beautifully landscaped four-square-block compound known as Temple Square, but downtown visitors will also enjoy the massive new commercial and shopping complex, City Creek, a walkable plaza that's home to restaurants, bars (yes, they have them here), theaters, and the Vivint Smart Home Arena. Bonus: attend Salt Lake City's Downtown Farmers Market every Saturday morning at Pioneer Park from June to October.

Wasatch Front Mountains: Trade in your heels or high-tops for hiking boots and enjoy the canyons, replete with winding rivers and breathtaking landscapes.

Olympic Legacy: The "Light the Fire Within" theme of the 2002 Winter Games is still present nearly two decades later; they helped put Salt Lake City on the tourist map, and many locations still emit the excitement of the games.

Inland Sea: Explore the city's namesake, the Great Salt Lake, by car, on foot, or by bicycle. If you're here in the summer, take a float off the beaches at Antelope Island—the water is so salty it's impossible to sink.

Pow-pow-powder: Experience the "greatest snow on earth" within an hour's drive of the airport at one of seven impressive resorts.

headquarters and the Tabernacle, home to the world famous Mormon Tabernacle Choir, call Temple Square home.

Increased commitment to the arts from both the public and private sector gave way to a booming cultural scene. Sports fans won't be disappointed as Salt Lake City is home to professional and amateur sports teams that provide family entertainment no matter the season. Particularly well-known are its two major-league franchises—basketball's Utah Jazz and soccer's Real Salt Lake, but an equally fervent crowd fills the bleachers for University of Utah and Brigham Young University athletics. Lesser known teams deserving credit include the Salt Lake Bee's, the minor league off-shoot of the Los Angeles Angels, as well as the Flying Aces, a team of Olympic and National Team skiers that put on an incredible freestyle show just up the mountain range in Park City.

Near Salt Lake City, the Wasatch Mountains and Antelope Island have superb hiking, mountain biking, skiing, and wildlife watching. Park City has a rich mining history and world-class skiing resorts. Five national parks are within a half-day's drive, and American history buffs enjoy well-preserved sections of the Pony Express Trail, the site of the Golden Spike railroad junction, and the Bonneville Salt Flats.

ORIENTATION AND PLANNING

GETTING ORIENTED

Salt Lake City proper is a modest sprawling city of about 194,000 people. Most visitors concentrate their time downtown (marked by the Mormon Temple, from which all addresses emanate), east side, and adjacent canyons and mountains. Locals live as far as 10 or 15 miles from the city's walkable center, and suburbs have created an almost uninterrupted residential metropolis from Ogden (30 miles to the north) to Provo (40 miles south).

Temple Square. Temple Square is the hub of Mormonism, home to both the Salt Lake Temple and Tabernacle, but it's also the cultural hub of this intermountain region, offering cultural experiences through museums and restaurants. An emphasis on green spaces by past and present city planners means you won't experience the claustrophobia present in many big cities. Visitors can even expect to see "pop-up" parks: part-art installation, part-accessible green space.

Downtown Salt Lake. The heart of Salt Lake's social, religious, and political institutions is within a few blocks of Temple Square, downtown, also home to the city's best outdoor gathering places. The $1.5 billion City Creek Center opened in 2012, introducing high-profile shopping (an Apple store, Tiffany & Co., Nordstrom, and more) to an open-air setting and bringing the once-buried City Creek waters back to the surface. Gallivan Center hosts midday and evening concerts throughout the summer and an outdoor skating rink in winter, and City Creek Canyon offers walking, running, and biking trails in close proximity to hotels downtown. The main library, The City Library, marks the east end of downtown, offering visitors views of its breathtaking design and the city's landscapes in one location.

Capitol Hill and the Avenues. Just a few blocks (and one significant hill) up from Temple Square is the state capitol, which was designed to resemble the nation's Capitol in Washington, D.C., a symbol of Utah Territory's loyalty as it emerged from its polygamous roots in the late 19th century. Surrounding the capitol on all sides are residential areas known for historic houses, hidden bistros, and the charm that makes this one of the most livable cities in America.

East Side and the University of Utah. Marked by a white U on the hillside is one of the leading centers of academia, research, and athletics in the West. Notable University distinctions include Distinguished Professor and Nobel Prize Winner, Dr. Mario Capecchi, and the 2008 Sugar Bowl champion football team. Many of the school's faculty and staff commute from the east-side neighborhoods of Federal Heights, Harvard-Yale, and Sugarhouse, enjoying 80- to 100-year-old homes, massive trees, and thriving restaurants and boutiques.

Great Salt Lake Salt Lake International Airport lies at the southern tip of Great Salt Lake, the remnants of the ancient Bonneville Lake that covered much of the northern half of Utah. With no place for the mountain stream-fed waters to go, the lake has a salinity level far higher than the Earth's oceans, creating a unique water world that revolves around brine shrimp. Explore the lake through Great Salt Lake State Park, about 13 miles west of the airport, or journey by causeway to Antelope Island (where you're more likely to encounter bison and birds than antelope), roughly 40 miles north of the airport.

Wasatch Front. The foothills of the Wasatch Range of the Rocky Mountains form the northern and eastern city limits. Several canyons bring water and cool breezes to the desert, and are the best way to enjoy the wilderness in summer. Trailheads for hikes can be reached from downtown via City Creek Canyon, on the east side in Emigration Canyon and Mill Creek Canyon, and near the city's southern limits in Big and Little Cottonwood Canyons. Four of the nation's top ski resorts, Snowbird, Alta, Solitude, and Brighton, are a short drive up Big and Little Cottonwood, with a full range of summer and winter activities, including concert series, family movie nights, Alpine sledding, and, of course, skiing.

PLANNING

WHEN TO GO
Spring and fall are the best times to visit Salt Lake City, as cooler afternoons give way to idyllic breezy evenings. Summertime high temperatures average more than 90° (June–August), with a few days above 100° each month. Winters bring snow, but abundant sunshine melts it quickly in the valley. If your plans include trips to Park City or the Cottonwood Canyons, follow weather forecasts closely, because a fluffy 6-inch snowfall in the city will often be accompanied by 3 to 5 feet "up the hill." Extreme heat or cold without any wind often brings about "inversions" of polluted air that sometimes linger for longer than a week and prompt red alert warnings against activity in the valley, especially for people who suffer from respiratory issues. The natives often escape to the mountains on these days to get some fresh air above the clouds. Most years, ski season kicks off by mid-November and ends in early April. (During a heavy snow year, Snowbird Ski Resort will stay open on weekends as late as July 4.) Expect heavier crowds at the airport and higher rates at hotels and resorts near the ski slopes on winter weekends, particularly around holidays such as Christmas, Martin Luther King Jr. Day, and Presidents' Day, as well as around the Sundance Film Festival, held in nearby Park City. City accommodations are cheaper than in other major cities across the country much of the rest of the year, but occasional large conventions significantly affect tourist travel to Salt Lake City.

Utahns reserve much of their patriotism for July 24, rather than July 4, as it is a recognized statewide holiday known as Pioneer Day, celebrated with a parade, a marathon, and fireworks; expect road and business closures.

FESTIVALS AND EVENTS
Gallery Stroll. Mingle with local artists and view their work at various art galleries on the third Friday of the month (or the first Friday of December). Stop at any gallery on the stroll to obtain a self-guiding

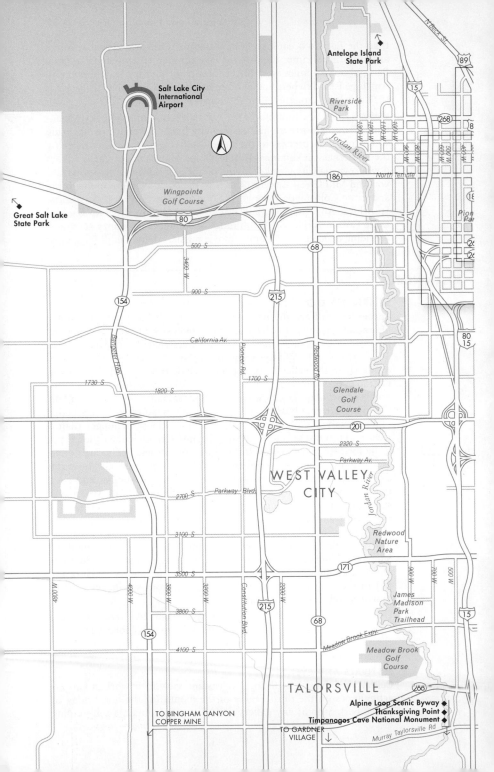

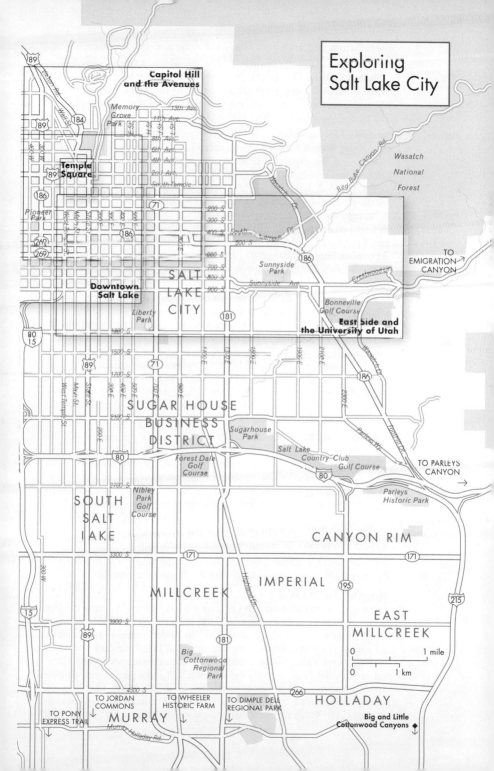

map. Artists and art lovers chat over wine and snacks at each stop. ⊠ *Salt Lake City* ☎ *801/870–0956* ⊕ *www.gallerystroll.org* 🎟 *Free.*

Phillips Gallery. One of the many galleries on the Salt Lake Gallery Stroll, Phillips Gallery is a great place to start the stroll. View artworks of various mediums inside and enjoy sculptures on their rooftop. ⊠ *444 E. 200 S, Downtown* ☎ *801/364–8284.*

Fodor's Choice
★

Sundance Film Festival. Movie buffs and casual fans will find much to love about Robert Redford's Sundance Film Festival. Each January, the crowds and the paparazzi tend to congregate in Park City, but savvy (and budget-conscious) moviegoers catch top picks in three venues in downtown Salt Lake City—the festival actually hosts events in three locations: Park City, Salt Lake City, and Sundance, Utah. With a focus on independent filmmakers, the festival has more than 100 screenings in Salt Lake City at the Tower Theatre, Broadway Center Theatre, and Rose Wagner Performing Arts Center. Ticket registration begins in September, but procrastinators can check for unsold day-of-show tickets at the Trolley Corners box office. ⊠ *Sundance Institute, 1825 Three Kings Dr., Park City* ☎ *435/776–7878* ⊕ *www.sundance.org/festival.*

FAMILY
Fodor's Choice
★

Utah Arts Festival. If you're in town on the fourth weekend in June, check out Salt Lake City's premier art event: the Utah Arts Festival. You can't miss this family-friendly event, which takes place over two full blocks downtown surrounding both Library and Washington squares. Browse original art at the Marketplace, create your own masterpiece at the Art Yard, treat your taste buds to a food truck-sponsored feast, and get down to live music on multiple stages. ⊠ *Library Square, 200 E. 400 S, Downtown* ✛ *Find Main Box Offices at the Library Arch Main Entrance, located midblock on 400 South between 200 East and 300 East* ☎ *801/322–2428* ⊕ *www.uaf.org* 🎟 *$6–$12.*

GETTING HERE AND AROUND

AIR TRAVEL

Locals say that Salt Lake City International Airport is closer to its downtown than any major airport in the country. It's 7 miles northwest of downtown via I–80, or you can take North Temple, which leads to the city center. A taxi ride from the airport to town costs about $20. The Utah Transit Authority (UTA) opened an aboveground light-rail extension (TRAX green line) in 2013 that ferries riders to and from the airport in less than 30 minutes for $2.50 each way.

Air Information Salt Lake City International Airport. ⊠ *776 N. Terminal Dr.* ☎ *801/575–2400, 800/595–2442 toll-free line* ⊕ *www.slcairport.com.*

BUS AND RAIL TRAVEL

Finding your way around Salt Lake City is easy, largely because the city is laid out on an orthogonal grid. However, the city blocks are longer than in many other cities, so distances can be deceiving. Salt Lake has a very workable public transportation system. A Free Fare Zone for travel by bus covers a roughly 36-square-block area downtown and on Capitol Hill. A light-rail system, called TRAX, moves passengers quickly around the city and to the suburbs south of Salt Lake. There are 41 stations, originating from Salt Lake Central Station, where you can connect to FrontRunner (inter-county light rail), Amtrak, and buses. The

Blue Line runs north–south from downtown to the suburb of Draper, serving the downtown landmarks (Temple Square, Vivint Smart Home Arena, Gallivan Center, Smith's Ballpark—home of the AAA baseball team—Fashion Place Mall) and Rio Tinto Stadium (home of Real Salt Lake soccer) in Sandy. The Red line extends eastward to the University of Utah and southwest to the suburb of South Jordan. The Green line originates at the airport and loops into downtown before heading west to the suburb of West Valley. More than 20 stations have free park-and-ride lots. One-way tickets are $2.50 and can be purchased on the platform through vending machines. Two children under five can ride free with a paying adult. For $15, up to four people can buy a Group Pass, good for unlimited rides on buses and TRAX. For trips that begin on a bus, you must purchase the day pass at selected UTA Pass outlets. For trips beginning on TRAX, day passes must be purchased at a ticket vending machine.

Bus and Rail Information Utah Transit Authority (UTA). ☎ 801/743-3882, 888/743-3882 ⊕ www.rideuta.com

TAXI TRAVEL

Though taxi fares are low, cabs can be hard to find on the street so it's best to call for one. Yellow Cab and City Cab provide 24-hour service throughout the Salt Lake Valley.

Taxi Contacts City Cab Company. ☎ 801/363-5550 ⊕ www.citycabut.com. **Yellow Cab.** ☎ 801/521-2100 ⊕ www.yellowcabutah.com.

TOURS

Most excursions run by City Sights include lunch at Brigham Young's historic living quarters. The Utah Heritage Foundation offers the most authoritative tours of Salt Lake's historic sights—the Kearns (Governor's) Mansion, McCune Mansion, and Union Pacific Depot—and their regularly scheduled public tours are free. The Utah Heritage Foundation website has downloadable self-guided tours.

Tour Contacts City Sights (AKA Salt Lake City Tours). ☎ 801/364-3333 ⊕ www.saltlakecitytours.org. **Utah Heritage Foundation.** ✉ 375 N. Canyon Rd., Temple Square ☎ 801/533-0858 ⊕ www.utahheritagefoundation.com.

VISITOR INFORMATION

Pick up maps, ask questions, and otherwise plan your stay at the Salt Lake Convention and Visitors Bureau, on the east side of the downtown convention center, open daily 9–5.

Contacts Salt Lake Convention and Visitors Bureau. ✉ 90 S. West Temple, Downtown ☎ 801/534-4900, 800/541-4955 ⊕ www.visitsaltlake.com. **Utah Office of Tourism.** ✉ 300 N. State St., Capitol Hill ☎ 800/200-1160 ⊕ www.visitutah.com.

EXPLORING

Start with a stroll around the city center, making sure to stop at the architecturally impressive Temple Square, the heart of the Church of Jesus Christ of Latter-day Saints. Within blocks, you'll find museums, theaters, historic buildings, and shopping havens, including the Gateway and Center outdoor malls. Then, branch out into the surrounding neighborhoods to capture more of the flavor of the city.

TEMPLE SQUARE

When Mormon pioneer and leader Brigham Young first entered the Salt Lake Valley, he chose this spot at the mouth of City Creek Canyon for the headquarters of the Mormon Church, a role it maintains to this day. The buildings in Temple Square vary in age, from the Tabernacle constructed in the 1860s to the Conference Center constructed in 2000. Perhaps the most striking aspect of the Square is the attention to landscaping, which turns the heart of downtown Salt Lake City into a year-round oasis. The Church takes particular pride in its Christmas decorations, which make a nighttime downtown stroll, or horse-and-buggy ride, a must on December calendars.

TOP ATTRACTIONS

The Mormon Tabernacle. The Salt Lake City Tabernacle, also known as the Mormon Tabernacle, is home to the famous Mormon Tabernacle Choir and its impressive organ with 11,623 pipes. From Memorial Day through Labor Day, visitors can hear organ recitals Monday through Saturday at noon and 2 pm, and Sunday at 2 pm. The rest of the year, recitals are held Monday through Saturday at noon and Sunday at 2 pm. Visitors are also welcome Thursday from 7:30 pm to 9:30 pm to listen to the choir rehearse Sunday hymns, as well as from 9:30 am to 10 am as the choir performs for the world's longest-running continuous network broadcast, *Music and the Spoken Word*. ⊠ *50 N. West Temple, Temple Square* ☏ *801/240–4872* ⊕ *www.lds.org/locations/temple-square-salt-lake-city-tabernacle?lang=eng&_r=1* ⛟ *Free.*

Fodor's Choice ★ **Salt Lake Temple.** The centerpiece and spiritual capital of the Church of Jesus Christ of Latter-day Saints, the Salt Lake Temple is a sacred pilgrimage destination for members of the faith. Brigham Young chose this spot for a temple as soon as he arrived in the Salt Lake Valley in 1847, but work on the building didn't begin for another six years. Built of blocks of granite hauled by oxen and train from Little Cottonwood Canyon, the Mormon Temple took 40 years to the day to complete. Its walls are 16 feet thick at the base. Enjoy the serene fountains and pristine landscaping that decorates the Temple area. ⊠ *50 N. West Temple, Temple Square* ☏ *801/240–2640* ⊕ *www.lds.org/temples.*

WORTH NOTING

Beehive House. Brigham Young's home, a national historic landmark, was constructed in 1854 and is topped with a replica of a beehive, symbolizing industry. Inside are many original furnishings; a tour of the interior will give you a fascinating glimpse of upper-class 19th-century life. ⊠ *67 E. South Temple, Temple Square* ☏ *801/240–2681* ⊕ *www.lds.org/locations* ⛟ *Free.*

Church of Jesus Christ of Latter-day Saints Conference Center. Completed in 2000, this massive center features a 21,000-seat auditorium and an 850-seat theater. Equally impressive are the rooftop gardens landscaped with native plants and streams to mirror the surrounding mountains. Visitors can find flexible tour times that last roughly 15 minutes, but all guests must be accompanied by a guide. The Center is home to the biannual General Conference and regular concerts by the Mormon Tabernacle Choir. ■ **TIP→ Groups are encouraged to call and schedule a tour.** ⊠ *60 W. North Temple, Temple Square* ☎ *801/240–0075, 801/240–4931 group tours* ⊕ *www.templesquare.com/explore* ⊠ *Free.*

Museum of Church History and Art. The museum houses a variety of artifacts and works of art relating to the history and doctrine of the Mormon faith, including personal belongings of church leaders Joseph Smith and Brigham Young. There are also samples of Mormon coins and scrip used as standard currency in Utah during the 1800s, and beautiful examples of quilting, embroidery, and other handicrafts. Upstairs galleries exhibit religious and secular works by Mormon artists from all over the world. ⊠ *45 N. West Temple, Temple Square* ☎ *801/240–3310* ⊕ *www.visitsaltlake.com* ⊠ *Free* ⊙ *Closed Sun.*

Temple Square Visitors' Center. The history of the Mormon Church and the Mormon pioneers' trek to Utah is outlined in a North and South Visitor's Center. Diligent missionaries stand by to offer tours and answer questions. ⊠ *Temple Sq.* ☎ *801/240–4872* ⊕ *www.templesquare.com* ⊠ *Free.*

DOWNTOWN SALT LAKE CITY

Although businesses and homes stretch in all directions, downtown's core is a compact, six-block area that includes multiple hotels, restaurants, historic buildings, and entertainment venues.

TOP ATTRACTIONS

FAMILY **Discovery Gateway Children's Museum.** The region's premier children's museum has three floors of lively hands-on experiences. Kids can participate in a television newscast, tell stories through pictures or radio, climb into a Life Flight helicopter, or revel in a kid-size town with grocery store, vehicles, a house, and a construction site. Plan on spending about two hours here if you have children ages 2 through 10. ⊠ *444 W. 100 S, Downtown* ☎ *801/456–5437* ⊕ *www.discoverygateway.org* ⊠ *Mon.–Sat. $10, Sun. $6.*

FAMILY **Gateway Mall.** Just west of downtown Salt Lake, Gateway is an all-in-one family destination with shopping, dining, movie theaters, museums, and a music venue. In summer, cool off in the Olympic Legacy Plaza, a choreographed fountain that sprays pillars of water in sync with the 2002 Olympic theme and other inspiring songs. Gateway Mall is also a great winter destination offering activities for all ages, including The Clark Planetarium, Discovery Gateway children's museum, the Depot (a live-music venue), and a 12-screen movie complex. ⊠ *400 W. 100 S, Downtown* ☎ *801/456–0000* ⊕ *www.shopthegateway.com.*

FAMILY
Fodor's Choice
★
The Leonardo. Salt Lake's first museum devoted to the convergence of science, art, and technology opened in late 2011, and has since become a bucket-list item for any family visit to Salt Lake. While it hosts large-scale national touring exhibits like the Dead Sea Scrolls, this museum is quintessentially a hands-on museum dedicated to inspiring children to

City and County
Building **9**

Clark
Planetarium **4**

Discovery
Gateway Children's
Museum **5**

Gallivan Center ..**7**

Gateway Mall **3**

The Leonardo .. **10**

Rio Grande
Depot **6**

Salt Lake City
Public Library **8**

Union
Pacific Building ..**2**

Vivint Smart
Home Arena **1**

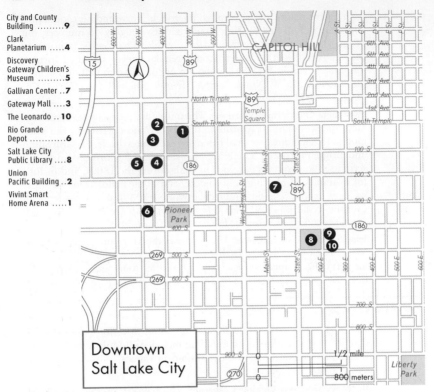

Downtown
Salt Lake City

explore. Revolving artists-in-residence offer a variety of free programs in the lab space on the main floor, including sculpting with clay, drawing, designing, or writing. Volunteers in the Tinkering Garage help you build with repurposed household objects, deconstruct electronics, create electric circuits, and much more. ⊠ *209 E. 500 S, Downtown* ☎ *801/531–9800* ⊕ *www.theleonardo.org* ⟟ *$9–$13.*

FAMILY
Fodor's Choice
★

Salt Lake City Public Library. Salt Lake City's Main Library is a must see, offering panoramic views of mountain ranges from the rooftop and breathtaking architecture inside. It truly is a novel experience. ⊠ *210 E. 400 S, Downtown* ☎ *801/524–8200* ⊕ *www.slcpl.org* ⟟ *Free.*

WORTH NOTING

City and County Building. Listed on the National Register of Historic Places, the castle-like seat of city government was the city's tallest building from its 1894 opening to 1973. On Washington Square, at the spot where the original Mormon settlers circled their wagons on their first night in the Salt Lake Valley, this building served as the state capitol for 19 years. Hundreds of trees, including species from around the world, and many winding paths and seating areas make the grounds a calm downtown oasis. In summer the grounds host major Salt Lake arts and music festivals. Free tours are given on Monday during the summer and by request outside the summer months through the Utah Heritage Foundation. ✉ 451 *S. State St., Downtown* ☎ *801/535–7280* ⊕ *www.visitsaltlake.com* ✉ *Free* ⊘ *Closed weekends.*

FAMILY **Clark Planetarium.** With an array of free hands-on exhibits and state-of-the-art 3-D and IMAX theaters, Clark Planetarium is an appealing, affordable family attraction. Traipse across a moonscape and learn about Utah's contributions to spaceflight, but save a few minutes for the Planet Fun store. ✉ *110 S. 400 W, Downtown* ☎ *385/468–7827* ⊕ *www.clarkplanetarium.org* ✉ *Exhibits free; movies $9.*

FAMILY **Gallivan Center.** Newly renovated, the John W. Gallivan Center offers an amphitheater, updated ice rink, various art projects, and a grand copper-finish facility perfect for any special occasion. Food Truck Thursdays are a staple you won't want to miss. Annual summer events include Craft Lake City, the Urban Arts Festival, and the Rock 'N' Ribs Festival. ✉ *239 S. Main St., Downtown* ☎ *801/535–6110* ⊕ *www.thegallivancenter.com.*

Union Pacific Building. This depot, built in 1909 at a cost of $300,000, is a striking monument to the importance of railroads in the settling of the West. The slate-shingle mansard roof sets a distinctive French Second Empire tone for the exterior. Inside, Western-theme murals and stained-glass windows create a setting rich with color and texture. The station has been restored and now functions as the entrance to the Gateway Mall and as a special-events venue. ✉ *400 W. South Temple, Downtown* ☎ *801/456–0000* ⊕ *www.shopthegateway.com* ✉ *Free.*

CAPITOL HILL AND THE AVENUES

These neighborhoods overlook the city from the foothills north of downtown. Two days after entering the future Salt Lake City, Brigham Young brought his fellow religious leaders to the summit of the most prominent hill here, which he named Ensign Peak, to plan out their new home. New arrivals built sod homes into the hillside of what is now the Avenues. Two-room log cabins and adobe houses dotted the area. Meanwhile, on the western slope of the hill, fruit and nut trees were planted. Some still remain, as does a neighborhood known as Marmalade, with streets named Apricot, Quince, and Almond.

With the coming of the railroad came Victorian homes. The city's rich and prominent families built mansions along South Temple. As the city has grown over the years, wealthy citizens have continued to live close to the city but farther up the hill where the views of the valley are better. Since the early 1970s the lower Avenues has seen an influx of residents interested in restoring the older homes, making this area a diverse and evolving community.

The state capitol, for which Capitol Hill is named, was completed in 1915. State offices flank the capitol on three sides. City Creek Canyon forms its eastern boundary. The Avenues denotes the larger neighborhood along the foothills, north of South Temple, extending from Capitol Hill east to the University of Utah. Getting around the Avenues is different from following the logic of the grid system of downtown.

Cathedral of the
Madeleine **4**

Governor's
Mansion **6**

Kearns
Mansion **5**

Memory Grove
Park **1**

Pioneer
Memorial
Museum **3**

Utah State
Capitol **2**

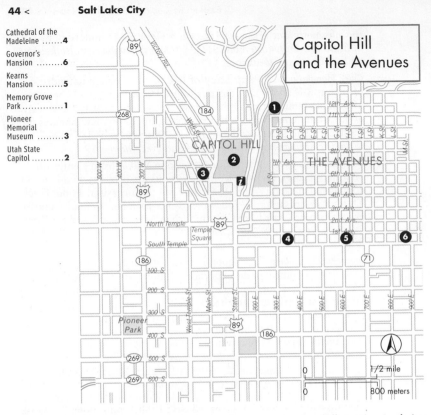

The Avenues increases in number as you head uphill, 1st Avenue being the beginning. From west to east, the streets are labeled alphabetically.

TOP ATTRACTIONS

Cathedral of the Madeleine. Although the Mormon Temple just to the west is Salt Lake's most prominent religious landmark, this cathedral stands high above the city's north side and is a stunning house of worship in its own right. The exterior sports gargoyles, and its Gothic interior showcases bright frescoes, intricate wood carvings, and a 4,066-pipe organ. The highly regarded Madeleine children's choir gives concerts regularly (especially during the Christmas season). The building is listed on the National Register of Historic Places. ⊠ *331 E. South Temple, The Avenues* ☎ *801/328–8941* ⊕ *www.utcotm.org* ⊠ *Free.*

Kearns Mansion. Built by silver-mining tycoon Thomas Kearns in 1902, this limestone structure—reminiscent of a French château with all its turrets and balconies—is now the official residence of Utah's governor. In its early days the mansion was visited by President Theodore Roosevelt and other dignitaries from around the world. The mansion was faithfully restored after Christmas lights caused a fire in 1993 that destroyed much of the interior. Tours are offered June through August and December, by appointment only. Call 24 hours in advance. ⊠ *603 E. South Temple, The Avenues* ☎ *801/533–0858* ⊕ *www.utah.gov/governor/mansion* ⊠ *Free.*

2

Utah State Capitol. The State Capitol, built in 1912, hosts Utah's legislature from January to March annually. The exterior steps offer marvelous views of the Salt Lake Valley. In the rotunda beneath the 165-foot-high dome, a series of murals, commissioned as part of a Works Progress Administration project during the Depression, depicts the state's history. Don't miss the gold-leafed State Reception Room, the original state supreme court, and the Senate gallery. Free guided tours are offered weekdays 9–5, on the hour, with the exception of holidays. ⊠ *350 N. State St., Capitol Hill* ☏ *801/538–1800* ⊕ *www. utahstatecapitol.utah.gov.*

QUICK BITE

✕ **Hatch Family Chocolates.** For a sweet treat, stop at Hatch Family Chocolates, a friendly candy- and ice-cream shop. Jerry Hatch uses his mother's secret recipe for creamy caramel, and each piece of chocolate is hand-dipped and sold by weight. Chocolate turtles here can weigh a full quarter pound. **Known for:** hand-dipped chocolates; best hot chocolate in the city. ⊠ *376 8th Ave., The Avenues* ☏ *801/532–4912* ⊕ *www. hatchfamilychocolates.com* ⊙ *Closed Sun.*

QUICK BITE

✕ **Cucina Deli.** Take a break from your tours with a picnic from this Italian deli specializing in gourmet lunches to eat in or take out. Bring your freshly packed lunch to Memory Grove or City Creek Canyon to relax and refuel amid beautiful surroundings. **Known for:** specialty sandwiches; Italian-inspired dishes. ⊠ *1026 E. 2nd Ave., The Avenues* ☏ *801/322–3055* ⊕ *www.cucinadeli.com.*

WORTH NOTING

Memory Grove Park. Severely damaged by a freak tornado in 1999, Memory Grove was carefully restored as a city park with veterans' monuments, beautiful landscaping, and the waters of City Creek. You can hike, jog, or bike on the paved road or dirt trails along **City Creek Canyon** . More trails take off from the road, including the 100-mile Bonneville Shoreline Trail. ⊠ *300 N. Canyon Rd., Capitol Hill* ⊕ *www. slcgov.com/cityparks.*

Pioneer Memorial Museum. Covering the pioneer era from the departure of the Mormons from Nauvoo, Illinois, to the hammering of the Golden Spike, this massive collection traces the history of Mormon settlers in 38 rooms—plus a carriage house—on four floors. Administered by the Daughters of Utah Pioneers, its displays include clothing, furniture, tools, wagons, and carriages. Be careful with kids—this museum is as cluttered as a westbound covered wagon loaded with all of a family's possessions. ⊠ *300 N. Main St., Capitol Hill* ☏ *801/532–6479* ⊕ *www. dupinternational.org* 🎟 *Free* ⊙ *Closed Sun.*

EAST SIDE AND THE UNIVERSITY OF UTAH

On one of the shorelines of ancient Lake Bonneville, the University of Utah is the state's largest higher-education institution and the oldest university west of the Mississippi. It is home to museums, the football stadium that was the site of the opening and closing ceremonies during the 2002 Winter Olympics, and a 15,000-seat indoor arena that played host to the 1979 NCAA basketball championship game, where Larry Bird faced off against Magic Johnson. The University Medical Center

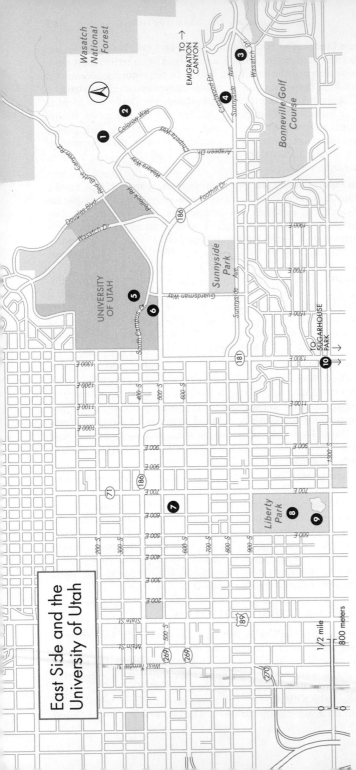

East Side and the University of Utah

Hogle Zoo **3**
Liberty Park **8**
Natural History Museum
of Utah **2**
Olympic Cauldron Park **6**
Red Butte Garden
and Arboretum **1**

Sugar House
Business District **10**
This is the Place
Heritage Park **4**
Tracy Aviary **9**
Trolley Square **7**
Utah Museum
of Fine Arts **5**

and its neighbor, Primary Children's Medical Center, east of the campus, are active in medical training and research. Research Park, located south of campus, houses scores of private companies and portions of 30 academic departments in a cooperative enterprise to combine research and technology to produce marketable products.

As you leave the downtown and university area, hiking trails lead across the foothills above the university. The scenic Red Butte Garden and Arboretum is a great place to learn about plants that thrive in dry climates such as Utah's. Since relocating to these foothills in 2011, the gleaming copper-colored Natural History Museum of Utah has become a must-visit destination. For living history, wander the boardwalks in This Is the Place Heritage Park, where volunteers don 19th-century costumes.

TOP ATTRACTIONS

FAMILY **Hogle Zoo.** This 42-acre zoo, nestled at the base of Emigration Canyon, has been a delightful half-day destination for families since 1931. Asian Highlands showcases big cats in natural surroundings; Rocky Shores includes underwater viewing of polar bears, sea lions, seals, and otters; and Elephant Encounter has elephants and white rhinos in a simulated African plain. In between you'll find many exhibits with species native to the West, including wolves and bison. A children's zoo, interactive exhibits, and special presentations make visits informative and engaging for both adults and children. Just for fun is the Lighthouse Point Splash Zone, with a tube slide, the Zoo Train, and a carousel. ⊠ *2600 E. Sunnyside Ave., East Side* ☎ *801/584–1700* ⊕ *www.hoglezoo.org* ☜ *$17 summer, $15 winter.*

FAMILY
Fodor's Choice
★

Natural History Museum of Utah. Stop and admire its copper and granite form before stepping inside to learn about the formation of the region's incredible landscape of parks, mountain ranges, lakes, and basins. Immerse yourself in prehistoric Utah, home to prolific research on dinosaurs and some of the most famous fossil recoveries in history. Since its opening in 2011, children and adults alike have counted this as an unforgettable highlight of any Salt Lake City visit. ⊠ *301 Wakara Way, University of Utah* ☎ *801/581–6927* ⊕ *www.nhmu.utah.edu* ☜ *$10–$15.*

Olympic Cauldron Park. Relive the 2002 Olympics through photographs, memorabilia, and a 10-minute film. Step outside to stand beneath the Olympic Torch (which is lit for special events), and Hoberman Arch, the backdrop for medal ceremonies that year. ⊠ *451 S. 1400 E, University of Utah* ☎ *801/581–5445* ⊕ *stadium.utah.edu* ☜ *Free.*

FAMILY
Fodor's Choice
★

Red Butte Garden and Arboretum. With more than 100 acres of gardens and undeveloped acres, the grounds here provide many enjoyable hours of strolling. Of special interest are the Perennial, Fragrance, and Medicinal gardens, the Daylily Collection, the Water Pavilion, and the Children's Garden. Lectures on everything from bugs to gardening in arid climates, workshops, and concerts are presented regularly. The popular Summer Concert Series attracts well-known musicians from Tony Bennett to Vampire Weekend. The pristine amphitheater seats approximately 3,000 people on its expansive lawn. The Botanic Gift Shop offers books, soaps, sculptures, and fine gifts. ⊠ *300 Wakara Way, University of Utah* ☎ *801/581–0556* ⊕ *www.redbuttegarden.org* ⊜ *$12.*

WORTH NOTING

FAMILY **Liberty Park.** Salt Lake's oldest park, Liberty Park features numerous amenities, including the Tracy Aviary, the Chase Home Museum, several playgrounds, a large pond, a swimming pool, and a tennis complex on its eight square city blocks. Weekly farmers' markets on Friday night and the city's biggest Pioneer Day celebration (July 24) mark a busy summer schedule annually. Make a wish and toss a coin into Seven Canyons Fountain, a symbol of the seven major canyons of the Wasatch Front. ⊠ *600 E. 900 S, East Side* ⊕ *www.slcgov.com/cityparks.*

Sugar House Business District. Utah pioneers tried to produce sugar out of beets at a mill here, and although sugar never made it to their tables, it is a sweet place to find eclectic shops and hip restaurants. The **Sprague Library** (*2131 S. 1100 E*), chosen as America's most beautiful library in 1935, is a historic Tudor-style building. Pick up picnic food and head for tiny Hidden Hollow Park, or cross 1300 East to the expansive Sugar House Park. View the city's most spectacular fireworks and arts festival every July 4. ⊠ *2100 S from 700 E to 1300 E, East Side.*

NEED A BREAK

Sugar House Park. Rolling grassy hills, athletic fields, multiple playgrounds, a creek, and a pond provide plenty of room to fly a kite or have a picnic at Sugar House Park. Take in stunning mountain views or head to the hill on the south end of the park—a go-to destination for sledding in winter. The park was once a federal prison famous for incarcerating Utah's polygamists. ⊠ *1330 E. 2100 S, East Side* ⊕ *www.sugarhousepark.org.*

FAMILY **This Is the Place Heritage Park.** On July 24, 1847, Brigham Young famously declared that this was the place for the Latter-day Saints to end their cross-country trek. A 60-foot-tall statue of Young, Heber Kimball, and Wilbur Woodruff stands prominently in the park, which includes Heritage Village, a re-created 19th-century community and visitor center. In summer volunteers dressed in period clothing demonstrate what Mormon pioneer life was like. ⊠ *2601 E. Sunnyside Ave., East Side* ☎ *801/582–1847* ⊕ *www.thisistheplace.org* ⊜ *Village: Mon.–Sat. $13, Sun. $7. Monument: free.*

FAMILY **Tracy Aviary.** The Tracy Aviary is a prime example of family-friendly fun in Salt Lake City. Easily walkable for even the smallest kids, this facility features more than 100 species of birds found on the Western Hemispheric Flyway, a migratory pattern that includes Great Salt Lake. You will see emus, bald eagles, flamingos, parrots, several types of waterfowl, and maybe even a wandering peacock. There are bird shows and educational activities daily. ⊠ *589 E. 1300 S, East Side* ☎ *801/596–8500* ⊕ *www.tracyaviary.org* ⊜ *$8–$12.*

Trolley Square. From 1908 to 1945 this sprawling redbrick structure held nearly 150 trolleys and electric trains for the Utah Light and Railway Company. As trolleys fell out of use, the facility was closed. In the early 1970s the mission-style edifice was completely overhauled.

Today it's listed on the National Register of Historic Places and houses a Whole Foods Market and lululemon in addition to dozens of boutiques and restaurants. ⊠ *602 S. 700 E, East Side* ☎ *801/521–9877* ⊕ *www.trolleysquare.com.*

Utah Museum of Fine Arts. Spanning 74,000 square feet and offering more than 20 galleries, you'll be glad this modern facility has a café and a sculpture court to rest in-between exhibits. In addition to their vast permanent collection of Egyptian, Greek, and Roman relics, Italian Renaissance and other European paintings, and Chinese ceramics and scrolls, special exhibits are mounted regularly. ⊠ *410 S. Campus Dr., University of Utah* ☎ *801/581–7332* ⊕ *www.umfa.utah.edu* ⊠ *$10–$13* ⊙ *Closed Mon.*

GREAT SALT LAKE

A visit to Utah is not complete without a trip to the Great Salt Lake.

EXPLORING

FAMILY **Great Salt Lake State Park.** The Great Salt Lake is eight times saltier than the ocean and second only to the Dead Sea in salinity. What makes it so briny? There's no outlet to the ocean, so salts and other minerals carried by rivers and streams become concentrated in this enormous evaporation pond. Ready access to this wonder is possible at Great Salt Lake State Park, 16 miles west of Salt Lake City, on the lake's south shore. A pavilion, souvenir shop, and dance floor honor the park's glory days when ballroom dancing and the lake brought thousands of visitors to its shores. The picnic beaches on Antelope Island State Park are the best places to float. If you can't take the time to get to Antelope Island, which is 25 miles north of Salt Lake City, you can walk down the boat ramp at the Great Salt Lake State Marina. You can also rent boats and stand-up paddleboards here. Shower off at the marina. ⊠ *13312 W. 1075 S, Magna* ⊕ *2 miles east of I–80 Exit 104* ☎ *801/828–0787* ⊕ *www.utah.com* ⊠ *$3 per vehicle.*

SPORTS AND THE OUTDOORS

Salt Lake City is a gateway to the excellent ski resorts strung along the Wasatch Range. There are also a handful of top-shelf golf courses. In town you can readily bicycle or jog along the wide streets and through the many parks.

TICKETS

Smith's Tix. Tickets to sporting events and concerts are available here. ⊠ *Salt Lake City* ☎ *801/467–8499, 800/888–8499* ⊕ *www.smithstix.com.*

Ticketmaster. Tickets here are primarily for music and sporting events at the Maverik Center in nearby West Valley City. ⊠ *West Valley City* ⊕ *www.ticketmaster.com.*

CLOSE UP

The Legendary Great Salt Lake

Legends of an enormous body of water with an outlet to the Pacific Ocean drew explorers north from Mexico as early as the 1500s. By the 1700s, other legends—about piles of gold and mines full of jewels—had been proven false by Spanish explorers, but the lake legend endured. Following a source of water through the West's harsh desert, and traveling along a flat riverbank instead of struggling over mountains, would make trade easier between New Mexico and the settlements springing up along California's coast. Perhaps goods could be shipped to the coast rather than hauled by mules, a trip the Spanish (correctly) predicted would take months.

Franciscan fathers Francisco Atanasio Dominguez and Francisco Silvestre Velez de Escalante came close to finding Great Salt Lake in 1776, but they cut through the Wasatch Mountains too far to the south. They did blaze a major trade route through Utah, but there is no record of any travelers wandering far enough off the route to see the lake of legend. In 1804–05 Lewis and Clark searched for a water route to the West Coast, but their focus on the Columbia River gave them no reason to travel south of Idaho. They, too, missed the lake.

Mountain men had heard of the lake. Legend has it that an argument about the lake broke out at the alcohol-soaked 1824 rendezvous in northern Utah—the trappers couldn't agree whether the nearby Bear River flowed into the lake. Jim Bridger was chosen to settle the argument, some say because he was the youngest. For whatever reason, he was set adrift on the Bear River in a rickety bull boat and told to report his findings at a future rendezvous—if he survived.

Jim Bridger did survive, and he was able to report that Bear River did flow into Great Salt Lake. However, his travels and those of fellow mountain man Jedediah Smith indicated that the lake was landlocked. Plus it was no good for drinking. Even worse, the explorers found that travel around the lake was hampered by vast expanses of marshland, a muddy shoreline, and hundreds of square miles of salt flats that looked solid but were often little more than a thin crust over layers of muck.

With dreams of a freshwater oasis and an easy route to the coast crushed, the legend of the lake changed. The lake became a place where monsters lurked in the water, giants rode elephant-like creatures on the islands, and the bottom periodically opened, swallowing everything nearby. The area became a place to avoid, or to pass by quickly, until 1847, when Brigham Young and the Mormon pioneers crossed the plains to settle on its shore.

BASEBALL

FAMILY **Salt Lake Bees.** Games are played in Smith's Ballpark; the backdrop of the Wasatch Mountains makes it one of the most picturesque baseball stadiums in America. Games run April through August offering fan-friendly, family fun. ✉ *77 W. 1300 S, Downtown* ☎ *801/325–2337* ⊕ *www.slbees.com* ✉ *Ticket prices start at $8 per person.*

BASKETBALL

Utah Jazz. Salt Lake's NBA team plays at the Vivint Smart Home Arena. Basketball buffs, check out the statues of Hall of Famers John Stockton and Karl Malone outside. ⊠ *Vivint Smart Home Arena, 301 W. South Temple, Downtown* 🕾 *801/325–2500* ⊕ *www.nba.com/jazz* 🖃 *Some tickets as low as $13 per person.*

BICYCLING

Bingham Cyclery. Bingham Cyclery operates four popular shops around the state, including one in downtown Salt Lake City across the street from Pioneer Park. The friendly staff sells and rents bikes or will tune up the one you already have. Other branches are in Ogden, Sunset, and Sandy. ⊠ *336 W. Broadway, Downtown* 🕾 *801/583–1940* ⊕ *www. binghamcyclery.com/home.*

Fodor's Choice ★ **City Creek Canyon.** Salt Lake City has fully integrated bicycles into its urban planning, and cyclists will love the 4-foot-wide bike lanes painted green on several downtown thoroughfares. Within minutes, road and mountain bikers alike can find all levels of challenge on roads and trails. A favorite is City Creek Canyon, east of the capitol, where cyclists can ride on odd-number days from Memorial Day through Labor Day, and every day between Labor Day and Memorial Day, when the road is closed to vehicles. Liberty Park and Sugar House Park also have good cycling and running paths. ⊠ *Salt Lake City* 🕾 *801/535–6630* ⊕ *www.bikeslc.com/ wheretoride/multi-usepavedtrails/citycreekmemorygrove.html.*

Fodor's Choice ★ **Contender Bicycles.** The store that vows to "make every bike a dream bike" is a must-visit for cyclists. The shop, which offers services and sales, has grown up like the trendy 9th & 9th neighborhood it anchors. You might catch Tour de France veterans Levi Leipheimer or Dave Zabriskie stopping by to chat or ride with this shop's competitive team. ⊠ *989 E. 900 S, Downtown* 🕾 *801/364–0344* ⊕ *www.contenderbicycles.com* ⊘ *Closed Sun.*

ICE SKATING

One legacy of the Salt Lake Olympics is the ZAP tax (that has since been renewed) to fund zoos, arts, and parks. As a result, some of the finest public facilities in the country are here.

Acord Ice Center. Built as a practice venue for the 2002 Winter Olympics, the rink hosts hockey, figure skating, and public skating. Call for public ice-skating times. ⊠ *5353 W. 3100 S, West Valley City* 🕾 *385/468–1965* ⊕ *slco.org/acord-ice.*

FAMILY **Cottonwood Heights Recreation Center.** Swim, jog, lift weights, play tennis, ice-skate, and much more at the Cottonwood Heights Recreation Center. ⊠ *7500 S. 2700 E, Cottonwood Heights* 🕾 *801/943–3190* ⊕ *www. cottonwoodheights.com.*

Fodor's Choice ★ **Salt Lake City Sports Complex.** With skating rinks, fitness equipment, and Olympic-size pools, this recreational complex is a year-round magnet for active families and individuals. ⊠ *645 S. 1580 E. Guardsman Way, University of Utah* ☎ *385/468–1925* ⊕ *slco.org/sports-complex.*

Fodor'sChoice **Utah Olympic Oval.** The stunning venue was built for the 2002 Winter
★ Olympics and is the home of the U.S. speed skating team. Watch the world's best skaters in major competitions every winter. It's open to the public year-round for myriad activities, including skating, curling, and running on the 442-meter indoor track. ⊠ *5662 S. Cougar La., Kearns* ☎ *801/968–6825* ⊕ *utaholympiclegacy.org/oval.*

PARKS

Most neighborhoods have a small park, usually with a children's playground.

FAMILY **Liberty Park.** Liberty Park is a local favorite running spot (it's about 1½ miles per lap on the jogging path), and also features tennis courts, an aviary, a swimming pool, picnic areas, a restaurant, and children's playgrounds. ⊠ *600 E. 900 S, East Side* ⊕ *www.slcgov.com/cityparks.*

FAMILY **Sugar House Park.** This is a favorite hangout spot for residents and visitors. Enjoy the open space where you can jog, ride a bicycle, fly a kite, enjoy a picnic, or soak up some rays. Feed the ducks in the large pond or skip rocks in the creek in the summer, or join dozens of sledders on its hills in winter. ⊠ *1330 2100 S, East Side* ⊕ *www.sugarhousepark.org.*

SKIING

Sports Den. A four-season store, Sports Den can handle any ski, snowboard, and snowshoeing need—as well as bicycles, golf, swimming, and summer gear. ⊠ *1350 S. Foothill Dr., East Side* ☎ *801/582–5611* ⊕ *www.sportsden.com.*

Utah Ski & Golf. Discounted lift tickets, advance equipment, and clothing rental reservations are available at Utah Ski & Golf's multiple downtown locations and in Park City, with free shuttle service from downtown hotels to their stores. ⊠ *134 W. 600 S, Downtown* ☎ *801/355–9088* ⊕ *www.utahskigolf.com.*

SOCCER

Real Salt Lake. Since 2005, Real Salt Lake has competed in Major League Soccer. The gleaming $100 million Rio Tinto Stadium also hosts concerts and other events. ⊠ *9256 S. State St., Sandy* ☎ *801/727–2700* ⊕ *www.rsl.com.*

WHERE TO EAT

The 2002 Winter Olympics cast Salt Lake City in a new, contemporary, more diverse light. Visitors discovered a panoply of cultural influences, brewpubs, ethnic flavors, and progressive chefs. Salt Lake City may not have the depth of restaurants seen in other big cities, but there are a couple of outstanding choices for nearly every budget and cuisine. Restaurants like Lamb's Grill Café, Hire's Big H, and Ruth's Diner

2

trace their roots back five-plus decades, and their colorful proprietors are more than willing to share the history they've witnessed from their kitchens. Returning LDS missionaries have brought back their favorite flavors from Asia, Europe, and Latin America, with impressive results. Seafood, Japanese, Tibetan, Indian, Spanish, and Italian are all suitably showcased in Salt Lake eateries, and when all else fails, there are great burgers and Rocky Mountain cuisine, a fusion inspired by frontier big game, seafood fresh from the great Pacific ports, and organic produce grown in Utah's fertile valleys. You'll also find creative wine lists and knowledgeable service. Bakers and pastry chefs defy the 4,400-foot altitude with rustic sourdoughs and luscious berry-filled treats. Multiple weekly summer farmers' markets are thriving, and chefs are building more and more of a food community.

Use the coordinates (✛ A1) at the end of each listing to locate a site on the corresponding map.

WHAT IT COSTS				
	$	$$	$$$	$$$$
Restaurants	under $12	$12–$20	$21–$30	over $30

Restaurant prices are the average cost of a main course at dinner or, if dinner is not served, at lunch.

DOWNTOWN SALT LAKE

$$$$
AMERICAN
✕ **Bambara.** Seasonal menus reflect regional American and international influences at this artfully designed destination restaurant. The setting, formerly an ornate bank lobby adjacent to swanky Hotel Monaco, is as much of a draw as the food. **Known for:** Scottish salmon; seared Alaskan halibut; steak frites. $ *Average main: $36* ⊠ *202 S. Main St., Downtown* ☎ *801/363–5454* ⊕ *www.bambara-slc.com* ✛ *C5.*

$$
AMERICAN
✕ **The Bayou.** You'll find more than 200 microbrews, both bottled and on tap, at chef-owner Mark Alston's lively, often crowded bar and restaurant. The menu offers everything from Cajun specialties such as gumbolaya (jambalaya smothered in gumbo) and étouffée to blackened seafood and a terrific garlicky hamburger with sweet-potato fries. **Known for:** alligator cheesecake; gumbolaya; bayou pizza. $ *Average main: $13* ⊠ *645 S. State St., Downtown* ☎ *801/961–8400* ⊕ *www.utahbayou.com* ⊗ *No lunch on weekends* ✛ *F3.*

$$$
MODERN
AMERICAN
Fodor's Choice
★
✕ **The Copper Onion.** Chef Ryan Lowder dazzles with the basics—artful salads, small plates, and charcuterie—and then overwhelms with mouthwatering locally sourced dishes, from Cast Iron Mary's Chicken to rainbow trout. The youthful Lowder studied at the Culinary Institute of America and apprenticed at Jean-Georges and with Mario Batali before bringing his own brand of sophisticated American cuisine to his hometown. **Known for:** house-made pastas; upscale Italian plates. $ *Average main: $23* ⊠ *111 E. Broadway, Downtown* ☎ *801/355–3282* ⊕ *thecopperonion.com* ✛ *F2.*

$$
PIZZA
FAMILY

✕**Este Pizzeria SLC.** At this New York–style pizzeria, try specials like Grandma Phi Phi's pie with marinara, mozzarella, and basil, or the Italian Flag pizza with marinara sauce, pesto, and ricotta sauce stripes. Vegans and gluten-free diners will also have plenty of options—and anyone with a sweet tooth will fall for zeppole (an Italian doughnut) and cream-filled cannoli. **Known for:** New York–style pizza; vegan and gluten-free options; zeppole. $ *Average main: $14* ⊠ *156 E. 200 S, Downtown* ☎ *801/363–2366* ⊕ *www.estepizzaco.com* ✛ *F2.*

$
CHINESE

✕**Hong Kong Tea House.** At lunch, ask for a dim sum menu and mark your choices, or wait until servers walk by with small dishes or bamboo baskets of Cantonese-style classics, from steamed pork buns to crunchy chicken feet. Dinner menus are more formal, with traditional Peking duck, spicy Szechuan-style chicken with green beans, and other authentic regional Chinese favorites. **Known for:** dim sum; steamed sea bass. $ *Average main: $12* ⊠ *565 W. 200 S, Downtown* ☎ *801/531–7010* ⊕ *hongkongteahouse.com* ☾ *Closed Mon.* ✛ *A5.*

$
VIETNAMESE

✕**La-Cai Noodle House.** Named for a historic restaurant district in Ho Chi Minh City, this place re-creates the cuisine of southern Vietnam. The menu ranges from traditional basics such as pho to unique entrées like walnut shrimp in a creamy white sauce, salt-baked calamari, and fondues. **Known for:** pho; large portions; Vietnamese cuisine. $ *Average main: $10* ⊠ *961 S. State St., Downtown* ☎ *801/322–3590* ⊕ *www.lacainoodlehouse.com* ☾ *Closed Sun.* ✛ *F3.*

$$$
SEAFOOD

✕**Market Street Grill.** This beautifully restored 1906 building is a popular breakfast, lunch, and dinner destination, where the selections range from daily fresh fish and seafood entrées to certified Angus beef. Portions are large, and include all the side dishes. **Known for:** delicious seafood entrées; historic setting. $ *Average main: $28* ⊠ *48 W. 340 S Market St., Downtown* ☎ *801/322–4668* ⊕ *www.marketstreetgrill.com* ✛ *C5.*

$$$
SEAFOOD

✕**Market Street Oyster Bar.** Popular items include oysters prepared a half-dozen ways, clam chowder, crab and shrimp cocktails, and more expensive seafood entrées. The decor features original hand-painted pillars, rounded booths that face the action, and televisions on at all hours. **Known for:** oysters; seafood entrées. $ *Average main: $26* ⊠ *54 W. Market St., Downtown* ☎ *801/531–6044* ⊕ *marketstreetgrill.com* ✛ *C5.*

$$$$
STEAKHOUSE

✕**New Yorker.** This subterranean location houses a clubby bar, café, and restaurant that exudes class with its modern continental menu, starched white tablecloths, stained-glass ceilings, and rounded banquette seating. If you're looking to celebrate a special occassion, promotion, or just wanting to treat yourself, spring for the filet mignon. **Known for:** filet mignon; crème brûlée; wine selection. $ *Average main: $35* ⊠ *60 W. 340 S Market St., Downtown* ☎ *801/363–0166* ⊕ *newyorkerslc.com* ☾ *Closed Sun.* ✛ *C6.*

$$
ECLECTIC

✕**Oasis Café.** From morning to well into the evening, a selection of fine teas and espresso drinks, big breakfasts, and fresh, innovative entrées draw regulars to this café and its serene patio courtyard. The menu leans toward vegetarian and seafood selections, and there are plenty of gluten-free options in addition to rich house-made pastries. **Known** for: seafood; vegetarian offerings. $ *Average main: $18* ⊠ *151 S. 500 L, Downtown* ▥ *801/322–0404* ⊕ *oasiscafeslc.com* ✛ *F2.*

$$ ╳ **Red Iguana.** Visitors seeking south-of-the-border cuisine need to look

MEXICAN no further than Salt Lake's Zagat-rated Red Iguana. This crown jewel

Fodor's Choice doesn't look like much, and it's off the beaten track, but it features

★ accommodating staff and incomparable house-made moles and chile verde. **Known for:** moles; chile verde; guacamole. $ *Average main: $16* ⊠ *736 W. North Temple, Downtown* ▥ *801/322–1489* ⊕ *www. rediguana.com* ✛ *E2.*

$$ ╳ **Red Rock Brewing Company.** Visitors looking for a chill atmosphere

AMERICAN with unique ales will enjoy this contemporary brewpub. Hungry? **Known for:** beer selection; fish-and-chips; on-site brewery. $ *Average main: $14* ⊠ *254 S. 200 W, Downtown* ▥ *801/521–7446* ⊕ *www. redrockbrewing.com* ✛ *B5.*

$ ╳ **Salt Lake Roasting Company.** Since 1981 the Roasting Company has

CAFÉ sourced, bought, imported, roasted, and sold dozens of varieties of coffees. Great pastries, desserts, light entrées, complimentary (although sometimes spotty) Wi-Fi, and friendly, knowledgeable staff make this a Salt Lake institution. **Known for:** coffee; pastries. $ *Average main: $8* ⊠ *820 E. 400 S, Downtown* ▥ *801/363–7572* ⊕ *www.roasting.com* ◷ *Closed Sun.* ✛ *F3.*

$$ ╳ **Settebello Pizzeria Napoletana.** Two ambitious restaurateurs set out to

PIZZA re-create authentic ultrathin pizza from Naples using an oven, flour, cheese, and other ingredients shipped from the Old Country. Settebello's pies hold their own and might even be the best thin-crust pizza anywhere outside of Italy. **Known for:** ultrathin pizza; authentic Italian ingredients. $ *Average main: $15* ⊠ *260 S. 200 W, Downtown* ▥ *801/322–3556* ⊕ *www.settebello.net* ✛ *B5.*

$$ ╳ **Squatters Pub Brewery.** This casual, high-energy brewpub located in

AMERICAN the 1906 Boston Hotel building is a happening spot for Sunday brunch. Featuring plenty of organic and locally sourced ingredients, the menu veers from locally made bratwurst to curry specials, fish tacos, and big, juicy buffalo burgers. **Known for:** Sunday brunch; house-made beer selection. $ *Average main: $14* ⊠ *147 W. 300 S Broadway, Downtown* ▥ *801/363–2739* ⊕ *www.squatters.com* ✛ *B5.*

$$ ╳ **Stoneground Kitchen.** On the top floor of a glass-fronted building across

ITALIAN the street from Salt Lake City's main public library, this is a casual hangout with New York–style pizza and "Grandma's" pasta dishes. The menu offers above-average pub food and pizzas at reasonable prices. **Known for:** thin-crust pizza; homemade pastas. $ *Average main: $15* ⊠ *249 E. 400 S, Downtown* ▥ *801/364–1368* ⊕ *www.stonegroundslc. com* ◷ *No lunch weekends* ✛ *F2.*

$$$ ╳ **Takashi.** One of Salt Lake's most popular Japanese restaurants, it is hip

JAPANESE and lively, and has the city's finest sushi, including *uni nigiri* (sea-urchin sushi) that defines melt-in-your-mouth. Owner-chef Takashi Gibo can be seen behind the sushi bar on any given day. **Known for:** sushi; uni nigiri; calamari. $ *Average main: $24* ⊠ *18 W. Market St., Downtown* ▥ *801/519–9595* ◷ *Closed Sun. No lunch Sat.* ✛ *C6.*

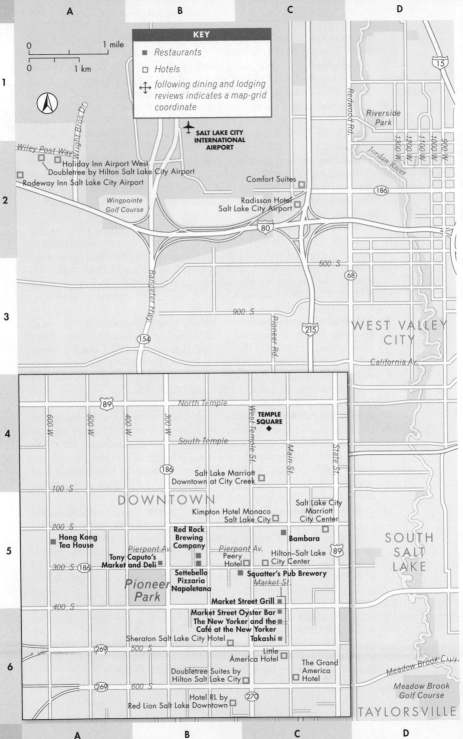

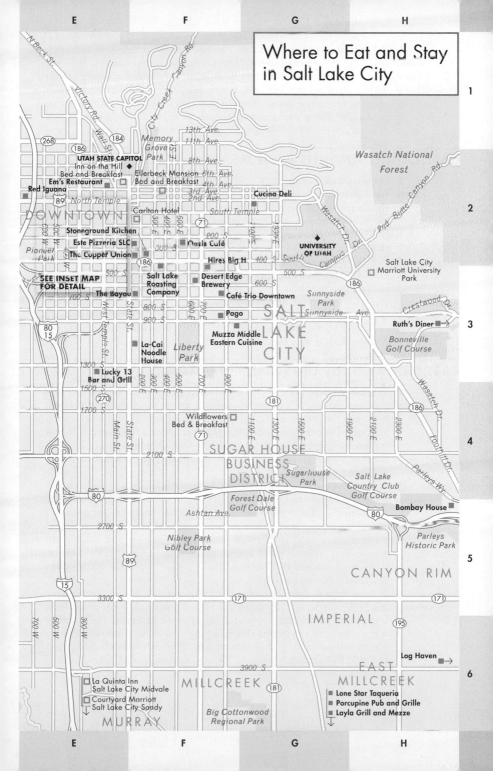

Where to Eat and Stay in Salt Lake City

$ ╳**Tony Caputo's Market and Deli.** Patrons line up at the door for sand-
ITALIAN   wiches at this stocked-to-the-rafters Italian deli and market. Whether
FAMILY   you fancy buffalo mozzarella with basil and fresh tomatoes, salami
Fodor's Choice   with roasted red peppers, or a daily special such as lasagna, it's a great
★   value in a no-frills eatery. **Known for:** cheese flights; gourmet Italian
sandwiches; busy on Saturday. $ *Average main: $8* ⊠ *314 W. 300 S,
Downtown* ☎ *801/531–8669* ⊕ *caputos.com* ⊹ *B5.*

CAPITOL HILL AND THE AVENUES

$ ╳**Cucina Deli.** Locals flock to this neighborhood café and take-away
ITALIAN   food market for the creative salads and colorful entrées. Also on
the menu are house-made soups, generous deli sandwiches, and hot
entrées such as meat loaf and mashed potatoes. **Known for:** salads; deli
sandwiches. $ *Average main: $10* ⊠ *1026 E. 2nd Ave., The Avenues*
☎ *801/322–3055* ⊕ *www.cucinadeli.com* ⊹ *G2.*

$$ ╳**Em's Restaurant.** Fresh, flavorful, creative, and artsy—chef Emily
ECLECTIC   Gassmann's small café combines it all in a renovated brick storefront
in the Marmalade District, west of the capitol. The café has an urban
feel with its modern art and polished wood floors. **Known for:** savory
crepes; vegetarian entrées; Sunday brunch. $ *Average main: $19* ⊠ *271
N. Center St., Capitol Hill* ☎ *801/596–0566* ⊕ *www.emsrestaurant.com*
⊘ *Closed Mon. and Tues.* ⊹ *E2.*

EAST SIDE AND THE UNIVERSITY OF UTAH

$$ ╳**Bombay House.** You're enveloped in exotic aromas the minute you
INDIAN   step into this dark, intimate restaurant. Enjoy good Indian standards,
including the softest naan and the spiciest of curries, tandoori dishes,
and lots of vegetarian options. **Known for:** attentive service; traditional
Indian specialties; long meal times. $ *Average main: $13* ⊠ *2731 E.
Parleys Way, East Side* ☎ *801/581–0222* ⊕ *www.bombayhouse.com*
⊘ *Closed Sun.* ⊹ *H5.*

$$ ╳**Café Trio Downtown.** Start with a selection of cheeses and flatbreads to
ITALIAN   tempt your appetite, but save room for balsamic-drizzled pizzas, hearty
baked pastas, and wood-roasted salmon, all of which vie for attention
at this constantly busy Italian eatery. Owner Mikel Trapp has created
a comfortable modern dining room with clean lines and sharp staff.
Known for: gourmet pizza and pasta; delicious crème brûlée; brunch.
$ *Average main: $16* ⊠ *680 S. 900 E, East Side* ☎ *801/533–8746*
⊕ *www.triodining.com* ⊹ *F3.*

$ ╳**Desert Edge Brewery.** For more than 40 years, this lively microbrewery
AMERICAN   inside Trolley Square has offered delicious pub food, house-made beer,
loft seating, a sheltered patio, and lots of music and noise. It also offers
a great view of the sunset through floor-to-ceiling windows. **Known
for:** french onion soup; delicious nachos; Reuben sandwich. $ *Average
main: $10* ⊠ *Trolley Square, 551 S. 600 E, East Side* ☎ *801/521–8917*
⊕ *www.desertedgebrewery.com* ⊹ *F3.*

$ BURGER FAMILY Fodor's Choice ★ 🍴 **Hires Big H.** Hires Big H elevates traditional diner favorites by incorporating fresh, local products prepared in-house. If you're nostalgic for good food with a vintage vibe, look no further than Utah's "Gathering Place." Roll down the car window and place your order at a burger joint that offers a menu, service, and groove that haven't changed much since its 1959 opening. **Known for:** car-side service; frosted root beer mugs; fry sauce. [$] *Average main: $8* ✉ *425 S. 700 E, East Side* ☎ *801/364–4582* 🌐 *www.hiresbigh.com* 🕑 *Closed Sun.* ⊕ *F3.*

$ BURGER Fodor's Choice ★ 🍴 **Lucky 13 Bar and Grill.** There is no better place in the valley to order a monstrous burger (with house-made ingredients, including fresh buns) and wash it down with a beer or a shot of whiskey. One of the few places in Salt Lake City that does not allow kids under 21, Lucky 13 is across the street from Smith's Ballpark, home to the Salt Lake Bees, the Triple A team for the Los Angeles Angels. **Known for:** signature burgers; house-made ingredients; whiskey from High West distillery. [$] *Average main: $11* ✉ *135 W. 1300 S, Downtown* ☎ *801/487–4418* 🌐 *www.lucky13slc.com* ⊕ *E3.*

$$ MIDDLE EASTERN 🍴 **Mazza Middle Eastern Cuisine.** Consistently voted the city's best Middle Eastern restaurant, Mazza is all about authentic and affordable fare in a casual setting. You can't go wrong with traditional dishes like falafel, stuffed vine leaves, and kebabs, but explore baked kafta, chicken and cauliflower kabseh, and musakhan to truly indulge your taste buds. **Known for:** honey-drenched baklava; stuffed vine leaves; tasty falafel. [$] *Average main: $15* ✉ *912 E. 900 S, East Side* ☎ *801/521–4572* 🌐 *www.mazzacafe.com* 🕑 *Closed Sun.* ⊕ *G3.*

$$$ MODERN AMERICAN 🍴 **Pago.** Pago more than lives up to its promise of farm-to-table freshness in a microscopic neighborhood bistro, putting their food forward with big-city ambition and tastes. The chef-driven restaurant capitalizes on local artisan farmers, with big and small plates anchored around simple ingredients like radishes, beets, or mountain stream trout. **Known for:** farm-to-table; fresh ingredients; excellent service. [$] *Average main: $25* ✉ *878 S. 900 E, East Side* ☎ *801/532–0777* 🌐 *www.pagoslc.com* 🕑 *No lunch weekdays. Closed 2:30–5 pm weekends* ⊕ *F3.*

$ AMERICAN FAMILY Fodor's Choice ★ 🍴 **Ruth's Diner.** Families love the gussied-up old railcar that serves as Ruth's dining room and the city's best creek-side patio in the city—you just have to navigate your way up gorgeous Emigration Canyon to find it. Breakfast (served until 4 pm) has been the diner's trademark since 1930, and starts with 3-inch-high biscuits followed by massive omelets like the King of Hearts (artichokes, garlic, mushrooms, and two cheeses). **Known for:** mile-high biscuits; Thursday night barbecue in summer; long wait times. [$] *Average main: $12* ✉ *4160 Emigration Canyon Rd., East Side* ☎ *801/582–5807* ⊕ *H3.*

FARTHER AFIELD

$$ MEDITERRANEAN Fodor's Choice ★ 🍴 **Layla Grill and Mezze.** Venture a few miles from downtown to find the Tadros family's Mediterranean restaurant that features savory dishes in a crisp, contemporary dining space. Tangy spices enliven old-world favorites such as shawarma and moussaka, and not-so-common dishes like muhamarra (think hummus but with walnuts) tempt you away from your comfort zone. **Known for:** signature fries; Lebanese-influenced

cocktails; both unique and standard Mediterranean dishes. $ *Average main: $15* ⊠ *4751 S. Holladay Blvd., Cottonwood* ☎ *801/272–9111* ⊕ *www.laylagrill.com* ✛ *G6.*

$$$
AMERICAN
Fodor's Choice
★

✕ **Log Haven.** This elegant mountain retreat brings inventive takes on American cuisine by incorporating Asian ingredients with a Rocky Mountain style. It excels with fresh fish, game, and seasonal local ingredients, creating dishes likes rabbit with white-corn polenta or ahi tuna served with lime sticky rice and baby bok choy. **Known for:** romantic mountain views; inventive entrées; upscale eats. $ *Average main: $25* ⊠ *6451 E. Millcreek Canyon Rd., Millcreek* ✛ *From I–15, take I–80 E to I–215 S; exit at 39th South; turn left at end of ramp, and left onto Wasatch Blvd., then turn right at 3800 South. Continue 4 miles up canyon* ☎ *801/272–8255* ⊕ *www.log-haven.com* ✛ *H6.*

$
MEXICAN

✕ **Lone Star Taqueria.** You can't miss this tiny lime green joint, marked by an old sticker-covered car off Fort Union Boulevard. The kitchen serves tasty and cheap Mexican food—including house special fish tacos, handmade tamales, burritos, and plenty of chilled Mexican beer. **Known for:** signature fish tacos, giant burritos; drive-through window. $ *Average main: $8* ⊠ *2265 E. Fort Union Blvd., Cottonwood* ☎ *801/944–2300* ⊕ *www.lstaq.com* ☽ *Closed Sun.* ✛ *G6.*

$$
AMERICAN

✕ **Porcupine Pub and Grille.** Above a ski- and board-rental shop at the mouth of Big and Little Cottonwood canyons sits one of the Valley's most lively pubs. The menu offers more than 40 variations on traditional pub foods, including buffalo wings, rock shrimp pizza, burgers, ribs, burritos, and ahi tuna. **Known for:** pub food; various microbrews; welcoming environment. $ *Average main: $15* ⊠ *3698 E. Fort Union Blvd., Cottonwood* ☎ *801/942–5555* ⊕ *www.porcupinepub.com* ✛ *G6.*

WHERE TO STAY

Luxury grand hotels, intimate bed-and-breakfasts, reliable national "all suites" chains—Salt Lake City has plenty of options when it comes to resting your head at night. Lodgings here cater to skiers in winter months, and many offer ski packages, transportation, and equipment-rental options, as well as knowledgeable staff who are probably on the slopes when they're not at work. Most of the hotels are concentrated in the downtown area and west of the airport, but there are also numerous options to the south of Salt Lake proper and closer to the canyon areas, where there are several high-tech companies and corporate headquarters. *Hotel reviews have been shortened. For full information, visit Fodors.com.*

Use the coordinates (✛ A1) at the end of each listing to locate a site on the corresponding map.

WHAT IT COSTS			
$	$$	$$$	$$$$
Hotels	under $100	$100–$150	$151–$200	over $200

Hotel prices are the lowest cost of a standard double room in high season.

DOWNTOWN SALT LAKE

$ — HOTEL — **Carlton Hotel.** An absolute steal on the quiet side of downtown, this 80-year-old hotel has a gorgeous brick exterior, but few to no amenities. **Pros:** family-owned for 50 years; pleasant service; made-to-order breakfast included. **Cons:** some small rooms; hemmed in by high-rises and a parking garage. $ *Rooms from: $79* ⊠ *140 E. South Temple, Downtown* ☎ *801/355-3418* ⊕ *www.carltonhotel-slc.com* ➘ *35 rooms* ⦿|*Breakfast* ⊹ *F2.*

$$ — HOTEL — **Doubletree Suites by Hilton Salt Lake City.** The sunlit atrium with its soaring ceiling gives the entire hotel a light, airy feeling, and the cool terracotta tile floors are soothing in the summer heat. **Pros:** suites are perfect for families; great on-site restaurant; two blocks from TRAX line. **Cons:** rooms fill up when conventions come to town; breakfast not included. $ *Rooms from: $109* ⊠ *110 W. 600 S, Downtown* ☎ *801/359-7800* ➘ *244 suites* ⦿|*No meals* ⊹ *C6.*

$$$$ — HOTEL — Fodor's Choice ★ **The Grand America Hotel.** With its white Bethel-granite exterior, this 24-story luxury hotel dominates the landscape a few blocks south of downtown. **Pros:** luxurious amenities; excellent pool and indoor spa; most rooms have a balcony. **Cons:** expensive for the area. $ *Rooms from: $235* ⊠ *555 S. Main St., Downtown* ☎ *801/258-6000, 800/304-8696 reservations* ⊕ *www.grandamerica.com* ➘ *775 rooms* ⦿|*No meals* ⊹ *C6.*

$$$ — HOTEL — **Hilton–Salt Lake City Center.** This Hilton is one of the city's largest and best-appointed places to stay, and it's within walking distance of all downtown attractions and many great restaurants. **Pros:** great location; on-site Spencer's steak house is a destination; on-site Starbucks. **Cons:** first hotel to sell out during conventions; fees for parking and Wi-Fi. $ *Rooms from: $167* ⊠ *255 S. West Temple, Downtown* ☎ *801/328-2000, 800/445-8667* ⊕ *www.hilton.com* ➘ *499 rooms* ⦿|*No meals* ⊹ *C5.*

$$ — HOTEL — **Hotel RL by Red Lion Salt Lake Downtown.** With its '70s-era architecture, this triangular high-rise is on the south end of downtown, and not a long walk from the Salt Palace Convention Center and Vivint Smart Home Arena (though the walk can be unpleasant in winter). **Pros:** easy access to I–15; free parking and airport shuttle; ski-rental shop across the street. **Cons:** could use update; not the best lodging for its price. $ *Rooms from: $111* ⊠ *161 W. 600 S, Downtown* ☎ *801/521-7373* ⊕ *www.redlion.com/salt-lake* ➘ *394 rooms* ⦿|*No meals* ⊹ *B6.*

$$$ — HOTEL — Fodor's Choice ★ **Kimpton Hotel Monaco Salt Lake City.** This swank hotel resides in a 14-story former bank (built in 1924), distinguished by an exterior decorated with classical cornices and cartouches. **Pros:** sparkling after $4 million renovation in 2013; restaurant has impeccable service and innovative food. **Cons:** parking is $19/day. $ *Rooms from: $180* ⊠ *15 W. 200 S, Downtown* ☎ *801/595-0000, 800/805-1801* ⊕ *www.monaco-saltlakecity.com* ➘ *223 rooms* ⦿|*No meals* ⊹ *C5.*

$$ — HOTEL — FAMILY — **Little America Hotel.** This reliably comfortable hotel stands in the shadow of its world-renowned sister property, but Little America actually has more rooms and its own loyal following. **Pros:** large indoor-outdoor pool; trees make the courtyard an oasis; elegant touches. **Cons:** restaurants and sports bar lack pizzazz of some downtown eateries. $ *Rooms from: $105* ⊠ *500 S. Main St., Downtown*

☎ 800/281–7899 *reservations*, 🌐 *www.saltlake.littleamerica.com* 🛏 *850 rooms* 🍴 *No meals* ✥ *C6.*

$ HOTEL 🏨 **Peery Hotel.** This historic building on the west side of downtown Salt Lake City is more than 100 years old, evidenced by its unique mulberry exterior, spacious antiques-filled lobby, and canopied beds in every room. **Pros:** well-maintained and charming; many "green" features; great location. **Cons:** occasional noise from local bars at night; $10 for valet parking; no on-site restaurant. [$] *Rooms from: $95* ✉ *110 W. Broadway, Downtown* ☎ *801/521–4300* 🌐 *www.peeryhotel.com* 🛏 *73 rooms* 🍴 *No meals* ✥ *C5.*

$$$ HOTEL 🏨 **Salt Lake City Marriott City Center.** If you want to be in the heart of the city, the Marriot City Center offers a superb location. **Pros:** close to downtown attractions; updated amenities. **Cons:** special events at Gallivan Center can bring big crowds; on-site parking fees can add up. [$] *Rooms from: $154* ✉ *220 S. State St., Downtown* ☎ *801/961–8700* 🌐 *www.marriott.com* 🛏 *359 rooms* 🍴 *No meals* ✥ *C5.*

$$ HOTEL 🏨 **Salt Lake Marriott Downtown at City Creek.** An extensive renovation in 2013 restored this property's status as one of the leading business and convention hotels in downtown Salt Lake City. **Pros:** location can't be beat; contemporary rooms; on-site restaurant, lounge, and Starbucks. **Cons:** not a lot of character; $15 parking. [$] *Rooms from: $146* ✉ *75 S. West Temple, Downtown* ☎ *801/531–0800* 🌐 *www.marriott.com* 🛏 *510 rooms* 🍴 *No meals* ✥ *C4.*

$$ HOTEL 🏨 **Sheraton Salt Lake City Hotel.** One of the city's major full-service hotels, this business-friendly place has a huge lobby with its own Starbucks coffee shop, oversize chairs, and fireplace. **Pros:** balcony rooms have great views; flat-panel TVs in rooms. **Cons:** far from heart of downtown; on busy stretch of 500 South. [$] *Rooms from: $108* ✉ *150 W. 500 S, Downtown* ☎ *801/401–2000, 800/364–3295* 🌐 *www.sheratonsaltlakecityhotel.com* 🛏 *362 rooms* 🍴 *No meals* ✥ *B6.*

CAPITOL HILL AND THE AVENUES

$$ B&B/INN 🏨 **Ellerbeck Mansion Bed and Breakfast.** A stay in this lovely Victorian mansion will give you a real appreciation of why city residents flock to live in the historic Avenues district. **Pros:** pleasant walk to Temple Square; fireplace in some rooms. **Cons:** surcharges and shortages when conventions are in town. [$] *Rooms from: $149* ✉ *140 N. B St., Capitol Hill* ☎ *801/699–0480* 🌐 *www.ellerbeckbedandbreakfast.com* 🛏 *6 rooms* 🍴 *Breakfast* ✥ *F2.*

$$$ B&B/INN 🏨 **Inn on the Hill Bed and Breakfast.** Owned and restored by former *Salt Lake Tribune* publisher Philip McCarthey, this turn-of-the-20th-century Renaissance Revival mansion makes a striking impression with its red-rock exterior. **Pros:** midway between Temple Square and the state capitol; each room is unique; rooms come with bathtubs and fireplaces. **Cons:** lots of steps and no elevator; kids only allowed in carriage house. [$] *Rooms from: $189* ✉ *225 N. State St., Capitol Hill* ☎ *801/328–1466* 🌐 *inn-on-the-hill.com* 🛏 *12 rooms* 🍴 *Breakfast* ✥ *E2.*

EAST SIDE AND THE UNIVERSITY OF UTAH

$$ HOTEL **Salt Lake City Marriott University Park.** Away from the downtown bustle and moments from hiking and biking trails, this spacious hotel is airy and inviting. **Pros:** near Natural History Museum and Red Butte Garden; close to hiking and biking trails. **Cons:** traditional amenities like shopping and restaurants are not within walking distance; less convenient to downtown. [$] *Rooms from: $100* ✉ *480 Wakara Way, University of Utah* ☎ *801/581–1000* 🌐 *www.marriott.com* 🛏 *218 rooms* 🍴 *No meals* ✣ *H3.*

$ B&B/INN **Wildflowers Bed & Breakfast.** An elegant "painted lady" with a private yard full of larkspur, columbine, and foxglove, this Victorian inn was built as a private home in 1891. **Pros:** friendly proprietors make you feel very welcome; listed on National Register of Historic Places; all the artwork is original, and much of it was painted by innkeeper Jeri Parker. **Cons:** clean and tidy—but may be ready for some updating. [$] *Rooms from: $90* ✉ *936 E. 1700 S, East Side* ☎ *801/466–0600, 800/569–0009 reservations* 🌐 *www.wildflowersbb.com* 🛏 *5 rooms* 🍴 *Breakfast* ✣ *F4.*

WEST SIDE AND THE AIRPORT

$$$ HOTEL **Comfort Suites.** This newer property is a great alternative if the downtown hotels are all booked, as it's closer than most other airport hotels to restaurants and other services. **Pros:** extensive renovations in rooms, hallways, and lobby in 2013; great value. **Cons:** very little within walking distance. [$] *Rooms from: $176* ✉ *171 N. 2100 W, Airport* ☎ *801/715–8688* 🌐 *www.choicehotels.com/comfort-inn* 🛏 *104 rooms* 🍴 *Breakfast* ✣ *C2.*

$ HOTEL **Doubletree by Hilton Salt Lake City Airport.** In its own self-contained world beside a man-made lake, this hotel meets business travelers' needs with plenty of business and personal services. **Pros:** completely renovated in 2013; many on-site services, including restaurant and bar; large weight room; it's ¼ mile around the lake if you're a jogger. **Cons:** nothing within walking distance; there's no downtown shuttle service. [$] *Rooms from: $85* ✉ *5151 Wiley Post Way, Airport* ☎ *801/539–1515* 🌐 *doubletree3.hilton.com* 🛏 *276 rooms, 12 suites* 🍴 *No meals* ✣ *A2.*

$ HOTEL **Holiday Inn Airport West.** This contemporary property, built in 2007, is a stunning departure from your grandfather's Holiday Inn, with stylish interiors and up-to-date amenities. **Pros:** staff is genuine and works hard to ensure your satisfaction; a great value for families or conventiongoers, as long as you have a car. **Cons:** the cluster of airport hotels feels like the last outpost before miles and miles of desert—and it is; there is nothing within walking distance; the nearest services are downtown. [$] *Rooms from: $90* ✉ *5001 W. Wiley Post Way, Airport* ☎ *801/741–1800* 🌐 *www.ihg.com* 🛏 *86 rooms* 🍴 *No meals* ✣ *A2.*

$ HOTEL **Radisson Hotel Salt Lake City Airport.** This comfortable hotel is a good bet between downtown and the airport. **Pros:** closer to downtown than other airport hotels. **Cons:** downtown Radisson offers nicer property, location, and amenities—often at nearly identical rate; too far to walk to downtown attractions. [$] *Rooms from: $85* ✉ *2177 W. North*

Temple, Airport ☎ *800/967–9033 Reservations* 🌐 *www.radisson.com* 🛏 *124 rooms* 🍴 *No meals* ✥ *C2.*

$$ 🏨 **Rodeway Inn Salt Lake City Airport.** Spacious, clean, and decked out HOTEL with amenities, this is a good value for a stay near the airport, with easy access to downtown. **Pros:** caters to business travelers. **Cons:** in a lifeless corporate park west of the airport. [$] *Rooms from: $129* ✉ *200 N. Admiral Byrd Rd., Airport* ☎ *801/746–5200, 800/535–8742* 🌐 *www.choicehotels.com/rodeway-inn* 🛏 *155 rooms* 🍴 *Breakfast* ✥ *A2.*

FARTHER AFIELD

$$ 🏨 **Courtyard Salt Lake City Sandy.** Excellent for business travelers visit- HOTEL ing Salt Lake's many South Valley corporations, this full-service hotel offers large in-room desks with broadband and spacious work areas. **Pros:** close to shopping; convenient if skiing in Cottonwood canyons. **Cons:** close to highway. [$] *Rooms from: $115* ✉ *10701 S. Holiday Park Dr., Sandy* ☎ *801/571–3600* 🌐 *www.marriott.com* 🛏 *124 rooms* 🍴 *No meals* ✥ *E6.*

$ 🏨 **La Quinta Inn Salt Lake City Midvale.** It may be a bit far from downtown, HOTEL but you have easy access to the TRAX line (there's a stop a block from the hotel), which will take you downtown, to the south suburbs, or to the University of Utah. **Pros:** interior hallways; breakfast included. **Cons:** industrial neighborhood is hardly family-friendly. [$] *Rooms from: $79* ✉ *7231 S. Catalpa St., Midvale* ☎ *801/566–3291* 🌐 *www.laquintasaltlakecitymidvale.com* 🛏 *125 rooms* 🍴 *Breakfast* ✥ *E6.*

NIGHTLIFE AND PERFORMING ARTS

For information on what's happening around town, pick up a *City Weekly* news and entertainment weekly, available at stands outside restaurants and stores in town.

NIGHTLIFE

Bars and clubs serving cocktails and providing live music abound in Salt Lake City, meeting diverse tastes. Yet remnants of the state's quirky liquor laws make for a few surprises to newcomers. Don't expect to spend the night barhopping along a single street—zoning prohibits more than two bars on one block. And you won't party until dawn here—last call is 1 am or earlier. Cabs are not on hand outside every bar or club, so you will probably have to call for one.

DOWNTOWN SALT LAKE

BARS AND LOUNGES

Lumpy's Downtown. This gathering place for sports fans is hopping seven nights a week until 2 am. You'll find televisions at every booth and a dance floor. Lumpy's is within walking distance of most downtown hotels ✉ *145 Pierpont Ave., Downtown* ☎ *801/883–8714* 🌐 *www.lumpysbar.com.*

The Red Door. Try a martini at this trendy bar with a cosmopolitan accent, where an eclectic crowd hangs out. The Red Door is closed on Sunday. ✉ 57 W. 200 S #102, Downtown ☎ 801/363–6030 ⊕ thereddoorslc.com.

Squatters Pub Brewery. This pub is lined with well-deserved awards from the Great American Beer Festival and World Beer Cup. The pub has friendly staff and a nice casual vibe, and is especially lively when conventions are in town; they serve great food, too. ✉ 147 W. 300 S. Broadway, Downtown ☎ 801/363–2739 ⊕ www.squatters.com.

Tavernacle Social Club. Dueling pianos (Wednesday through Saturday) and karaoke (Sunday to Tuesday) make for a festive atmosphere in this bar just east of downtown. The musicians only play requests, and if you don't like the current song, you can pay $1 to change it. ✉ 201 E. 300 S, Downtown ☎ 801/519–8900 ⊕ www.tavernacle.com.

PERFORMING ARTS

Salt Lake City's arts tradition officially started in 1847 with the Deseret Musical and Dramatic Society, founded by Brigham Young. The city has continued to give strong support for the arts, even voting for a special tax to support cultural organizations such as the opera and symphony. Ballet West, the Utah Symphony, and Utah Opera have kept the state on the nation's cultural map. The Capitol Theatre and Rose Wagner Performing Arts Center host Broadway touring companies. The Pioneer Theatre Company and Plan-B Theatre produce the most successful theater productions. Many film lovers forgo the snow and the crowds of Park City to enjoy the 10-day Sundance Film Festival at a half-dozen Salt Lake City venues every January. Lesser-known and locally written plays are presented in small theaters throughout the valley.

TICKETS

ArtTix. Salt Lake City's main ticketing service for various shows at locations like Eccles Theater and Abravanel Hall, to name a few. ✉ Downtown ☎ 801/355–2787, 888/451–2787 ⊕ artsaltlake.org/events.

MAJOR PERFORMANCE VENUES

There are three main performance spaces in Salt Lake City.

Fodor's Choice
★ **Abravanel Hall.** Home of the Utah Symphony and other distinguished events like the Wasatch Speaker Series featuring names such as Dr. Sanjay Gupta, Former Vice President Joe Biden, and Jane Goodall. ✉ 123 W. South Temple, Downtown ☎ 801/468–1010 ⊕ artsaltlake. org/venue/abravanel-hall.

Capitol Theatre. The Janet Quinney Lawson Capitol Theatre features Ballet West and the Utah Opera in addition to hosting Broadway touring companies. ✉ 50 W. 200 S, Downtown ☎ 801/355–2787 ⊕ artsaltlake. org/venue/capitol-theatre.

Rose Wagner Performing Arts Center. Comprising the Black Box Theatre, the Jeanné Wagner Theatre, and the Studio Theatre, the Center is home to the Ririe-Woodbury Dance Company and the Repertory Dance Theatre, providing performance space for many of the city's smaller theater and dance companies. ✉ 138 W. 300 S. Broadway, Downtown ☎ 801/355–2787 ⊕ artsaltlake.org/venue/rose-wagner-center.

DANCE

Ballet West. This respected professional ballet company performs both classic and original works at the Capitol Theatre. Its inner-workings featured in the multiseason reality show *Breaking Pointe.* ⊠ *Capitol Theatre, 50 W. 200 S, Downtown* ☎ *801/869–6900* ⊕ *www.balletwest.org.*

Repertory Dance Theatre. This company presents modern-dance performances that portray art in motion. ⊠ *Rose Wagner Performing Arts Center, 138 W. 300 S. Broadway, Downtown* ☎ *801/534–1000* ⊕ *www. rdtutah.org.*

Ririe-Woodbury Dance Company. This is Salt Lake City's premier modern dance troupe, recognized for its innovation and commitment to community education. ⊠ *138 W. 300 S. Broadway, Downtown* ☎ *801/297–4241* ⊕ *www.ririewoodbury.com.*

FILM

Brewvies Cinema Pub. A variety of new releases and independent films are shown here. You can have a beer and dinner with the show. ⊠ *677 S. 200 W, Downtown* ☎ *801/322–3891* ⊕ *www.brewvies.com.*

Broadway Centre Theatre. The Salt Lake Film Society shows newly released, independent, and foreign films here. ⊠ *111 E. Broadway, Downtown* ☎ *801/321–0310* ⊕ *www.saltlakefilmsociety.org.*

Tower Theatre. See newly released, independent, and foreign films at this historic art deco theater that's also a Sundance Film Festival venue. ⊠ *876 E. 900 S, East Side* ☎ *801/321–0310* ⊕ *www.saltlakefilmsociety.org.*

MUSIC

Mormon Tabernacle Choir. Nearly 400 volunteers make up this famous choir, which performs sacred music, with some secular (classical and patriotic) works. You can hear them during their weekly broadcast, "Music and the Spoken Word," Sunday morning from 9:30 to 10 in the Tabernacle most of the year. Their weekly rehearsal, also open to the public, is on Thursday evening from 7:30 to 9:30 in the Tabernacle. ⊠ *50 N. West Temple, Temple Square* ☎ *801/240–4150* ⊕ *www.mormontabernaclechoir.org.*

Utah Symphony. The premier orchestra in the state, if not the region, the Utah Symphony performs in the acoustically acclaimed Maurice Abravanel Concert Hall and calls the Deer Valley Music Festival its summer home. ⊠ *Abravanel Hall, 123 W. South Temple, Downtown* ☎ *801/533–6683* ⊕ *www.utahsymphony.org.*

OPERA

Utah Opera. Since 1978, this company has performed new and classical works at Capitol Theatre and throughout the state. ⊠ *123 W. South Temple, Downtown* ☎ *801/533–6683* ⊕ *www.utahopera.org.*

THEATER

Off Broadway Theatre. Musicals and plays here include comedies, parodies, and improvisational comedy events. ⊠ *272 S. Main St., Downtown* ☎ *801/355–4628* ⊕ *www.theobt.org.*

Pioneer Theatre Company. This professional company, in residence at the University of Utah, stages classic and contemporary musicals and plays. From *Les Misérables* to *The Producers*, it has proven it can put on large-scale and commercially viable theater. ⊠ *300 S. 1400 E, Room 325, University of Utah* ☎ *801/581–6961* ⊕ *www.pioneertheatre.org.*

Fodor's Choice **Plan-B Theatre.** The resident company of the Rose Wagner Performing
★ Arts Center stages modest productions built on fine original scripts and timely social and cultural themes. Two shows became hits outside of Utah: *Facing East ,* which went to New York off-Broadway, and *Exposed ,* which drew considerable acclaim for tackling the issue of fallout from nuclear testing in the 1950s. ⊠ *138 W. 300 S, Downtown* ☎ *801/297–4200* ⊕ *planbtheatre.org.*

Salt Lake Acting Company. Recognized for its development of new regionally and locally written plays, this company's performances run year-round. The Company brings thought-provoking plays to the Salt Lake Area while promoting arts education for Utahns in kindergarten up through the university level. ⊠ *168 W. 500 N, Capitol Hill* ☎ *801/363–7522* ⊕ *www.saltlakeactingcompany.org.*

SHOPPING

Salt Lake's shopping is concentrated downtown as well as in several malls. Good bets for souvenirs include books, Mormon crafts, and Western collectibles. The vicinity of 300 South and 300 East streets has several shops that specialize in antique jewelry, furnishings, art, and knickknacks.

DOWNTOWN SALT LAKE

PLAZAS AND MALLS

City Creek Center. The City Creek Center is the centerpiece of a $1 billion downtown redevelopment across from Temple Square in 2012. To date, City Creek has brought luxury shopping to the city with stores like Nordstrom, Tiffany & Co., Porsche Design, and Pandora. Although the outdoor mall is gorgeous and developers were credited with bringing historic City Creek waterway back above ground, it's somewhat controversial—the Mormon Church owns the land and most shops are closed on Sunday. ⊠ *50 S. Main St., Downtown* ☎ *801/521–2012* ⊕ *www.shopcitycreekcenter.com* ☉ *Closed Sun.*

FAMILY **Gateway Mall.** Gateway Mall brings together a shopping mall, children's museum, restaurants, and business and residential center, all accessible by TRAX, Salt Lake's mass transit. ⊠ *400 W. 100 S, Downtown* ☎ *801/456–0000* ⊕ *www.shopthegateway.com.*

OUTDOOR MARKETS

Farmers bring produce, flowers, and other goodies to the popular downtown farmers' market at **Pioneer Park,** at 300 West and 300 South streets, each Saturday from June through mid-October. Local bakeries and restaurants also sell tasty treats ranging from fresh salsa to cinnamon rolls, and there is live music, too. Find fresh markets in Park City, Murray, South Jordan, and at the University of Utah in the summer as well.

ART GALLERIES

Alice Gallery at Glendinning. This gallery is housed in Glendinning Mansion, which is also home to the Utah Arts Council. ⌧ *617 E. South Temple, Downtown* ☎ *801/245–7272* ⊕ *heritage.utah.gov/arts-and-museums/things-galleries-alice* ⊗ *Closed weekends.*

Phillips Gallery. Phillips Gallery features three floors of local artists' work, including mixed media, paintings, and sculptures. Check out the sculptures on their rooftop for a view of art and nature. ⌧ *444 E. 200 S, Downtown* ☎ *801/364–8284* ⊕ *www.phillips-gallery.com* ⊗ *Closed Sun. and Mon.*

BOOKS

Ken Sanders Rare Books. More than 100,000 titles await in this store that specializes in literature about Utah, Mormons, and Western exploration. ⌧ *268 S. 200 E, Downtown* ☎ *801/521–3819* ⊕ *www.kensandersbooks.com.*

Weller Book Works. The name of this store has been synonymous with independent book sales in Salt Lake City since 1929. Catherine and Tony Weller are the third generation to operate this bookstore, which relocated to the historic former train yard in 2012. Bibliophiles will love the space and the helpful and knowledgeable staff. ⌧ *607 Trolley Sq., East Side* ☎ *801/328–2586* ⊕ *www.wellerbookworks.com.*

EAST SIDE AND UNIVERSITY OF UTAH

Explore the smaller neighborhood clusters of shops such as 9th & 9th (900 South, 900 East), Foothill Village, or Trolley Square to find unique souvenirs of Utah.

BOOKS

FAMILY **The King's English Bookshop.** This converted cottage is a great place to browse. Works by local authors, a wide selection of children's books, a dozen reading groups, and a community writing series can all be found here. ⌧ *1511 S. 1500 E, East Side* ☎ *801/484–9100* ⊕ *www.kingsenglish.com.*

PLAZAS AND MALLS

Sugar House Business District. The Sugar House Business District is a funky mix of locally owned shops and restaurants between 1700 South and 2700 South streets, from 700 East to 1300 East streets. ⌧ *East Side.*

Trolley Square. The wares here run the gamut from estate jewelry and designer clothes to bath products, baskets, and saltwater taffy. Stores include Pottery Barn, Weller Books, lululemon, Tabula Rasa, and an assortment of restaurants, as well as a Whole Foods Market. ⌧ *600 S. 700 E, East Side* ☎ *801/521–9877.*

FARTHER AFIELD

SPORTING GOODS

Backcountry.com. This is one of the best-known outdoor-equipment retailers. Visit their small showroom and massive (200,000-square-foot) back room where you can shop or pick up products you've ordered online. Skiers, boarders, campers, and climbers are all welcome. ⊠2607 *S. 3200 W, West Side* ☎ *800/409–4502* ⊕ *www.backcountry.com.*

Kirkham's Outdoor Products. Locally owned, this store carries a wide spectrum of outdoor gear. ⊠*3125 S. State St., The Suburbs* ☎*801/486–4161, 800/453–7756* ⊕ *www.kirkhams.com.*

SIDE TRIPS FROM SALT LAKE CITY

BIG COTTONWOOD CANYON

31 miles from Downtown Salt Lake City.

The history of mining and skiing in Utah often go hand in hand, and that's certainly true of Big Cottonwood Canyon, with its adjacent ski resorts of **Brighton** and **Solitude.** In the mid-1800s, 2,500 miners lived at the top of this canyon in a rowdy tent city. The old mining roads make great hiking, mountain-biking, and backcountry ski trails. Rock climbers congregate in the lower canyon for excellent sport and traditional climbing.

Opened in 1936, Brighton is the second-oldest ski resort in Utah, and one of the oldest in North America. Just down the canyon, Solitude has undergone several incarnations since it opened in 1957, and has invested heavily in overnight accommodations and new base facilities since the early 1990s. As an area, Big Cottonwood is quieter than Park City or neighboring Little Cottonwood Canyon, home of Alta and Snowbird resorts.

GETTING HERE AND AROUND

From downtown Salt Lake City it's a 40-minute drive to Big Cottonwood via Interstate 80 and Interstate 215, then Highway 190 E. Most downtown hotels offer free shuttles to the ski resorts, and Utah Transit Authority runs bus shuttles for $4.50 each way.

SPORTS AND THE OUTDOORS

BICYCLING

Solitude Mountain Resort. Mountain bikers will love Solitude for its single-track trails that span 20 miles within Big Cottonwood Canyon as well as routes that connect neighboring canyons. Solitude Mountain Resort offers lift-served mountain biking with rentals available at Solitude Village from mid-to-late June to early October, weather permitting. ⊠ *12000 Big Cottonwood Canyon Rd.* ☎*801/748–4754* ⊕ *solitudemountain.com.*

HIKING

Brighton Lakes Trail. The upper section of Big Cottonwood Canyon is a glacier-carved valley with many side drainages that lead to picturesque alpine lakes. In the Brighton area, you can access beautiful mountain lakes (Mary, Margaret, and Catherine) just a short jaunt from the highway. The elevation at Brighton's parking lot is 8,700 feet, so take it easy, rest often, drink plenty of water, and keep an eye on the weather no matter the season. A beautiful hike is along the Brighton Lakes Trail past four alpine lakes and then ascending to Catherine Pass. From here

Ride on the Pony Express Trail

Imagine a young man racing over the dusty trail on the back of a foaming mustang. A cloud of dust rises to announce him to the station manager, who waits with a new mount, some beef jerky, and water. The rider has galloped 11 miles since breakfast and will cover another 49 before he sleeps. That was the daily life of a courier with the Pony Express.

A rider had to weigh less than 120 pounds. He was allowed only 25 pounds in gear, which included four leather mail pouches, a light rifle, a pistol, and a Bible. The standard uniform consisted of a bright red shirt and blue pants. Hostile Indians, bandits, and rattlesnakes were handled with the guns. The blazing heat of the desert in the summer and blinding blizzards in the winter were his constant foes.

There are few places in the United States where the original trail and stations of the Pony Express survive in such pristine condition as they do in Utah. One of the best-preserved sections of the original Pony Express Trail, which was in operation for 19 months in the mid-19th century, is the 133-mile section through the desert of west-central Utah. You'll see territory that remains much as it was during the existence of the Pony Express, and many of the sights you'll see along the way haven't changed perceptibly since that time. The desert has preserved them.

If you want to traverse the route, the logical starting point is Camp Floyd–Stagecoach Inn State Park in Fairfield. The end is in Ibapah, 133 miles away

on the Utah-Nevada border. Stone pillars with metal plaques mark the route that starts and ends on pavement, then becomes a dirt road for 126 miles that is passable when dry. The Bureau of Land Management maintains a campground at Simpson Springs, one of the area's most dependable water sources. Some interesting ruins are still visible at the Faust, Boyd, and Canyon stations. A brochure describing the major stops along the trail is available from the U.S. Bureau of Land Management's Salt Lake Field Office.

It takes a certain breed of romantic to appreciate the beauty of the land and life lived by those who kept the mail moving during the short time that the Pony Express existed. For those with a similar sense of adventure as the wiry young riders, who included "Buffalo Bill" Cody, traveling this trail is a chance to relive history. Historians say that the enterprise enabled communications between Washington, D.C. and California, keeping the state in the Union and helping to secure the North's eventual success in the Civil War. Stagecoaches, freight wagons, the Transcontinental Railroad, and the Lincoln Highway all followed the route pioneered by the Pony Express. Before the Pony Express, it took mail six to eight weeks to travel from Missouri to California; by Pony Express, the mail took 10 days to arrive. This labor-intensive system of communicating cross-country ended with the invention of the telegraph—once it was put into wide use, telegraphed messages went across the continent in a mere four hours.

2

you can choose to descend into Little Cottonwood's Albion Basin near Alta (but remember, you'll need a car for the 45-minute ride back to Brighton), or back along the Brighton Lakes Trail.

Sunset Peak. At Catherine Pass you have the option of continuing up to Sunset Peak, which, at 10,648 feet, is one of the most accessible summits in the Wasatch Range. It's another short grunt to the top, but well worth the effort for the unsurpassed, nearly 360-degree view. The breathtaking vistas include the Heber Valley, Park City, Mount Timpanogos, Big and Little Cottonwood Canyons, and even a portion of the Salt Lake Valley.

SKIING

CROSS-COUNTRY
Solitude Nordic Center. Accessible from Solitude Village, the Solitude Nordic Center has 20 km (12 miles) of groomed cross-country trails, 10 km (6 miles) of snowshoe trails, and a small shop offering rentals, lessons, food, and guided tours. For $20 you can use the trails all day, for $62 you can get a private lesson as well as an all-day trail pass. ⊠ *12000 Big Cottonwood Canyon Rd.* ☎ *801/534–1400* ⊕ *solitudemountain.com.*

DOWNHILL
Brighton Ski Resort. The smallest of the Cottonwood resorts just outside Salt Lake City, Brighton is nonetheless a favorite among serious snowboarders, parents (who flock to the resort's ski school), and some extreme skiers and riders. There are no megaresort amenities here, just a nice mix of terrain for all abilities, and a basic lodge, ski shop, and ski school. The snow is as powdery and deep as nearby Alta and Snowbird, and advanced (and prepared) skiers can access extensive backcountry areas. There's something for everyone here at a fraction of the cost of the bigger resorts. ⊠ *8302 S. Brighton Loop Rd., Brighton* ☎ *801/532–4731, 855/201–7669,* ⊕ *www.brightonresort. com* ⊠ *Lift tickets $72* ⌖ *1,745-ft vertical drop; 1,050 skiable acres; 21% beginner, 40% intermediate, 39% advanced/expert; 5 high-speed quad chairs, 1 triple chair.*

Solitude Mountain Resort. Since 1957, Solitude Mountain Resort offers Big Cottonwood Canyon's most intense ski experience. It has since grown into a European-style village with lodges, condominiums, a luxury hotel, and good restaurants. Downhill skiing and snowboarding are still the main attractions, with steep, pristine terrain in Honeycomb Canyon attracting the experts, and a mix of intermediate cruising runs and beginner slopes beckoning the less accomplished. Day guests will enjoy relaxing after a hard day on the slopes at the comfortable Solitude Mountain Spa. ⊠ *12000 Big Cottonwood Canyon Rd., Solitude* ☎ *801/534–1400, 800/748–4754, 801/536–5774 Nordic Center, 801/536–5777 snow report* ⊕ *www.solitudemountain.com* ⊠ *Lift tickets $88* ⌖ *2,047-ft vertical drop; 1,200 skiable acres; 20% beginner, 50% intermediate, 30% advanced; 3 high-speed quad chairs, 2 quad chairs, 1 triple chair, 2 double chairs.*

WHERE TO STAY

$$
HOTEL
Brighton Lodge. There are no frills at Brighton, and if you blink you might miss this inn at the base of the ski hill, but in an area where skiing is increasingly expensive, you can save money and enjoy fantastic family skiing here. **Pros:** unpretentious in every way; a good deal for families. **Cons:** if you don't have kids, the family atmosphere

may not appeal. $ *Rooms from: $139* ✉ *8302 S. Brighton Loop Rd.* ☎ *801/532–4731, 855/201–7669 reservations* ⊕ *www.brightonresort.com* 🛏 *16 rooms* ⃝ *No meals.*

$$$$ 🖼 **The Inn at Solitude.** You get ski-in ski-out luxury and VIP treatment
RESORT at this well-appointed hotel with comfortable and spacious rooms. **Pros:** guest-only wine tasting events; outdoor heated pool. **Cons:** "solitude" equals "quiet.". $ *Rooms from: $386* ✉ *12000 Big Cottonwood Canyon Rd., Solitude* ☎ *800/748–4754* ⊕ *solitudemountain. com/explore-lodging/the-inn-at-solitude* ⊘ *Closed May–Nov.* 🛏 *42 rooms, 4 suites* ⃝ *No meals.*

$$$$ 🖼 **Powderhorn Lodge.** The spacious condo-style units and convenient
RENTAL location allow for the perfect family ski trip. **Pros:** handsome furnishings and full kitchens; convenient to slopes and Solitude's village; condos have private balconies and fireplaces. **Cons:** early-to-bed spot. $ *Rooms from: $250* ✉ *12000 Big Cottonwood Canyon Rd.* ☎ *800/748–4754, 801/534–1400* ⊕ *solitudemountain.com/explore-lodging/powderhorn-lodge* 🛏 *60 units* ⃝ *No meals.*

$$$ 🖼 **Silver Fork Lodge.** Log furniture and wood paneling make the rooms
B&B/INN here warm and inviting; the views are unbeatable and the food is a major attraction. **Pros:** renowned dining; breakfast on patio in warmer months; attentive service. **Cons:** nightlife is lacking; no in-room phones or TVs. $ *Rooms from: $165* ✉ *11332 Big Cottonwood Canyon Rd.* ☎ *801/533–9977, 888/649–9551* ⊕ *www.silverforklodge.com* 🛏 *6 rooms, 1 suite* ⃝ *Breakfast.*

NIGHTLIFE

Molly Green's. Once referred to as the "Majestic Manor," ski bums and snowboarders come together to tip back a few at Molly Green's, a 60-plus year-old watering hole in the A-frame at the base of Brighton Ski Resort. ✉ *Brighton Ski Resort, 12601 Big Cottonwood Rd.* ☎ *801/532–4731* ⊕ *brightonresort.com/stay/dining* ⊘ *Call for hrs, May–Nov.*

Thirsty Squirrel. A good place to unwind after a day on the slopes, Thirsty Squirrel quiets down once the après-ski crowd leaves. ✉ *Powderhorn Bldg., Solitude Village, 12000 Big Cottonwood Canyon Rd.* ☎ *801/534–1400* ⊕ *solitudemountain.com/village-dining/thirsty-squirrel* ⊘ *Closed May–Oct.*

LITTLE COTTONWOOD CANYON

25 miles from Brighton and Solitude; 20 miles from Salt Lake City.

Skiers have been singing the praises of Little Cottonwood Canyon since 1938, when the Alta Lifts Company pieced together a ski lift using parts from an old mine tram to become the **Alta Ski Resort,** the second ski resort in North America. With its 500 inches per year of dry, light snow and unparalleled terrain, this canyon is legendary among diehard snow enthusiasts. A mile down the canyon from Alta, **Snowbird Ski and Summer Resort,** which opened in 1971, shares the same mythical snow and terrain quality. Since 2001 Alta and Snowbird have been connected via the Mineral Basin area. You can purchase an Alta Snowbird One Pass that allows you on the lifts at both areas, making this a huge skiing complex.

But skiing isn't all there is to do here. Many mountain-biking and hiking trails access the higher reaches of the Wasatch-Cache National Forest, and the trails over Catherine Pass will put you at the head of Big Cottonwood Canyon at the Brighton Ski Area. The hike to Catherine Pass is relatively easy and quite scenic. Formed by the tireless path of an ancient glacier, Little Cottonwood Canyon cuts a swath through the Wasatch-Cache National Forest. Canyon walls are composed mostly of striated granite, and traditional climbing routes of varied difficulty abound. Down the canyon from Alta and Snowbird is the trailhead for the Red Pine Lake and White Pine Lake trails. Some 3½ miles and 5 miles in, respectively, these mountain lakes make for great day hikes.

At Snowbird's base area, modern structures house guest rooms, restaurants, and nightclubs. The largest of these buildings, the Cliff Lodge, is an entire ski village under one roof. The resort mounts a variety of entertainment throughout the year, including live jazz shows, rock, blues, folk, and bluegrass concerts, and an Oktoberfest in fall. You can enjoy a drink at any of several base-area lounges.

GETTING HERE AND AROUND

Travelers to Little Cottonwood Canyon take I–80 East to I–215 South, then hop off the highway at Exit 6 and venture into Little Cottonwood Canyon, following signs for Alta and Snowbird. The canyon's dramatic topography invites very occasional avalanches that block the road, the only entrance and egress.

ESSENTIALS

Visitor Information Alta Chamber & Visitors Bureau. ☏ 435/633–1394 ⊕ www.discoveralta.com.

EXPLORING

Snowbird Ski and Summer Resort. The resort is transformed into a playground in summer with rides and games for children of all ages, plus concerts, outdoor sports, dining, and more. Thrill-seekers will love the mountain coaster, the alpine slide, the zip line, and the mountain flyer, which resembles a roller coaster. You'll also find a climbing wall, trampoline, ropes course, inflatables, and more man-made fun. There are ample options to access stunning hiking terrain and views, including the tram to 11,000-foot Hidden Peak. ✉ 9385 Snowbird Center Trail, Sandy ☏ 801/933–2222 ⊕ www.snowbird.com ✉ All-day activity pass $49 (individual ride tickets are also available); $24 tram ride only.

SPORTS AND THE OUTDOORS

BICYCLING

Snowbird Ski and Summer Resort. Other than a mile-long beginner-to-intermediate single-track trail, the steep, rocky terrain here is not recommended for novices. Advanced mountain bikers can ride the tram at Snowbird Ski and Summer Resort to the top of the mountain and access a network of trails. Adventure addicts should check out the brand new Big Mountain Trail, which is downhill riding only with a 2,900-foot descent over 7½ miles from the top of Hidden Peak down to Snowbird Center. Road cyclists should note that Little Cottonwood Canyon has been part of the most grueling stage of the Tour of Utah bike race several times. Bike rentals are available. Summer tram tickets are $24/day, with family passes and season passes available. ✉ *9385 Snowbird Center Trail, Sandy* ☎ *801/933–2222* ⊕ *www.snowbird.com.*

HIKING

The upper canyons provide a cool haven during the hot summer months. Wildflowers and wildlife are plentiful, and most trails provide a good balance of shade and sun. Due to high altitude, even fit hikers often become fatigued and dehydrated faster than they would otherwise, so remember to take it easy, rest often, and drink plenty of water.

Sunset Peak. The trailhead for the 4-mile out-and-back hike to Sunset Peak starts high in Little Cottonwood Canyon, above Alta Ski Resort, in Albion Basin. This is a popular area for finding wildflowers in July and August. After an initial steep incline, the trail wanders through flat meadows before it climbs again to Catherine Pass at 10,240 feet. From here intermediate hikes continue along the ridge in both directions. Continue up the trail to the summit of Sunset Peak for breathtaking views of the Heber Valley, Park City, Mount Timpanogos, Big and Little Cottonwood Canyons, and even a part of the Salt Lake Valley. You can alter your route by starting in Little Cottonwood Canyon and ending your hike in neighboring Big Cottonwood Canyon: from Catherine Pass descend into Big Cottonwood Canyon, passing four lakes and finally ending up at Brighton Ski Resort. If you choose to end your hike in Big Cottonwood, make sure you aren't left stranded without a car.

White Pine Trailhead. White Pine Trailhead, ¾ mile below Snowbird on the south side of the road, accesses some excellent easy hikes to overlooks. If you want to keep going on more intermediate trails, continue up the trail to the lakes in White Pine Canyon, Red Pine Canyon, and Maybird Gulch. All of these hikes share a common path for the first mile.

SKIING

Fodor'sChoice
★
Alta Ski Area. Alta Ski Area has perhaps the best snow anywhere in the world—up to 500 inches a year, and terrain to match it. Alta is one of the few resorts left in the country that doesn't allow snowboarding. Sprawling across two large basins, Albion and Wildcat, Alta has a good mixture of expert, intermediate, and beginner terrain. Much of the best skiing (for advanced or expert skiers) requires either finding obscure traverses or doing some hiking. It takes some time to get to know this mountain so if you can find a local to show you around you'll be ahead of the game. Albion Basin's lower slopes have a terrific expanse of novice and lower-intermediate terrain. Rolling meadows, wide trails, and light dry snow create one of the best places in the country for less-skilled skiers to learn to ski powder. Two-hour lessons start at $70. In addition to downhill skiing, Alta also has 3 km of groomed track for skating and classic skiing (on a separate ticket), plus a good selection of rental equipment at Alta Ski Shop. ✉ *10230 UT-210, Alta* ☎ *801/359–1078, 801/572–3939 snow report* ⊕ *www.alta.com* ✉ *Lift tickets $104; Alta Snowbird Day Pass $139* ✑ *2,020-ft vertical drop; 2,200 skiable acres; 25% novice, 40% intermediate, 35% advanced; 2 high-speed quads, 2 triple chairs, 3 double chairs.*

Fodor'sChoice
★
Snowbird Ski and Summer Resort. For many skiers, this is as close to heaven as you can get. Soar aboard Snowbird's signature 125-passenger

tram straight from the base to the resort's highest point, 11,000 feet above sea level, and then descend into a playground of powder-filled chutes, bowls, and meadows—a leg-burning top-to-bottom run of more than 3,000 vertical feet if you choose. The terrain here is weighted more toward experts—35% of Snowbird is rated black diamond—and if there is a drawback to this resort, it's a lack of beginner terrain. The open bowls, such as Little Cloud and Regulator Johnson, are challenging; the Upper Cirque and the Gad Chutes are hair-raising. On deep-powder days—not uncommon at the Bird—these chutes are exhilarating for skiers who like that sense of a cushioned free fall with every turn. With a nod to intermediate skiers, Snowbird opened North America's first skier tunnel in 2006. Skiers and boarders now ride a 600-foot magic carpet through the Peruvian Tunnel, reducing the trek to Mineral Basin. If you're looking for intermediate cruising runs, there's the long, meandering Chip's Run. After a day of powder turns, you can lounge on the 3,000-square-foot deck of Creekside Lodge at the base of Gad Valley. Beginner's lessons start at $130 and include lift ticket, tuition, and rentals. ⊠ *Hwy. 210, Snowbird* ☎ *801/933–2222, 800/232–9542 lodging reservations, 801/933–2110 special events, 801/933–2100 snow report* ⊕ *www.snowbird.com* ⊠ *Lift tickets $106* ⌁ *3,240-ft vertical drop; 2,500 skiable acres; 27% novice, 38% intermediate, 35% advanced; 125-passenger tram, 4 quad lifts, 6 double chairs, 1 gondola, and a skier tunnel with surface lift.*

SKI TOURS

Ski Utah Interconnect Adventure Tour. Strong intermediate and advanced skiers can hook up with the Ski Utah Interconnect Adventure Tour for a guided alpine ski tour that takes you to as many as six resorts (including Brighton, Solitude, Alta, and Snowbird) in a single day, all connected by backcountry ski routes with unparalleled views of the Wasatch Mountains. Guides test your ski ability before departure. The tour includes guide service, lift tickets, lunch, and transportation back to the point of origin. You'll even walk away with a finisher's pin. The Deer Valley Departure Tour operates Sunday, Monday, Tuesday, Wednesday, and Friday; the Snowbird Departure Tour operates Thursday and Saturday. Reservations are required. ⊠ *2749 Parleys Way #310* ☎ *801/534–1907* ⊕ *www.skiutah.com* ⊠ *$395.*

Wasatch Powderbird Guides. If you don't mind paying for it, the best way to find untracked Utah powder is with Wasatch Powderbird Guides. A helicopter drops you on the top of the mountain, and a guide leads you back down. Itineraries are always weather dependent. Call to inquire about departures from Snowbird (Little Cottonwood Canyon) or Park City Mountain Resort (Canyons Village). ⊠ *3000 Canyons Resort Dr., Park City* ☎ *801/742–2800* ⊕ *www.powderbird.com* ⊠ *From $1260.*

WHERE TO EAT

$$$
AMERICAN

✕ **The Aerie Restaurant, Lounge and Sushi Bar.** Spectacular panoramic views through 15-foot windows, white-linen tablecloths, and dark Oriental rugs set a romantic mood at Little Cottonwood's most elegant dining option on the 10th floor of the Cliff Lodge. Pleasant surprises dot the menu, with entrées like lobster mac-and-cheese and the BBQ whiskey-braised pork shank. **Known for:** game dishes; lobster mac-and-cheese.

[$] *Average main: $30* ✉ *Snowbird Ski and Summer Resort, Cliff Lodge, Hwy. 210, 10th fl., Snowbird* ☎ *801/933–2160* 🌐 *www.snowbird.com/dining/the-aerie* ⏲ *No lunch.*

$$$$ AMERICAN 🍴 **Shallow Shaft.** For fine American Kobe beef, seafood, poultry, and pasta dishes, Alta's only sit-down restaurant not in a hotel is the place to go. The cuisine has a regional focus, with dishes like Willis lamb T-bone and boneless beef short rib. **Known for:** upscale dining; Kobe beef; delicious steaks. [$] *Average main: $38* ✉ *10199 E. Hwy. 210, Alta* ☎ *801/742–2177* 🌐 *www.shallowshaft.com* ⏲ *No lunch. Closed Apr.–Nov.*

$$$$ STEAKHOUSE 🍴 **Steak Pit.** Views and food take precedence over interior design at Snowbird's oldest restaurant, with a menu full of well-prepared steak and seafood choices. Whether you opt for the oven-baked scallops or filet mignon, you can't go wrong. **Known for:** prime rib eye with smoked sea salt; Alaskan king crab split legs. [$] *Average main: $35* ✉ *Snowbird Plaza Center, 9385 S # 092, Snowbird Center Trail, Snowbird* ☎ *801/933–2222* 🌐 *www.snowbird.com/dining/the-steak-pit* ⏲ *No lunch.*

WHERE TO STAY

$$$$ B&B/INN 🏨 **Alta Lodge.** This is a homey place, where many families have been booking the same week each year for several generations. **Pros:** close to Alta's steep slopes; views of the Wasatch Mountains; pleasant staff. **Cons:** few amenities for price; no TVs in guest rooms. [$] *Rooms from: $360* ✉ *10230 Little Cottonwood Canyon Rd., Alta* ☎ *801/742–3500, 800/707–2582* 🌐 *www.altalodge.com* ⏲ *Closed mid-Apr.–May and early Oct.–mid-Nov.* 🛏 *53 rooms, 4 dorms* 🍽 *Some meals.*

$$$$ HOTEL 🏨 **Alta's Rustler Lodge.** Alta's fanciest lodge resembles a traditional full-service hotel and the interior is decidedly upscale. **Pros:** mountain views; on the slopes of Alta Ski Resort; unpretentious service. **Cons:** avalanches are rare, but you could get snowed in. [$] *Rooms from: $450* ✉ *10380 E. Hwy. 210, Alta* ☎ *801/742–4200* 🌐 *www.rustlerlodge.com* ⏲ *Closed May–mid-Nov.* 🛏 *85 rooms, 4 dorms* 🍽 *Some meals.*

$$$$ RESORT 🏨 **Cliff Lodge.** The stark concrete walls of this 10-story structure, designed to complement the surrounding granite cliffs, enclose a self-contained village with restaurants, bars, shops, and a high-end, two-story spa. **Pros:** windows facing the Wasatch Range; nice rooftop spa; several eateries and bars on-site. **Cons:** outdated furniture; poor lighting in rooms. [$] *Rooms from: $240* ✉ *Snowbird Ski and Summer Resort, 9320 Cliff Lodge Dr., Snowbird* ☎ *801/933–2222, 800/232–9542* 🌐 *www.snowbird.com/lodging/the-cliff-lodge* 🛏 *511 rooms* 🍽 *No meals.*

$$$$ RESORT 🏨 **Iron Blosam Lodge.** A utilitarian lobby with a lot of exposed concrete belies attractive condo-style lodging with accommodations and amenities to suit most any traveler's needs, including studios, bedrooms with lofts, and one-bedroom suites. **Pros:** many rooms have fireplaces and balconies; close to the slopes. **Cons:** guests booking through Saturday will be required to change rooms due to property's fix week ownership. [$] *Rooms from: $240* ✉ *Hwy. 210, Resort Entry 2, Snowbird* ☎ *801/933–2222, 800/232–9542* 🌐 *www.snowbird.com/lodging/the-iron-blosam* ⏲ *Closed 1 wk fall and 1 wk late spring* 🛏 *159 rooms* 🍽 *No meals.*

NIGHTLIFE AND PERFORMING ARTS

NIGHTLIFE

Almost all the lodges in Little Cottonwood have their own bar or lounge, and tend to be on the quiet side, centering on the après-ski scene.

Aerie Lounge. Lots of couches and a fireplace give the Aerie Lounge a relaxed feel. You can listen to live music every Wednesday, Saturday, and Sunday night during the winter. ⊠ *Snowbird Ski and Summer Resort, Cliff Lodge, Hwy. 210, 10th fl., Snowbird* ☎ *801/933–2222* ⊕ *www.snowbird.com/dining/the-aerie.*

The Sitzmark Club. Upstairs at the Alta Lodge, the Sitzmark Club is a small, comfortable bar that is a favorite with many of the freeskiers who call Little Cottonwood home. ⊠ *Alta Lodge, Hwy. 210, Alta* ☎ *801/742–3500* ⊕ *www.altalodge.com.*

Tram Club. Windows looking into the grais of the Snowbird tram give the Tram Club its name. Swank leather couches, live music, pool tables, big screens, and video games draw a younger crowd. ⊠ *Snowbird Center, Hwy. 210, Snowbird* ☎ *801/933–2222* ⊕ *www.snowbird. com/dining/the-tram-club.*

PERFORMING ARTS

Snowbird Ski and Summer Resort. Even after the snow melts, this is one of the top spots to go in the mountains for special events, including the Friday night films, free outdoor music, and two months of Oktoberfest. ⊠ *Hwy. 210, Snowbird* ☎ *801/933–2222* ⊕ *www.snowbird.com.*

ANTELOPE ISLAND STATE PARK

25 miles north of Salt Lake City.

The best way to experience Great Salt Lake is a half-day excursion to Antelope Island. There's no place in the country like this state park, home to millions of waterfowl and hundreds of bison and antelope, and surrounded by some of the saltiest water on earth. Drive the 7-mile narrow causeway that links the shoreline, then explore the historic ranch house and miles of hiking trails, and try a buffalo burger at the small café.

GETTING HERE AND AROUND

Take Exit 332 off Interstate 15, then drive west on Antelope Drive for 7 miles to the park entrance.

EXPLORING

Antelope Island State Park. Hiking and biking trails crisscross the island. You can go saltwater bathing at several beach areas. Since the salinity level of the lake is always greater than that of the ocean, the water is extremely buoyant. Hot showers at the marina remove the chill and the salt afterward.

The island has historic sites, as well as desert wildlife and birds in their natural habitat. The island's most popular inhabitants are the members of a herd of more than 500 bison descended from 12 brought here in 1893. Each October at the **Buffalo Roundup** more than 250 volunteers on horseback round up the free-roaming animals and herd them to the island's north end to be counted. The island's **Fielding-Garr House,** built in 1848 and now owned by the state, was the oldest continuously inhabited home in Utah until the last resident moved out in 1981. The house displays assorted ranching artifacts, and guided horseback riding is available from the stables next to the house. Sample a bison burger at the stand that overlooks the lake to the north. Access to the island is via a 7½-mile causeway. ✉ *4528 W. 1700 S, Syracuse* ☎ *801/773–2941* 🌐 *stateparks.utah.gov* 🎫 *$10 per vehicle, $3 per pedestrian.*

SPORTS AND THE OUTDOORS

HIKING

Antelope Island State Park offers plenty of space for the avid hiker to explore, but keep a few things in mind. All trails are also shared by mountain bikers and horseback riders—not to mention the occasional bison. Trees are few and far between on the island, making for high exposure to the elements, so bring (and drink) plenty of water and dress appropriately. In the spring, biting insects make bug repellent a must-have. Pick up a trail map at the visitor center.

Once you're prepared, hiking Antelope Island can be a very enjoyable experience. Trails are fairly level except for a few places, where the hot summer sun makes the climb even more strenuous. Mountain ranges, including the Wasatch Front to the east and the Stansbury Mountains directly to the west, provide beautiful background in every direction, though haze sometimes obscures the view. Aromatic sage plants offer shelter for a variety of wildlife, so don't be startled if your next step flushes a chukar partridge, horned lark, or jackrabbit. A bobcat is a rarely seen island resident that will likely keep its distance.

MOUNTAIN AND ROAD BIKING

Bountiful Bicycle Center. Bountiful Bicycle Center rents mountain and road bikes and offers great advice on trails. ✉ *2482 S. U.S. 89, Woods Cross* ☎ *801/295–6711* 🌐 *www.bountifulbicycle.com.*

WHERE TO EAT

You'll pass a smorgasbord of fast-food outlets in Davis County north of Salt Lake City, including most of the national chain restaurants and a few that are found mainly in Utah. Unless you go as far north as Ogden, there aren't too many choices.

$ BURGER 🍴 **Island Buffalo Grill.** Some people may have an issue with eating buffalo burgers on a bison sanctuary, but they don't know what they're missing. No frills here, but there is an unparalleled view. **Known for:** buffalo burgers; spectacular views. [$] *Average main: $8* ✉ *Antelope Island Rd., 4528 W. 1700 S, Syracuse* ☎ *801/897–3452* 🕒 *No dinner. Closed Nov.–Feb.*

$$ BURGER 🍴 **Roosters Brewing Company.** Even in conservative Davis County north of Salt Lake City, you can find one couple with a passion for beer and quality brewpub fare. The original Roosters is farther north in Ogden, but for nearly a decade, the Layton location has served the array of Roosters beers (from stouts to pale ales), accompanied by individual-size pizzas, full-meal salads, burgers, and pasta. **Known for:** homemade root beer; Naughty fries. [$] *Average main: $15* ✉ *718 W. Heritage Park Blvd., Layton* ☎ *801/774–9330* 🌐 *www.roostersbrewingco.com.*

THANKSGIVING POINT

28 miles south of Salt Lake City.

Heading south toward ultraconservative Utah County (home of Brigham Young University), make Thanksgiving Point your first stop. Founded by WordPerfect computing giant Alan Ashton, Thanksgiving Point is home to museums, gardens, championship golf, restaurants, and a movie theater.

2

GETTING HERE AND AROUND

Thanksgiving Point is centrally located about halfway between Salt Lake City and Provo just off Interstate 15 at the Point of the Mountain. Look for the water tower, which can be seen from the freeway. From Salt Lake City, take Interstate 15 south to Exit 284 (Alpine/Highland). Turn right and proceed west to the light. Turn left onto Thanksgiving Way and proceed ½ mile to Water Tower Plaza.

EXPLORING

FAMILY **Thanksgiving Point.** Founded by the Ashton family (Alan Ashton founded computer-software giant WordPerfect), Thanksgiving Point is now an ever-evolving destination for all visitors to enjoy. Wander among 60 dinosaur skeletons in the Museum of Ancient Life; play golf on an 18-hole Johnny Miller–designed course; or meditate in 55 acres of carefully landscaped gardens. There are also farm animals, shops, restaurants, and a movie theater. The museum is open year-round, but gardens and other attractions are seasonal. ⊠ *3003 N. Thanksgiving Way, Lehi* ☎ *801/768–2300, 801/768–2300* ⊕ *www.thanksgivingpoint. com* 🖃 *$15 museum, $15 gardens, $8 Farm Country* ⊘ *Closed Sun.*

SHOPPING

PLAZAS AND MALLS

Outlets at Traverse Mountain. Utah's newest outlet mall has some of the top names in retail, including Nike, Gap, J.Crew, Polo Ralph Lauren, Coach, and Michael Kors. ⊠ *3700 N. Cabelas Blvd., Lehi* ☎ *801/901–1200* ⊕ *www.outletsattraversemountain.com.*

TIMPANOGOS CAVE NATIONAL MONUMENT

36 miles from Salt Lake City.

Although visitors of all ages and abilities can find easy exploring in the canyons surrounding the Wasatch Front, Timpanogos Cave is suitable only for robust and prepared hikers. The journey is well worth it.

GETTING HERE AND AROUND

From Salt Lake City, take Interstate 15 to Exit 284 (Alpine/Highland exit), then turn east on State Highway 92 for 10 miles to the monument. The highway runs east—west through the monument.

EXPLORING

Timpanogos Cave National Monument. Soaring to 11,750 feet, Mount Timpanogos is the centerpiece of a wilderness area of the same name and towers over Timpanogos Cave National Monument along Highway 92 within American Fork Canyon. After a strenuous hike up the paved 1½-mile trail to the entrance, you can explore three caves connected by two man-made tunnels. Stalactites, stalagmites, and other formations make the three-hour round-trip hike and tour worth the effort. No refreshments are available on the trail or at the cave, and the cave temperature is 45°F throughout the year, so bring water and warm clothes. Although there's some lighting inside the caves, a flashlight will make your explorations more interesting; it will also come in handy should you have to head back down the trail at dusk. These popular tours are often sold out; to guarantee your place on Saturday and holidays, purchase tickets in advance. ⊠ *2038 Alpine Loop Rd., American Fork* ☎ *801/756–5239 cave info, 801/756–5238 advance tickets* ⊕ *www.nps. gov/tica* ⊠ *$8* ⊙ *Closed Nov.–Apr.*

OFF THE
BEATEN
PATH

Alpine Loop Scenic Byway. Beyond Timpanogos Cave, Highway 92 continues up American Fork Canyon before branching off to climb behind Mount Timpanogos itself. Designated the Alpine Loop Scenic Byway, this winding road offers stunning mountain views and fall foliage in the latter months before dropping into Provo Canyon to the south. The 9-mile Timpooneke Trail and the 8-mile Aspen Trail, both off the byway, reach the summit of Mount Timpanogos. Closed in winter, the Alpine Loop isn't recommended for motor homes and trucks pulling trailers. This is the roundabout way to get to scenic Provo Canyon from I–15; the more direct route is U.S. 189 east from Orem (stop by Bridal Veil Falls on your way in). ⊠ *Provo* ⊕ *utah.com/scenic-drive/alpine-loop*.

PARK CITY AND
THE SOUTHERN
WASATCH

Updated by
Caitlin Martz
Streams

The Wasatch Range shares the same desert climate as the Great Basin, which it rims, but these craggy peaks rise to more than 11,000 feet, and stall storms moving in from the Pacific causing massive precipitations. The 160-mile stretch of verdure is home to 2 million people, or three-fourths of all Utahns. Although its landscape is crisscrossed by freeways and dappled by towns large and small, the Wasatch still beckons adventurers with its alpine forests and windswept canyons.

Where three geologically distinct regions—the Rocky Mountains, the Colorado Plateau, and the Basin and Range provinces—converge, the Wasatch Range combines characteristics of each. You'll find broad gla-cial canyons with towering granite walls, stream-cut gorges through purple, tan, and green shale, and red-rock bluffs and valleys.

Most people associate Park City with its legendary skiing in winter, but this is truly a year-round destination. Bright-blue lakes afford fantastic boating and water sports, and some of the West's best trout streams flow from the high country. Add miles of hiking and biking trails, the Sundance Film Festival, and an increasing number of nightclubs and music venues, and you have a vacation that's hard to beat.

ORIENTATION AND PLANNING

GETTING ORIENTED

Each canyon of the Wasatch is different in topography and scenery. The back (eastern) side of the range is rural, with high-mountain pas-tures, farms, and small towns, whereas the front side is a long stretch of metropolis.

Park City and the Wasatch Back. This is the hospitality heart of the moun-tains, and you'll be spending a good deal of your time in Park City whatever your budget. There's everything from fine dining on Main Street to athlete training and shows at Utah Olympic Park to nonstop year-round activity at the resorts. Mountain valleys north and south of Park City are home to stunning wildlife.

South of Salt Lake City. It's worth venturing south to the glorious Sundance Resort for a slice of rural Utah. Even farther south, Provo, home to Brigham Young University, counters Park City's "Sin City" reputation with an overwhelming Mormon temperance.

TOP REASONS TO GO

Outdoor fun: Regardless of the season, Park City is the epicenter of mountain adventure. You come here to play, not to watch, whether your speed is a hot-air balloon float or an 80 mph bobsled run.

Two top-tier resorts: No place in North America has two world-class and distinct resorts so close to one another, not to mention as expansive, dynamic, luxurious, and unique as Deer Valley and Park City Mountain Resort, and it's not only skiing on offer—the resorts provide year-round adventures and hospitality.

Olympic spirit: This town seems to contain more Olympians per capita than any town in the country, if not the world; nearly every U.S. winter

Olympian trains in Park City at some point every four years.

Old Town Park City: First laid out by silver miners in the late 1800s, Park City's historic Main Street has dozens of fine restaurants, bars, galleries, and boutiques. Always vibrant, its hub is especially lively during big events like the Sundance Film Festival and Kimball Arts Festival.

Sundance Resort: At the base of Mount Timpanogos, Robert Redford's intimate resort pays homage to art and nature, with artists in residence creating works before your eyes, and the chance to bond with Mother Nature. You can ski here, too, but the calendar of performances and speakers is the biggest attraction.

PLANNING

WHEN TO GO

Winter is long in the mountains (ski resorts buzz from November to mid-April) but much more manageable in the valleys. The snow stops falling in April or May, and a month later the temperatures are in the 80s. In spring and fall, rates drop and crowds lessen. Spring is also a good time for fishing, rafting on rivers swollen with snowmelt, birding, and wildlife viewing. In summer, water-sports enthusiasts of all stripes flock to the region's reservoirs, alpine lakes, rivers, and streams. The Wasatch Mountains draw those seeking respite from the heat of the valley from June through Labor Day. Fall's colors rival those of New England; a tradition here is to drive along the Alpine Loop east of Provo or up Pine Canyon out of the Heber Valley.

PLANNING YOUR TIME

At your home base in Park City you can ski, snowboard, hike, mountain bike, or simply take in the scenery at the local resorts. Head east to Heber City or Midway for golfing at Wasatch State Park, cross-country skiing at Soldier Hollow, or fly-fishing on the Provo River. Plan at least a half-day trip to Sundance Resort. For a glimpse of Utah's Mormon culture, spend a day in the college town of Provo, particularly if home team Brigham Young University is playing rival University of Utah. Warm-weather drives along the Alpine Loop or Mirror Lake scenic byways are great opportunities for snapping photos of mountain vistas and wildlife.

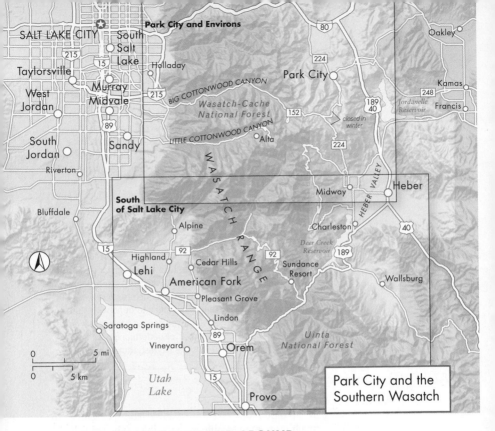

Park City and the Southern Wasatch

GETTING HERE AND AROUND

AIR TRAVEL

Commercial air traffic flies in and out of Salt Lake International Airport, which is less than an hour from all destinations in the Wasatch and 7 miles northwest of downtown Salt Lake City. The airport is served by Alaska, American, Delta, Southwest, jetBlue, Frontier, United, Air Canada, and KLM. Provo Airport has commercial flights from Los Angeles, Oakland, San Diego, and Mesa, Arizona, on Allegiant Airlines. Heber's airport is open to private planes only.

Contacts Salt Lake City International Airport. ⊠ 776 N. Terminal Dr., Salt Lake City ☎ 801/575–2400 ⊕ www.slcairport.com.

CAR TRAVEL

Highway travel around the region is quick and easy. The major routes in the area include the transcontinental I–80, which connects Salt Lake City and Park City; and U.S. 40/189, which connects southwest Wyoming, Utah, and northwest Colorado via Park City, Heber City, and Provo. Along larger highways, roadside stops with restrooms, fast-food restaurants, and sundries stores are well spaced. Scenic routes and lookout points are clearly marked, enabling you to slow down and pull over to take in the views. Off the main highways, roads range from well-paved multilane blacktop routes to barely graveled backcountry trails. Watch out for wildlife on the roads just about anywhere in Utah.

Road Conditions Utah Highway Patrol; Wasatch, Summit and Rich Counties. ✉ *10420 No. Jordanelle Blvd., Heber* ☎ *435/655-3445* ⊕ *highwaypatrol.utah.gov.* **Utah Road Condition Information.** ☎ *511 Salt Lake City area, 866/511-8824 within Utah* ⊕ *www.udot.utah.gov.*

SHUTTLE TRAVEL

Shuttles are the best way to travel between the airport and Park City, and fares start at $39 per person one way. A free, efficient Park City transit system operates a reliable network of bus routes, connecting Old Town, the local ski resorts, Kimball Junction, and most neighborhoods.

Shuttle Contacts Canyon Transportation. ☎ *801/255-1841* ⊕ *www.canyontransport.com.* **Park City Direct Shuttle.** ☎ *866/655-3010 toll free, 435/655-3010* ⊕ *www.parkcitydirectshuttle.com.*

RESTAURANTS

American cuisine dominates the Wasatch dining scene, with great steaks, barbecue, and traditional Western fare. There's also an abundance of good seafood, which the busier eateries fly in daily from the West Coast. Restaurants range from Swiss to Japanese, French, and Mexican. Hours vary seasonally, so it's a good idea to call ahead. Reservations are essential during winter holiday weekends and the Sundance Film Festival. Park City restaurants offer great deals, such as two-for-one entrées from spring to fall, so check the local newspaper for coupons or ask your concierge which eateries are offering discounts.

HOTELS

Chain hotels and motels dot I–15 all along the Wasatch Front and nearly always have availability. Every small town on the back side of the range has at least one good bed-and-breakfast, and most towns have both independent and chain motels. Condominiums dominate Park City lodging, but you also find high-end hotels, luxurious lodges, and well-run bed-and-breakfast inns. All this luxury means prices here tend to be higher than in other areas in the state during the winter. Prices drop significantly in the warmer months, when package deals or special rates are offered. Lodging in Provo tends to be most expensive during the week. Make reservations well in advance for busy ski holidays like Christmas, Presidents' Day, and Martin Luther King Jr. Day, and during January's Sundance Film Festival. As the mountain country is often on the cool side, lodgings at higher elevations generally don't have air-conditioning. *Hotel reviews have been shortened. For full information, visit Fodors.com.*

CAMPGROUNDS

There are a number of wonderful campgrounds across the Wasatch–Cache National Forest. Between Big and Little Cottonwood canyons there are four higher-elevation sites. In the vicinity of Provo, American Fork, Provo Canyon, and the Hobble Creek drainage, there are dozens of possibilities. Additional campgrounds are at the region's state parks and national monuments.

Sites range from rustic (pit toilets and cold running water) to posh (hot showers, swimming pools, paved trailer pads, full hookups). Fees vary from $6 to $20 a night for tents and up to $50 for RVs, but are usually waived once the water is turned off for the winter. Site reservations are accepted at most campgrounds, but are usually limited to seven days (early birds reserve up to a year in advance). Campers who prefer a more remote setting may camp in the vast National Forest Service and Bureau of Land Management backcountry. You might need a permit, which is available from park visitor centers and ranger stations.

WHAT IT COSTS			
	$	$$	$$$	$$$$
Restaurants	under $12	$12–$20	$21–$30	over $30
Hotels	under $100	$100–$150	$151–$200	over $200

Restaurant prices are the average cost of a main course at dinner or, if dinner is not served, at lunch. Hotel prices are the lowest cost of a standard double room in high season.

VISITOR INFORMATION

Park City Convention and Visitors Bureau. ⊠ *1850 Sidewinder Dr., #320, Park City* ☎ *800/453–1360* ⊕ *www.visitparkcity.com.*

Ski Utah. ⊠ *2749 E. Parleys Way, Suite 310, Salt Lake City* ☎ *801/534–1779, 800/754–8824* ⊕ *www.skiutah.com.*

Utah Valley Convention and Visitors Bureau. ⊠ *220 W. Center St., Suite 100, Provo* ☎ *801/851–2100, 800/222–8824* ⊕ *www.utahvalley.com.*

PARK CITY AND THE WASATCH BACK

The best-known areas of the Wasatch Mountains lie east of Salt Lake City. Up and over Parley's Canyon via I-80 you'll find the sophisticated mountain town of Park City, with its world-class ski resorts and myriad summer attractions.

After silver was discovered in Park City in 1868, it quickly became a rip-roaring mining town with more than two-dozen saloons and a thriving red-light district. In the process, it earned the nickname "Sin City." A fire destroyed many of the town's buildings in 1898; this, combined with declining mining fortunes in the early 1900s, caused most of the residents to pack up and leave. It wasn't until 1946 that its current livelihood began to take shape in the form of the small Snow Park ski hill, which opened where Deer Valley Resort now sits.

Park City once again profited from the generosity of the mountains as skiing became popular. In 1963 Treasure Mountain Resort began operations with its skier's subway—an underground train and hoist system that ferried skiers to the mountain's summit via old mining tunnels. Facilities were upgraded over time, and Treasure Mountain became the Park City Mountain Resort. Although it has a mind-numbing collection of condominiums, at Park City's heart is a historic downtown that rings with the authenticity of a real town with real roots.

GETTING HERE AND AROUND

If you're arriving via Salt Lake City, a rental car or shuttle bus will get you to Park City in about 35 minutes. Park City has a free transit system running between neighborhoods and to the ski resorts. It operates from roughly 6 am to midnight in summer and winter. The schedule is more limited in fall and spring, so be sure to check schedules at the Transit Center on Swede Alley or on the buses.

Old Town is walkable, but the rest of greater Park City is best explored by bicycle in the spring, summer, and fall. More than 400 miles of bike trails help Park City earn accolades as one of the top cycling communities in the world, including the designation of Gold Level Ride Center by International Mountain Biking Association. Automobile traffic is relatively minimal and limited to slowdowns during morning and evening commutes and the postski exodus from the resorts. There are several local taxi businesses.

ESSENTIALS

Visitor Information Park City Visitor Information Center. ⊠ *1794 Olympic Pkwy., Kimball Junction* ☎ *435/658–9616, 435/649–6100* ⊕ *www.visitparkcity. com* ⊠ *Park City Museum, 528 Main St., Park City* ☎ *435/649–7457.*

FESTIVALS

Robert Redford's Sundance Film Festival comes to Park City every January, but the city hosts a number of other festivals and events that might sway your decision about when to visit.

FAMILY **Canyons Village Summer Concert Series.** Rock, reggae, funk, and country bands draw fans of all ages to Park City Mountain Resort's village stage at Canyons Village in July and August. Food vendors and family activities surround the Resort Village, and picnics are welcome. ⊠ *4000 Canyons Resort Dr., Park City* ☎ *435/649–8111* ⊕ *www.parkcitymountain.com.*

Fodor's Choice **Deer Valley Snow Park Amphitheater.** Everything from Utah Symphony ★ performances to country music features on stage. Big names like Willie Nelson, Bonnie Raitt, Chris Isaak, and Judy Collins have graced the outdoor amphitheater, which sits on the resort's beginner ski area. ■TIP➔ Go on Wednesday evenings for free concerts with local and regional bands and pack a picnic. ⊠ *Park City* ☎ *435/649–1000* ⊕ *www.deervalley.com.*

FAMILY **Independence Day Celebration.** A traditional celebration, complete with a pancake breakfast, parade down Main Street, fireworks, and all-day activities in City Park, is a sure sign that summer has arrived. It culminates in fireworks that illuminate the sky over Old Town. ⊠ *Park City* ☎ *435/649–6100* ⊕ *www.visitparkcity.com.*

FAMILY **Miner's Day.** The end of the summer season is heralded with an old-fashioned parade down Main Street and the Rotary Club's "Running of the Balls"—with golf balls in place of Pamplona-style bulls—followed by miners' competitions of mucking and drilling at Library Park. This

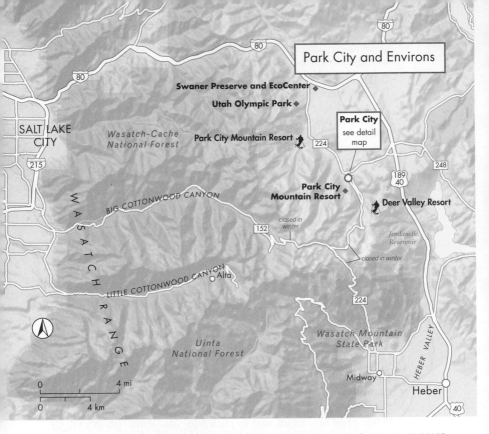

Park City and Environs

Swaner Preserve and EcoCenter

Utah Olympic Park

Park City Mountain Resort

Park City
see detail
map

Wasatch-Cache
National Forest

Salt Lake City

Big Cottonwood Canyon

Park City
Mountain Resort

Deer Valley Resort

closed in
winter

Jordanelle
Reservoir

Little Cottonwood Canyon

Alta

closed in winter

Wasatch Mountain
State Park

Uinta
National Forest

Midway

Heber Valley

Heber

0   4 mi

0   4 km

Labor Day tradition is a Park City favorite. ⊠ *Park City* ☎ *435/649–6100* ⊕ *www.visitparkcity.com.*

Park City Food & Wine Classic. Held in early July, this festival offers tastings of hundreds of wines from seemingly every continent, paired with great food, educational seminars, and gourmet dinners around town. It culminates in a grand tasting at Montage Deer Valley. ■TIP→ **It's increasingly popular, and many events now sell out in advance, so plan ahead.** ⊠ *Park City* ☎ *877/328–2783* ⊕ *www.parkcityfoodandwine-classic.com.*

Fodor'sChoice ★ **Park City Kimball Arts Festival.** Celebrating visual and culinary art, this three-day festival, held the first weekend in August, is the biggest summer event in town. More than 200 artists from all over North America exhibit and offer their work to 40,000 festival attendees. Culinary vendors and beer and wine gardens offer plenty of refreshment to art lovers, and live music is around every corner. ⊠ *Main St., Park City* ☎ *435/649–8882* ⊕ *www.parkcitykimballartsfestival.org.*

Savor the Summit. When more than 25 of Park City's restaurants—from gourmet to on-the-go—take over Main Street for the Saturday nearest the Summer Solstice in June, it's a spectacle of food, drink, and music that is unmatched in the country. Restaurateurs line the length of Main Street with a mile-long "Grande Table," creating the largest dinner party you'll witness in Utah. Pick one restaurant (many sell out) and be treated to a special menu, often with a theme related to Park City's colorful history. Visit the website for participating restaurants and reservation information. ⊠ *Main St., Park City* ☎ *435/640–7921* ⊕ *www. parkcityrestaurants.com/savor-the-summit.*

Fodor's Choice ★ **Sundance Film Festival.** For 10 days each January, Park City morphs into a mountain version of Hollywood as movie stars and film executives gather for the internationally recognized Sundance Film Festival, hosted by Robert Redford's Sundance Institute. In addition to panels, tributes, premieres, and screenings of independent films at various venues in Park City, Sundance, Ogden, and Salt Lake City, there are music and culinary events as well.

■**TIP→** **Book your hotel months in advance. Skip the rental car and use the free shuttle. Park City's legendary ski slopes empty out while the filmgoers pack the screenings, so build in a day of crowd-free skiing.** ⊠ *Park City* ☎ *435/658–3456* ⊕ *www.sundance.org/festival.*

EXPLORING

Park City and the surrounding area hosted the lion's share of skiing and sliding events during the 2002 Winter Olympic Games, and the excited spirit of the Games is still evident around town. Visitors often enjoy activities at the Utah Olympic Park or simply taking candid photos at various memorable sports venues.

The city also serves as an excellent base camp for summer activities. Hiking trails are plentiful. A scenic drive over Guardsman Pass is now mostly paved and passable for most vehicles, providing incredible mountain vistas. There are top-rated golf courses, hot-air ballooning is popular, and mountain bikers find the ski slopes and old mining roads truly exceptional pedaling. With so much to offer both summer and winter visitors, dozens of hotels of all levels have sprung up to complement the three resorts, each with its own scene.

Both Park City ski resorts consistently earn high skier-snowboarder rankings. Whereas Park City Mountain Resort is known for its central location, superb family amenities, and gnarly parks and pipes for snowboarders and free skiers, Deer Valley is in a peaceful spot at the edge of town and is renowned for its creature comforts—and its prohibition on snowboarding. A city-run free shuttle-bus system serves the resorts.

TOP ATTRACTIONS

FAMILY **Park City Mountain Resort.** In the warmer months, the resort transforms itself into a mountain amusement park, with attractions such as the Alpine Slide, zip lines, Alpine Coaster, and a climbing wall. The Alpine Slide begins with a chairlift ride up the mountain, and then special sleds carry sliders down 3,000 feet of winding concrete and fiberglass track at speeds controlled by each rider. Two zip lines offer high-flying adrenaline rushes as riders strap into a harness suspended from a cable. The gravity-propelled Alpine Coaster (which operates year-round) zooms through aspen-lined twists and turns at speeds up to 35 mph. There's also a climbing wall, miniature golf course, trampolines,

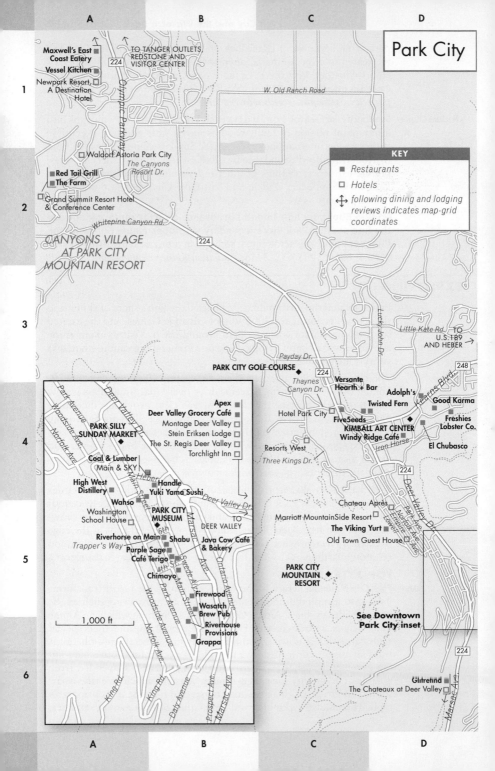

Park City

KEY
- ■ Restaurants
- □ Hotels
- ⬌ following dining and lodging reviews indicates map-grid coordinates

TO TANGER OUTLETS, REDSTONE AND VISITOR CENTER

224

Maxwell's East Coast Eatery ■
Vessel Kitchen ■
Newpark Resort, A Destination Hotel □

W. Old Ranch Road

Olympic Parkway

□ Waldorf Astoria Park City
The Canyons Resort Dr.

■ Red Tail Grill
■ The Farm

□ Grand Summit Resort Hotel & Conference Center

Whitepine Canyon Rd.

CANYONS VILLAGE
AT PARK CITY
MOUNTAIN RESORT

224

Little Kate Rd.
TO U.S.189 AND HEBER

Lucky John Dr.

248

Payday Dr.

PARK CITY GOLF COURSE ◆

224
Thaynes Canyon Dr.

Versante Hearth + Bar ■
Adolph's ■
Twisted Fern ■
Good Karma ■

Hotel Park City □

Five5eeds ■
KIMBALL ART CENTER
Windy Ridge Café ■

Freshies Lobster Co. ■

Iron Horse

El Chubasco ■

Resorts West
Three Kings Dr.

224

Chateau Après □
Marriott MountainSide Resort □

The Viking Yurt ■
Old Town Guest House □

PARK CITY MOUNTAIN RESORT ◆

See Downtown
Park City inset

224

Glitretind ■
The Chateaux at Deer Valley □

Downtown Park City inset

Park Avenue
Deer Valley Dr.
Norfolk Ave.

PARK SILLY SUNDAY MARKET ◆

Apex ■
Deer Valley Grocery Café ■
Montage Deer Valley □
Stein Eriksen Lodge □
The St. Regis Deer Valley □
Torchlight Inn □

Coal & Lumber ■
Main & SKY

Heber

High West Distillery ■
Handle ■
Yuki Yama Sushi ■

Wahso ■
Washington School House □

PARK CITY MUSEUM

Main Street

Deer Valley Dr.

TO DEER VALLEY

Riverhorse on Main ■
Shabu ■
Java Cow Café & Bakery ■

Purple Sage ■
Café Terigo ■
Trapper's Way

6th

Marsac Ave.

Sweete Ally

Chimayo ■

4th St.

Ontario Avenue

Firewood ■
Wasatch Brew Pub ■

1,000 ft

Riverhouse Provisions ■
Grappa ■

Woodside Avenue
Park Avenue
King Rd.
Norfolk Ave.
Prospect Ave.
Daly Avenue
Marsac Ave.

an adventure zone for younger children, and some of the West's best lift-served mountain biking and hiking. ✉ *1345 Lowell Ave., Park City* ☎ *435/649–8111, 800/222–7275* ⊕ *www.parkcitymountain.com.*

Park City Museum. A must-see for history buffs, this museum is housed in the former library, city hall, and the Bell Tower on Main Street. With a two-story scale model of the 19th-century Ontario Mine, a 20th-century gondola hanging overhead, and the old jail below, this is an authentic tribute to Park City's mining and skiing past. Climb aboard a re-created Union Pacific train car, hold on to a quivering and noisy jack drill for a feel of the mining experience, and, if you dare, step inside a jail cell. Tours of historic Main Street also depart from here. ✉ *528 Main St., Park City* ☎ *435/649–7457* ⊕ *www.parkcityhistory.org* ✑ *$12.*

FAMILY
Fodor's Choice
★
Utah Olympic Park. An exciting legacy of the 2002 Winter Olympics, this is a mecca of bobsled, skeleton, luge, and ski jumping. As it is one of the only places in America where you can try these sports, you might have to wait your turn behind U.S. Olympians and aspirants who train here year-round. In summer or winter, screaming down the track in a bobsled at nearly 80 mph with a professional driver is a ride you will never forget. In summer, check out the freestyle ski jumpers doing flips and spins into a splash pool and Nordic jumpers soaring to soft landings on a synthetic outrun. Ride the zip lines or Alpine Slide, or explore the adventure course. There's also an interactive ski museum and an exhibit on the Olympics; guided tours are offered year-round, or you can take a self-guided tour. ✉ *3419 Olympic Pkwy., Park City* ☎ *435/658–4200* ⊕ *www.utaholympiclegacy.com* ✑ *Museum and self-guided tours free, guided tours $13.*

WORTH NOTING

Kimball Art Center. A thriving nonprofit community art center, this venue hosts national and regional exhibitions, sells art supplies, provides educational opportunities including seminars and art classes for all ages, and hosts special events. ✉ *1404 Kearns Blvd., Park City* ☎ *435/649–8882* ⊕ *www.kimballartcenter.org* ✑ *Free.*

Park Silly Sunday Market. A funky and constantly changing assortment of artisans, entertainers, and culinary vendors transform Old Town into a street festival complete with beer garden and Bloody Mary bar on Sunday, June through September. The Silly Market strives to be a no-waste event with everything recycled or composted. Look for the free bike valet to park your ride while you walk through the crowds. ✉ *Lower Main St., Park City* ☎ *435/714–4036* ⊕ *www.parksillysun-daymarket.com.*

Swaner Preserve and EcoCenter. Home to an array of birds (most notably sandhill cranes) and small critters (like the spotted frog), as well as more elusive larger inhabitants such as foxes, deer, elk, moose, and coyotes, this 1,200-acre preserve is both a bird-watchers' paradise and an example of land restoration in action. Naturalist-led walks, snowshoe tours in winter, and other environmentally friendly events are hosted by this nonprofit throughout the year. The EcoCenter is filled with interactive exhibits, such as a climbing wall with microphones emitting the sounds of the wetlands as climbers move through habitats. The facility serves as an exhibit in itself, given its eco-friendly construction, incorporating everything from recycled denim insulation to solar panels. More than 10 miles of hiking and biking trails encompass both sides of I–80. ✉ *1258 Center Dr., Newpark* ☎ *435/649–1767* ⊕ *www.swanerecocenter.org* ⊡ *Free (donation appreciated)* ⊙ *Closed Mon. and Tues.*

SPORTS AND THE OUTDOORS

BICYCLING

In 2012, Park City was the first community ever designated a Gold Level Ride Center by the International Mountain Bicycling Association, thanks in large part to the relentless work of the Mountain Trails Foundation, which oversees and maintains more than 400 miles of area trails. The accolade is based upon bike shops, trail access, variety, and more. Pick up a map at any local bike shop or get details from the Mountain Trails Foundation (☎ *435/649 6839* ⊕ *www.mountaintrails.org*). You can join local road or mountain bikers most nights in the summer for free group rides sponsored by Park City bike shops.

Cole Sport. Road bikers of all abilities can ride with a pack one evening a week from June to mid-September from this shop. You can rent mountain and road bikes here, too; be ready to ride at 6 pm. ✉ *1615 Park Ave., Park City* ☎ *435/649–4806* ⊕ *www.colesport.com* ☞ *Call in advance for weekly schedule.*

Deer Valley Resort. Mountain bikers from across the world flock to Deer Valley's single track trails for mountain biking each summer, and it's easy to see why with the variety of terrain and bike offerings available. Nearly 70 miles of trails can be accessed from three chairlifts, spanning all levels of ability, including down-hill flow trails. Bike clinics and lessons, both group and private, are offered through the Deer Valley Mountain Bike School, and rentals are available at the base areas. Trails are open June through September. ✉ *2250 Deer Valley Dr. S, Park City* ☎ *435/649–1000* ⊕ *www.deervalley.com.*

Jans Mountain Outfitters. When the snow melts, Jans has everything you need to hit the road on two wheels. Whether you're into mountain bikes, road bikes, or cruisers, stop by to rent or demo something new, or to tune your own wheels. ✉ *1600 Park Ave., Park City* ☎ *435/649–4949* ⊕ *www.jans.com.*

Park City Mountain Resort. Utah's largest ski resort transforms into a summer adventure land for cyclists, with a lift-served bike park at Canyons Village and miles of cross-country and downhill trails across the whole resort. Park City Base Area provides a number of trails accessible directly from the base, or haul your bike up the lift for some downhill riding. Canyons Village is the home of Park City Bike Park, with a dozen downhill flow and jump trails, many of which are accessible to all skill levels. Lessons are available with certified instructors for those who are new to the sport, and cyclists can find bike rentals at both base areas. ✉ *Park City Base Area, 1345 Lowell Ave., Park City* ☎ *435/649–8111* ⊕ *www.parkcitymountain.com.*

Silver Star Ski & Sport. Look for Tallulah, the English bulldog at Silver Star Ski & Sport. While the dog watches the shop, friendly staff help find the best bike to suit your needs. In addition to the retail area of the store offering top-of-the-line gear and clothing, Silver Star offers cruiser, road, and mountain bike rentals. ⊠ *1825 Three Kings Dr. #85, Park City* ☎ *435/645–7827* ⊕ *www.silverstarskiandsport.com.*

White Pine Touring. Every Thursday in summer, mountain bikers of all levels gather at 6 pm for a free guided mountain-bike ride. On the last Thursday of June, July, and August, the White Pine guides prepare a barbecue, too. There's also a women-only ride on Tuesday. For both rides, meet at the shop at 6 pm—earlier if you need to rent a bike. Guided road-biking, mountain-biking, climbing, and hiking tours are also available throughout the summer. ⊠ *1790 Bonanza Dr., Park City* ☎ *435/649–8710* ⊕ *www.whitepinetouring.com.*

FLY-FISHING

The mountain-fed waters of the Provo and Weber rivers and several smaller streams near Park City are prime trout habitat.

Jans Mountain Outfitters. During the summer, the entire upstairs of this store is dedicated solely to fly-fishing, and knowledgeable staff will help you find the best equipment and gear for your time on the river. Specializing in trout fishing, guides lead fly-fishing excursions year-round in nearby rivers, rent equipment, and provide insight and advice to the local area. Jans also has exclusive access to private waters in the surrounding areas. Guides also give free casting lessons at the Deer Valley ponds on Monday at 5 pm from Memorial Day to Labor Day. ⊠ *1600 Park Ave., Park City* ☎ *435/649–4949* ⊕ *www.jans.com.*

Park City Fly Shop and Guide Service. See Chris Kunkel, the owner of this shop, for good advice, guide service, and a modest selection of fly-fishing necessities. ⊠ *2065 Sidewinder Dr., Park City* ☎ *435/640–2864* ⊕ *www.pcflyshopguideservice.com.*

Trout Bum 2. This full-service fly shop can outfit you with everything you need, then guide you to where the fish are. This shop has the largest selection of flies in town, and is the only guide service in all of Park City to have access to the renowned Green River below Flaming Gorge Reservoir. Check the website for fishing reports of the areas rivers and streams. ⊠ *4343 N. Hwy. 224, Suite 101, Park City* ☎ *435/658–1166, 877/878–2862* ⊕ *www.troutbum2.com.*

HIKING

The Wasatch Mountains surrounding Park City offer more than 400 miles of hiking trails, ranging from easy, meandering meadow strolls to strenuous climbs up wind-blown peaks. Getting away from civilization and into the aspens is easy, and lucky hikers might spy foxes, coyotes, moose, elk, deer, and red-tailed hawks. Many of the trails take off from the resort areas, but some of the trailheads are right near Main Street. For beginners, or for those acclimating to the elevation, the Rail Trail is a good place to start. Another alternative is to take the McLeod Creek Trail from behind The Market all the way to the Redstone Center. The Round Valley and Lost Prospector trails are still mellow but slightly more challenging. To really get the blood pumping, head up Spiro or do a lengthy stretch of Mid-Mountain.

For interactive trail maps, up-to-date information about trail conditions and events, and answers to your trail questions, contact the nonprofit Mountain Trails Foundation (⊕ *www.mountaintrails.org*) whose mission is to promote, preserve, advocate for, and maintain Park City's local trail system. Maps detailing trail locations are available at most local gear shops.

HORSEBACK RIDING

Blue Sky Adventures. Located just outside of Park City in Wanship, this Vaquero-style equestrian center sits on 3,500 acres of land available for exploring. Using the vaquero method of finding harmony and togetherness between horse and rider, each ride is private and includes a unique gourmet culinary experience. ⊠ *Blue Sky Ranch, 27659 Old Lincoln Hwy.* ☎ *435/252–0662* ⊕ *www.blueskyutah.com.*

Red Pine Adventures. This outfitter leads trail rides through thousands of acres of private land. ⊠ *2050 W. White Pine Canyon Rd., Park City* ☎ *435/649–9445* ⊕ *www.redpinetours.com* ⊟ *From $75.*

Rocky Mountain Recreation. Saddle up for a taste and feel of the Old West with guided mountain trail rides, from one hour to all-day or overnight excursions, departing from several locations in the Park City area, complete with fantastic scenery and good cowboy grub. ⊠ *Stillman Ranch, Oakley* ☎ *435/645–7256* ⊕ *www.rockymtnrec.com* ⊟ *From $66.*

Wind In Your Hair Riding. Only experienced riders who are looking for a get-up-and-go kind of mountain riding adventure are allowed on these trail rides, so there will be no inexperienced riders to slow you down, and the Paso Fino horses are noted for their smooth ride. Plan to tip the trail leader. Lessons are available for beginners. ⊠ *Cherry Canyon Ranch, 46 E. Cherry Canyon Dr., Wanship* ☎ *435/336–4795, 435/901–4644* ⊕ *www.windinyourhair.com* ⊟ *From $150.*

HOT-AIR BALLOONING

Park City Balloon Adventures. Hour-long scenic sunrise flights are offered daily, weather permitting. Fliers meet at Starbucks in Kimball Junction and are shuttled to the take-off site, which varies from day to day. A champagne or nonalcoholic toast is offered on touchdown. Reservations are required. ⊠ *Park City* ☎ *435/645–8787, 800/396–8787* ⊕ *www.pcballoonadventures.com* ⊟ *$225 per person.*

ICE-SKATING

Park City Ice Arena. The Olympic-size rink here provides plenty of space for testing out that triple-toe loop or slap shot. The hill outside the building is popular sledding terrain. ⊠ *600 Gillmor Way, Park City* ☎ *435/615–5700* ⊕ *www.parkcityice.org* ⊟ *$11.*

RAFTING

Utah Outdoor Adventures. This company specializes in half-day and full-day excursions, all of which are private groups. Tours take place on the Weber river on class II and class III rapids. Perfect for all age groups. ⊠ *3310 Mountain Lane, Park City* ☎ *801/703–3357* ⊕ *www.utahoutdooradventures.com* ⊟ *$60.*

Park City Rafting. Two-hour, mostly class II rafting adventures are offered, as well as full-day trips that end with a class III splash. Given the Weber's mostly benign water, there are plenty of breaks between plunges to look for moose, deer, beavers, badgers, and feathered friends along the shore. ✉ *1245 Taggart La., Morgan* ☎ *435/655–3800, 866/467–2384* ⊕ *www. parkcityrafting.com* 🎟 *From $49.*

ROCK CLIMBING

White Pine Touring. If you're looking for some hang time on the local rocks but don't know the area, White Pine Touring offers guided climbing tours, equipment rental, and private and group lessons. Reservations are required. ✉ *1790 Bonanza Dr., Park City* ☎ *435/649–8710* ⊕ *www. whitepinetouring.com* 🎟 *From $325.*

SKIING AND SNOWBOARDING

FAMILY
Fodor'sChoice
★

Deer Valley Resort. Just to the south of downtown Park City, this resort set new standards in the ski industry by providing such amenities as ski valets and slope-side dining of the highest caliber. For such pampering, the resort has drawn rave reviews from virtually every ski and travel magazine, consistently rated #1 Ski Resort in America by *SKI* magazine. The careful layout of runs and the impeccable grooming makes this an intermediate skier's heaven. With the Empire Canyon and Lady Morgan areas, the resort also offers bona fide expert terrain. For many, part of the ski experience includes a two- to three-hour midday interlude of feasting at one of the many world-class dining locations on the mountain and catching major rays on the snow-covered meadow in front of Silver Lake Lodge. The ski experience fits right in with the resort's overall image. With lessons for kids from preschool through teens, Deer Valley's acclaimed children's ski school is sure to please both children and parents. Note: this is one of the only ski resorts in the United States that prohibits snowboards. ✉ *2250 Deer Valley Dr., Park City* ☎ *435/649–1000, 800/424–3337 reservations* ⊕ *www.deervalley.com* 🎟 *Lift ticket $135* ✂ *3,000-ft vertical drop; 2,026 skiable acres; 27% beginner, 41% intermediate, 32% advanced; 101 total runs.*

FAMILY
Fodor'sChoice
★

Park City Mountain Resort. Although this has been one of North America's most popular ski and snowboard destinations for quite some time, in 2015 Vail Resorts joined neighboring Canyons Resort to Park City Mountain, creating the largest ski resort in the United States. With more than 300 trails, 7,300 skiable acres, and 41 lifts, it is almost impossible to ski the entire resort in one day. The trails provide a great mix of beginner, intermediate, and advanced terrain, with Jupiter Peak providing the highest elevation and steepest terrain in town. Three distinct base areas provide a great starting point for the ski day—Park City Base Area has a variety of dining and retail options, along with a stellar après-ski scene. Park City is the only resort with lift access to Historic Main Street with Town Lift, allowing for guests staying near or on Main Street direct access to the slopes. Canyons Village, located on the other side of the mountain, gives ski-in/ski-out access to many of the base area's hotels and lodging properties. The resort is widely acclaimed for being a free-skiing and snowboarding mecca with official Olympic qualifying events each year; you're likely to see Olympic athletes training and playing on the slopes. ⊠ *1345 Lowell Ave., Park City* ☎ *435/649–8111* ⊕ *www.parkcitymountain.com* ☜ *Lift ticket prices change daily; check online for daily rate* ☞ *3,200-ft vertical drop; 7,300 skiable acres; 8% beginner, 42% intermediate, 50% advanced; 41 lifts; 2 halfpipes (including 1 super pipe) and 8 terrain parks.*

Wasatch Powderbird Guides. If you don't mind paying for it, the best way to find untracked Utah powder is with Wasatch Powderbird Guides. A helicopter drops you on the top of the mountain, and a guide leads you back down. Itineraries are always weather dependent. Call to inquire about departures from Snowbird (Little Cottonwood Canyon) or Park City Mountain Resort (Canyons Village). ⊠ *3000 Canyons Resort Dr., Park City* ☎ *801/742–2800* ⊕ *www.powderbird.com* ☜ *From $1260.*

White Pine Nordic Center. Just outside Old Town, White Pine Nordic Center offers around 20 km (12 miles) of set track, in 3-km (2-mile), 5-km (3-mile), and 10-km (6-mile) loops, plus cross-country ski instruction, equipment rentals, and a well stocked cross-country ski shop. The fee to use the track is $18, or $10 after 3 pm. Reservations are required for their guided backcountry ski and snowshoe tours in the surrounding mountains. ⊠ *On Park City Golf Course, 1541 Thaynes Canyon Dr., Park City* ☎ *435/649–6249* ⊕ *www.whitepinetouring.com.*

SKI RENTALS AND EQUIPMENT

Many shops in Park City rent equipment for skiing and other sports. From old-fashioned rental shops that also offer discount lift tickets to luxurious ski-delivery services that will fit you in your room, you have dozens of choices. Prices tend to be slightly lower if you rent in Salt Lake City. ■ TIP→ **If you happen to be visiting during holidays, reserve skiing and snowboarding gear in advance.**

Breeze Winter Sports Rentals. You can reserve your equipment online in advance with this company (often for less than day-of rentals), which has two locations in Park City. You'll find them near Canyons Village and at Park City Base Area. They're owned by Vail Resorts, and you can expect good quality and service at a value price. ⊠ *4343 N. Hwy. 224, Park City* ☎ *435/655–7066, 888/427–3393* ⊕ *www.skirentals.com.*

Cole Sport. With four locations from Main Street to Deer Valley, Cole Sport carries all of your winter ski, snowboard, and snowshoe rental needs. Come back in summer for bikes, stand-up paddleboards, hiking gear, and more. No matter the season, Cole Sport offers expert fitting and advice with a broad range of equipment. ⊠ *1615 Park Ave., Park City* ☎ *435/649–4806, 800/345–2938* ⊕ *www.colesport.com.*

Jans Mountain Outfitters. For almost 40 years, this has been the locals' choice for gear rentals, with ski and snowboard equipment packages and clothing in winter, and bikes and fly-fishing gear in summer. With the most knowledgeable staff around, they'll assist you with any outdoor adventure. There are multiple locations, including the flagship Park Avenue store, Deer Valley, and Park City Mountain Resort. ⊠ *1600 Park Ave., Park City* ☎ *435/649–4949* ⊕ *www.jans.com.*

Park City Sport. At the base of Park City Mountain Resort, this is a convenient place to rent ski and snowboard equipment, goggles, and clothing. You can drop off your personal gear at the end of a ski day, and they'll have it tuned and ready for you the next morning with free overnight storage for customers. A second location on Main Street is across from Town Lift. ⊠ *1335 Lowell Ave., #104, Park City* ☎ *435/645–7777, 800/523–3922* ⊕ *www.parkcitysport.com.*

Silver Star Ski & Sport. This company rents, tunes, and repairs ski equipment, snowshoes, bike gear, and stand-up paddleboards. It doesn't get much more convenient for winter rentals/gear adjustments, as the shop is located at the base of the Silver Star lift at Park City Mountain Resort. ⊠ *1825 Three Kings Dr., #85, Park City* ☎ *435/645–7827* ⊕ *www. silverstarskiandsport.com.*

Ski Butlers. The most prominent of a number of companies offering ski and snowboard delivery, Ski Butlers carries top-of-the-line Rossignol equipment. Their experts will fit you in your hotel room or condo and meet you at any of the resorts should something go wrong. You'll pay a little more, but you'll avoid the hassle of rentals when the snow is falling on your first morning in the mountains. ⊠ *Park City* ☎ *877/754–7754* ⊕ *www.skibutlers.com.*

Utah Ski & Golf. Downhill equipment, snowshoes, clothing, and golf-club rental are available here, at Park City Base Area and Town Lift, as well as in downtown Salt Lake City. ⊠ *698 Park Ave., Park City* ☎ *435/649–3020* ⊕ *www.utahskigolf.com.*

SKI TOURS

Ski Utah Interconnect Tour. Strong intermediate and advanced skiers can hook up with the Ski Utah Interconnect Tour for a guided alpine ski tour that takes you to as many as six resorts, including Deer Valley and Park City, in a single day, all connected by backcountry ski routes with unparalleled views of the Wasatch Mountains. Guides test your ski ability before departure. The tour includes guide service, lift tickets, lunch, and transportation back to the point of origin. You'll even walk away with a finisher's pin. Reservations are required. ⊠ *Park City* ☎ *801/534–1907* ⊕ *www.skiutah.com* ⊠ *$395.*

Fodor'sChoice
★ **White Pine Touring.** Specializing in telemark, cross-country, and alpine touring gear and guided tours, White Pine Touring also has top of the line clothing, as well as mountain bikes, fat bikes, snowshoes, and climbing shoes. ⊠ *1790 Bonanza Dr., Park City* ☎ *435/649–8710* ⊕ *www.whitepinetouring.com.*

SNOWMOBILING

Red Pine Adventures. For a winter speed thrill of the machine-powered variety, hop on a snowmobile and follow your guide along private groomed trails adjacent to Park City Mountain Resort. Pick up is in Park City. ⊠ *2050 W. White Pine Canyon Rd., Park City* ☎ *435/649–9445* ⊕ *www.redpinetours.com* ⊠ *From $199 single rider, $239 double.*

Thousand Peaks Snowmobile Adventures. Backcountry snowmobile tours are on one of Utah's largest private mountain ranches, just outside of Park City. Clothing is available to rent. ⊠ *Office, 698 Park Ave., Park City* ☎ *888/304–7669* ⊕ *www.powderutah.com* ⊠ *From $169 single rider, $218 double.*

SNOW TUBING

FAMILY **Gorgoza Park.** Lift-served snow tubing (with 7 lanes) and minisnowmobile rentals bring families here. ✉ *3863 W. Kilby Rd., Park City* ☎ *435/658–2648* 🌐 *www.gorgoza.com* 🎟 *$10 single ride; $30 for 2 hrs; $44 for 4 hrs.*

WHERE TO EAT

Use the coordinates (✥ A1) at the end of each listing to locate a site on the corresponding map.

$$$ SWISS 🍴 **Adolph's.** The Swiss Alps meet Park City at this beloved stomping ground of longtime locals and athletes from around the globe. Chef Adolph Imboden's food is European, with strong ties to his Alpine roots. **Known for:** Swiss fondue; escargots; rack of lamb; European-inspired ambience. [$] *Average main: $30* ✉ *1500 Kearns Blvd., Park City* ☎ *435/649–7177* 🌐 *www.adolphsrestaurant.com* ✥ *D4.*

$$$$ STEAKHOUSE 🍴 **Apex.** Suitably named as this restaurant is the highest year-round restaurant in Park City, Apex is also at the top of its class for dining and service. The restaurant is within Montage Deer Valley, and at dinner transforms into a mountain steak house. **Known for:** steak; superior service. [$] *Average main: $50* ✉ *9100 Marsac Ave., Park City* ☎ *435/604–1402* 🌐 *www.montagedeervalley.com* ✥ *B4.*

$$$ ITALIAN 🍴 **Café Terigo.** This Main Street staple has delighted guests for more than 25 years with a modern Italian menu in an airy café with the best patio in town. The restaurant serves well-prepared pasta and seafood dishes using only fresh ingredients for lunch and dinner. **Known for:** traditional bolognese; hearty salads; alfresco dining. [$] *Average main: $30* ✉ *424 Main St., Park City* ☎ *435/645–9555* 🌐 *www.cafeterigo.com* 🕒 *Call for seasonal hrs* ✥ *B5.*

$$$$ SOUTHWESTERN 🍴 **Chimayo.** Star-shape lanterns illuminate the Mission-style wrought iron and terra-cotta tiles of this upscale southwestern restaurant. Chef Arturo Flores will delight and surprise you with tantalizing flavors in his menu, with items such as duck breast enchiladas, tortilla soup (his grandmother's recipe), a giant ahi tuna taco, or the melt-off-the-bone spareribs you won't soon forget. **Known for:** upscale southwestern fare; margaritas; friendly staff. [$] *Average main: $40* ✉ *368 Main St., Park City* ☎ *435/649–6222* 🌐 *www.chimayorestaurant.com* 🕒 *Call for seasonal hrs* ✥ *B5.*

$$$$ AMERICAN 🍴 **Coal & Lumber.** This chef-driven, modern American restaurant opened in late 2016, but has quickly established a presence among the culinary greats in Park City. A seasonal focus means menus change frequently, but you'll find a creative blend of seafood, local meats, and seasonal vegetables served in an inventive fashion. **Known for:** house-cured charcuterie; beautiful open kitchen; seasonal menu. [$] *Average main: $36* ✉ *201 Heber Ave., Main Street* ☎ *435/658–9425* 🌐 *www.skyparkcity.com* ✥ *B4.*

$ AMERICAN FAMILY 🍴 **Deer Valley Grocery Cafe.** An extension of the ski resort's famous culinary offerings, this gourmet grocery/café serves breakfast, lunch, and early dinner and features menu items ranging from the famous Deer Valley turkey chili, to shrimp tacos, to a chicken tandoori wrap, and everything in between. The expansive outdoor deck provides waterfront al fresco dining (the only place in Park City) and views of the ski resort. **Known for:** waterfront dining; high-quality ingredients; fast-casual atmosphere. $ *Average main: $10* ⊠ *1375 Deer Valley Dr., Park City* ☎ *435/615–2400* ⊕ *www.deervalley.com* ✛ *B4*.

$ ✗ **El Chubasco.** For quick and hearty traditional Mexican food, this
MEXICAN popular place is perfect. Favorites are *camarones a la diabla* (spicy
Fodor's Choice shrimp), chiles rellenos, and fish tacos. **Known for:** extensive salsa bar;
★ fast-casual dining. $ *Average main: $10* ⊠ *1890 Bonanza Dr., Park City* ☎ *435/645–9114* ⊕ *www.elchubascomexicangrill.com* ✛ *D4*.

$$$ ✗ **The Farm.** The team at The Farm relentlessly seeks new, fresh, and
MODERN unique ingredients to infuse into memorable meals in the restaurant's
AMERICAN open kitchen. Seasonal menus always spotlight items from regional sus-
Fodor's Choice tainable farmers, including root vegetables, truffles, berries, and meat.
★ **Known for:** charcuterie board; fresh ingredients; cozy atmosphere. $ *Average main: $30* ⊠ *Canyons Village, 4000 Canyons Resort Dr., Park City* ☎ *435/615–8080* ⊕ *www.canyonsresort.com* ☾ *Call for seasonal hrs* ✛ *A2*.

$$$$ ✗ **Firewood.** At this warm establishment, dishes are cooked over an
AMERICAN open flame, and antique leather chairs look out onto the open kitchen.
Fodor's Choice Self-described as "heirloom American," the seasonal, locally sourced
★ menu changes frequently. **Known for:** open-fire cooking; locally sourced menu; downstairs bar. $ *Average main: $36* ⊠ *306 Main St., Main Street* ☎ *435/252–9900* ⊕ *firewoodonmain.com* ☾ *Call for seasonal closures* ✛ *B5*.

$$ ✗ **Five5eeds.** This breakfast and lunch restaurant pulls in flavors from all
CONTEMPORARY over the globe while using Utah-sourced ingredients. Breakfast is served all day, and the hearty pulled pork Benedict will hit the spot no matter what time it is. **Known for:** iced coffee with ice cream; global flavors; breakfast served all day. $ *Average main: $14* ⊠ *1600 Snow Park Dr., #EF, Park City* ☎ *435/901–8242* ☾ *No dinner* ✛ *C4*.

$$ ✗ **Freshies Lobster Co.** It may seem a bit out of place, but Freshie's Lob-
SEAFOOD ster Co started as a food truck by East Coast natives, and became so
Fodor's Choice popular in the mountains of Utah that a brick-and-mortar location
★ opened in 2016. Lobsters are flown in fresh daily, and the lobster roll is now nationally recognized as the "World's Best Lobster Roll" after taking home the win at a competition in Portland, Maine, in 2017. **Known for:** lobster rolls; casual atmosphere. $ *Average main: $20* ⊠ *1897 Prospector Ave., Prospector* ☎ *435/631–9861* ⊕ *www. freshieslobsterco.com* ✛ *D4*.

$$$$ ✗ **Glitretind.** Wood trim, white tablecloths, crystal glasses, and fresh-
MODERN cut flowers set the scene for executive chef Zane Holmquist's creative
AMERICAN dishes. Try specialties like Iberico pork chop or rabbit succotash. **Known for:** private wine seminars and tastings; excellent wine pairings; Sunday brunch. $ *Average main: $40* ⊠ *7700 Stein Way, Deer Valley* ☎ *435/645–6455* ⊕ *www.steinlodge.com/dining* ✛ *D6*.

$$ ✗ **Good Karma.** This Indo-Persian restaurant is a nice break from the
INDIAN New American found all over town, and you'll immediately feel at home in the intimate, comfortable dining room where chef-owner Houman Gohary personally greets guests. Open for breakfast, lunch, and

dinner, locals love the house-made lamb curry and the tandoori shrimp vindaloo. **Known for:** house-made curries; vegetarian and gluten-free friendly; welcoming and friendly atmosphere. [$] *Average main: $20* ✉ *1782 Prospector Ave., Prospector* ☎ *435/658–0958* 🌐 *www.goodkarmarestaurants.com* ✥ *D4.*

$$$$ ITALIAN 🍴 **Grappa.** This restaurant specializes in regional Italian cuisine with impeccable presentation. Heavy floor tiles, rustic bricks, and exposed timbers lend a warm, rustic farmhouse feel. **Known for:** ambience; osso bucco; wine list. [$] *Average main: $40* ✉ *151 Main St., Main Street* ☎ *435/645–0636* 🌐 *www.grapparestaurant.com* 🕒 *No lunch* ✥ *B6.*

$$$ AMERICAN Fodor's Choice ★ 🍴 **Handle.** Handle was voted Best Restaurant in Park City in 2017 thanks to chef Briar Handly's inventive American dishes. Small plates make it easy to try everything, and you'll want to with dishes like buffalo cauliflower, smoked trout sausage, and the chef's famous fried chicken. **Known for:** chef's fried chicken; creative cocktails; $10 burger Wednesday (during off-season). [$] *Average main: $30* ✉ *136 Heber Ave., Old Town* ☎ *435/602–1155* 🌐 *www.handleparkcity.com* 🕒 *Call for seasonal closures* ✥ *B4.*

$$$ AMERICAN Fodor's Choice ★ 🍴 **High West Distillery.** Touted as the only ski-in, ski-out distillery in the world, High West Saloon sits at the base of the Park City Mountain's Town Lift, serving an eclectically Western, locally focused menu that changes seasonally, and specialty handcrafted cocktails using the distillery's own whiskey and vodka. The family-friendly restaurant and bar, housed in a historical home and livery, is a favorite among locals and visitors alike. **Known for:** whiskey; handcrafted cocktails; lively atmosphere. [$] *Average main: $21* ✉ *703 Park Ave., Old Town* ☎ *435/649–8300* 🌐 *www.highwest.com* ✥ *A4.*

$ DELI FAMILY 🍴 **Java Cow Cafe & Bakery.** Java Cow has long been a staple on Main Street. Stop in for a panini, a caffeine pick-me-up, or delicious ice cream to satisfy your sweet tooth. **Known for:** excellent coffee; house-made ice cream; quick breakfast or lunch spot. [$] *Average main: $10* ✉ *402 Main St., Main Street* ✥ *B5.*

$$$ PIZZA FAMILY 🍴 **Maxwell's East Coast Eatery.** Located between the Swaner Preserve and a swath of shops, this unpretentious eatery is popular with locals and welcomes the late-night crowd. Nearly 2 feet in diameter, the Fat Kid "pie" will remind you of Brooklyn or the Bronx—grab a slice of the "Goodfella" veggie pizza or the "Italian Stallion" meat-lovers version. **Known for:** east coast-style pizza; sports bar; family-friendly. [$] *Average main: $21* ✉ *1456 Newpark Blvd., Newpark* ☎ *435/647–0304* 🌐 *www.maxwellsparkcity.com* ✥ *A1.*

$$$ AMERICAN 🍴 **Purple Sage.** Plenty of purple-hue touches—velvet upholstered booths, hand-painted scrims, and Western murals—brighten the 1898 brick building that was once the local telegraph office. "Fancy cowboy" cuisine includes such dishes as grilled veal meat loaf with poblano peppers and pine nuts or the lime-grilled black tiger shrimp. In summer, eat on the back deck under the charming bistro lights. **Known for:** Western fare; meat loaf; intimate dining. [$] *Average main: $30* ✉ *434 Main St., Main Street* ☎ *435/655–9505* 🌐 *www.purplesageparkcity.com* 🕒 *Call for seasonal hrs* ✥ *B5.*

$$$$ AMERICAN Fodor's Choice ★

🍴 **Riverhorse on Main.** With two warehouse loft rooms, exposed wood beams, sleek furnishings, and original art, this award-winning restaurant feels like a big-city supper club where chef-owner Seth Adams pairs imaginative fresh food with an elegant—but ski-town relaxed—atmosphere. The menu changes seasonally, but look out for the braised buffalo short rib, pan-roasted tomahawk pork, or signature macadamia-nut-crusted Alaskan halibut. **Known for:** Alaskan halibut; vegan and gluten-free friendly; Sunday brunch. [$] *Average main: $42* ✉ *540 Main St., Park City* ☎ *435/649–3536* 🌐 *www.riverhorseparkcity.com* ⏲ *No lunch Mon.–Sat.* ✣ *B5.*

3

$ CAFÉ

🍴 **Riverhorse Provisions.** A casual sister to Riverhorse on Main (with the same award-winning chef behind it), Riverhorse Provisions is a café, specialty market, and deli all in one. Come here for one of the few breakfasts served on Main Street, or stop in on your way to an outdoor concert and pick up a signature picnic basket filled with everything from fried chicken with cornbread and peach cobbler, to chilled lobster salad. **Known for:** signature picnic baskets; gourmet market; café-style fare. [$] *Average main: $12* ✉ *221 Main St., Main Street* ☎ *435/649–0799* 🌐 *www.riverhorseprovisions.com* ✣ *B6.*

$$$$ ASIAN

🍴 **Shabu.** The wagyu hot rock, volcano sushi roll (tuna, wasabi, pine apple, jalapeño, and cilantro) and shabu shabu, a Japanese hot pot, are all favorites at this trendy eatery. Go for a Ginger Snap sake martini (saketini) in the red-hued dining room. **Known for:** excellent sushi; wagyu hot rock; trendy spot. [$] *Average main: $33* ✉ *442 Main St., Main Street* ☎ *435/645–7253* 🌐 *www.shabuparkcity.com* ⏲ *Call for seasonal hrs* ✣ *B5.*

$$$ MODERN AMERICAN

🍴 **Twisted Fern.** After 10 years of working in the kitchens of Park City's top restaurants, chef/owner Adam Ross ventured out on his own and opened Twisted Fern in 2017. A seasonal, ingredient-driven menu with comfort food favorites such as pork chop, open-faced short-rib sandwich, and ratatouille, this restaurant is quickly becoming a hot spot in town, offering lunch, après-ski, and dinner daily. **Known for:** welcoming atmosphere; friendly staff. [$] *Average main: $21* ✉ *1300 Snow Creek Dr., Suite RS, Park City* ☎ *435/731–8238* 🌐 *www.twistedfern.com* ✣ *C4.*

$$ AMERICAN

🍴 **Versante Hearth + Bar.** Located in the newly remodeled Park City Peaks Hotel, Versante opened in January of 2017 and quickly became a favorite among locals. The welcoming, casual atmosphere paired with menu favorites such as flatbread pizzas, hearty pastas, and specialty cocktails is hard to beat. **Known for:** flatbread pizzas; welcoming atmosphere. [$] *Average main: $18* ✉ *2346 Park Ave., Park City* ☎ *435/649–5000* ⏲ *No lunch* ✣ *C4.*

$ FAST FOOD

🍴 **Vessel Kitchen.** In an area of town where fast-food reigns, Vessel Kitchen has a sustainable and healthy menu without sacrificing the fast-casual environment and reasonable prices. Here, you'll find hearty grain bowls, proteins such as braised beef and pork confit, and seasonal vegetables for sides. **Known for:** healthy dining; hearty grain bowls; fast-casual dining. [$] *Average main: $12* ✉ *1784 Uinta Way, #1E, Kimball Junction* ☎ *435/200–8864* 🌐 *www.vesselkitchen.com* ✣ *A1.*

$$$$ EUROPEAN

🍴 **The Viking Yurt.** Don your Scandinavian sweater for the 23-minute snow-cat-pulled sleigh ride up to this Nordic hut, located mid-mountain at Park City Mountain Resort. After a hot cup of glogg, tuck into a four-hour, six-course feast that might feature braised short ribs, lobster soup, and a traditional cheese course. **Known for:** unique dining experience; traditional Nordic cuisine. [$] *Average main: $140* ✉ *1345 Lowell Ave., Old Town* ☎ *435/615–9878* 🌐 *www.thevikingyurt.com* 🕓 *Closed Apr.–Nov.* ⊕ *D5.*

$$$$ ASIAN Fodor's Choice ★

🍴 **Wahso.** This restaurant instantly transports you to Shanghai in the 1930s, with art deco decor and Asian artifacts from around the world. Start your evening with a sake martini shaken table-side, then ask your server about starters that span the continent, from steamed Chinese buns to *tom kha gai*, a delicious chicken-and-lemongrass soup from Thailand. **Known for:** warm atmosphere; steamed Chinese buns; attentive service. [$] *Average main: $41* ✉ *577 Main St., Main Street* ☎ *435/615–0300* 🌐 *www.wahso.com* 🕓 *Call for seasonal hrs* ⊕ *A5.*

$$ AMERICAN FAMILY

🍴 **Wasatch Brew Pub.** It's hard to believe it's been more than 30 years since Wasatch became Park City's first brewery in the post-Prohibition era. At the top of Main Street, this pub stays on top of its game with celebrated beers and down-to-earth yet elevated pub food. **Known for:** local craft beer; outdoor dining in summer; elevated pub food. [$] *Average main: $18* ✉ *250 Main St., Park City* ☎ *435/645–0900* 🌐 *www.wasatchbeers.com* ⊕ *B5.*

$$ AMERICAN FAMILY

🍴 **Windy Ridge Café.** Don't overlook Windy Ridge because of its industrial park neighborhood, as the dining room is warm and inviting. Lighter appetites might fancy the homemade chicken noodle soup and a Southwest salad, or if you've spent the day skiing or biking, tackle the meat loaf or a rack of smoked ribs. **Known for:** comfort food; warm atmosphere; Taco Tuesdays. [$] *Average main: $20* ✉ *1250 Iron Horse Dr., Prospector* ☎ *435/647–0880* 🌐 *www.windyridgecafe.com* ⊕ *D4.*

$$ SUSHI

🍴 **Yuki Yama Sushi.** The name means "snow mountain" in Japanese, and the menu has a whirling blend of sushi, sashimi, and maki, as well as hot entrées, including noodle dishes. Observe sushi-making theatrics at the bar while they prepare the 84060 roll in homage to the local zip code, or retreat to the sunken seating of the tatami room. **Known for:** fresh sushi; sake; lively atmosphere. [$] *Average main: $18* ✉ *586 Main St., Main Street* ☎ *435/649–6293* 🌐 *www.yukiyamasushi.com* 🕓 *Check for seasonal closures* ⊕ *A4.*

WHERE TO STAY

Use the coordinates (⊕ A1) at the end of each listing to locate a site on the corresponding map.

$$ B&B/INN

🏨 **Chateau Après.** In one of the most expensive ski towns around, this reasonably priced classic skiers' lodge is a throwback to bygone ski days. **Pros:** comfortable rooms; close to the slopes; longtime local owners. **Cons:** basic accommodations. [$] *Rooms from: $145* ✉ *1299 Norfolk Ave., Park City* ☎ *435/649–9372, 800/357–3556* 🌐 *www.chateauapres.com* 🛏 *32 rooms* 🍽 *Breakfast* ⊕ *D5.*

$$$$
HOTEL
FAMILY
The Chateaux at Deer Valley. Just steps away from the Deer Valley lifts at Silver Lake Village, this modern interpretation of a luxury European château incorporates designer furnishings, heated towel racks, full kitchens in suites, gas fireplaces, and numerous windows with spectacular mountain views. **Pros:** luxury digs without stuffy atmosphere; great Italian dining at Cena; rooms can accommodate any family size. **Cons:** too far from Old Town to walk; evenings are quiet. $ *Rooms from: $448* ✉ *7815 Royal St. E, Park City* ☎ *435/658–9500, 877/288–2978* ⊕ *www.the-chateaux.com* ↻ *160 rooms* ⓘ *No meals* ✛ *D6.*

$$$$
RESORT
FAMILY
Grand Summit Resort Hotel & Conference Center. Located in the heart of Canyons Village, the hotel is just steps from a heated chairlift and golf course, making lodgings here ideal year-round. **Pros:** luxury accommodations; countless activities; on-site spa. **Cons:** very large, can sometimes feel cavernous; expensive daily resort fee; no nightlife on property. $ *Rooms from: $368* ✉ *4000 Canyons Resort Dr., Park City* ☎ *435/615–8040 front desk, 888/226–9667 reservations* ⊕ *www.parkcitymountain.com* ↻ *375 units* ⓘ *No meals* ✛ *A2.*

$$$$
HOTEL
Hotel Park City. On the Park City golf course, this all-suites hotel is built in the tradition of the grand old stone-and-timber lodges of the West. **Pros:** close to town and the ski hills; grand lodge-style rooms with views; on 18-hole golf course. **Cons:** rooms are expensive; must drive to restaurants and resorts; long outdoor walk to some of the rooms. $ *Rooms from: $569* ✉ *2001 Park Ave., Park City* ☎ *435/200–2000* ⊕ *www.hotelparkcity.com* ↻ *100 suites* ⓘ *No meals* ✛ *C4.*

$$$$
HOTEL
Main & SKY. Smack in the middle of Old Town, this contemporary hotel blends chic modern design with a mountain feel. **Pros:** prime location; large, luxurious rooms; great views. **Cons:** location on Main Street means no escaping the action; large suites mean expensive rates; pricey valet parking. $ *Rooms from: $650* ✉ *201 Heber Ave., Park City* ☎ *435/658–2500* ⊕ *www.skyparkcity.com* ↻ *33 suites* ⓘ *No meals* ✛ *A4.*

$$$$
HOTEL
Marriott MountainSide Resort. Watch skiers go by from the heated outdoor pool at this hotel near the lifts in arguably the most ideal location at Park City Base Area, offering traditional rooms and one- and two-bedroom suites. **Pros:** ski-in, ski-out convenience; heated outdoor pool and hot tubs; helpful, pleasant staff. **Cons:** busy and somewhat congested area; rooms are plain; no great dining nearby. $ *Rooms from: $400* ✉ *1305 Lowell Ave., Park City* ☎ *435/940–2000, 800/845–5279* ⊕ *www.marriott.com* ↻ *365 rooms* ⓘ *No meals* ✛ *D5.*

$$$$
RESORT
Fodor'sChoice
★
Montage Deer Valley. The jewel on the top of the crown of Park City, Montage is breathtakingly nestled in Empire Pass at 9,000 feet above sea level like a grand Alpine luxury chalet. **Pros:** exquisite location with beautiful views; top level dining; ample amenities and activities on-site. **Cons:** remote location; car or shuttle required to get to Main Street; can feel cavernous at times. $ *Rooms from: $805* ✉ *9100 Marsac Ave., Park City* ☎ *435/604–1300* ⊕ *www.montagedeervalley.com* ↻ *88 rooms, 66 suites* ⓘ *No meals* ✛ *B4.*

$$$
HOTEL
Newpark Resort, A Destination Hotel. At Newpark you'll find a busy shopping and dining scene on one side, and a gorgeous nature preserve on the other. **Pros:** comfortable suites; affordable rates; within walking

distance of shops and restaurants. **Cons:** a drive to ski resorts and Main Street; location is in congested area; not all rooms have views. [$] *Rooms from: $180* ✉ *1476 Newpark Blvd., Newpark* ☎ *435/649–3600, 877/649–3600* 🌐 *www.newparkresort.com* 🛏 *126 rooms, 24 townhomes* 🍴 *No meals* ✥ *A1.*

$$$ B&B/INN Fodor's Choice ★ 🏨 **Old Town Guest House.** Listed on the National Register of Historic Places, this four-room inn, steps from the slopes and trails, is warm and cozy with its country style and lodgepole-pine furniture. **Pros:** walking distance to Park City Base Area and Main Street; hearty mountain breakfast and afternoon snacks included; year-round hot tub. **Cons:** rooms are small; only one suite can accommodate more than two people; strict cancellation policy. [$] *Rooms from: $169* ✉ *1011 Empire Ave., Park City* ☎ *435/649–2642, 800/290–6423* 🌐 *www.oldtownguesthouse.com* 🛏 *4 rooms* 🍴 *Breakfast* ✥ *D5.*

$$$$ RESORT Fodor's Choice ★ 🏨 **The St. Regis Deer Valley.** A 90-second ride up the funicular will take you to one of the most luxurious hotels at any alpine resort. **Pros:** glitz, glam, and butlers; ski-in, ski-out convenience; award-winning dining on property. **Cons:** additional restaurants are a drive away; layout is confusing, easy to get lost inside; après is popular with locals, get there early. [$] *Rooms from: $946* ✉ *2300 Deer Valley Dr. E, Park City* ☎ *435/940–5700, 866/932–7059* 🌐 *www.stregisdeervalley.com* 🛏 *115 rooms, 66 suites* 🍴 *No meals* ✥ *B4.*

$$$$ RESORT Fodor's Choice ★ 🏨 **Stein Eriksen Lodge.** As enchanting as it gets for a slope-side retreat, this lodge is as perfectly groomed, timelessly gracious, and uniquely charming as its namesake founder, the winner of an Olympic Gold Medal in 1952. **Pros:** award-winning dining on property; service is impeccable and exemplary; only five-star-rated spa in Utah. **Cons:** isolated location means a drive to Main Street and Park City; rooms require a walk outside, which can be cold in the winter; the high-altitude location (8,000-plus feet) can be difficult for some. [$] *Rooms from: $900* ✉ *7700 Stein Way, Park City* ☎ *435/649–3700, 800/453–1302* 🌐 *www.steinlodge.com* 🛏 *112 rooms, 68 suites* 🍴 *No meals* ✥ *B4.*

$$$$ B&B/INN 🏨 **Torchlight Inn.** This bed-and-breakfast inn offers a nice mix of contemporary and traditional style and incredible views from its rooftop deck and hot tub. **Pros:** rooms are spacious; delicious and personal breakfast; one block from Main Street and a short drive to the slopes. **Cons:** location is near a loud congested traffic circle; no a/c; limited parking. [$] *Rooms from: $361* ✉ *255 Deer Valley Dr., Park City* ☎ *435/612–0345* 🌐 *www.torchlightinn.com* 🛏 *6 rooms* 🍴 *Breakfast* ✥ *B4.*

$$$$ RESORT Fodor's Choice ★ 🏨 **Waldorf Astoria Park City.** A sweeping staircase, Baccarat crystal chandelier, and 300-year-old marble fireplace lend grandeur to the first Waldorf Astoria hotel in an alpine location. **Pros:** celebrated restaurant; steps from the gondola; decadent spa. **Cons:** very little within walking distance; gondola nearby is very slow; only one dining option on-site. [$] *Rooms from: $740* ✉ *2100 Frostwood Dr., Park City* ☎ *435/647–5500, 866/279–0843* 🌐 *www.waldorfastoriaparkcity.com* 🛏 *178 rooms, 37 suites* 🍴 *No meals* ✥ *A2.*

3

$$$$
B&B/INN
Fodor's Choice
★

☷ **Washington School House.** Since 2011, this spectacular boutique hotel has been the hottest "must-stay" destination in Old Town Park City, providing beautifully designed and well-appointed rooms within a National Historic Registry landmark. **Pros:** central location; stellar service (they'll even pack and unpack for you); chefs provide delicious (included) breakfast and après-ski. **Cons:** not family-friendly; rooms fill up quickly, so book far in advance. $ *Rooms from: $875* ✉ *543 Park Ave., Box 536, Park City* ☎ *435/649–3800, 800/824–1672* ⊕ *www. washingtonschoolhouse.com* ⇌ *12 rooms* ⊚ *Breakfast* ✦ *A5.*

CONDOS

Deer Valley Resort Lodging. The reservationists at Deer Valley Resort Lodging are knowledgeable and the service is efficient at this high-end property-management company. They can book distinctive hotel rooms, condominiums, or private homes throughout Deer Valley and Park City. Complimentary shuttle service to/from resorts and around town in Cadillac Escalades is a perk. ✉ *Park City* ☎ *435/645–6428, 800/558–3337* ⊕ *www.deervalley.com.*

Resorts West. Resort West manages roughly 150 properties around town, ranging from two-bedroom condos to eight-bedroom ski homes. More than 90% of their properties are on the slopes or a short walk to the lifts. Your concierge will take care of everything from grocery delivery and private chefs to ski rental delivery, and each reservation includes daily housekeeping and shuttle service around town. ✉ *1795 Sidewinder Dr., Suite 100, Park City* ☎ *435/655–7006* ⊕ *www.resortswest.com.*

NIGHTLIFE AND PERFORMING ARTS

NIGHTLIFE

In a state where nearly every town was founded by Mormons who eschewed alcohol and anything associated with it, Park City has always been an exception. Founded by miners with healthy appetites for whiskey, gambling, and ladies of the night, Park City has been known since its mining heyday as Utah's "Sin City." The miners are gone, but their legacy lives on in this town that has far more bars per capita than any other place in Utah.

Boneyard Saloon and Kitchen. This hot spot is in a somewhat unlikely place—in fact, you might think you're lost as you pull into the industrial-looking area in Prospector. But its off-Main location means it's popular with the locals, and ample parking is a huge plus. TVs lining the wall and a special weekend breakfast menu have made Boneyard the new go-to for Sunday football, and the rooftop deck has stunning views of the mountains. A sister restaurant of No Name on Main Street, Boneyard features beers on tap and an extensive bottle list. Head next door to Wine Dive (same ownership) to find 16 wines on tap and artisan pizza. ✉ *1251 Kearns Blvd., Prospector* ☎ *435/649–0911* ⊕ *www. boneyardsaloon.com.*

Fodor's Choice
★

No Name Saloon. A Park City favorite anchoring Main Street's nightlife, this is a classic wood-backed bar with lots of memorabilia, a shuffleboard table, and a regular local clientele. The upstairs outdoor deck is great for enjoying cool summer nights, but heaters in the winter make this deck comfortable year-round. The eclectic decor looks like everything was purchased at a flea market in the best way possible. If you are looking for some late-night grub, No Name has the best buffalo burgers in town. ⊠ *447 Main St., Park City* ☏ *435/649–6667* ⊕ *www. nonamesaloon.net.*

Old Town Cellars. The first of its kind in the area, this private label winery opened on Main Street in 2016. Stop in to learn about the urban wine-making process, buy a bottle of their house wine, or enjoy an après-ski tasting in their Bar and Lounge where local beers and spirits are also available. Local meats and chocolate, available on their fare menu, pair perfectly with the experience. ⊠ *890 Main St., Main Street* ☏ *435/649–3759* ⊕ *www.otcwines.com.*

The Spur Bar and Grill. If you are looking for live music, look no further than The Spur, which hosts bands seven nights a week. A renovation in 2016 more than doubled the size of The Spur, adding two additional bar areas and a Main Street entrance. The front room provides a lively bar atmosphere; head upstairs if you want to hear your conversation. The back room is where you'll find the live music and the dancing. A full kitchen means breakfast, lunch, and dinner are served until 10 pm. ⊠ *352 Main St., Park City* ☏ *435/615–1618* ⊕ *www.thespurbarandgrill.com.*

Troll Hallen Lounge. If quiet conversation and a good single-malt scotch or Swiss raclette in front of a fire is your idea of nightlife, this is the place for you. ⊠ *Stein Eriksen Lodge, 7700 Stein Way, Park City* ☏ *435/645–6455.*

PERFORMING ARTS

MUSIC

FAMILY
Fodor'sChoice
★

Mountain Town Music. This nonprofit organization books dozens of local, regional, and national musical acts in the Park City area, using many different venues around town including the ski resorts and Main Street. No matter what show you go to, you're likely to see every age group represented and enjoying the music. Most performances are free. ⊠ *Park City* ☏ *435/901–7664* ⊕ *www.mountaintownmusic.org.*

THEATER AND DANCE

Eccles Center for Performing Arts. Dance, theater, wide-ranging concerts, family shows, and other performances are on the bill in a state-of-the-art auditorium that also holds the biggest premieres during the Sundance Film Festival. ⊠ *1750 Kearns Blvd., Park City* ☏ *435/655–3114* box office ⊕ *www.ecclescenter.org.*

Egyptian Theatre. This historical building has been a Park City theater since its mining days in the 1880s. In 1922 the Egyptian Theatre was constructed on the site of the original Dewey Theatre that collapsed under record-breaking snow. Patrons enjoy an eclectic array of local and regional music, theater, and comedy in the 266-seat space. ⊠ *328 Main St., Park City* ☏ *435/649–9371* ⊕ *www.egyptiantheatrecompany.org.*

SHOPPING

Within the colorful structures that line Park City's Main Street are a number of clothing boutiques, sporting-goods stores, and gift shops. In recent years, brand name stores like lululemon, Patagonia, and Gorsuch have opened their doors along Historic Main Street, but alongside these recognizable names are locally owned boutiques and shop that help preserve the Park City charm.

ART GALLERIES

Park City Gallery Stroll. Main Street is packed with great art galleries, and the best way to see them all is the Park City Gallery Stroll, a free event hosted by the Park City Gallery Association on the last Friday of the month 6–9 pm, sun or snow. ⊠ *Park City* ⊕ *www.parkcitygalleryassociation.com.*

BOOKS AND TOYS

FAMILY **Dolly's Bookstore.** For many returning visitors, the first stop in town is Dolly's Bookstore to check on the two cats: Dolly and Pippi Longstocking. Oh, and to browse a great selection of regional books as well as national best-sellers. Dolly's also has a uniquely complete selection of children's books and toys. While you are at it, swing through neighboring Rocky Mountain Chocolate Factory to satisfy your sweet tooth. ⊠ *510 Main St., Park City* ☎ *435/649–8062.*

FAMILY **J.W. Allen & Sons Toys & Candy.** Jam-packed with classic toys and modern fun, J.W. Allen & Sons rescues parents who forgot to pack toys for their kids on family vacation. Scary dinosaurs, giant stuffed bears, dolls, sleds, scooters, and kites are as irresistible as the candy. ⊠ *1675 W. Redstone Center, No. 105, Park City* ☎ *435/575–8697.*

CLOTHING

Indigo Highway. This eclectic boutique, located in Newpark Town Center, is worth a visit. Here you'll find clothing, gifts, scented candles, Park City keepsakes, and more, all with a modern nomad twist. They sell handmade bags from all over the world (with notes about the women who made them) next to Park City embroidered caps. There's even a full section of small batch, artisanal apothecary items (think body oils, detoxifying bath salts, and more). ⊠ *1241 Center Dr. #L170, Newpark* ☎ *435/214–7244* ⊕ *www.indigohighway.com.*

Mary Jane's. This independently owned boutique has an eclectic selection of trendy clothing and designer jeans, lingerie, statement jewelry, shoes, and handbags. ⊠ *613 Main St., Park City* ☎ *435/645–7463* ⊕ *www.maryjanesshoes.com.*

Olive and Tweed. This artist-driven boutique sells local handmade jewelry, women's clothing accessories, home decor, baby items, and local art. ⊠ *608 Main St., Park City* ☎ *435/649–9392* ⊕ *www.oliveandtweed.storeenvy.com.*

FOOD AND CANDY

Rocky Mountain Chocolate Factory. You'll find a quick fix for your sweet tooth here, and you can watch them make fudge, caramel apples, and other scrumptious treats. There's another location at 1385 Lowell Avenue. ⊠ *510 Main St., Park City* ☎ *435/649–0997, 435/649–2235.*

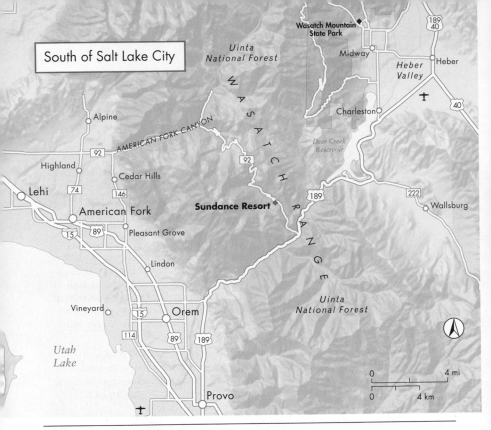

Uinta National Forest

Wasatch Mountain State Park

Midway

Heber Valley

Heber

AMERICAN FORK CANYON

Alpine

92

Charleston

Deer Creek Reservoir

Highland

92

Cedar Hills

146

189

222

Wallsburg

Lehi

74

Sundance Resort

American Fork

15

89

Pleasant Grove

Lindon

Uinta National Forest

Vineyard

15

Orem

114

89

189

Utah Lake

Provo

0   4 mi

0   4 km

SOUTH OF SALT LAKE CITY

The Utah Valley was a busy place long before the Mormons settled here in 1851. With Utah Lake teeming with fish, and game plentiful in the surrounding mountains, several bands of Native Americans lived in the area, and Spanish explorers passed through in 1775. Traders from several countries used the explorers' trail to bring goods here and to capture slaves to sell in Mexico, and fur trappers spent winter seasons in the surrounding mountains. With so many groups competing for the area's resources, conflicts were inevitable. The conflicts became more intense when Mormons settled Provo in 1851 and then began claiming land in other parts of the valley, land that had always been used by Native Americans. Several battles were fought here between Mormon settlers and Native American groups during the Walker and Black Hawk wars.

SUNDANCE RESORT

35 miles south of Park City; 12 miles northeast of Provo.

As Thoreau had Walden Pond, so does Redford have Sundance. Lucky for the rest of us, the "Sundance Kid" shares his 5,000-acre bounty. Several miles up a winding mountain lane, Sundance Resort is a full-service ski resort with bustling slopes in winter, except during the Sundance Film Festival. In summer, it's a destination for filmmakers, writers, craftsmen, and artists of all sensibilities. It also caters to visitors looking to relax at spas, shop, or dine.

GETTING HERE AND AROUND

From Park City, take Highway 40 and 189 south. From Provo, head northeast on Highway 92.

EXPLORING

Fodor's Choice **Sundance Resort.** Set on the eastern slopes of the breathtaking 11,750-foot
★ Mount Timpanogos, the 5,000-acre resort came into being when Robert Redford purchased the land in 1969. No matter the season, you'll find plenty of recreational opportunities, including hiking, biking, fly-fishing, horseback riding, alpine and cross-country skiing, snowboarding, snowshoeing, and zip lining. Relax with a body treatment in the Spa at Sundance or take one of many creative classes in the Art Studios. The Sundance Film Festival, based in nearby Park City each January, is an internationally recognized showcase for independent films. Festival screenings and summer workshops are held at the resort. ⊠ *8841 N. Alpine Loop Rd., Sundance* ☎ *866/259–7468, 800/892–1600* ⊕ *www. sundanceresort.com* ⊠ *Lift tickets $80* ⊂ *2,150-ft vertical drop; 450 skiable acres; 35% novice, 45% intermediate, 20% advanced; 3 quad lifts, 1 triple chair, 1 surface lift.*

SPORTS AND THE OUTDOORS

FLY-FISHING

The Provo River, minutes from Sundance Resort, is a fly-fishing catch-and-release waterway. Access to the rainbow, cutthroat, and German brown trout found in the river is year-round. Tours are provided by Wasatch Guide Service, and include all necessary gear, guides, and some may include drinks and snacks.

Wasatch Guide Service. The preferred outfitter of Sundance Resort, Wasatch Guide Service provides access to some of the best fly-fishing in the state. Guides will take you to the world-class Provo River, right near Sundance Resort, or up to the Weber River, and can even provide access to private waters and lesser-known streams in the area. One guide to every two guests ensures personalized experiences, and they provide all necessary equipment. Half-day and full-day tours are available year-round, with lunch provided in the full-day tour. ⊠ *Sundance* ☎ *801/830–3316* ⊕ *www.wasatchguideservice.com* ⊠ *From $280 half-day; from $400 full-day.*

HIKING

Hiking trails in the Sundance area vary from the easy 1.25-mile Nature Trail and the popular lift-accessed Stewart Falls Trail (3 miles) to the 7½-mile Big Baldy Trail, which leads past a series of waterfalls up steep, rugged terrain. You can access moderate- to expert-level trails from the resort base or chairlift. Select from three routes to summit the 11,000-foot Mount Timpanogos. Guided naturalist hikes are available.

MOUNTAIN BIKING

You'll find more than 25 miles of ski lift–accessed mountain-biking trails at Sundance Resort, extending from the base of Mount Timpanogos to Ray's Summit at 7,250 feet. High-tech gear rentals are available for full or half days, as is individual or group instruction.

Sundance Mountain Outfitters. Rent all the gear you need for mountain biking, skiing, or snowboarding. ⊠ *8841 N. Alpine Loop Rd., Sundance* ☎ *801/223–4121* ⊕ *www.sundanceresort.com.*

SKIING

CROSS-COUNTRY Enjoy terrain suitable for all skill levels on nearly 10 miles of groomed trails. Six miles of dedicated snowshoeing trails wind through mature aspen groves and pines. Lessons and equipment rentals, including telemark gear, are available for all techniques of cross-country skiing and snowshoeing at the Sundance Nordic Center.

DOWNHILL Skiers and snowboarders at Sundance Resort will find 44 trails on 450 acres of varied terrain. Services include specialized ski workshops (including ladies' day clinics and personal coaching), a PSIA-certified ski school, and a ski school just for children, with programs that include all-day supervision, lunch, and ski instruction. Children as young as four are eligible for group lessons. Rentals are available for all skill levels. Night skiing is also available four nights a week.

WHERE TO EAT AND STAY

$$$
AMERICAN
Fodor'sChoice
★

✕ **Foundry Grill.** Wood-oven pizzas, sizzling steaks, and spit-roasted chicken are among the hearty staples on the menu at this restaurant. Like the rest of Sundance, everything here, from the food presentation to the interior design to the staff, is natural, beautiful, and pleasant. **Known for:** Sunday brunch; open kitchen; wood-burning pizza oven. Ⓢ *Average main: $30* ⊠ *Sundance Resort, 8841 N. Alpine Loop Rd., Sundance* ☎ *866/932–2295* ⊕ *www.sundanceresort.com.*

$$$$
AMERICAN
Fodor'sChoice
★

✕ **Tree Room.** It's easy to imagine that you're a personal guest of Robert Redford at this intimate, rustic restaurant with its exquisite collection of Native American art and Western memorabilia from the famed actor's private collection. The servers look like they double as Sundance catalog models. **Known for:** fine dining; candlelit atmosphere; interesting art. Ⓢ *Average main: $37* ⊠ *Sundance Resort, 8841 N. Alpine Loop Rd., Sundance* ☎ *866/627–8313* ⊕ *www.sundanceresort.com* ☽ *No lunch.*

$$$$
RESORT
Fodor'sChoice
★

▦ **Sundance Resort.** With 11,750-foot Mount Timpanogos serving as a backdrop, Robert Redford's 5,000-acre retreat is a genuine tribute to arts and nature. **Pros:** retreat from urban hubbub; glorious scenery; culinary magic. **Cons:** cell reception is spotty; far drive to other restaurants and nightlife; limited ski terrain compared to other Utah resorts. Ⓢ *Rooms from: $285* ⊠ *8841 N. Alpine Loop Rd., Sundance* ☎ *866/259–7468, 800/892–1600* ⊕ *www.sundanceresort.com* ⇆ *95 rooms* ⓘⓞⓛ *No meals.*

NIGHTLIFE AND PERFORMING ARTS

NIGHTLIFE

Owl Bar. Whether you feel like a quiet midday chess game or more lively atmosphere at night, the Owl Bar is a good gathering space. Here you'll find live music on weekends and a wide selection of beers and spirits to

The Geology of the Wasatch Mountains

The geology of the Wasatch Mountains gives the Salt Lake Valley its character. Few places in the world can show off such distinct geologic features in an area as small as the 50 to 70 miles along the Wasatch Front. One section, from City Creek Canyon in the north to Bells Canyon in the south, has 10 distinct geologic zones. Each canyon, some formed by glaciers, others by flowing water, has a different look, with rocks of varying ages and colors.

The reddish rocks visible on a drive up Parley's Canyon come from the Jurassic period. Suicide Rock, at the canyon's mouth, dates from the earlier Triassic age. Lower portions of Big Cottonwood Canyon have billion-year-old Precambrian rock. To the south, Little Cottonwood Canyon has comparatively new formations: a molten igneous mass pushed its

way almost to the surface a mere 32 million years ago. Granite formed here was used to build the Mormon Temple in Salt Lake City.

Tongues of the Wasatch Fault run along the front of the Wasatch Mountains. This fault is where the earth cracks as the Great Basin stretches by a couple of centimeters annually. For this to happen, the valleys from California through the Wasatch Range must fall slightly. Portions of Salt Lake Valley's Wasatch Boulevard and 1300 East Street are on fault lines. You can tell that you're near a fault when the east–west streets suddenly get steeper. Although geologists say that a quake could happen any time, the valley hasn't experienced a major one in recorded history. Where to grab some dinner should be a bigger concern than being shaken by an earthquake.

accompany a limited but satisfying menu. Classic photographs of Paul Newman and Robert Redford as Butch Cassidy and the Sundance Kid hang on the walls, and with the worn plank floors, stone fireplace, and original 1890s rosewood bar (said to have been favored by Cassidy's Hole-in-the-Wall Gang) transported from Thermopolis, Wyoming, you might just feel like cutting loose. ⊠ *Sundance Resort, 8841 N. Alpine Loop Rd., Sundance* ☎ *801/223–4222* ⊕ *www.sundanceresort.com.*

PERFORMING ARTS

Sundance Art Studio. The studios offer workshops in photography, jewelry making, wheel-thrown pottery, watercolor painting, and charcoal or pencil drawing. Mirroring the Sundance ethic, these classes blend the natural world with the artistic process. All workshops and classes are open to resort guests as well as day visitors. ⊠ *Sundance Resort, 8841 N. Alpine Loop Rd., Sundance* ☎ *801/225–4107* ⊕ *www.sundanceresort.com.*

Sundance Author Series. For more over 15 years, the Sundance Author Series has brought literary and political icons like Sue Monk Kidd and Jimmy Carter to the Tree Room for an intimate brunch and lecture. As an added bonus, you'll walk away with a signed copy of the author's book. ⊠ *Sundance Resort, 8841 N. Alpine Loop Rd., Sundance* ☎ *801/223–4567* ⊕ *www.sundanceresort.com* ☒ *$85.*

Sundance Bluebird Café Concert Series. Each summer, Sundance brings a little Nashville to Utah with the Bluebird Café series. Singer-songwriters take the outdoor stage on select summer Fridays to share stories and music in the serene Utah mountains. ⊠ *8841 N. Alpine Loop, Sundance* ☎ *866/734–4428* ⊕ *www.sundanceresort.com* ⊠ *$30.*

Fodor's Choice   **Sundance Film Festival.** Add this to your bucket list. Every January the
★   Sundance Institute, a nonprofit organization supporting independent filmmaking, screenwriters, playwrights, composers, and other film and theater artists, presents the Sundance Film Festival. A world-renowned showcase for independent film, the 10-day festival is based in Park City, but has screenings and workshops at Sundance Resort, Salt Lake City, and Ogden. ⊠ *Sundance* ☎ *435/658–3456* ⊕ *www. sundance.org/festival.*

SHOPPING

General Store. Step inside the Sundance catalog, which features distinctive home furnishings, clothing, and jewelry reflecting the rustically elegant Sundance style. Ask about many items that are organic or made of recycled materials. ⊠ *Sundance Resort, 8841 N. Alpine Loop Rd., Sundance* ☎ *801/223–4250* ⊕ *www.sundanceresort.com.*

Sundance Deli. Selling foods from American cottage farmers and artisans as well as homemade oils, soaps, and bath salts, the Deli also has a juice bar and is a good place to get tea, coffee, shakes, pastries, deli meats, organic produce, and other tasty snacks. Stop here before your hike to pick up a fresh sandwich. ⊠ *Sundance Resort, 8841 N. Alpine Loop Rd., Sundance* ☎ *801/223–4211* ⊕ *www.sundanceresort. com* ☉ *Closed Sun.*

NORTH OF SALT LAKE CITY

Updated
by Johanna
Droubay

When most people think of Utah, they picture the red-rock crags and canyons of the south, but the north, with its cattail marshes and pasture lands framed by the gray cliffs of the Wellsville Mountains and the Bear River Range, has its own kind of beauty—without the throngs of tourists you'll encounter in the south.

Here the Shoshones (Sacagawea's tribe) made their summer camps, living on roots, berries, and the plentiful game of the lowlands. In the 1820s and '30s mountain men came to trap beavers, foxes, and muskrats, taking time out for their annual rendezvous on the shores of Bear Lake. Some, like the famous Jim Bridger, took Native American wives and settled here; to this day, Cache, Rich, and Box Elder counties are collectively known as "Bridgerland." In the 1850s Mormon pioneers were sent by Brigham Young to settle here, and their descendants still populate this rugged land. In 1869 an event occurred here that would change the face of the West, and indeed the nation, forever: the completion of the Transcontinental Railroad was celebrated officially at Promontory Summit.

ORIENTATION AND PLANNING

GETTING ORIENTED

With two mountain ranges, Mother Nature has neatly divided northern Utah into three major sightseeing areas, each with its own attractions. Ogden is one of the main towns that anchors the region. Forty minutes north of the state capital in Salt Lake City, Ogden served as a major railroad hub in the 19th and 20th centuries, and goods, services, wealth, brothels, and religion all found their way on the rails to this once-rough town. Northwest of Ogden is the Golden Spike Empire, home to the union of transcontinental railroads in 1869 and a thriving agricultural community. Turquoise-colored Bear Lake straddles the Idaho border farther north.

Ogden City and Valley. The largest city north of Salt Lake City is Ogden, with more than 86,000 residents. Its growth was spurred by the coming of the railroads and Hill Air Force Base, but its 21st-century renaissance is oriented around the easygoing outdoorsy lifestyle here. Hiking, skiing, golf, kayaking, boating, and more are all available either within city limits or in the beautiful valley that lies 8 miles up the canyon.

The Golden Spike Empire. Heading north up I–15 from Ogden (or, if you're in no hurry, up Highway 89, where you'll find plenty of farm stands), you'll come upon the Golden Spike Empire. Pleasant farmlands in the shadow of the Wellsvilles give way to rolling sagebrush-covered hills and eventually the desolate salt flats of the Great Salt Lake. Visit the Bear River Migratory Bird Refuge and the Golden Spike National Historic Site.

TOP REASONS TO GO

Ski Ogden: Park City gets the accolades, but locals know that the snow is just as good, the slopes less crowded, and the prices much more reasonable at Snowbasin, Powder Mountain, and Nordic Valley. The most memorable moments on skis in the 2002 Winter Olympics happened here, not in Park City.

Hill Air Force Base: One of Utah's largest employers, the base provides worldwide logistics support for America's F-16s and A-10s. Look for Hill's fighters crisscrossing the skies, or get up close with more than 90 air- and spacecraft at the Hill Aerospace Museum.

Logan Canyon National Scenic Byway: A favorite with locals and visitors, the winding Highway 89 from Logan to Bear Lake is best

enjoyed in the fall when changing leaves create stunning panoramas of red, gold, and green. The route offers scenic picnic spots and fun hiking trails, with plenty of historic sites to explore along the way.

Historic 25th Street, Ogden: Once home to brothels and unsavory railside establishments, the community of Ogden has banded together to revitalize 25th Street with art galleries, museums, restaurants, and several unique shops. Downtown Ogden also has one of minor-league baseball's most beautiful ballparks.

Bear Lake: A favorite retreat on the Utah-Idaho border during the hot summer months, this modestly developed lake has a reputation for azure-blue water and the best raspberry shakes in America.

Bear Lake Country. It's almost incomprehensible that a lake as blue as the Mediterranean exists in the Intermountain West—but it's true. Straddling the Utah-Idaho border, Bear Lake is relatively undeveloped, with a quaint cluster of old-fashioned burger and shake shops on the southwest side, and only a few small motels and campgrounds. At 109 square miles, it will give you plenty to explore for a few days in the hot summer.

PLANNING

WHEN TO GO

Northern Utah offers four seasons of outdoor fun. Be prepared for hot summer days and extremely cold winter nights. Spring brings vistas of verdant pastures under the still snowcapped mountains. Hot summer afternoons prepare you for a dip in Bear Lake followed by an evening at the Festival Opera. On crisp fall days, breathtaking hues of red scrub oak, orange maple, and bright yellow aspen rub shoulders with blue-green firs. Winter is the domain of skiers, snowshoers, and snowmobilers. This region drops dozens of inches of snow annually in the valleys and hundreds of inches in the mountains. You'll never battle hordes of tourists in this less-discovered part of the state, but you might have to wait in a line of locals for a raspberry shake at Bear Lake on a hot summer weekend.

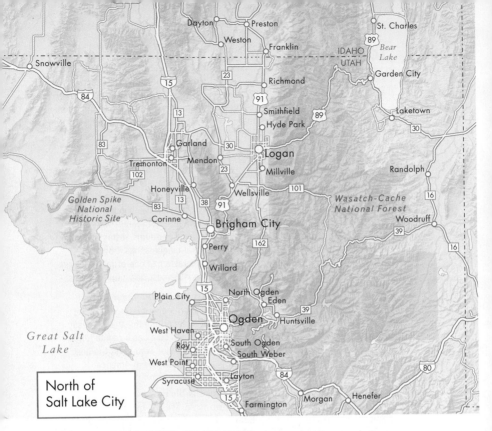

PLANNING YOUR TIME

Ogden serves as a great base to begin your exploration of this corner of Utah, offering plenty of family-friendly and outdoor activities. Plan on a day in Ogden to check out the **Salomon Center, Treehouse Museum,** and **Historic 25th Street.** Head west on Highway 83 to **Golden Spike National Historic Site.** If you've had your fill of railroad history, make your way to Honeyville for a cleanse at **Crystal Hot Springs.** Heading north to Logan, enjoy one of the region's more scenic drives, before settling into this college town with plenty to see both in town and on the Utah State University campus. Stock up on cheese, ice cream, and local produce before the leisurely drive up beautiful **Logan Canyon** to **Bear Lake State Park,** where boating, swimming, or lounging await at Rendezvous Beach.

If it's wintertime, a few days is enough time to get a good sense of skiing in northern Utah. Pick from **Nordic Valley, Powder Mountain,** and **Snowbasin** ski resorts in the Ogden Valley. For a taste of what skiing was like before it became a rich person's sport, drive farther north to **Cherry Peak** or **Beaver Mountain.**

GETTING HERE AND AROUND
AIR TRAVEL

Salt Lake International is the primary airport for northern Utah. Thirty-eight miles north, Ogden-Hinckley Airport is one of Utah's busiest general aviation airports. The Logan-Cache airport is capable of handling small charter jets, and Brigham City has an airport for propeller planes.

Airport Information Brigham City Municipal Airport. ✉ *1800 N. 2000 W, Brigham City* ☎ *435/734–6615* ⊕ *brighamcity.utah.gov/airport.htm.* **Logan-Cache Airport.** ✉ *2500 N. 900 W, Logan* ☎ *435/752–8111* ⊕ *logancacheairport.org.* **Ogden-Hinckley Airport.** ✉ *3909 Airport Rd., Ogden* ☎ *801/629–8251* ⊕ *www.flyogden.com.* **Salt Lake International Airport.** ✉ *776 N. Terminal Dr., Salt Lake City* ☎ *801/575–2400* ⊕ *www.slcairport.com.*

AIRPORT TRANSFERS Express Shuttle offers round-trip shuttles to Ogden, and Salt Lake Express makes several stops in Logan including the Transit Center, where you can transfer to local buses. Prices vary by day and time.

Shuttle Information Express Shuttle. ☎ *800/397–0773* ⊕ *www.expressshuttleutah.com.* **Salt Lake Express.** ☎ *800/356–9796* ⊕ *www.saltlakeexpress.com.*

BUS TRAVEL

The Utah Transit Authority (UTA) is a good option for getting to and from the Wasatch Front.

Bus Information Cache Valley Transit District. ☎ *435/752–2877* ⊕ *www.cvtdbus.org.* **Utah Transit Authority.** ☎ *801/743–3882, 888/743–3002* ⊕ *www.rideuta.com.*

CAR TRAVEL

Northern Utah has two main highways: I-15 running north–south and Highway 89 running northeast–southwest. The latter is a national scenic byway, and the hour's drive between Logan and Bear Lake will reward you with breathtaking vistas and plenty of places to pull off for a picnic. Off the main highways, roads range from well-paved multilane blacktop routes to barely graveled backcountry trails.

Information Utah Highway Patrol Brigham City Office. ✉ *20 W. 700 N, Brigham City* ☎ *435/723–1094* ⊕ *highwaypatrol.utah.gov.* **Utah Highway Patrol Ogden Office.** ✉ *461 Stewart Dr., Ogden* ☎ *801/393–1136* ⊕ *highwaypatrol. utah.gov.*

Road Conditions Utah Road Condition Information. ☎ *511 within Utah, 866/511–8824 outside Utah* ⊕ *udot.utah.gov/traffic.*

TRAIN TRAVEL

The FrontRunner high-speed commuter train operates every hour on weekdays and Saturday, and every half-hour during weekday rush hour, between the downtowns of Ogden and Salt Lake City, with a half-dozen stops in between. Fares are based on the distance traveled, starting at $2.50 one-way.

Train Information Utah Transit Authority. ☎ *801/743–3882, 888/743–3882* ⊕ *www.rideuta.com.*

RESTAURANTS

Ogden has fine restaurants, but in general the fare in northern Utah is your basic Western-style grub. Be sure to sample the Aggie ice cream made at Utah State University, Cache Valley Swiss cheese, and fresh fruit and vegetables from this rich agricultural area.

HOTELS

Some reputable chains service Ogden, along with interesting family-owned inns and B&Bs in a full range of prices. In the Ogden Valley and at Bear Lake, your best option may be a condo or cabin. Make reservations, especially on summer weekends and holidays; during fall and winter many hotels get booked far in advance when conventions are in town. *Hotel reviews have been shortened. For full information, visit Fodors.com.*

VISITOR INFORMATION

Bear Lake Convention and Visitors Bureau. ☎ *435/946–2197, 800/448–2327 ⊕ www.bearlake.org.*

Cache Valley Visitors Bureau. ✉ *199 N. Main St., Logan ☎ 435/755–1890, 800/882–4433 ⊕ www.visitloganutah.com ⊙ Closed Sun.*

OGDEN CITY AND VALLEY

Settled several years prior to Salt Lake City's historic Mormon influx (in 1847), Ogden has nonetheless been trumped by the capital city to the south for most of its history. Recently, however, a thriving outdoor recreation industry, Hill Air Force Base, three ski areas, and the renovation of Historic 25th Street have brought jobs, recreation, and redevelopment to a community once known as a seedy railroad junction. The city is a small, affordable alternative to Salt Lake City—or head "up the canyon" to the Ogden Valley to enjoy a marvelously pastoral community surrounding the Pineview Reservoir, and bordered by mountains with some of America's best skiing.

OGDEN

35 miles from Salt Lake City.

With a population of more than 86,000, Ogden combines a small-town feel with the infrastructure of a larger city. The oldest town in Utah, Ogden was founded by mountain man Miles Goodyear, who settled here with his family in the early 1840s. The Mormons arrived in the area in 1847, and in 1869 Ogden became a hub for the Transcontinental Railroad. The city quickly became a major Western crossroads. During World War II there was a considerable military presence here. This continues today at Hill Air Force Base. Ogden is also a college town; Weber State University is within the city limits.

Today, Ogden has become a multisport mecca, where outdoor adventure blends with emerging urban chic. You can head east into the Ogden Valley—only 25 minutes from downtown—for climbing, biking, hiking, and world-class skiing. After your adrenaline binge, recharge on Historic 25th Street, the metropolitan complement to this recreation-heavy stronghold. During the railroad heyday, 25th Street, directly east of the railroad depot, was infamous for its bars and bordellos. The buildings that once housed them have been preserved and now house quirky, locally owned restaurants, clubs, art galleries, and clothing boutiques.

GETTING HERE AND AROUND

Ogden is about 40 minutes north of Salt Lake City on I–15, with several suburbs and Hill Air Force base in between. Most commuters and visitors take the highway and enter Ogden via Exit 341, 343, or 344. Highway 89 hugs the foothills of the Wasatch Mountains and offers an alternative route and a shortcut for drivers headed to Ogden Valley from Salt Lake City. FrontRunner trains, taxis, or UTA buses are public options if you don't have a car.

ESSENTIALS

Ogden Convention and Visitors Bureau. ⊠ *2438 Washington Blvd.* ☎ *800/255–8824, 866/867–8824* ⊕ *www.visitogden.com.*

Ogden–Weber Chamber of Commerce. ⊠ *2380 Washington Blvd., Suite 290* ☎ *801/621–8300* ⊕ *www.ogdenweberchamber.com.*

EXPLORING

TOP ATTRACTIONS

FAMILY **George S. Eccles Dinosaur Park.** The 8-acre dinosaur park near the mouth of Ogden Canyon is the stomping ground for about 100 life-size dinosaur models and the delighted children who come to see them. A playground with dinosaurs to crawl on is a lure for the younger set, and grown-ups can brush up on their geology and paleontology in two indoor natural history museums. The gift shop is brimming with dinosaur toys, T-shirts, games, and souvenirs. Technicians working with excavated dinosaur bones are on view in the paleontology laboratory, and educational activities for kids put a lot of fun into learning. ⊠ *1544 E. Park Blvd.* ☎ *801/393–3466* ⊕ *www.dinosaurpark.org* ⊠ *$7* ⊗ *Closed Sun. and Mon. in winter.*

FAMILY **Hill Aerospace Museum.** If you like airplanes old or new, you'll love this museum 5 miles south of downtown Ogden at Hill Air Force Base in Roy, off I–15 at Exit 338. There are more than 90 aircraft on display along with missiles, military vehicles, munitions, uniforms, and thousands of artifacts. ⊠ *Hill Air Force Base, 7961 Wardleigh Rd., Roy* ☎ *801/825–5817* ⊕ *www.aerospaceutah.org* ⊠ *Free* ⊗ *Closed Sun.*

Fodor's Choice **Historic 25th Street.** This quaint section of downtown Ogden has been the
★ centerpiece of a 30-year urban-renewal initiative. On 25th Street you'll find the color, flavor, and vitality of its 19th-century roots without the grime and crime that once made it infamous. The three-block stretch from Union Station to Washington Boulevard includes more than a dozen restaurants and bars, plus galleries, and boutiques. Historical markers tell the story of the rough pubs, brothels, and gambling houses that were the anomaly in heavily Mormon Utah a century ago. Check out the farmers' market Saturday mornings in the summer. ⊠ *Ogden* ⊕ *www.historic25.com.*

FAMILY   **Salomon Center.** This massive center is a high-adventure recreational playground, complete with a climbing wall, indoor surfing, simulated skydiving, a bowling alley, laser tag, an arcade, bumper cars, and billiards. ⊠ *2261 Kiesel Ave.* ☎ *801/399–4653* ⊕ *www.visitogden.com/ salomon-center* ⊠ *Admission varies.*

FAMILY   **Union Station.** Incorporating elements of Ogden's original 1870s train depot, which was destroyed by fire in 1923, the impressive Spanish Revival replacement houses two art galleries and four museums: the John M. Browning Firearms Museum, the Browning-Kimball Classic Car Museum, the Utah State Railroad Museum, the Utah Cowboy & Western Heritage Museum, the Myra Powell Gallery, and the Gallery at the station. ⊠ *2501 Wall Ave.* ☎ *801/393–9890* ⊕ *theunionstation. org* ⊠ *Combined ticket to all 4 museums $5* ⊘ *Closed Sun.*

WORTH NOTING

Eccles Community Art Center. Housed in an impressive Victorian mansion, the museum has a permanent collection of works by such contemporary artists as LeConte Stewart, Henri Mosher, Pilar Pobil, David Jackson, and Richard Van Wagoner. There is also a sculpture garden. Special exhibits change periodically, and there are monthly displays of works by emerging Utah artists. ⊠ *2580 Jefferson Ave.* ☎ *801/392–6935* ⊕ *www. ogden4arts.org* ⊠ *Free* ⊘ *Closed Sun.*

FAMILY   **Fort Buenaventura Park.** Highlighting a chapter in history that unfolded decades prior to the railroad era, this 84-acre tract along the Weber River has replicas of the fort and cabins that mountain man Miles Goodyear built in 1846. Picnicking facilities are available and canoes may be rented ($3 for a half-hour, $5 for an hour) in warmer months. Campsites and teepees may also be reserved. In June the park hosts acoustic, folk, bluegrass, and roots artists at the Ogden Music Festival. ⊠ *2450 A Ave.* ☎ *801/399–8099* ⊕ *www.webercountyutah.gov/parks/fortb* ⊠ *Free.*

FAMILY   **Ogden Nature Center.** As one of very few wildlife sanctuaries set within a
Fodor's Choice   city, the 152-acre center is home to thousands of trees, marshlands, and
★   ponds, with nature trails used for cross-country skiing in winter. You can see Canada geese, great blue herons, red foxes, mule deer, and porcupines in the wild, as well as rescued bald eagles, owls, and other spectacular species up close. The nature center museum has activities for children, and the Nest gift shop sells nature-oriented goods. ⊠ *966 W. 12th St.* ☎ *801/621–7595* ⊕ *www.ogdennaturecenter.org* ⊠ *$5* ⊘ *Closed Sun.*

FAMILY   **Treehouse Museum.** Offering a hands-on learning experience where children literally can step into a story, the downtown museum features interactive exhibits for kids ages 2–12. Visit Jack's Fairy Tale Diner, a Japanese House, the Jupiter Train Locomotive, or the German House Puppet Theater. Other fun activities include songs, theater, and art workshops. ⊠ *347 22nd St.* ☎ *801/394–9663* ⊕ *www.treehousemu-seum.org* ⊠ *$5* ⊘ *Closed Sun.*

   The Ice Sheet. This popular indoor ice-skating arena hosted the 2002 Olympic curling events and offers open skating daily; call for hours. Individual instruction is also available. ⊠ *Weber County Sports Complex, 4390 Harrison Blvd.* ☎ *801/778–6360* ⊕ *www.co.weber.ut.us/ icesheet* ⊠ *$7 (includes skate rental)* ⊘ *Closed Sun.*

SPORTS AND THE OUTDOORS

More than 250 miles of trails for hiking, mountain biking, and horseback riding surround the Ogden area, and the scenic roads are perfect for biking enthusiasts. The Weber and Ogden rivers provide high-adventure rafting and kayaking. Olympic-caliber skiing is just up the canyon.

2nd Tracks Sports. Conveniently located close to the mouth of Ogden Canyon, 2nd Tracks has the gear and equipment you'll need to explore the area's mountains, waters, and snow. Rent or buy a paddleboard, tube, kayak, bike ($25–$65 per day), skis, or a snowboard, and then head up the canyon to the recreational paradise that is the Ogden Valley. Be sure to allot some time for perusing the selection of discounted and secondhand name-brand outdoor apparel. Ski and bike tuning services are also available. ⊠ *1273 Canyon Rd.* ☎ *801/466–9880* ⊕ *2ndtracks. com.*

BICYCLING

The Bike Shoppe. Specializing in bikes and bike service for more than 40 years, this shop favored by bike enthusiasts sells and repairs top-of-the-line brands and offers bike rentals by the day ($30–$80). You can also rent snowshoes and wetsuits here. ⊠ *4390 S. Washington Blvd.* ☎ *801/476–1600* ⊕ *www.thebikeshoppe.com* ☉ *Closed Sun.*

HIKING

From an urban stroll along the Ogden River Parkway to a challenging hike on the Beus Canyon Trail to the summit of Mount Ogden, hikes in the Ogden area provide something for everyone. Most of the trail system is connected in some way to the North–South Bonneville Shoreline Trail, a pathway following the high mark of prehistoric Lake Bonneville along the Wasatch Front.

Ogden Trails Network. Choose from 25 different adventures identified on a handy online trail map, including the Ogden River Parkway and the Ogden Bike Park. ⊠ *Ogden* ☎ *801/629–8271* ⊕ *www.ogdencity. com/545/Ogden-Trails-Network.*

Weber Pathways. This local nonprofit organization is dedicated to preserving and maintaining trails in Weber County. Its online trail map includes detailed elevation information and covers the greater Ogden area. ⊠ *Ogden* ☎ *801/393–2304* ⊕ *www.weberpathways.org*

KAYAKING AND RAFTING

WSU Outdoor Program. Weber State University offers an affordable outdoor program designed for students, residents, and visitors seeking custom guided tours. Activities include white-water rafting, kayaking, rock climbing, snowshoeing, and cross-country skiing. All guides are experienced with insider's knowledge of the area. Equipment rentals are available. ⊠ *Weber State University, 4022 Stadium Way* ☎ *801/626–6373* ⊕ *www.weber.edu/outdoor* ⌨ *$25–$125.*

WHERE TO EAT

$$$

CONTEMPORARY

✗ **Hearth on 25th.** With an emphasis on wood-fired cooking and farm-to-table freshness, the menu at this fine-casual gem includes fish presented in creative ways and house-made pastas, breads, and dressings. Diners enjoy a patio overlooking the historic district and the Wasatch Mountains, wine on tap, a selection of more than 70 whiskeys, and a seasonally changing array of fresh desserts. **Known for:** wild game; grass-fed yak; intimate setting. [$] *Average main: $22* ⊠ *195 25th St.* 🕾 *801/399–0088* ⊕ *www.hearth25.com* ⊗ *Closed Sun.*

$$
AMERICAN

✕ **Rooster's Brewing Company and Restaurant.** On Historic 25th Street, this brewpub offers excellent libations brewed on-site. Set in a 128-year-old building, the pub offers pizzas created with locally made cheeses, steak, sandwiches, salads, and daily seafood specials. **Known for:** buzzing atmosphere; people-watching on the patio; beer brewed on-site. [$] *Average main: $16* ⊠ *253 25th St.* 🕾 *801/627–6171* ⊕ *www.roostersbrewingco.com* ⊗ *No brunch weekdays.*

$
PIZZA

✕ **Slackwater Pizzeria & Pub.** This casual stop along the Ogden River Parkway boasts hundreds of craft beers, mountain and river views, and a festive, friendly vibe. Try the boldly unorthodox pizza toppings, which are internationally inspired, verdant, and piled high. **Known for:** expansive regional beer selection; live music; adventurous brick-oven pizzas. [$] *Average main: $12* ⊠ *1895 Washington Blvd.* 🕾 *801/399–0637* ⊕ *slackwaterpizzeria.com.*

$$$
JAPANESE
Fodor's Choice
★

✕ **Tona Sushi Bar and Grill.** Sushi is hardly regional cuisine in Utah, but you wouldn't know it at Tona. Named the best restaurant north of SLC by Salt Lake Magazine in 2017, this chic little spot has a modern focus, offering much more than just sushi rolls (although the rolls alone would keep the doors open). **Known for:** sashimi; impressively plated Green Globe; homemade desserts. [$] *Average main: $22* ⊠ *210 25th St.* 🕾 *801/622–8662* ⊕ *tonarestaurant.com* ⊗ *Closed Sun.*

WHERE TO STAY

$$
HOTEL

🏨 **Courtyard Ogden.** Renovated in 2014, the former Ogden Marriott has a convenient downtown location close to government offices and businesses and in walking distance of Historic 25th Street. **Pros:** modern amenities; close to businesses, restaurants and nightlife; comfortable and spacious business center and lounge area. **Cons:** no complimentary breakfast without more expensive package. [$] *Rooms from: $129* ⊠ *247 24th St.* 🕾 *801/627–1190, 800/321–2211* ⊕ *www.marriott.com* ⟿ *193 rooms* ⦿ *No meals.*

$$
HOTEL
Fodor's Choice
★

🏨 **Hampton Inn and Suites.** Gray marble, bright bay windows, and soaring ceilings with ornate crown molding greet you in the lobby of this art deco beauty. **Pros:** free Wi-Fi; complimentary hot breakfast; walking distance to Historic 25th Street. **Cons:** frequently booked with business travelers; higher rates during special events. [$] *Rooms from: $150* ⊠ *2401 Washington Blvd.* 🕾 *801/394–9400* ⊕ *www.ogdensuites.hamptoninn.com* ⟿ *145 rooms* ⦿ *Breakfast.*

$$
HOTEL

🏨 **Hilton Garden Inn.** Near the Ogden Eccles Conference Center and Union Station, this modern hotel, built in 2012, is an ideal choice for both business or leisure travelers. **Pros:** convenient to businesses, attractions and Historic 25th Street; on-site restaurant serves breakfast and dinner and offers room service; scenic view suites have fireplaces. **Cons:** frequently booked up for conventions and conferences; outdoor parking. [$] *Rooms from: $109* ⊠ *2271 S. Washington Bd.* 🕾 *801/399–2000* ⊕ *www.hilton.com* ⟿ *134 rooms* ⦿ *Breakfast.*

NIGHTLIFE AND PERFORMING ARTS

NIGHTLIFE

At the height of the railroad era Ogden's 25th Street was lined with saloons and gambling halls, opium dens, and a thriving red-light district. It has become more gentrified since then, but is still the center of one of Utah's most vibrant nightlife scenes.

Alleged. Although there are other dance clubs in Ogden, this one is by far the most modern and sceney. The first floor is for dancing, and gets progressively more packed as the night goes on. The second floor is more of a lounge; you can order pizza from Lucky Slice across the street and bring it into the bar. On the top floor, a rooftop bar overlooks Historic 25th Street, with sunsets to the west, and mountains to the east. ⊠ *201 25th St.* ☎ *801/990–0692* ⊕ *www.alleged25th.com.*

Brewskis. Big-screen TVs, pool tables, and live music are the big draws at this popular bar. The menu features pub fare including burgers, sandwiches, and pizzas. On weekends, live acts range from country to hard rock and indie folk. ⊠ *244 25th St.* ☎ *801/394–1713* ⊕ *www. brewskisonline.net.*

City Club. Decorated with an impressive collection of Beatles memorabilia, this unique bar caters to an upscale crowd, generally in their 30s. Patrons enjoy a friendly, attentive staff and a menu offering appetizers, specialty drinks, sandwiches, and salads. ⊠ *264 25th St.* ☎ *801/392–4447* ⊕ *www.thecityclubonline.net.*

Lighthouse Lounge. This upscale lounge and music venue is a great spot for sipping a cocktail, sharing some appetizers, and listening to live performers in the Listening Room; some performances are free of a cover charge. ⊠ *130 25th St.* ☎ *801/392–3901* ⊕ *lighthouseloungeogden.com.*

PERFORMING ARTS

FAMILY **Ogden Amphitheater.** From June through August at this venue with gorgeous views, local and regional artists give free outdoor concerts Tuesday at noon and Wednesday night, and there are free movies on Monday. ⊠ *Municipal Gardens, 343 25th St.* ☎ *801/629–8307* ⊕ *www. ocae.org.*

Fodor'sChoice **Peery's Egyptian Theater.** Built in the 1920s then abandoned for years,
★ Peery's Egyptian Theater is a restored art deco jewel that hosts concerts ranging from world music to national blues, jazz, and country acts, as well as an ongoing film series and musical theater. ⊠ *2415 Washington Blvd.* ☎ *801/689–8600* ⊕ *www.peerysegyptiantheater.com.*

Val A. Browning Center for the Performing Arts. Theater, music, and dance performances by students and visiting artists are offered frequently at Weber State University's performing arts center, home stage for the Ogden Symphony Ballet Association. ⊠ *Weber State University, 3950 W. Campus Dr.* ☎ *801/626–7015* ⊕ *www.weber.edu/browningcenter.*

SHOPPING

As with nightlife and dining, you'll find the most interesting concentration of shops on Historic 25th Street, with a few don't-miss shopping stops scattered around the rest of town.

ART GALLERIES

Art Stroll. The first Friday of each month, 20 or so downtown galleries, shops, and restaurants showcase the work of local artists during a street stroll that stretches from the gallery inside Union Station to the Eccles Community Art Center on the corner of 26th and Jefferson streets. ⊠ *2501 Wall Ave.* ☎ *801/629–8718* ⊕ *ogdencity.com/arts.*

FOOD

FAMILY **Farmers Market Ogden.** Find fresh local produce and the work of local artists here on Saturday, late June through mid-September from 9 am to 2 pm. There's live music and food stalls, too. ⊠ *25th St. and Municipal Park* ☎ *385/333–7119* ⊕ *farmersmarketogden.com.*

GIFTS AND SOUVENIRS

Fodor's Choice **Ailulia.** This large, beautifully staged boutique carries vintage-inspired ★ clothing for women and children, gifts, soaps, party supplies, toys, and much more. Allot ample time for exploring the delightful displays spread across the store's two floors. ⊠ *236 25th St.* ☎ *801/628–2213* ⊗ *Closed Sun. and Mon.*

Rainbow Gardens and Planet Rainbow. If you're looking for a gift or memento that says Utah, these unique stores at the mouth of Ogden Canyon are fun to browse. Rainbow Gardens' 20-plus departments offer souvenirs, cowboy nostalgia, books, garden ornaments, gadgets, regional food items, and more. Planet Rainbow features artisan jewelry, collectibles, new-age crystals, and espresso. ⊠ *1851 Valley Dr.* ☎ *801/621–1606 Rainbow Gardens, 801/392–3902 Planet Rainbow* ⊕ *www.rainbowgardens.com.*

SPIRITS

Fodor's Choice **Ogden's Own Distillery.** Stop in for a tasting at Ogden's Own (and only) ★ Distillery, and try one of their six handcrafted liquors. An herbal liqueur known as Underground is a local favorite. Five Wives Vodka is made from water hiked out five gallons at a time from a hidden spring in nearby Ogden Canyon. ⊠ *3075 Grant Ave.* ☎ *801/458–1995* ⊕ *www.ogdensown.com* ⊗ *Closed Sun. and Mon.*

SPORTING GOODS

Alpine Sports. If you're in Utah for a ski vacation, you can't beat Alpine Sports for high-performance winter gear, stylish outdoor apparel, and design-conscious gadgets and accessories. The selection here is painstakingly curated by buyers who know their stuff, and you can't walk through the door without falling in love with something a little outside your budget. Rentals, tuning, and repair are also available. ⊠ *1165 Patterson St.* ☎ *801/393–0066* ⊕ *alpinesportsutah.com* ⊗ *Closed Sun. and Apr.–Aug. Open Sat. only in Sept.*

OGDEN VALLEY

8 miles east of Ogden City.

With its world-class skiing, accessible water sports, great fishing, golf, climbing, hiking, biking, and camping, the Ogden Valley is a recreation mecca still largely waiting to be discovered.

GETTING HERE AND AROUND

Most visitors approach the valley from Ogden via 12th Street, which becomes Highway 39. Pineview Reservoir lies at the center of the valley, and resembles an airplane with the nose pointing west, and wings (arms of the lake) extending north and south. You can circle the reservoir in about 30 minutes by car, although it's tempting to stop for the beaches, boat access, milk shakes, and more.

Trapper's Loop (Highway 167) is the scenic shortcut expanded for the 2002 Olympics from I–84 to the south end of the reservoir. It's beautiful in spring and fall, and well maintained for access to Snowbasin ski resort in the winter.

Ogden Valley Business Association. ⊠ *Eden* ☎ *801/745–2550* ⊕ *www.visitogdenvalley.com.*

EXPLORING

FAMILY

Fodor'sChoice

★

Pineview Reservoir. In summer, this 2,800-acre lake and its sandy beaches are festooned with colorful umbrellas and the graceful arcs of water-skiers and wakeboarders. In winter it's a popular spot for ice-fishing. The fishing is good, and campgrounds and marinas dot the shore. Middle Inlet, Cemetery Point, and Anderson Cove are the three developed beaches (fee), but Anderson Cove is the only one that allows overnight camping. The Cove has a boat launch. **Amenities:** parking (fee); toilets; water sports. **Best for:** partiers; swimming. ⊠ *Ogden* ☎ *801/625–5112* 🖅 *$13–$16 day use; access to some beaches is free* ⊙ *Beach amenities closed Oct.–Apr.*

SPORTS AND THE OUTDOORS

HIKING

Many of the beautiful hikes in the Ogden Valley enable you to discover ski terrain in the off-season. For detailed trail maps and information, contact the Ogden Ranger District at ☎ *801/625–5112*; if you're at Snowbasin you can get maps in the Grizzly Center.

FAMILY

Snowbasin. Starting at 6,500 feet and ending at 9,600 feet, the moderate 2½-mile trail (one-way) from the upper parking lot at Snowbasin leads to the saddle south of Mount Ogden. Hikers pass through bowls filled with colorful summer wildflowers. On weekends, you can ride the gondola ($14) to Needles lodge, eat lunch, and then hike along the ridge to Mt. Ogden peak. June through September, the resort hosts the popular Blues, Brews & BBQ every Sunday, bringing free musical acts to the base of the mountain. ⊠ *Ogden* ⊕ *www.snowbasin.com.*

HORSEBACK RIDING

Red Cliff Ranch and Outfitters. Visitors in summer enjoy scenic mountain views on horseback. Guided trail rides are offered, as well as guiding and outfitting for big game hunting in the summer, and bobcat and mountain lion hunting in the winter. ⊠ *13554 E. Hwy. 39, Huntsville* ☎ *801/745–6900* ⊕ *www.redcliffranch.com.*

SKIING

FAMILY

CROSS-

COUNTRY

North Fork Park. North Fork's well-maintained 14 miles of cross-country trails, plus 6 miles of snowshoe trails, are perfect for beginners, intermediates, and families looking for a day of fun in the snow. Cross-country ski and snowshoe rentals are available for adults and kids. The trails are also popular for hiking and biking in warmer months. ✉ *1984 North Fork Park Rd., Eden* ☎ *801/648–9020 rentals, 801/399–7275 grooming report* ⊕ *www.ogdennordic.com* 🖃 *$6 cross-country ski; $3 snowshoe.*

DOWNHILL If you're staying in Ogden and want to head for the mountains for a day of skiing or snowboarding, you can catch the Ski Bus, which runs between several downtown Ogden hotels and the ski resorts in the Ogden Valley. For details of schedules and routes, call ☎ *888/743–3882*, or ask at the front desk of your local hotel. Black Diamond Shuttle also offers taxi service from hotels and the airport. Call ☎ *801/920–1774.*

Fodor's Choice **Powder Mountain.** This classic ski resort offers huge terrain (more skiable
★ acres than any other resort in North America) even though it doesn't have as many lifts as some of the destination resorts. Two terrain parks and a half-pipe are popular with snowboarders. Snowcat skiing (for an additional $25) and night skiing are also popular. Although plenty challenging, the intermediate options are heavenly in contrast to nearby Snowbasin, which is generally steeper and more exposed. You won't find fancy lodges or haute cuisine here, but with caps on season and day passes, crowds are nonexistent, and the laid-back slope-side eateries serve everything from scones and hot soup to sandwiches or a flame-broiled burger at the Powder Keg. ✉ *6965 E. Hwy. 158, Eden* ☎ *801/745–3772* ⊕ *www.powdermountain.com* 🖃 *Lift tickets $85* ⛷ *2,205-ft vertical drop; 8,464 skiable acres; 25% beginner, 40% intermediate, 35% advanced; 4 quad chairs, 1 triple chair, 3 surface lifts.*

Snowbasin. A vertical drop of 2,959 feet and a dramatic start at the pinnacle of Mount Ogden made this ski resort, 17 miles from Ogden, the perfect site for the downhill ski races during the 2002 Olympic Winter Games. With nine lifts accessing more than 2,800 acres of steep, skiable terrain, this is one of Utah's largest resorts. It also offers miles of Nordic trails for cross-country skiing. Served in spectacular lodges, the on-mountain food was ranked #2 by Ski Magazine. Snowbasin also regularly ranks in the magazine's top 10 for service, lifts, and grooming. ✉ *3925 E. Snowbasin Rd. (Hwy. 226), Huntsville* ☎ *801/620–1000, 888/437–5488* ⊕ *www.snowbasin.com* 🖃 *Lift tickets $109* ⛷ *2,959-ft vertical drop; 2,820 skiable acres; 20% beginner, 50% intermediate, 30% advanced; 2 high-speed gondolas, 1 tram, 1 high-speed six-pack chair, 2 high-speed quad chair, 3 triple chairs, 2 surface lifts.*

FAMILY **Nordic Valley.** Utah's smallest ski resort was used for downhill training for the 2002 Olympics. A great place to learn, this charming family-oriented resort is one of the most affordable in the state, and the whole mountain is lighted for night skiing and boarding. ✉ *3567 E. Nordic Valley Way, Eden* ☎ *801/745–3511* ⊕ *www.nordicvalley.com* 🖃 *Lift tickets $50* ⛷ *1,000-ft vertical drop; 140 skiable acres; 35% beginner, 45% intermediate, 20% advanced; 2 double chairs, 1 triple chair, 1 surface lift.*

SNOWMOBILING

Club Rec. This outdoor recreation shop rents Jet Skis, speed boats, double-decker pontoon boats, and other watercraft so you can enjoy Pineview Reservoir to the fullest. In the winter time, a guided tour of

Monte Cristo is one of the best snow adventures in the West. ✉ *3718 N. Wolf Creek Dr., Eden* ☎ *801/614–0500* 🌐 *www.clubrecutah.com.*

WHERE TO EAT AND STAY

There are no real hotels or motels in the Ogden Valley, but you will find a few tucked-away B&Bs and condos that accommodate groups of all sizes.

$$ MEXICAN 🍴 **Carlos & Harley's.** This fun Mexican restaurant specializes in "fresh-Mex" cuisine, a contemporary spin on Tex-Mex, using all made-from-scratch ingredients. **Known for:** festive vibe; sizzling fajitas; margaritas on the outdoor patio. [$] *Average main: $17* ✉ *5510 E. 2200 N, Eden* ☎ *801/745–8226.*

$ AMERICAN Fodor's Choice ★ 🍴 **Red Rock Grill.** It can be hard to find good food in the Ogden Valley, not to mention good service, which is why it's well worth your effort to veer off the beaten path in pursuit of this tiny but excellent barbecue joint. Their pulled pork is the star, and it's always crispy, juicy, and tasty, whether in sandwich form, loaded on top of fries, or nestled inside Carolina tacos. **Known for:** slow-smoked BBQ; remote but scenic location; specialty burgers. [$] *Average main: $11* ✉ *13555 E. Hwy. 39, Huntsville* ☎ *801/745–3060* 🌐 *www.theredrockgrill.com* ⏲ *Closed Mon. and Tues. Apr.–Oct.; closed Mon.–Thurs. Nov.–Mar.*

$ AMERICAN Fodor's Choice ★ 🍴 **Shooting Star Saloon.** The only Utah bar listed in *Esquire* magazine's ranking of top bars in the United States is also the oldest remaining saloon in the state. In operation since the 1880s, it's a favorite hangout of skiers in winter and a beloved destination for bikers in summer. **Known for:** the Star Burger (double cheeseburger topped with a Polish hot dog); the Saint Bernard head mounted on the wall; Old West charm. [$] *Average main: $7* ✉ *7350 E. 200 S, Huntsville* ☎ *801/745–2002.*

$$$ RENTAL 🏨 **Moose Hollow at Wolf Creek Resort.** The condos at Wolf Creek's Moose Hollow property are just a few miles from Powder Mountain and within walking distance of Wolf Creek's scenic 18-hole golf course. **Pros:** spacious units; outdoor pool; gorgeous views of the lake and mountains. **Cons:** two-night minimum stay (some exceptions when space is available); no pets. [$] *Rooms from: $200* ✉ *3718 N. Wolf Creek Dr., Eden* ☎ *801/745–3737* 🌐 *wolfcreekrentals.com* 🛏 *30 units.*

THE GOLDEN SPIKE EMPIRE

Deserts, marshes, farmlands, mountains: there's enough landscape in the vast reaches of eastern Box Elder County to please any palate. The star attraction here, though, is history, specifically one day in history that changed the world: May 10, 1869. That's the date the Union Pacific and Central Pacific railroad officials met to drive their symbolic golden spike in celebration of the completion of the First Transcontinental Rail route. It happened at Promontory Summit, an ironically desolate spot about 15 miles north of the Great Salt Lake. The Wild West was about to be tamed.

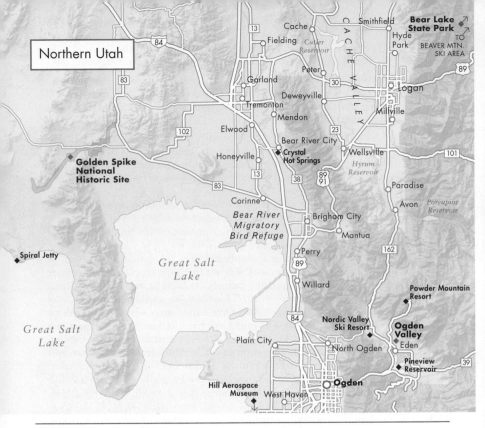

GOLDEN SPIKE NATIONAL HISTORIC SITE

32 miles west of Brigham City.

Golden Spike National Historic Site offers a variety of activities in addition to the annual reenactment that celebrates the anniversary of the completion ceremony for the nation's first Transcontinental Railroad. Replicas of the 1869 steam locomotives operate May to October, and visitors can hike on Big Fill Loop Trail or take two auto tours that detail how the railroad was constructed. In the winter, engine house tours are offered.

GETTING HERE AND AROUND

One of the more remote outposts in the National Park System, Golden Spike is almost two hours north and west of Salt Lake City and not on the way to anywhere. Be aware that once you leave I–15, there are virtually no services. Make sure you have enough gas to make the round-trip.

EXPLORING

Golden Spike National Historic Site. The Union Pacific and Central Pacific railroads met here at Promontory Summit on May 10, 1869, to celebrate the completion of the first transcontinental rail route. Under the auspices of the National Park Service, the site has a visitor center and two beautifully maintained locomotives that are replicas of the

LOGAN CANYON DRIVE

Logan Canyon Scenic Byway. Connecting the Cache Valley to Bear Lake via Highway 89, Logan Canyon is perhaps best known for its vibrant fall colors. A photographer's dream in autumn, the canyon also thrills snowmobilers in the winter and fishermen in the warmer months. Towering limestone walls follow the path of the Logan River through the Bear River Mountains and provide ample opportunity for rock climbing. Hiking, biking, and horseback riding are also popular. High in the canyon's mountains, Tony Grove Lake and its campground are a serene escape, and a trail from the lake leads to Naomi Peak, the highest point in the Bear River Mountains. ⊠ *Logan Ranger District Visitor's Center, 1500 East Hwy. 89, Logan* ☎ *534/755–3620.*

4

originals that met here for the "wedding of the rails." Every May 10 (and on Saturday and holidays in summer), a reenactment of the driving of the golden spike is held. In August, boiler stoking, rail walking, and buffalo-chip throwing test participants' skills at the Railroader's Festival. The Winter Steam Festival around Christmas time gives steam buffs opportunities to photograph the locomotives in the cold, when the steam from the smokestacks forms billowing clouds. ⊠ *Golden Spike Rd., off Hwy. 83, Promontory* ☎ *435/471–2209* ⊕ *www.nps.gov/gosp* ⊠ *$5–$7 per vehicle.*

OFF THE
BEATEN
PATH

Spiral Jetty. It may look strange from the road but this 1,500-foot-long, 15-foot-wide earthen creation that juts out into Great Salt Lake was created by artist Robert Smithson in 1970. The jetty, 16 miles from the Golden Spike site via dirt road, was submerged for much of the subsequent 30 years, before the lake level fell precipitously in 2002 revealing the structure again. The snail shell-shape land art structure is considered one of the most remote sculptures in modern American art history, and it is Utah's state work of art. ⊠ *N. Rozel Flats Rd. W, Rozel Point* ☎ *212/989–5566* ⊠ *Free.*

BEAR LAKE COUNTRY

Bear Lake is one of the most beautiful alpine lakes in America, nearly 6,000 feet above sea level and extremely remote. The handful of lodgings fill quickly, and some are closed in winter.

BEAR LAKE STATE PARK

41 miles from Logan (to Garden City).

GETTING HERE AND AROUND

Perhaps the remote nature of Bear Lake explains why it's such a well-kept secret in the West. The only way to get here is by driving 41 miles on Highway 89 from Logan. Once you're here, it can take an hour and a half or longer to circle the lake by car, especially if it's a busy summer weekend (it may be impossible to access in the winter due to weather). Services are limited and clustered on the lake's western shore. Garden

City (population 587) is the largest town and the best place to stock up on gas, basic groceries, and other supplies. Otherwise, it's mostly no-stoplight communities on the lakefront.

EXPLORING

FAMILY **Bear Lake State Park.** Eight miles wide and 20 miles long, Bear Lake is an unusual shade of blue, thanks to limestone particles suspended in the water. It is home to four species of fish found nowhere else, including the Bonneville cisco, which draws anglers during its spawning season in January. The abundance of Bear Lake's raspberries is celebrated each year in early August at **Raspberry Days.** A parade, a rodeo, fireworks, and entertainment are almost eclipsed by the main event: sampling myriad raspberry concoctions. You'll find several hotel and restaurant options nearby at the junction of U.S. 89 and Route 30, and you can follow the ¼-mile boardwalk through a small wetlands preserve to the lakeshore. On the less developed east side, the lake bottom drops off quickly making it a favorite spot among anglers and scuba divers. ⊠ *Hwy. 89* ☎ *435/946–3343* ⊕ *stateparks.utah.gov/parks/bear-lake* 🖃 *$5–$10 per vehicle.*

Bear Lake Marina. Visitors to Bear Lake won't want to miss the marina. It has a picnic area, campground, and the floating Marina Grill. Pull your boat up to its dock and order a hamburger and a shake right on the water. Buy a bag of fish food at the marina store and watch swarms of fish suddenly materialize in the lake's clear turquoise waters. You can also rent boats, paddleboards, kayaks, a water trampoline, and other watercraft from the marina's concessions, run by Bear Lake Fun. ⊠ *Hwy. 89, Garden City* ⊕ *bearlakefun.com* 🖃 *$8–$10/vehicle, day use.*

Rendezvous Beach. On the south shore of Bear Lake, mountain men gathered for their annual rendezvous in 1827 and 1828. Today this area has more than a mile of sandy beaches, three lakeside campgrounds (many sites have ample shade), and picnic areas. There is also a marina with concessions, including watercraft rentals and a burger-and-shake shack. If you're hoping to camp here, book as early as possible. **Amenities:** food and drink; parking (fee); toilets; water sports. **Best for:** partiers; swimming. ⊠ *Hwy. 30, Laketown* 🖃 *$10/vehicle, day use* ☉ *Closed Nov.–Apr.*

SPORTS AND THE OUTDOORS

BICYCLING

Cyclists of all abilities can enjoy all or any portion of the level 48-mile ride on the road circling Bear Lake. The paved Lakeside Bicycle Path curves from Bear Lake Marina south and east along the shore, with several rest stops. Interpretive signs relate stories about Bear Lake's history and local lore.

BOATING

Personal watercraft, kayaks, pontoons, and motorboats are available at the Bear Lake Marina and in the surrounding towns. Prices vary from about $70 per hour for a PWC to $150 an hour and up for large motorboats capable of towing water skiers and wakeboarders. Be advised that the winds at this mountain lake can change 180 degrees within minutes (or go from 30 knots to completely calm), so be cautious. Life jackets are required for everyone on board vessels up to 40 feet.

FISHING

The Logan River and Blacksmith Fork are blue ribbon trout streams. You can pull Bear Lake cutthroat, out of Bear Lake from mid-April through June, or join the locals in dip-netting Bear Lake cisco when they come to shore to spawn in January. Warm-water species are found in abundance in Mantua Reservoir, 4 miles east of Brigham City on Highway 89. In the Bear River you'll find mostly carp. For a novelty fishing experience, boat out to the middle of Tony Grove Lake and use a long line with plenty of sinkers to land one of the rare albino rainbow trout that frequent the depths of the lake.

Utah Division of Wildlife Resources. You can get a fishing license at most local sporting goods stores, but if you want to obtain your license online, go to the Utah Division of Wildlife Resources website. ⊠ *Bear Lake State Park* ☎ *801/476–2740* ⊕ *www.wildlife.utah.gov.*

GOLF

Bear Lake Golf Course. Golfers looking for a quick game can play nine holes in this beautiful lakeside setting when the weather permits (generally May to October). It's suitable for all levels of play, good for beginners, but also with some challenging greens and water hazards, generally calling for accurate shots—not easy, given the distraction of the stunning views and activity on the lake. ⊠ *222 E. Clubhouse Dr., Garden City* ☎ *435/946–8742* ⊕ *bearlakegolfcourse.com* ⌷ *$23 weekdays, $25 weekends (includes cart)* ⅃ *9 holes, 3376 yards, par 36.*

HIKING

At 9,980 feet, Naomi Peak is the highest point of the Bear River Range in Cache National Forest. The 3.2-mile **Naomi Peak Trail** starts in the parking lot of the Tony Grove Campground and gains almost 2,000 feet in elevation. You hike through conifer forests and open meadows and along subalpine basins and rocky ledges. A shorter hike to **White Pine Lake,** which begins on the same trail and splits after a quarter of a mile, is also lovely. To reach the trailhead, take Highway 89 southwest from Garden City for approximately 15 miles to the Tony Grove turnoff, then follow the signs. Closer to Garden City is the **Limber Pine Nature Trail,** a popular and easy hike (1 mile round-trip) at the summit between Logan Canyon and Bear Lake that features interpretive information especially designed for children.

SKIING

FAMILY **Beaver Mountain Ski Area.** Owned and operated by the same family since 1939, this locals' favorite offers skiing as it was before it became a rich man's sport. See aerial tricks, or try night skiing (until 9 pm) at the two terrain parks. There aren't any trendy nightspots at the foot of this mountain, just an old-fashioned A-frame lodge with burgers and chili. ⊠ *40000 E. Hwy. 89* ☎ *435/946–3610, 435/753–0921* ⊕ *www.skithebeav.com* ⌷ *Lift tickets $50* ⌁ *1,700-ft vertical drop; 828 skiable acres; 48 runs; 25% beginner, 40% intermediate, 35% advanced; 3 triple chairs, 1 double chair, 1 surface lift.*

WHERE TO EAT AND STAY

$ MEXICAN 🍴 **Café Sabor.** Offering a welcome respite for hungry tourists, fishermen, and water-sports enthusiasts returning from a day on Bear Lake, this family-owned Mexican restaurant treats diners to a fiesta-like atmosphere with comfortable indoor seating or outdoor dining on the spacious patio. Featuring a full lunch and dinner menu filled with traditional favorites like quesadillas, tacos, and burritos, the options also include sizzling fajita platters for two, chicken mole, shrimp enchiladas, and homemade tortilla soup. **Known for:** house-made chips, tortillas, and guacamole; margaritas; fried ice cream. [$] *Average main: $12* ✉ *100 N. Bear Lake Bd., Garden City* ☎ *435/946–3297* 🌐 *www.cafesabor.com* 🕒 *Closed Sun.–Wed. in winter.*

$ FAST FOOD 🍴 **LaBeau's Drive-in.** The Bear Lake region is well known for its locally grown raspberries, and this is the most popular spot in town to enjoy a thick and creamy raspberry shake. Choose from 45 other shake flavors along with a menu of old-fashioned hamburgers, hot dogs, and chicken sandwiches. **Known for:** raspberry shakes; people-watching at outdoor picnic tables; long lines. [$] *Average main: $9* ✉ *69 N. Bear Lake Blvd., Garden City* ☎ *435/946–8821* 🕒 *Closed Sun. and mid-Oct.–late Apr.*

$$$ RESORT FAMILY 🏨 **Ideal Beach Resort.** A private beach awaits at this family-style resort open year-round, and there's a wide range of accommodations options, from rooms for two to condos sleeping up to 20. **Pros:** a wonderful place for families; lots of activities; within walking distance of the lake. **Cons:** with so many kids around, it's not a spot for peace and quiet; limited amenities in winter. [$] *Rooms from: $200* ✉ *2176 S. Bear Lake Blvd., Garden City* ☎ *435/946–3364, 800/634–1018* 🌐 *www.ideal-beachresort.com* 🛏 *8 rooms, 200 condos* 🍽 *No meals.*

DINOSAURLAND
AND EASTERN UTAH

Updated by
Aly Capito

The rugged beauty of Utah's northeastern corner, wedged neatly between Wyoming to the north and Colorado to the east, is the reward for those willing to take the road less traveled. Neither I–80 nor I–70 enters this part of the state, so most visitors who pass through the western United States never even see it—that is part of its appeal. Small towns, rural attitudes, and a more casual and friendly approach to life are all part of the eastern Utah experience.

Northeastern Utah is home to superb boating and fishing at Flaming Gorge, Red Fleet, and the Steinaker reservoirs. Hundreds of miles of hiking and mountain-biking trails (available to cross-country skiers, snowmobilers, or snowshoers in winter) crisscross the region. The Green and Yampa rivers entice white-water rafters as well as less ambitious float-trippers. The pine- and aspen-covered Uinta Mountains offer campers and hikers hidden, pristine lakes and streams surrounded by amazing mountain views. Even if you don't get out of the car, exploring this region on the road takes you through vast red-rock basins, over high mountain passes, and between geologic folds in the earth.

Dinosaurs once dominated this region, and in many ways, they still do. Excavation sites such as Dinosaur National Monument make northeastern Utah one of the most important paleontological research areas in the world. Paleontology labs and fossil displays can be found at roadside stops and on off-road adventures, as well as kitschy dino statues and impressive life-size skeleton casts.

Ancient Native American cultures also left their marks throughout the region. Cliff walls and boulders are dotted with thousands of examples of rock art of the Fremont people (AD 600 to 1300), so called because they inhabited the region near the Fremont River. Today, the Uintah and Ouray Reservation is the second largest in the United States. It covers a significant portion of eastern Utah, though much of the reservation's original land grant was reclaimed by the U.S. government for its mineral and timber resources. The Ute Tribe, whose 3,000-some members inhabit the land, hold powwows and host other cultural ceremonies, which help visitors understand their way of life.

Museums throughout the region are full of fascinating pioneer relics, and there are a number of restored homesteads in and around Vernal. The rich mining and railroad history of the Price–Helper area fuels the tall tales you're certain to hear of outlaws, robberies, mine disasters, and heroes of the past.

TOP REASONS TO GO

One great gorge: The most jaw-dropping spot in northeastern Utah is the Flaming Gorge National Recreation Area. The deep-blue water under the gorge's reddish, steep walls is a serene place for fishing and boating. The surrounding open space makes for good camping, biking, and hiking.

Famous fossils: Come to Dinosaur National Monument to see the famous dinosaur fossils or just to explore some truly remote country. For the most exciting introduction to the monument, take a guided river-rafting trip through it.

Ancient art: The cliffs near Vernal and Price are striking not only for their interesting rock formations,

but also for numerous displays of ancient petroglyphs and picto-graphs, drawn once upon a time by members of the Fremont tribe.

Bike Vernal: In the last decade, almost 200 miles of former cow trails around Vernal have been converted for use by mountain bikes. The sport is taking a foothold in the area, so that means the paths are sometimes busy.

Alone in the swell: The San Rafael Swell is one of the least crowded spots in a region that's already known for its sparse population. If you're looking for solitude while hiking, biking, and boating, these miles of domed rock might be exactly what you need.

ORIENTATION AND PLANNING

GETTING ORIENTED

This section of Utah is large, but it's easy to get around. With few towns in the area, traffic is almost always light. The main highways to explore this area are U.S. 191 and U.S. 40, which run north–south. The biggest towns are Vernal and Price, both of which make comfortable bases for the backcountry.

Northeast–Central Utah (Castle Country). Nicknamed for the impressive castle-like rock formations that dot the landscape, Castle Country is one of those secret spots that many vacationers miss out on. Most of the attractions are near the town of Price, such as the huge crop of petroglyphs at Nine Mile Canyon. The San Rafael Swell, one of the largest and wholly unvisited natural wonders, lies 25 miles south of Price.

The Uinta Basin (Dinosaurland). Dubbing the Uinta Basin "Dinosaurland" is no overstatement. Named in honor of the large quantity of dinosaur fossils in the area (and especially the 1909 discovery of a huge cache of dino fossils in what is now Dinosaur National Monument), this slice of Utah boasts about its paleontological history whenever possible. Here you can see the ancient bones at the monument and get a crash course in dinosaur history at Vernal's Utah Field House of Natural History State Park. The breathtaking Flaming Gorge National Recreation Area is an excellent place to fish, boat, swim, and catch up-close glimpses of wildlife such as bighorn sheep and wild turkeys.

PLANNING

WHEN TO GO

In northeastern Utah most museums, parks, and other sights extend their hours from Memorial Day to Labor Day or through the end of September. (Some museums and parks are open only in summer.) Summer (when temperatures can reach 100°F) also brings art festivals, pioneer reenactments, rodeos, and other celebrations. Spring and autumn are cooler and less crowded. Some campgrounds are open year-round, but the drinking water is usually turned off after Labor Day. In winter you can cross-country ski or snowshoe on many of the hiking trails.

> ### CAMPING
>
> Wilderness makes up the majority of this beautifully undeveloped region. Many visitors choose to immerse themselves in the outdoors by camping for at least part of their stay. For campground information contact **Dinosaur National Monument Quarry Visitor Center** (☎ 435/781–7700 ⊕ www.nps.gov/dino), the state government's recreation department (☎ 877/444–6777 ⊕ www.recreation.gov), or **Utah State Parks** (☎ 800/322–3770 ⊕ www.stateparks.utah.gov).

PLANNING YOUR TIME

The two biggest draws in this area are **Flaming Gorge National Recreation Area** and **Dinosaur National Monument**. While it's reasonable to see the fossils on display at Dinosaur in just a day, you'll get a better sense of the park's untouched natural beauty if you stay overnight. Likewise, you can spend a day or several hiking the trails and playing in the water at Flaming Gorge. Many of the towns in the area can be driven through or stopped in without spending the night. The one exception is **Price**, a pleasant town that's less than two hours from the stunning **San Rafael Swell**, a huge, oval-shape, geologic dome that's far from everything but worth the trek. You could easily spend a few days exploring these unique areas. If you can make the time, a one or multiday excursion on the **Green, White,** or **Yampa river** would be an unforgettable—and occasionally heart-pounding—addition to your stay.

GETTING HERE AND AROUND

AIR TRAVEL

The closest major airport is Salt Lake City International Airport—two hours from Price and three hours from Vernal; it's served by most major airlines.

CAR TRAVEL

Both U.S. 40 and U.S. 191 are well maintained but have some curvy, mountainous stretches, and away from major towns, be prepared for dirt roads. Keep your vehicle fueled up, because gas stations can be far apart, and some are closed on Sunday. Watch for wildlife on the road, especially at night. Price is the largest city on U.S. 6, the major route between the Wasatch Front and the southeastern part of the state. Dinosaur National Monument (which spans the Utah–Colorado border) is three hours east of Salt Lake City on U.S. 40, or three hours northeast of Price via U.S. 191 and U.S. 40. Flaming Gorge is 40 miles north of Vernal via U.S. 191. The Uinta Mountains and the High Uintas Wilderness

Area are about 1½ hours east of Salt Lake City, first via I–80, U.S. 40, and Highway 248 to Kamas and then via Highway 150.

Information Road Conditions. ☎ 866/511-8824 ⊕ www.udottraffic.utah.gov.

RESTAURANTS

Because the towns in eastern Utah are small, dining options are generally more casual and less innovative than you may find in urban settings. The best dining in this part of the state can be found in upscale lodges—Red Canyon Lodge and Flaming Gorge Resort, both near Flaming Gorge—which pride themselves on gourmet menus. Vernal, a farming and ranching town, has good steak houses and tasty diner eats. The area is known for the refreshingly trendy Vernal Brewing Company, which opened just off Vernal's Main Street in 2013. Bear in mind that most locally owned restaurants are closed on Sunday.

HOTELS

Most hotels and motels in eastern Utah are chains, and you can expect clean, comfortable rooms and standard amenities. The area's lodges make for a nice change of pace when desired, surrounding you with natural beauty and more individualized rooms and services. Though it goes against logic, many hotels here offer cheaper rates on weekends than weekdays, due to the high number of workers who stay during the week. On weekends, hotels and motels do their best to attract tourists. *Hotel reviews have been shortened. For full information, visit Fodors.com.*

WHAT IT COSTS			
$	**$$**	**$$$**	**$$$$**
Restaurants under $12	$12–$20	$21–$30	over $30
Hotels under $100	$100–$150	$151–$200	over $200

Restaurant prices are the average cost of a main course at dinner or, if dinner is not served, at lunch. Hotel prices are the lowest cost of a standard double room in high season.

VISITOR INFORMATION

Visitor Information Bureau of Land Management. ✉ 125 S. 600 W, Price ☎ 435/636-3600 ⊕ www.blm.gov/ut ✉ 170 S. 500 E, Vernal ☎ 435/781-4400 ⊕ www.blm.gov/ut. **Visit Dinosaurland.** ✉ 149 E. Main St., Vernal ☎ 435/781-6765 Uintah County Travel and Tourism, 800/477-5558 visits and more info ⊕ www.dinoland.com.

NORTHEAST–CENTRAL UTAH (CASTLE COUNTRY)

While Castle Country feels desolate, people have been in the area for centuries. Spanish explorers and traders crossed northeast–central Utah as early as 1598, on a trail now followed by Highway 10. In the 19th century fur trappers passed through the mountains in their search for beaver and other animals, and in the 1870s some of them decided to

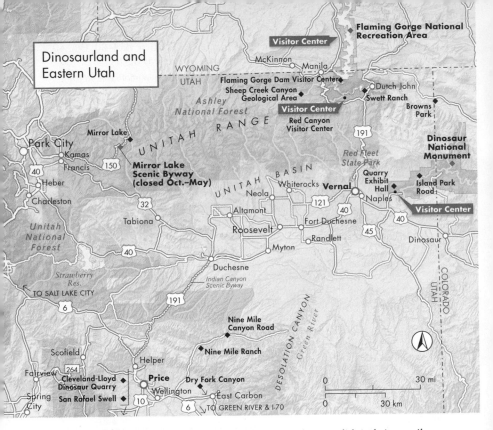

Dinosaurland and Eastern Utah

return to do some ranching. However, the area didn't thrive until a new kind of wealth was discovered in the mountains—coal. Railroad tracks were laid in the valley in 1883 to bring miners from around the world to dig the black mineral and to carry the coal out to markets across the country. Coal continues to provide the economic base for many towns in Castle Country, but so does tourism, which is growing every year.

PRICE

120 miles southeast of Salt Lake City.

Thousands of visitors travel to Price every year to experience Utah's past through fossils, exhibits, and preservation sites at the Prehistoric Museum, USU Eastern. For being a quite small, mostly blue-collar town, one may not expect to find much excitement here, but they'd be wrong. While Price began as a Mormon farming settlement in the late 1800s, in 1883 the railroad arrived, bringing with it immigrants from around the world to mine coal reserves. As the town expanded, coal became the cash crop of the area, and mining remains the town's primary industry to this day.

GETTING HERE AND AROUND

To get to Price from Salt Lake City, travel on I–15 South for 50 miles, and then take U.S. 6 for 70 miles toward the southeastern corner of the state. This drive contains many of the area's breathtaking views and rock formations. Be aware that mountain and canyon roads can seem unpredictable if you're not used to them.

If you're heading to Price from Green River or the surrounding area, take U.S. 191 north for 65 miles. The town is easy to navigate, with most of the main attractions on or close to Main Street.

FESTIVALS

Greek Festival Days. A sizable number of Greek immigrants arrived in the area of Price to work in the mines throughout the early 1900s. This annual festival in mid-July celebrates that heritage with two days of traditional Greek food, dance, and music. ☒ *Assumption Greek Orthodox Church, 61 S. 200 E* ☎ *435/636–3701* ⊕ *www.castlecountry.com/greek-festival-days.*

Price City International Days. Held annually at the end of each July, this festival uses music, dance, and food to celebrate the many nationalities that make up the Price community. Find yourself in cultures from around the world. Enjoy all that this amazing festival has to offer, right on the heels of the Pioneer Days festivities (July 24) throughout the state. ☒ *Pioneer Park, 100 E. 550 N* ☎ *435/636–3701* ⊕ *www.castlecountry.com/Price-City-International-Days.*

ESSENTIALS

Visitor Information Carbon County Office of Tourism and Visitors Center. ☒ *751 E. 100 N #2100* ☎ *435/637–3701* ⊕ *www.castlecountry.com.*

EXPLORING

FAMILY **Cleveland-Lloyd Dinosaur Quarry.** Paleontologists and geologists have excavated more than 15,000 dinosaur bones from the Cleveland-Lloyd Dinosaur Quarry, making this "predator trap" the densest concentration of Jurassic fossils ever found. The center is 15 miles on a gravel road from the nearest services, so bring food and water and dress for desert conditions. It's 32 miles south of Price: take Highway 10 south to the Cleveland/Elmo turnoff and follow the signs. Free admission for ages 15 and younger. ☒ *Off Hwy. 10* ☎ *435/636–3600* ⊕ *www.blm.gov/ut* 🔛 *$5.*

Fodor's Choice **Nine Mile Canyon.** The hundreds of petroglyphs etched into the boulders and cliffs of Nine Mile Canyon may be one of the world's largest
★ outdoor art galleries. They're the handiwork of the Fremont people, who lived in much of what is now Utah from AD 600 to 1300. The canyon also shelters the remnants of many early homesteads, stage stops, and ranches. It's important not to touch the fragile rock art because oils from your fingers can damage them. The drive through Nine Mile Canyon spans about 100 miles round-trip. ☒ *Nine Mile Canyon Rd.* ✛ *To reach canyon, go 7½ miles southeast of Price on U.S. 6 and then turn north on Soldier Creek Rd., which eventually connects with Nine Mile Canyon Rd.* ☎ *435/637–3701* ⊕ *www.castlecountry.com/nine-mile-canyon.*

FAMILY **The Prehistoric Museum, USU Eastern.** Miners working in the coal pits around Price in the late 1800s often saw and excavated rare treasures that most scientists could only dream of finding—dinosaur bones, eggs, skeletons, and fossilized tracks. These are all on exhibit at the Prehistoric Museum, USU Eastern. For families, this museum offers a small but excellent kids' discovery area where children can experiment with excavating dino bones all on their own. A second hall is devoted to early humans, with displays of beadwork, clay figurines, a walk-in teepee, and other area artifacts. You can't miss the museum's gigantic wooly mammoth and saber-toothed tiger replicas. ✉ *155 E. Main St.* ☎ *435/613–5060, 800/817–9949* 🌐 *www.usueastern.edu/museum* 🎟 *$6* 🕒 *Closed Sun.*

Fodor's Choice ★ **San Rafael Swell.** Tremendous geological upheavals pushed through the Earth's surface eons ago, forming a giant oval-shape dome of rock about 80 miles long and 30 miles wide, giving rise to the name "swell." Over the years, the harsh climate beat down the dome, eroding it into a wild array of multicolor sandstone and creating buttes, pinnacles, mesas, and canyons that spread across more than 600,000 acres. In the northern Swell, the Wedge Overlook peers into the Little Grand Canyon and the San Rafael River below. The strata at the edges of the southern Swell are angled near vertical, creating the San Rafael Reef. Both are known for fantastic hiking, canyoneering, and mountain biking. ✉ *125 S. 600 W* ☎ *435/636–3600* 🌐 *www.blm.gov/ut.*

SPORTS AND THE OUTDOORS

Carbon County covers a wide range of geography, from mountains to gorges to plateaus. Hundreds of miles of hiking and biking trails crisscross the region.

HIKING AND MOUNTAIN BIKING

The canyons and surrounding landscapes of Price include trails that rival the slickrock of Moab, minus the crowds. The visitor center in Price has a mountain biking guide that shows several trails you can challenge yourself on, including Nine Mile Canyon. Adventurous hikers can use many of these trails as well. Bicyclewerks is a great source of information for those looking to explore.

Bicyclewerks. The co-owners here—Fuzzy "the Bike Guy" Nance and Mark Jespersen—are Price's go-to guys for trail details, fix-its, or area information. ✉ *82 N. 10 W* ☎ *435/637–7676.*

WHERE TO EAT

$ AMERICAN 🍴 **Farlaino's Café.** Found in a historic building along Main Street, this casual restaurant attracts locals with large portions of American fare for breakfast, lunch, and early dinners (it closes at 7 pm). **Known for:** hand-cut curly fries; homemade soups (on weekdays); giant pancakes. [$] *Average main: $9* ✉ *87 W. Main St.* ☎ *435/637–9217* 🕒 *Closed Sun.*

$ GREEK 🍴 **Greek Streak.** In what used to be a Greek coffeehouse in the early 1900s, this low-key café is a reminder of Price's strong Greek heritage. The menu includes traditional recipes from Crete, like gyros, dolmades, and lemon-rice soup. **Known for:** traditional Greek recipes; outstanding baklava. [$] *Average main: $9* ✉ *84 S. Carbon Ave.* ☎ *435/637–1930* 🕒 *Closed Sun.*

$ ITALIAN 🍴 **Nicki Spaghetti.** In a welcome departure from the region's typical bar and grill fare, this restaurant serves traditional Italian dishes at very reasonable prices. The atmosphere evokes the Rat Pack era with a Sinatra soundtrack, black-and-white photographs of Bogart and gang, and a low-light ambience. **Known for:** family recipes; traditional Italian. [$] *Average main: $8* ✉ *40 W. Main St.* ☎ *435/637–4393* 🌐 *www.nickispaghetti.com* 🕒 *Closed Sun. No lunch.*

$ FAST FOOD FAMILY Fodor's Choice ★ 🍴 **Sherald's.** If you hanker for the nostalgia, and the prices, of an old-fashioned hamburger stand, you're in luck. Order at the window and eat outside at picnic tables, or use the car-side service. **Known for:** long lines; delicious burgers and fries; very thick milk shakes. [$] *Average main: $5* ✉ *434 E. Main St.* ☎ *435/637–1447* 🕒 *Closed Sun.*

WHERE TO STAY

$ HOTEL 🏨 **Greenwell Inn & Convention Center.** With more amenities than most of the local hotels, but still reasonably priced, the Greenwell is a great choice for most travelers. **Pros:** convenient downtown location; nice pool; fireplaces in some rooms. **Cons:** motel-style room entrances are a downside in inclement weather; fitness center is large but is in lobby/pool area. [$] *Rooms from: $90* ✉ *655 E. Main St.* ☎ *435/637–3520, 800/666–3520* 🌐 *www.greenwellinn.com* 🛏 *130 rooms, 6 suites* 🍽 *No meals.*

$ B&B/INN 🏨 **Nine Mile Ranch.** Ben Mead grew up in beautiful Nine Mile Canyon, and now runs this "bunk and breakfast" establishment on his working cattle ranch. **Pros:** a true cowboy experience; unrivaled silence. **Cons:** remote location; breakfast not included with cabin rental. [$] *Rooms from: $90* ✉ *Nine Mile Canyon Rd., Post 24, Wellington* ✥ *To reach ranch, travel 7 miles southeast of Price to Wellington via Hwy. 6, then make left onto Soldier Creek Canyon Rd., which will become Nine Mile Canyon Rd., and drive north for 25 miles* ☎ *435/637–2572* 🌐 *9mileranch.com* 🛏 *2 rooms, 3 cabins* 🍽 *Breakfast; No meals.*

$$ HOTEL 🏨 **Ramada.** This stylishly decorated hotel has a large atrium surrounding the pool area; rooms are clean and comfortable, offering kitchenettes, jetted tubs, and comfy beds. **Pros:** many amenities; pleasant and well-lit interiors; restaurant open Sunday. **Cons:** no meals included; a bit expensive for the area, but worth it. [$] *Rooms from: $124* ✉ *838 Westwood Blvd.* ☎ *435/637–8880, 877/492–4803* 🌐 *www.ramada.com/hotel/48661* 🛏 *137 rooms, 14 suites* 🍽 *No meals.*

NIGHTLIFE

The Club at the Tuscan. This club's classy atmosphere renders it a pleasant place to park for the evening. Come early for dinner; it's attached to a tasty fine dining restaurant with extremely reasonable prices. Afterwards, step across the hall for a drink and maybe a game of pool. The atmosphere livens up on the weekends, when the doors stay open until 2 am and a live DJ brings the dance floor to life. ✉ *23 E. 100 N* ☎ *435/613–2582.*

5

THE UINTA BASIN

The Uinta Basin, the original home of the ancient Fremont people, is a vast area of sprawling high-desert at its finest. Bordered by the Uinta Mountains to the north, the Wasatch Mountains to the west, and a series of high plateaus and cliffs to the south, you may feel as if you've journeyed through several different states all in one drive.

In the 1860s the Mormons thought about settling here, but decided the land was not fit for agriculture. At their suggestion, President Abraham Lincoln set aside several million acres of the basin as a Native American reservation. Members of Ute and other tribes were relocated to the basin from their traditional lands in the Salt Lake and Utah Lake valleys. In the 1900s, the U.S. government took back much of the Uinta Basin land that had been set aside as a reservation and opened it to settlers from the east. However, following the Indian Reorganization Act of 1934, the Northern Ute Tribe purchased the majority of this land, and it now constitutes the second-largest reservation in the United States.

As with much of this region, it was discovered that an unbelievably rich trove of dinosaur fossils lie in the sandstone layers near the eastern Utah border. Since the discovery in the early 1900s, archaeologists have unearthed hundreds of tons of fossils, and the region encompassing Daggett, Duchesne, and Uintah counties has become known as Dinosaurland. An area particularly rich in fossils, straddling the Utah and Colorado borders, has been preserved as Dinosaur National Monument.

VERNAL

22 miles east of Fort Duchesne.

Vernal is the hub of Dinosaurland, mixing the region's ancient heritage with a certain kitschy charm—think down-home diners and giant dino statues. Dinosaurs aren't the only things they're proud of in Vernal, though. The town claims a connection to the ancient Fremont people, a rowdy ranching past, and more than a passing acquaintance with outlaws like Butch Cassidy, who frequented the area whenever he felt it was safe to be seen around town.

GETTING HERE AND AROUND

Though secluded, it's easy to get to Vernal. From Salt Lake City, head 25 miles via I–80, then 145 miles east via U.S. 40/U.S. 191; from Price go east on U.S. 40. Most of Vernal's attractions are right on Main Street. From Vernal, take U.S. 40 east to reach Dinosaur National Monument, or head north on U.S. 191 to explore Flaming Gorge National Recreation Area.

FESTIVALS

Dinosaur Roundup Rodeo. For three days in early or mid-July each year, Vernal celebrates the town's Western heritage when it hosts the Dinosaur Roundup Rodeo. Three days of rodeo events, dances, and parades on Main Street celebrate the real-life cowboys who wear cowboy boots because they're practical, not because they're fashionable. ⊠ *Western Park Convention Center, 302 E. 200 S* ☎ *435/781–6765* ⊕ *vernalrodeo. com* ⊡ *$14–$17.*

ESSENTIALS

Visitor Information Vernal Area Chamber of Commerce. ⊠ *134 W. Main St.* ☎ *435/789–1352* ⊕ *www.vernalchamber.com.* **Visit Dinosaurland.** ⊠ *149 E. Main St.* ☎ *435/781–6765 Uintah County Travel and Tourism, 800/477–5558 visits and more info* ⊕ *www.dinoland.com.*

EXPLORING

FAMILY **Dry Fork Canyon.** An impressive array of easily accessible Native American petroglyphs and pictographs adorn the 200-foot-high cliffs in Dry Fork Canyon, making the 22-mile round-trip drive from Vernal well worth your time. Two trails leading to the rock art are on **McConkie Ranch,** a privately owned property that asks only for a $4 per vehicle donation and respect for the art and trails. ⊠ *3500 West St. (Dry Fork Canyon Rd.)* ☎ *435/789–6733* ⊠ *$4 per vehicle donation requested.*

Uintah County Heritage Museum. Inside the Uintah County Heritage Museum are collections of Fremont and Ute Indian artifacts, including baskets, water jugs, and beadwork, as well as pioneer items like carriages, guns, saddles, and old-fashioned toys. Kids can try out an old-school typewriter, while their parents check out the most off-beat installation: a collection of handmade porcelain dolls modeled after the nation's First Ladies, from Martha Washington to Nancy Reagan; they are a kitschy delight. ⊠ *155 E. Main St.* ☎ *435/789–7399* ⊕ *www. uintahmuseum.org* ⊠ *Free.*

FAMILY
Fodor's Choice
★

Utah Field House of Natural History State Park. Around 150 million years ago, this was the stomping ground of dinosaurs, and you can see rock samples, fossils, Fremont and Ute nation artifacts, and a viewing lab where you can watch paleontologists restore actual fossils. The biggest attraction for kids is undoubtedly the outdoor Dinosaur Garden with its 18 life-size models of prehistoric creatures, including a T-rex and a woolly mammoth. The Field House also doubles as a visitor center for all of Dinosaurland, so stop here for maps and guides for the entire area. ⊠ *496 E. Main St.* ☎ *435/789–3799* ⊕ *stateparks.utah.gov/parks/ utah-field-house* ⊠ *$6.*

OFF THE
BEATEN
PATH

Browns Park. Along a quieter stretch of the Green River and extending into Colorado, this area features plenty of high-desert scenery, a national waterfowl refuge. Explore several buildings on the **John Jarvie Ranch.** Buildings date from 1880 to the early 1900s, and there's also a cemetery with graves of a few men who met violent ends nearby. Jarvie also ran a post office, store, and river ferry, and his spread was a major hideout on the so-called Outlaw Trail. In late May, the **Jarvie Festival** celebrates this past with mountain men, wagon rides, pioneer demonstrations, rope- and leather-making, and live music. A similar festival takes place the last Saturday of October. Reach the park and ranch by driving 65 miles north of Vernal on U.S. 191, then 22 miles east on a gravel road. ⊠ *Browns Park Rd., Browns Park* ☎ *435/885–3307 John Jarvie Ranch* ⊕ *www.blm.gov/utah* ⊠ *Free.*

SPORTS AND THE OUTDOORS

BICYCLING

Because Dinosaurland is lesser-known than other parts of the state, bikers can often escape the crowds and enjoy some scenic solitude. The Uinta Basin has some 100 miles of trails. Bring plenty of water and sunblock.

Altitude Cycle. To talk to knowledgeable cyclists about local trails off the beaten path, stop in here; they can set you up with trail guides, repairs, and accessories. Ask for a map of biking hot spot **McCoy Flats**, just 6½ miles west of the shop, off Highway 40. There you'll find 45 miles of trails to explore. ⊠ *580 E. Main St.* ☏ *435/781–2595* ⊕ *www. altitudecycle.com.*

Dinosaur River Expeditions. Explore the best local mountain biking trails with guides from Dinosaur River Expeditions. Most of the biking tours take you just west of Vernal to McCoy Flats. There, your guide will lead you on the best trails for your abilities. Novices might start on the 1½-mile Milk and Cookies loop, while advanced riders may head for the 5½-mile technical singletrack of Slippery When Wet. For a discounted rate, tack on a full-day rafting excursion on the Green River the day before or after. ⊠ *550 E. Main St.* ☏ *800/345–7238* ⊕ *www.dinosaurriverexpeditions.com* ⊠ *$65 for half-day tour; does not include bike rental.*

HIKING

Dinosaur National Monument Quarry Visitor Center. Check with the rangers at this visitor center, 20 miles east of Vernal, for information about the numerous hiking trails in the area. ⊠ *Hwy. 149, Dinosaur National Monument* ☏ *435/781–7700* ⊕ *www.nps.gov/dino.*

Jones Hole Creek. One of the most beautiful hikes in the area begins at the Jones Hole National Fish Hatchery, 40 miles northeast of Vernal on the Utah-Colorado border, and follows Jones Hole Creek through riparian woods and canyons, past petroglyphs and wildlife. The full trail is an 8-mile round-trip to the Green River and back, but you can stop halfway at Ely Creek and return for an easier, but still lovely, 4-mile hike. There are numerous trails in this area that are unmarked and not maintained, but easy to follow if you use reasonable caution. ⊠ *24495 E. Jones Hole Hatchery Rd.*

SCENIC FLIGHTS

Dinaland Aviation. For a bird's-eye view of Dinosaurland's deep canyons, wide-open deserts, and blue reservoirs, take to the air with Dinaland Aviation. They offer flight-seeing tours from 30 minutes to more than an hour. ⊠ *830 E. 500 S* ☏ *435/789–4612* ⊠ *From $39 per person.*

WHERE TO EAT

$ ✕ **Betty's Café.** The atmosphere says "dive bar" and the food may inch
AMERICAN you a notch closer to a heart attack, but your taste buds will loudly sing the praises of Betty's Café. Locals swear by the breakfasts, especially the biscuits, jams, and scalloped-cut home fries—all homemade. **Known for:** homemade strawberry jam; large portions; friendly staff. $ *Average main: $9* ⊠ *416 W. Main St.* ☏ *435/781–2728* ☉ *No dinner.*

$$$ STEAKHOUSE 🍴 **Club XS.** The atmosphere is odd at this combo nightclub and family steak house, but the steaks are the best in town, as locals will attest. Seafood, sandwiches, and salads are also available. **Known for:** amazing service; signature steaks; variety of cuisine and cultural choices. [$] *Average main: $24* ✉ *1080 E. Hwy. 40* ☎ *435/781–0122* 🌐 *www.clubxsrocks.com* 🕒 *Closed Sun. No lunch Sat.*

$ AMERICAN FAMILY 🍴 **Dinosaur Brew Haus.** This friendly spot serves higher quality food than your average sports pub, including hand-cut fries (try them cajun-style), house-smoked meats, and grilled salmon. Snack on peanuts and watch a game on one of the TVs while you wait for your food, or drop a coin in the jukebox and shoot some pool. **Known for:** burgers; beer selection; affordable prices. [$] *Average main: $12* ✉ *550 E. Main St.* ☎ *435/781–0717.*

$$ MEXICAN 🍴 **Plaza Mexicana.** Festive, colorful interiors and authentic Mexican specialties make Plaza Mexicana a sure bet if you need a break from Vernal's ubiquitous American eateries. There are 22 varieties of burritos to choose from, as well a large selection of seafood options. [$] *Average main: $14* ✉ *55 E. Main St.* ☎ *435/781–2931.*

$$ MODERN AMERICAN Fodor's Choice ★ 🍴 **Vernal Brewing Company.** Breweries are rare in this corner of the state, as are eateries with modern style and trendy menu items such as tempura-fried portobello or honey-glazed cornish game hen with watermelon salsa. The VBC fits both bills, with a half-dozen home brews on tap and a creative array of menu items, ranging from thin-crust pizzas to delectable dishes served in mini cast-iron skillets. **Known for:** skillet cookie; burger selection; atmosphere. [$] *Average main: $15* ✉ *55 S. 500 E* ☎ *435/781–2337* 🌐 *www.vernalbrewingcompany.com.*

WHERE TO STAY

$$$ HOTEL FAMILY 🏨 **Best Western Dinosaur Inn.** Remodeled rooms and a new pizza place spruce up this comfortable chain motel located within blocks of all downtown attractions. **Pros:** family-friendly; central location. **Cons:** Main Street location leads to traffic noise in some rooms; feels pricey considering that it's a basic chain offering. [$] *Rooms from: $160* ✉ *251 E. Main St.* ☎ *435/789–2660, 800/780–7234* 🌐 *www.bestwestern.com* 🛏 *55 rooms, 5 suites* 🍽 *Breakfast.*

$$ HOTEL 🏨 **Landmark Inn and Suites.** Just one block off Main Street, this inn offers rooms that are classy for the area and come with kitchenettes. **Pros:** central location; well-appointed rooms. **Cons:** the area isn't very pretty; in-room fans are loud. [$] *Rooms from: $119* ✉ *301 E. 100 S* ☎ *435/781–1800, 888/738–1800* 🛏 *36 rooms, 3 suites* 🍽 *Breakfast.*

DINOSAUR NATIONAL MONUMENT

20 miles east of Vernal.

Dinomania rules at this 330-square-mile park that straddles the Utah–Colorado border. Although the main draws are obviously the ancient dinosaur fossils, the park's setting is something to savor as well, from craggy rock formations to waving grasslands to the Green and Yampa rivers. The best part is that complete solitude is easy to find, as desolate wilderness surrounds even the busiest spots within the park.

GETTING HERE AND AROUND

Coming from Vernal, go east about 10 miles to the town of Jensen, via U.S. 40. Once there, be on the lookout for Utah Highway 149 on your left and then follow the signs to the park.

EXPLORING

FAMILY

Fodor's Choice

★

Quarry Exhibit Hall. Here you can view some 1,500 genuine fossils, displayed in their original burial positions in an excavated river bed, several stories high, 150-feet long, and now enclosed by a large, airy museum. ⊠ *Hwy. 149, 20 miles east of Vernal* ☎ *435/781–7700* ⊕ *www.nps.gov/ dino* ⊠ *$20 per vehicle to enter monument.*

SCENIC DRIVES

Island Park Road. A scenic drive on the unpaved Island Park Road, along the northern edge of the park, not only passes some impressive Fremont petroglyph panels but also reaches a put-in point for rafters. ⊠ *Dinosaur National Monument.*

Tour of the Tilted Rocks. This scenic 20-mile round-trip drive goes from the Quarry Visitor Center east to the Josie Morris Cabin. Josie's sister, Ann Bassett, was reputedly the "Etta Place" of Butch Cassidy legends. Morris lived alone for 50 years at her isolated home. Along the drive, watch for ancient rock art, geological formations, views of Split Mountain, the Green River, and hiking trails. ⊠ *Dinosaur National Monument.*

SPORTS AND THE OUTDOORS

HIKING

Desert Voices Nature Trail. Four miles past the Quarry Visitor Center, the moderate 1½-mile trail has interpretive signs (including some designed by children for children) that describe the arid environment you're hiking through. You can make a longer hike by using the Connector Trail to link up with the Sound of Silence Trail. ⊠ *Dinosaur National Monument.*

Sound of Silence Trail. More challenging than the Desert Voices trail, this 3-mile trail begins 2 miles past the Dinosaur Quarry, and delivers excellent views of Split Mountain. To hike both trails without returning to your car, use the easy ¼-mile Connector Trail , which links the two. ⊠ *Dinosaur National Monument.*

RAFTING

The best way to experience the geologic depths of Dinosaur National Monument is to take a white-water rafting trip on the Green or Yampa river. Joining forces near Echo Park in Colorado, the two waterways have each carved spectacular canyons through several eons' worth of rock, and contain thrilling white-water rapids. River-running season is May through September. ■TIP➔ **Permits are required for all boaters.**

Adrift Adventures. The closest guide service to the Dinosaur National Monument, this outfitter offers one-day or multiday rafting trips on the Green and Yampa rivers. ⊠ *9500 E. 6000 S, Jensen* ☎ *435/789–3600, 800/824–0150* ⊕ *www.adrift.com* ⊠ *From $96 (day trip, including lunch and pass to Dinosaur National Monument).*

Dinosaur River Expeditions. Single-day trips on the Green River and multiday trips on both the Green and Yampa rivers are available. Ask

about custom trips as well. ⊠ *550 E. Main St., Vernal* ☎ *800/345–7238* ⊕ *www.dinosaurriverexpeditions.com* ✉ *From $90.*

Don Hatch River Expeditions. The region's original river-running company, Don Hatch River Expeditions has been operating since 1929. Their one-day and multiday rafting trips take you through both calm and white waters on the Green and Yampa rivers. ⊠ *221 N. 400 E, Vernal* ☎ *800/342–8243* ⊕ *www.hatchriver.com* ✉ *From $99.*

FLAMING GORGE NATIONAL RECREATION AREA

40 miles north of Vernal (to Flaming Gorge Dam).

If you are standing in front of the Flaming Gorge or its reservoir with a crowd of people, you'll likely hear gasps and exclamations of amazement. The sheer size of these bodies of water is astounding, as are the red, narrow walls on either side of the gorge. Though not far from the suburban town of Vernal, the Flaming Gorge area offers a lesson in stillness and serenity. The lake and 91-mile gorge also has some of the best boating and fishing in the state. The Flaming Gorge Reservoir stretches north into Wyoming, but most facilities lie south of the state line in Utah.

A BRIEF HISTORY OF FLAMING GORGE

In May 1869, during his mapping expedition on the Green and Colorado rivers, explorer John Wesley Powell named this canyon Flaming Gorge for its "flaming, brilliant red" color. Flaming Gorge remained one of Utah's most remote and least-developed inhabited areas well into the 1950s. In 1964 Flaming Gorge Canyon and the Green River running through it were plugged with a 500-foot-high wall of concrete, creating the gorge of today.

5

GETTING HERE AND AROUND

From Vernal, getting to the gorge is a straight shot north via U.S. 191. Follow the highway for about 38 miles, which will take you into some magnificent country at high elevations. Then, simply follow the signs to the gorge. The road will veer downward for a few miles before you reach it. From Salt Lake City, go 30 miles east via I–80 past Evanston, Wyoming. Take the Fort Bridge exit, and drive to Manila via Highway 414, which becomes Highway 43. Once in Manila, turn right on Highway 44 for 38 miles until you reach U.S. 191 and follow signs.

ESSENTIALS

Flaming Gorge Dam Visitor Center. The main information center for the Utah side of the gorge, 2 miles north of Greendale Junction, includes displays and an explanatory movie, and, depending on national terrorism alert levels and the weather, this engineering marvel may be open for free guided tours. ⊠ *U.S. 191* ☎ *435/885–3135* ⊕ *www. flaminggorgecountry.com.*

Red Canyon Visitor Center. Displays here explain the geology, flora and fauna, and human history of the Flaming Gorge area. But the best thing has to be the clifftop location 1,300 feet above the lake. The views are outstanding, and you can enjoy them while having a picnic.

To get here, head west from the Greendale Junction of U.S. 191 and Highway 44, and follow the signs. ☒ *Hwy. 44* ☎ *435/889–3713* ⊕ *www.flaminggorgecountry.com.*

EXPLORING

Sheep Creek Canyon Geological Area. A scenic 13-mile drive on paved and gravel roads crosses the Sheep Creek Canyon Geological Area, which is full of upturned layers of rock, craggy pinnacles, and hoodoos. Watch for a herd of bighorn sheep, as well as a popular cave alongside the road. In the fall, salmon return to Sheep Creek to spawn; a kiosk and several bridges provide unobtrusive viewing. The area, 28 miles west of Greendale Junction off U.S. 191 and Highway 44, is open from May to October. ☒ *Forest Service Rd. 218* ☎ *435/784–3445.*

Spirit Lake Scenic Backway. This 17-mile round-trip add-on to the Sheep Creek Canyon Loop road leads past the **Ute Lookout Fire Tower,** which was in use from the 1930s through the 1960s. ☒ *Flaming Gorge National Recreation Area.*

Swett Ranch. This isolated homestead belonged to Oscar and Emma Swett and their nine children through most of the 1900s. The U.S. Forest Service has turned the ranch into a working historical site, complete with restored and decorated houses and buildings. ☒ *Off U.S. 191* ✛ *At Greendale Junction of U.S. 191 and Hwy. 44, stay on U.S. 191; about ½ mile north of junction there's a sign for 1½-mile dirt road to ranch* ☎ *435/784–3445* ⊕ *www.flaminggorgecountry. com/swett-ranch* ☒ *Free.*

SPORTS AND THE OUTDOORS

BICYCLING

Because it mixes high-desert vegetation—blooming sage, rabbit brush, cactus, and wildflowers—and red-rock terrain with a cool climate, Flaming Gorge is ideal for road and trail biking. The 3-mile round-trip **Bear Canyon–Bootleg** ride begins south of the dam off U.S. 191 at the Fire-fighters' Memorial Campground, and runs west to an overview of the reservoir. For the intermediate rider, **Dowd Mountain Hideout** is a 10-mile ride with spectacular views through forested single-track trail, leaving from Dowd Springs Picnic Area off Highway 44. Fliers describing cycling routes are at area visitor centers or online at ⊕ *www.dinoland. com.* Several local lodges rent bikes.

BOATING AND FISHING

Flaming Gorge Reservoir provides ample opportunities for boating and water sports of all kinds. Most boating facilities close from October through mid-March.

Cedar Springs Marina. If you have your own boat, this is your one-stop shop. You can launch, fuel up, or rent a slip here. You can also rent a boat or hire a fishing guide. The marina is approximately 2 miles southwest of Flaming Gorge Dam. ☒ *U.S. 191* ☎ *435/889–3795* ⊕ *www. cedarspringsmarina.com.*

Flaming Gorge Recreation Services. Boat rentals, guided fishing trips, and daily float trips on the Green River are available here. ☒ *U.S. 191 at Dutch John Blvd.* ☎ *435/885–3191* ⊕ *www.fishthegreen.com.*

Lucerne Valley Marina. Seven miles east of Manila you'll find this marina, with just about any amenity you may need for your water-top adventure. With a boat launch, slips, mooring buoys, boat rentals, fishing licenses, mechanical services, gas, RV camping with electricity, and houseboat and floating-cabin rentals, you can't ask for much more. ⊠ *5570 E. Lucerne Valley Rd.* ☎ *435/784–3483, 888/820–9225* ⊕ *www.flaminggorge.com.*

HIKING

There's plenty of hiking in the Flaming Gorge area and any of the local visitor centers or lodges can recommend hikes. From the Red Canyon Visitor Center, three different hikes traverse the **Canyon Rim Trail** through the pine forest: an easy ½-mile round-trip trek leads to the Red Canyon Rim Overlook (above 1,300-foot cliffs), a moderate 3½-mile round-trip hike finds you at the Swett Ranch Overlook, and a 7-mile round-trip hike winds through brilliant layered colors to the Green River at the canyon's bottom below the dam. In the Sheep Creek Canyon Geological Area, the 4-mile **Ute Mountain Trail** leads from the Ute Lookout Fire Tower down through pine forest to Brownie Lake, and back the same way. The **Tamarack Lake Trail** begins at the west end of Spirit Lake (on Highway 44, go past the Ute Lookout Fire Tower turnoff and take F.S. Road 221 to Spirit Lake) and goes to Tamarack Lake and back for a moderate 3-mile trek, round-trip.

RAFTING

For information on rafting, see Dinosaur National Monument.

WHERE TO STAY

$$
HOTEL

Flaming Gorge Resort. With motel rooms and condo-style suites, a good American-cuisine restaurant, and a store just a short drive from the water, this is a practical home base for activities. **Pros:** plenty of amenities and recreational options; good restaurant. **Cons:** aging rooms and suites; motel rooms don't have air-conditioning; can be very busy in summer, and too quiet in winter. Ⓢ *Rooms from: $125* ⊠ *1100 E. Flaming Gorge Resort Rd., off U.S. 191, Dutch John* ☎ *435/889–3773* ⊕ *www.flaminggorgeresort.com* ⌁ *21 rooms, 24 suites* ⦿ *No meals.*

$$
RESORT
FAMILY
Fodor's Choice
★

Red Canyon Lodge. A pleasant surprise in the woods, this lodge is surrounded by well-built, handcrafted log cabins with kitchenettes (some with wood-burning stoves) that face a private trout-stocked lake. **Pros:** beautiful setting; cabins are comfortable for families or groups. **Cons:** must book 3–6 months in advance in summer; Wi-Fi only in restaurant; no air-conditioning; some beds are small. Ⓢ *Rooms from: $119* ⊠ *2450 W. Red Canyon Lodge Rd., Dutch John* ☎ *435/889–3759* ⊕ *www.red-canyonlodge.com* ⌁ *18 cabins* ⦿ *No meals.*

MIRROR LAKE SCENIC BYWAY

Kamas is 42 miles from Salt Lake City.

Although the Wasatch may be Utah's best-known mountain range, the Uinta Mountains, the only major east–west mountain range in the United States, are its tallest, topped by 13,528-foot Kings Peak. This area, particularly in the High Uintas Wilderness where no vehicles are allowed, is great for pack trips, horseback day rides, hiking, and overnight backpacking in summer. The Uintas are ribboned with streams and dotted with small lakes set in rolling meadows.

GETTING HERE AND AROUND

From Salt Lake City, take I–80 and Highway 32 south to Kamas. You can access the Uinta Mountains either from Kamas or Evanston, Wyoming. From Kamas, go 65 miles east via Highway 150. From Evanston, travel 30 miles south on the same highway.

EXPLORING

Mirror Lake. A mile north of the crest of Bald Mountain Pass on Highway 150, this is arguably the best-known lake in the High Uintas Wilderness. At an altitude of 10,000 feet, it offers a cool respite from summer heat. It's easy to reach by car, and families enjoy fishing, hiking, and camping along its rocky shores. Its campgrounds provide a base for hikes into the surrounding mountains, and Highline Trail accesses the 460,000-acre High Uintas Wilderness Area to the east. There's a $6 day-use fee for Mirror Lake, but it's good for three days. ⊠ *Hwy. 150, mile marker 32.*

Fodor'sChoice **Mirror Lake Scenic Byway.** This scenic road begins in Kamas and winds its
★ way up to the High Uinta country. The 65-mile drive follows Highway 150 through heavily wooded canyons past mountain lakes and peaks, cresting at 10,687-foot Bald Mountain Pass. Because of heavy winter snows, much of the road is closed from October to May. A three-day pass is required to use facilities in the area. You can buy a guide to the byway from the Wasatch-Cache National Forest's Kamas Ranger District office in Kamas (50 E. Center St. ☎ *435/783–4338* ⊕ *www.utah. com/byways*). ⊠ *Kamas* ⊠ *$6 for 3-day pass.*

Upper Provo Falls. This is a good place to stop en route, near mile marker 24, where you can stroll the boardwalk to the terraced falls cascading with clear mountain water.

SPORTS AND THE OUTDOORS

Bear River Lodge. This is an ideal jumping-off spot to explore the Uinta Mountains. Well-informed employees can steer you to the right hiking trails for you, and the lodge rents fishing gear, ATVs, snowmobiles, kayaks, cross-country skis, and snowshoes. ⊠ *Mirror Lake, Hwy. 150, mile marker 49* ☎ *435/642–6289* ⊕ *www.bearriverlodge.com.*

WHERE TO STAY

$$$$ 🏨 **Bear River Lodge.** Log cabins in the forest let you reconnect with nature
RENTAL via a range of on-site activities without giving up creature comforts. **Pros:** comfortable cabins; plenty of activities. **Cons:** prices seem high for the level of amenities; no other restaurants within 30 miles. $ *Rooms from: $289* ⊠ *Mirror Lake Hwy., mile marker 49* ☎ *435/642–6289* ⊕ *www.bearriverlodge.com* 🛏 *16 cabins* 🍴*No meals.*

6

CAPITOL REEF
NATIONAL PARK

Visit Fodors.com for advice, updates, and bookings

WELCOME TO CAPITOL REEF NATIONAL PARK

TOP REASONS TO GO

★ **The Waterpocket Fold:** See an excellent example of a monocline—a fold in the Earth's crust with one very steep side in an area that is otherwise horizontal. This one's almost 100 miles long.

★ **No crowds:** Experience the best of southern Utah weather, rock formations, and wide open spaces without the crowds of nearby parks such as Zion and Bryce Canyon.

★ **Fresh fruit:** Pick apples, pears, apricots, and peaches in season at the pioneer-planted orchards at historic Fruita. These trees still produce plenty of fruit.

★ **Rock art:** View pictographs and petroglyphs left by Native Americans who lived in this area from AD 700 to 1300.

★ **Pioneer artifacts:** Buy faithfully reproduced tools and utensils like those used by Mormon pioneers at the Gifford Homestead.

1 Fruita. This historic pioneer village is at the heart of what most people see of Capitol Reef. The one and only park visitor center nearby is the place to get travel and weather information and maps. The scenic drive through Capitol Gorge provides a view of the Golden Throne.

2 Cathedral Valley. The views are stunning and the silence deafening in the park's remote northern section. High-clearance vehicles are required, as is crossing the Fremont River. Driving in this valley is next to impossible when the Cathedral Valley Road is wet, so ask at the visitor center about current weather and road conditions.

3 Muley Twist Canyon. At the southern reaches of the park, this canyon is accessed via Notom-Bullfrog Road from the north, and Burr Trail Road from the west and southeast. High-clearance vehicles are required for much of it.

GETTING ORIENTED

At the heart of this 378-square-mile park is the massive natural feature known as the Waterpocket Fold, which runs roughly northwest to southeast along the park's spine. Capitol Reef itself is named for a formation along the fold near the Fremont River. A historic pioneer settlement, the green oasis of Fruita is easily accessed by car, and a 9-mile scenic drive provides a good overview of the canyons and rock formations that populate the park. Colors here range from deep, rich reds to sage greens to crumbling gray sediments. The absence of large towns nearby ensures that night skies are brilliant starscapes.

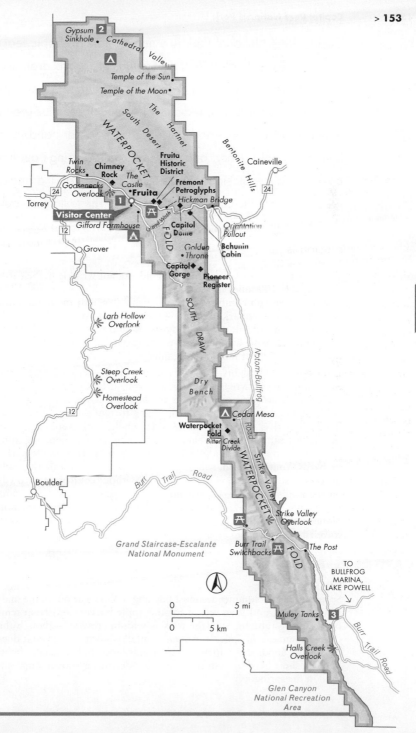

Gypsum
Sinkhole
Cathedral Valley

2

Temple of the Sun

Temple of the Moon

The Hartnet

South Desert

WATERPOCKET

Bentonite Hills

Caineville

24

Twin
Rocks

**Chimney
Rock**

Goosenecks
Overlook

**Fruita
Historic
District**

**Fremont
Petroglyphs**

The
Castle

Fruita

Hickman Bridge

Torrey

24

Visitor Center

1

Grand Wash

FOLD

Orientation
Pullout

Gifford Farmhouse

12

**Capitol
Dome**

**Behunin
Cabin**

Golden
Throne

Grover

**Capitol
Gorge**

**Pioneer
Register**

6

Larb Hollow
Overlook

SOUTH DRAW

Dry
Bench

Steep Creek
Overlook

Homestead
Overlook

12

Notom-Bullfrog

Cedar Mesa

**Waterpocket
Fold**

*Bitter Creek
Divide*

Boulder

Strike Valley

WATERPOCKET

Burr Trail Road

Notom-Bullfrog Road

**Grand Staircase-Escalante
National Monument**

*Strike Valley
Overlook*

*Burr Trail
Switchbacks*

The Post

FOLD

TO
BULLFROG
MARINA,
LAKE POWELL

0   5 mi

0   5 km

Muley Tanks

3

Burr Trail Road

*Halls Creek
Overlook*

**Glen Canyon
National Recreation
Area**

Updated by
John Blodgett

Capitol Reef National Park is a natural kaleidoscopic feast for the eyes, saturated with colors that are more dramatic than anywhere else in the West. The dominant Moenkopi rock formation is a rich, red-chocolate hue; deep blue-green juniper and pinyon stand out against it. Other sandstone layers are gold, ivory, and lavender. Sunset brings out the colors in an explosion of copper, platinum, and orange, then dusk turns the cliffs purple and blue. The texture of rock deposited in ancient inland seas and worn by subsequent erosion is pure art.

The park preserves the Waterpocket Fold, a giant wrinkle in the earth that extends 100 miles between Thousand Lake Mountain and Lake Powell. When you climb high onto the rocks or into the mountains, you can see this remarkable geologic wonder and the jumble of colorful cliffs, massive domes, soaring spires, and twisting canyons that surround it. It's no wonder Native Americans called this part of the country the "land of the sleeping rainbow."

Beyond incredible sights, the fragrance of pine and sage rises from the earth, and canyon wrens sing to you as you sit by the water. Flowing across the heart of Capitol Reef is the Fremont River, a narrow little creek that can turn into a swollen, raging torrent during desert flash floods. The river sustains cottonwoods, wildlife, and verdant valleys rich with fruit. During the harvest, your sensory experience is complete when you bite into a perfect ripe peach or apple from the park's orchards. Your soul, too, will be gratified here. You can walk the trails in relative solitude and enjoy the beauty without confronting crowds on the roads or paths. All around you are signs of those who came before: ancient Native Americans of the Fremont culture, Mormon pioneers who settled the land, and other courageous explorers who traveled the canyons.

CAPITOL REEF PLANNER

WHEN TO GO

Spring and early summer are most bustling. Folks clear out in the mid-summer heat, and then return for the apple harvest and crisp temperatures of autumn. Still, the park is seldom crowded—though the campground can fill quickly. Annual rainfall is scant, but when it does rain, flash floods can wipe out park roads. Snowfall is usually light. Sudden, short-lived snowstorms—and thunderstorms—are not uncommon in the spring.

AVG. HIGH/LOW TEMPS.

Jan.	Feb.	Mar.	Apr.	May	June
41/20	46/26	57/33	66/40	76/49	86/58

July	Aug.	Sept.	Oct.	Nov.	Dec.
92/65	88/63	80/54	66/43	51/30	41/21

FESTIVALS AND EVENTS
AUGUST

FAMILY **Wayne County Fair.** The great American county fair tradition is at its finest in Loa in mid-August. A demolition derby, rodeo, horse shows, and a parade are all part of the fun. You'll also find crafts such as handmade quilts, agricultural exhibits, children's games, and plenty of good food. ☎ *435/836–1300* ⊕ *waynecountyutah.org.*

Women's Redrock Music Festival. Held at the Robbers Roost Bookstore, this two-day event has been attracting independent female musicians from all corners of the globe, as well as hundreds of fans, since 2007. Run by the nonprofit Entrada Institute, a regional arts and education organization, the festival benefits Utah women through donations and scholarships. ✉ *185 W. Main St., Torrey* ☎ *435/425–3265* ⊕ *womensredrockmusicfest.com.*

OCTOBER

Harvest Time Scarecrow Festival. Events for this month-long celebration marking the end of another busy season are held throughout Wayne County. In addition to a scarecrow contest, there are plenty of family-friendly events, including live music, arts and crafts, pumpkin carving, and a Halloween party. ✉ *Torrey* ☎ *435/425–3265* ⊕ *www.entradainstitute.org.*

PLANNING YOUR TIME
CAPITOL REEF IN ONE DAY

Pack a picnic lunch, snacks, and cold drinks to take with you (there are no restaurants in the park). As you enter the park, look to your left for Chimney Rock; in a landscape of spires, cliffs, and knobs, this deep-red landmark is unmistakable. Start your journey at the **visitor center,** where you can study a three-dimensional map of the area, watch a short film, and browse the many books and maps related to the park. Then, head for the park's scenic drive, stopping at the **Fruita Historic District** to see some of the sites associated with the park's Mormon history. Visit **Gifford Homestead** for a tour and to browse the gift shop. That lunch you packed can be enjoyed at picnic tables on rolling green lawns lining both sides of the road between the orchard and Gifford Farmhouse.

Check out the **Fremont Indian Petroglyphs,** and if you feel like some exertion, take a hike on the Hickman Bridge Trail. From the trail (or 2 miles east of the visitor center from Highway 24 if you skip the hike), you'll see **Capitol Dome.** Along this stretch of Highway 24 stop to see the old one-room **Fruita Schoolhouse,** the **petroglyphs,** and the **Behunin Cabin.** Next you'll have to backtrack a few miles on Highway 24 to find the **Goosenecks Trail.** At the same parking lot you'll find the trailhead for

Sunset Point Trail; take this short hike in time to watch the setting sun hit the colorful cliffs.

GETTING HERE AND AROUND

AIR TRAVEL

The nearest major airports are in Salt Lake City and Las Vegas, about 3½ and 5½ hours away by car, respectively.

BUS TRAVEL

Once inside the park, there is no shuttle service like there is at nearby Zion and Bryce Canyon national parks.

CAR TRAVEL

Though far from big cities, Capitol Reef country can be reached by a variety of approaches. The main high-speed arteries through the region are Interstates 70 and 15, but any route will require travel of some secondary roads such as U.S. 50, U.S. 89, Highway 24, or Route 72. All are well-maintained, safe roads that bisect rich agricultural communities steeped in Mormon history (such as the nearby towns of Bicknell and Loa). Interstate 15 is the fastest way through central Utah, but U.S. 89 and the local roads that feed onto it will give you a more direct path into Utah's past and present-day character. Highway 24 runs across the middle of Capitol Reef National Park, offering scenic views for anyone passing through.

PARK ESSENTIALS

ACCESSIBILITY

Capitol Reef doesn't have many trails that are accessible to people in wheelchairs. The visitor center, museum, film, and restrooms are all accessible, as is the campground amphitheater where evening programs are held. The Fruita Campground Loop C restroom is accessible; so is the boardwalk to the petroglyph panel on Highway 24, 1.2 miles east of the visitor center.

PARK FEES AND PERMITS

There is no fee to enter the park, but it's $10 per vehicle (or $7 per bicycle) to travel on Scenic Drive beyond Fruita Campground; this fee is good for one week, paid via the "honor system" at a drop box versus a staffed entry gate. Backcountry camping permits are free; pick them up at the visitor center. An annual pass that allows unlimited access to Scenic Drive is $30.

PARK HOURS

The park is open 24/7 year-round. It is in the Mountain time zone.

CELL-PHONE RECEPTION

Cell-phone reception is best near the visitor center and campground areas. Pay phones are at the visitor center and at Fruita Campground.

EDUCATIONAL OFFERINGS

RANGER PROGRAMS

From late May to October, ranger programs are offered at no charge. You can obtain current information about ranger talks and other park events at the visitor center or campground bulletin boards.

FAMILY **Evening Program.** Learn about Capitol Reef's geology, American Indian cultures, wildlife, and more at the campground amphitheater about a mile from the visitor center. Programs typically begin around sunset. A schedule with topics and times is posted at the visitor center. ⊠ *Amphitheater, Loop C, Fruita Campground, Scenic Dr.* ☎ *435/425–3791.*

FAMILY **Junior Ranger Program.** Each child who participates in this self-guided, year-round program completes a combination of activities in the Junior Ranger booklet, attends a ranger program, watches the park movie, interviews a park ranger, and/or picks up litter. ⊠ *National Park Visitor Center, 16 Scenic Dr.* ☎ *435/425–3791* ☜ *Free.*

FAMILY **Ranger Talks.** Typically, the park offers a daily morning geology talk at the visitor center and a daily afternoon petroglyph-panel talk. Occasional geology hikes and history tours are also sometimes offered. Times vary. ⊠ *National Park Visitor Center, 16 Scenic Rd.* ☎ *435/425–3791* ☜ *Free.*

RESTAURANTS

Inside Capitol Reef you won't find any restaurants, though there is a small store selling baked goods and ice cream. More dining options exist close by in the town of Torrey, where you can find everything from high-end Southwestern cuisine to basic hamburger joints serving consistently good food.

HOTELS

There are no lodging options within Capitol Reef, but clean and comfortable accommodations for all budgets exist in nearby Torrey, and not far beyond in Bicknell and Loa. Drive farther into the region's towns, and you're more likely to find locally owned low- to moderately priced motels, and a few nice inns and bed-and-breakfasts. Reservations are recommended in summer. *Hotel reviews have been shortened. For full information, visit Fodors.com.*

WHAT IT COSTS			
	$	**$$**	**$$$**	**$$$$**
Restaurants	under $13	$13–$20	$21–$30	over $30
Hotels	under $101	$101–$150	$151–$200	over $200

Restaurant prices are the average cost of a main course at dinner, or if dinner is not served, at lunch. Hotel prices are the lowest cost of a standard double room in high season.

VISITOR INFORMATION

Park Contact Information Capitol Reef National Park. ⊠ *Off Hwy. 24* ☎ *435/425–3791* ⊕ *nps.gov/care.*

VISITOR CENTERS

FAMILY **Capitol Reef Visitor Center.** Watch a park movie, talk with rangers, or peruse the many books, maps, and materials for sale in the bookstore. Towering over the center (11 miles east of Torrey), is the Castle, one of the park's most prominent rock formations. ⊠ *Hwy. 24 and Scenic Dr.* ☎ *435/425–3791.*

6

EXPLORING

SCENIC DRIVES

FAMILY   **Capitol Reef Scenic Drive.** This 8-mile road, simply called Scenic Drive by locals, starts at the visitor center and winds its way through the Fruita Historic District and colorful sandstone cliffs into Capitol Gorge; a side road, Grand Wash Road, provides access into the canyon. At Capitol Gorge, the canyon walls become steep and impressive but the route becomes unpaved for about the last 2 miles, and road conditions may vary due to weather and usage. Check with the visitor center before setting out. ⊠ *Off Hwy. 24, 11 miles east of Torrey.*

SCENIC STOPS

FAMILY   **Behunin Cabin.** Elijah Cutlar Behunin used blocks of sandstone to build this cabin in 1882. Floods in the lowlands made life too difficult, and he moved before the turn of that century. The house, 5.9 miles east of the visitor center, is empty, but you can peek through the window to see the interior. ⊠ *Hwy. 24.*

FAMILY   **Capitol Dome.** One of the rock formations that gave the park its name, this giant sandstone dome is visible in the vicinity of the Hickman Bridge trailhead, 1.9 miles east of the visitor center. ⊠ *Hwy. 24.*

Fodor's Choice **Capitol Gorge.** At the entrance to this gorge, 9 miles south of the visi-
★   tor center, Scenic Drive is unpaved. The narrow, twisting road on the floor of the gorge was a route for pioneer wagons traversing this part of Utah starting in the 1860s. After every flash flood, pioneers would laboriously clear the route so wagons could continue to go through. The gorge became the main automobile route in the area until 1962, when Highway 24 was built. The short drive to the end of the road has striking views of the surrounding cliffs and leads to one of the park's most popular walks: the hiking trail to the water-holding "tanks" eroded into the sandstone. ⊠ *Scenic Dr.*

Chimney Rock. Even in a landscape of spires, cliffs, and knobs, this deep-red landform, 3.9 miles west of the visitor center, is unmistakable. ⊠ *Hwy. 24.*

FAMILY   **Fremont Petroglyphs.** Between AD 600 and 1300 the Capitol Reef area was occupied by Native Americans who were eventually referred to as Fremonts, named after the Fremont River that flows through the park. A nice stroll along a boardwalk bridge, 1.1 miles east of the visitor center, allows close-up views of ancient rock art, which can be identified by the large trapezoidal figures often depicted wearing headdresses and ear baubles. ⊠ *Hwy. 24.*

FAMILY   **Fruita Historic District.** In the 1880s Nels Johnson became the first homesteader in the Fremont River Valley, building his home near the confluence of Sulphur Creek and the Fremont River. Other Mormon settlers followed and established small farms and orchards, creating the village of Junction. The orchards thrived, and by 1900 the name was changed to Fruita. The orchards, less than a mile from the visitor center, are preserved and protected as a Rural Historic Landscape. ⊠ *Scenic Dr.*

Pioneer Register. Travelers passing through Capitol Gorge in the 19th and early 20th centuries etched the canyon wall with their names and the date. Directly across the canyon from the Pioneer Register and about 50 feet up are signatures etched into the canyon wall by an early United States Geologic Survey crew. Though it's illegal to write or scratch on the canyon walls today, plenty of damage has been done by vandals over the years. You can reach the register via an easy hike from the sheltered trailhead at the end of Capitol Gorge Road, 10.3 miles south of the visitor center; the register is about 10 minutes along the hike to the sandstone "tanks." ⊠ *Off Scenic Dr.*

The Waterpocket Fold. A giant wrinkle in the earth extends almost 100 miles between Thousand Lake Mountain and Lake Powell. You can glimpse the fold by driving south on Scenic Drive after it branches off Highway 24, past the Fruita Historic District. For complete immersion enter the park via the 36-mile Burr Trail from Boulder. Roads through the southernmost reaches of the park are largely unpaved. The area is accessible to most vehicles during dry weather, but check with the visitor center for current road conditions. ⊠ *Capitol Reef National Park*

SPORTS AND THE OUTDOORS

The main outdoor activity at Capitol Reef is hiking. There are trails for all levels. Remember to bring and drink plenty of water wherever you go in Capitol Reef.

MULTISPORT OUTFITTER

Hondoo Rivers & Trails. This tour company has been providing high-quality backcountry trips into Capitol Reef National Park, Escalante Canyons, and the High Plateaus for 40 years. From April to October, they'll take you on hiking, horseback-riding, and Jeep day tours. Trips are designed to explore the geologic landforms in the area, seek out wildflowers in season, and to encounter free-roaming mustangs, bison, and bighorn sheep when possible. Multiday trips can also be arranged. ⊠ *90 E. Main St., Torrey* ☎ *435/425–3519* ⊕ *www.hondoo. com* ⊠ *From $120.*

BICYCLING

Bicycles are allowed only on established roads in the park. Highway 24 is a state highway and receives a substantial amount of through traffic, so it's not the best place to pedal. Scenic Drive is better, but the road is narrow, and you have to contend with drivers dazed by the beautiful surroundings. In fact, it's a good idea to traverse it in the morning or evening when traffic is reduced, or in the off-season. Four-wheel-drive roads are certainly less traveled, but they are often sandy, rocky, and steep. You cannot ride your bicycle in washes or on hiking trails.

GOOD READS

■ *Capitol Reef: Canyon Country Eden,* by Rose Houk, is an award-winning collection of photographs and lyrical essays on the park.

■ *Dwellers of the Rainbow, Fremont Culture in Capitol Reef National Park,* by Rose Houk, offers a brief background of the Fremont culture in Capitol Reef.

■ *Explore Capitol Reef Trails,* by Marjorie Miller and John Foster, is a comprehensive hiking guide.

■ *Geology of Capitol Reef National Park,* by Michael Collier, teaches the basic geology of the park.

■ *Red Rock Eden,* by George Davidson, tells the story of historic Fruita, its settlements, and its orchards.

Cathedral Valley Scenic Backway. Located in the remote north of the park, you can enjoy solitude and a true backcountry ride on this trail. The entire route is about 58 miles long and can be accessed at Caineville, off Highway 24, or at River Ford Road, 5 miles west of Caineville; for a multiday trip, there's a primitive campground about midway through the loop. ⊠ *Off Hwy. 24.*

South Draw Road. This is a very strenuous ride that traverses dirt, sand, and rocky surfaces, and crosses several creeks that may be muddy. It's not recommended in winter or spring because of deep snow at higher elevations. The route starts at an elevation of 8,600 feet on Boulder Mountain, 13 miles south of Torrey, and ends 15¾ miles later at 5,500 feet in the Pleasant Creek parking area at the end of Scenic Drive. ⊠ *Bowns Reservoir Rd. and Hwy. 12.*

FOUR-WHEELING

You can explore Capitol Reef in a 4X4 on a number of exciting backcountry routes. Road conditions can vary greatly depending on recent weather patterns.

Cathedral Valley Scenic Backway. The north end of Capitol Reef, along this backcountry road, is filled with towering monoliths, panoramic vistas, two water crossings, and a stark desert landscape. The area is remote and the road through it unpaved, so do not enter without a high-clearance vehicle, some planning, and a cell phone (although reception is virtually nonexistent). The drive through the valley is a 58-mile loop that you can begin at River Ford Road, 11¾ miles east of the visitor center off Highway 24; allow half a day. If your time is limited, you can tour only the Caineville Wash Road, which takes about two hours. Pick up a self-guided auto tour brochure at the visitor center. ⊠ *River Ford Rd., off Hwy. 24.*

HIKING

Many park trails in Capitol Reef include steep climbs, but there are a few easy-to-moderate hikes. A short drive from the visitor center takes you to a dozen trails, and a park ranger can advise you on combining trails or locating additional routes.

EASY

Goosenecks Trail. This nice little walk gives you a good introduction to the land surrounding Capitol Reef. Enjoy the dizzying views from the overlook on this 0.3-mile round-trip jaunt. *Easy.* ⊠ *Capitol Reef National Park* ✛ *Trailhead: at Hwy. 24, about 3 miles west of visitor center.*

Grand Wash Trail. At the end of unpaved Grand Wash Road you can continue on foot through the canyon to its end at Highway 24. This flat hike takes you through a wide wash between canyon walls, and is an excellent place to study the geology up close. The round-trip hike is 4½ miles; allow two to three hours for your walk. Check at the ranger station for flash-flood warnings before entering the wash. *Easy.* ⊠ *Capitol Reef National Park* ✛ *Trailhead: at Hwy. 24, east of Hickman Bridge parking lot, or at end of Grand Wash Rd., off Scenic Dr. about 5 miles from visitor center.*

Sunset Point Trail. The trail starts from the same parking lot as the Goosenecks Trail. Benches along this easy hike (0.8 mile round-trip) invite you to sit and meditate surrounded by the colorful desert. At the trail's end you'll be rewarded with broad vistas into the park; it's even better at sunset. *Easy.* ⊠ *Capitol Reef National Park* ✛ *Trailhead: at Hwy. 24, about 3 miles west of visitor center.*

MODERATE

Capitol Gorge Trail and the Tanks. Starting at the Pioneer Register, about a mile from the Capitol Gorge parking lot, is a trail that climbs to the Tanks—holes in the sandstone, formed by erosion, that hold water after it rains. After a scramble up about ¼ mile of steep trail with cliff drop-offs, you can look down into the Tanks and see a natural bridge below the lower tank. Including the walk to the Pioneer Register, allow an hour or more for this interesting hike, one of the park's most popular. *Moderate.* ⊠ *Capitol Reef National Park* ✛ *Trailhead: at end of Scenic Dr., 10 miles south of visitor center.*

FAMILY **Cohab Canyon Trail.** Find rock wrens and Western pipistrelles (canyon bats) on this trail. One end is directly across from the Fruita Campground on Scenic Drive; the other is across from the Hickman Bridge parking lot. The first ¼ mile from Fruita is strenuous, but the walk becomes easier except for turnoffs to the overlooks, which are short. You'll find miniature arches, skinny side canyons, and honeycombed patterns on canyon walls where the wrens make nests. The trail is 3.2 miles round-trip to the Hickman Bridge parking lot (two to three hours). The Overlook Trail adds 1 mile. Allow one to two hours to over-looks and back. *Moderate.* ⊠ *Capitol Reef National Park* ✛ *Trailheads: Scenic Dr., about 1 mile south of visitor center, or Hwy. 24, about 2 miles east of visitor center.*

6

Fremont River Trail. What starts as a quiet little stroll beside the river turns into an adventure. The first ½ mile of the trail is wheelchair accessible as you wander past the orchards next to the Fremont River. After you pass through a narrow gate, the trail changes personality and you're in for a steep climb on an exposed ledge with drop-offs. The views at the top of the 480-foot ascent are worth it. It's 2 miles round-trip; allow two hours. *Moderate.* ⊠ *Capitol Reef National Park* ✢ *Trailhead: near amphitheater off Loop C of Fruita Campground, about 1 mile from visitor center.*

Hickman Bridge Trail. This trail leads to a natural bridge of Kayenta sandstone, with a 133-foot opening carved by intermittent flash floods. Early on, the route climbs a set of steps along the Fremont River. The trail splits, leading along the right-hand branch to a strenuous uphill climb to the Rim Overlook and Navajo Knobs. Stay to your left to see the bridge, and you'll encounter a moderate up-and-down trail. Up the wash on your way to the bridge is a Fremont granary on the right side of the small canyon. Allow about two hours for the 2-mile round-trip. Expect lots of company. *Moderate.* ⊠ *Capitol Reef National Park* ✢ *Trailhead: Hwy. 24, 2 miles east of visitor center.*

DIFFICULT

Chimney Rock Trail. You're almost sure to see ravens drifting on thermal winds around the deep-red Mummy Cliff that rings the base of this trail. This loop trail begins with a steep climb to a rim above Chimney Rock. The trail is 3.6 miles round-trip, with a 590-foot elevation change. No shade. Use caution during monsoon storms due to lightning hazards. Allow three to four hours. *Difficult.* ⊠ *Capitol Reef National Park* ✢ *Trailhead: Hwy. 24, about 3 miles west of visitor center.*

Golden Throne Trail. As you hike to the base of the Golden Throne, you may be lucky enough to see one of the park's elusive desert bighorn sheep, but you're more likely to spot their split-hoof tracks. The trail is about 2 miles of gradual rise with some steps and drop-offs. The Golden Throne is hidden until you near the end of the trail, then suddenly you see the huge sandstone monolith. If you hike near sundown the throne burns gold. The round-trip hike is about 3.8 miles and will take two to three hours. *Difficult.* ⊠ *Capitol Reef National Park* ✢ *Trailhead: at end of Capitol Gorge Rd., 10 miles south of visitor center.*

WHAT'S NEARBY

NEARBY TOWNS

Probably the best home base for exploring the park, the pretty town of **Torrey,** just outside the park, has lots of personality. Giant old cottonwood trees make it a shady, cool place to stay, and the townspeople are friendly and accommodating. A little farther west on Highway 24, tiny **Teasdale** is a charming settlement cradled in a cove of the Aquarius Plateau. The homes look out onto brilliantly colored cliffs and green fields. Quiet **Bicknell** lies another few miles west of Capitol Reef. The Wayne County seat of **Loa,** 10 miles west of Torrey, was settled by pioneers in the 1870s. If you head south from Torrey instead of west, you can take a spectacular 32-mile drive along Highway 12 to **Boulder,** a town so remote that its mail was carried on horseback until 1940. Nearby is Anasazi State Park. In the opposite direction, 51 miles east, **Hanksville** is a place to stop for food and fuel stop.

Visitor Information Garfield County Office of Tourism. ✉ *55 S. Main St., Panguitch* ☎ *800/444-6689, 435/676-8585* ⊕ *www.brycecanyoncountry.com.* **Wayne County Office of Tourism.** ☎ *435/425-3365, 800/858-7951* ⊕ *www. capitolreef.org.*

NEARBY ATTRACTIONS

FAMILY **Anasazi State Park.** This former archaeological site includes portions of an Ancestral Puebloan (Anasazi) village occupied sometime between AD 1160 and 1235, a small but informative museum with artifacts discovered on-site, and a reconstructed pueblo dwelling. ✉ *460 N. Hwy. 12, Boulder* ☎ *435/335-7308* ⊕ *stateparks.utah.gov* 🎟 *$5.*

FAMILY **Goblin Valley State Park.** Strange-looking "hoodoos" rise up from the desert landscape 12 miles north of Hanksville, making Goblin Valley home to hundreds of strange goblin-like rock formations with a dramatic orange hue. Short, easy trails wind through the goblins making it a fun walk for kids and adults. ✉ *Hwy. 24* ☎ *435/275-4584* ⊕ *stateparks. utah.gov* 🎟 *$13 per vehicle.*

Fodor's Choice **San Rafael Swell.** Tremendous geological upheavals pushed through the
★ Earth's surface eons ago, forming a giant oval-shape dome of rock about 80 miles long and 30 miles wide, giving rise to the name "swell." Over the years, the harsh climate beat down the dome, eroding it into a wild array of multicolor sandstone and creating buttes, pinnacles, mesas, and canyons that spread across more than 600,000 acres. In the northern Swell, the Wedge Overlook peers into the Little Grand Canyon and the San Rafael River below. The strata at the edges of the southern Swell are angled near vertical, creating the San Rafael Reef. Both are known for fantastic hiking, canyoneering, and mountain biking. ✉ *125 S. 600 W, Price* ☎ *435/636-3600* ⊕ *www.blm.gov/ut.*

AREA ACTIVITIES

SPORTS AND THE OUTDOORS
FISHING
Fishlake National Forest. At an elevation of 8,800 feet is Fish Lake, which lies in the heart of its namesake 1.4-million-acre forest. The area has several campgrounds and wonderful lodges. The lake is stocked annually with lake and rainbow trout, mackinaw, and splake. A large population of brown trout is native to the lake. The Fremont River Ranger District office (*138 S. Main St., Loa*) can provide all the information you need for fishing, camping, and hiking in the forest. ✉ *Off Hwy. 24* ☎ *435/836-9233* ⊕ *www.fs.usda.gov/fishlake.*

Alpine Adventures. With a stellar reputation for personalized attention during fly-fishing trips into the high backcountry around Capitol Reef and the Fremont River, Alpine Adventures also leads trophy hunting tours. ✉ *Torrey* ☎ *435/425-3660* ⊕ *alpineadventuresutah.com* 🎟 *From $225.*

6

SCENIC DRIVES

Burr Trail Scenic Backway. Branching east off Highway 12 in Boulder, Burr Trail travels through the Circle Cliffs area of Grand Staircase–Escalante National Monument into Capitol Reef. The views are of backcountry canyons and gulches. The road is paved between Boulder and the eastern boundary of Capitol Reef. It leads into a hair-raising set of switchbacks—not suitable for RVs or trailers—that ascend 800 feet in ½ mile. Before attempting to drive this route, check with the Capitol Reef Visitor Center for road conditions. From Boulder to its intersection with Notom-Bullfrog Road the route is 36 miles long. ⊠ *Off Hwy. 12, Boulder* ⊕ *www.scenicbyway12.com.*

Utah Scenic Byway 24. For 62 miles between Loa and Hanksville, you'll cut right through Capitol Reef National Park. Colorful rock formations in all their hues of red, cream, pink, gold, and deep purple extend from one end of the route to the other. The closer you get to the park the more colorful the landscape becomes. The vibrant rock finally gives way to lush green hills and the mountains west of Loa.

NIGHTLIFE AND PERFORMING ARTS

PERFORMING ARTS

Robbers Roost. This shop, named after Butch Cassidy's hideout, is home base for the Entrada Institute, an alliance of arts and outdoors enthusiasts that holds musical events and talks, usually on Saturday nights, from May through October. The annual women's music festival, held each August, attracts more than 600 attendees to hear performance art, blues, rock, jazz, and folk. ⊠ *185 W. Main St. (Hwy. 24), Torrey* ☎ *435/425–3265* ⊕ *robbersroostbooks.com.*

SHOPPING

Flute Shop Trading Post. Unique and unexpected, the nifty Flute Shop, open year-round, sells American Indian jewelry, rocks, fossils, and flutes, handcrafted by owner Vance Morrill. A quiet and inexpensive four-unit motel has been added to the premises. You'll find it 4 miles south of the junction of Highways 12 and 24. ⊠ *1705 S. Scenic Rte. 12, Torrey* ☎ *435/425–3144* ⊕ *www.fluteshopmotel.com.*

Gallery 24. This pleasing space sells contemporary fine art from southern Utah–based artists that includes paintings, photography, ceramics, and sculpture. ⊠ *135 E. Main St., Torrey* ☎ *435/425–2124* ⊕ *www.gallery24.biz* ☞ *Closed Nov.–Mar.*

Torrey Gallery. Located in a pioneer home off Main Street, this lovely gallery specializes in regional art. Its offerings include paintings, sculpture, and photographs, as well as antique and contemporary Navajo rugs discovered by the longtime collectors who own the gallery. ⊠ *160 W. Main St., Torrey* ☎ *435/425 3909* ⊕ *torreygallery.com.*

FAMILY **Torrey Trading Post.** Come here for Native American jewelry and pottery, T-shirts, wood carvings, stone figures, gifts for children, and more. The trading post also has a handful of deluxe and camping cabins for lodging. ⊠ *25 W. Main St., Torrey* ☎ *435/425–3716* ⊕ *torreytradingpost.com.*

WHERE TO EAT

OUTSIDE THE PARK

$$$ ✕ **Cafe Diablo.** Nestled in the tiny hamlet of Torrey is one of the better
AMERICAN restaurants in the state, with innovative Southwestern fare that has
Fodor's Choice included dishes such as rosemary and pine nut-crusted beef sirloin,
★ and pumpkin seed trout. Visit the dining room to see work of local artists, or enjoy the peaceful patio surrounded by gardens and a view of distant red-rock mountains. **Known for:** rattlesnake cakes; delicious desserts; tequila list. $ *Average main: $26* ⊠ *599 W. Main St. (Hwy. 24), Torrey* ☎ *435/425–3070* ⊕ *cafediablo.net* ☉ *Closed late Oct.–early Apr.*

$$ ✕ **Capitol Reef Café.** For a varied selection of solid and healthy fare,
AMERICAN visit this unpretentious eatery. Favorites include the vegetable salad and the flaky smoked or grilled fillet of rainbow trout, and the breakfasts are both delicious and hearty. **Known for:** hearty breakfasts; friendly service; guide books. $ *Average main: $14* ⊠ *360 W. Main St. (Hwy. 24), Torrey* ☎ *435/425–3271* ⊕ *capitolreefinn.com* ☉ *Closed late Oct.–mid-Mar.*

$$$ ✕ **Hell's Backbone Grill.** On the grounds of the Boulder Mountain Lodge
ECLECTIC and voted Best Restaurant in Southern Utah for eight years in a row
Fodor's Choice by *Salt Lake Magazine,* this remote eatery is worth the drive. The
★ menu is inspired by American Indian, Western range, Southwestern, and Mormon pioneer recipes. **Known for:** peaceful vibe; farmfresh ingredients; Thanksgiving feast. $ *Average main: $25* ⊠ *20 N. Hwy. 12, Boulder* ☎ *435/335–7464* ⊕ *www.hellsbackbonegrill.com* ☉ *Closed Dec.–early Mar.*

$ ✕ **Stan's Burger Shak.** This is the traditional pit stop between Lake Powell
FAST FOOD and Capitol Reef, featuring great burgers, fries, a generous selection of flavored shakes, and the best homemade onion rings around. Keep in mind it generally closes for the winter. **Known for:** homemade onion rings; thick shakes; homestyle burgers. $ *Average main: $8* ⊠ *140 S. Hwy. 95, Hanksville* ☎ *435/542–3330* ⊕ *www.stansburgershak.com* ☉ *Closed Dec.–early to mid-Feb.*

6

CLOSE UP

Best Campgrounds in Capitol Reef

Campgrounds in Capitol Reef fill up fast between Memorial Day and Labor Day, though that goes mainly for the highly convenient Fruita Campground, and not the more remote backcountry sites. Most of the area's state parks have camping facilities, and the region's two national forests offer many wonderful sites.

Cathedral Valley Campground. This small, basic (no water, pit toilet), no-fee campground in the park's remote northern district touts sprawling views, but the bumpy road there is hard to navigate. ✉ *Hartnet Junction, on Caineville Wash Rd.* ☎ *435/425–3791.*

Cedar Mesa Campground. Wonderful views of the Waterpocket Fold and Henry Mountains surround this primitive, no-fee campground in the park's southern district. ✉ *Notom-Bullfrog Rd., 22 miles south of Hwy. 24* ☎ *435/425–3791.*

Fruita Campground. Near the orchards and the Fremont River, the park's developed (flush toilets, running water), shady campground is a great place to call home for a few days. The sites require a $20 nightly fee and those nearest the Fremont River or the orchards are the most coveted. ✉ *Scenic Dr., about 1 mile south of visitor center* ☎ *435/425–3791.*

WHERE TO STAY

OUTSIDE THE PARK

$$ B&B/INN 🏨 **Muley Twist Inn.** This gorgeous inn sits on 15 acres of land, with expansive views of the colorful landscape in just about every direction. **Pros:** dramatic setting against a beautiful rock cliff; knowledgeable and friendly owner; all rooms have private baths. **Cons:** a bit removed from civilization. [$] *Rooms from: $145* ✉ *249 W. 125 South St., Teasdale* ☎ *435/425–3640, 800/530–1038* 🌐 *www.muleytwistinn.com* 🕒 *Closed Nov.–Mar.* 🛏 *5 rooms* 🍴 *Breakfast.*

$ HOTEL 🏨 **Rim Rock Inn.** On a bluff with outstanding views into the desert, this motel was the first one to accommodate visitors to Capitol Reef. **Pros:** immaculate rooms; pub and fine dining restaurant on-site; breakfast included. **Cons:** a bit removed from town; no shade. [$] *Rooms from: $94* ✉ *2523 E. Hwy. 24, Torrey* ☎ *435/425–3398* 🌐 *therimrock.net* 🕒 *Closed Nov.–Mar.* 🛏 *19 rooms* 🍴 *Breakfast.*

$$$ B&B/INN 🏨 **SkyRidge Inn Bed and Breakfast.** Each of the inn's windows offers an exceptional year-round view of the desert and mountains surrounding Capitol Reef National Park. **Pros:** cozy; close to gas station and other amenities; local artwork and unique decor. **Cons:** rooms fill quickly in high season. [$] *Rooms from: $170* ✉ *1092 E. Hwy 24, Torrey* ☎ *435/425–3775* 🌐 *skyridgeinn.com* 🛏 *6 rooms* 🍴 *Breakfast.*

ZION NATIONAL PARK

WELCOME TO ZION NATIONAL PARK

TOP REASONS TO GO

★ **Eye candy:** Pick just about any trail in the park and it's all but guaranteed to culminate in an astounding viewpoint full of pink, orange, and crimson rock formations.

★ **Auto immunity:** From spring through autumn, cars are generally not allowed in Zion Canyon, allowing for a quiet and peaceful park.

★ **Botanical wonderland:** Zion Canyon is home to approximately 900 species of plants, more than anywhere else in Utah.

★ **Animal tracks:** Zion has expansive hinterlands where furry, scaly, and feathered residents are common. Hike long enough and you'll encounter deer, elk, rare lizards, birds of prey, and other zoological treats.

★ **Unforgettable canyoneering:** Zion's array of rugged slot canyons is the richest place on Earth for scrambling, rappelling, climbing, and descending.

1 Zion Canyon. This area defines Zion National Park for most people. Free shuttle buses are the only vehicles allowed during the crowded high season. The backcountry is accessible via the West Rim Trail and the Narrows, and 2,000-foot cliffs rise all around.

2 The Narrows. A quintessential slot canyon, this is one of the national park system's best hiking trails. Following the north fork of the Virgin River, there's something for everyone in the Narrows, whether you're a day-tripper or an overnight explorer.

3 Kolob Canyons. The northwestern corner of Zion is a secluded 30,000-acre wonderland that can be reached only via a special entrance. Don't miss the West Temple and the Kolob Arch, and keep looking up to spot Horse Ranch Mountain, the park's highest point.

4 Lava Point. Infrequently visited, this area has a primitive campground and two nearby reservoirs that offer the only significant fishing opportunities. Lava Point Overlook provides a view of Zion Canyon from the north.

GETTING ORIENTED

The heart of Zion National Park is Zion Canyon, which follows the North Fork of the Virgin River for 6½ miles beneath cliffs that rise 2,000 feet from the river bottom. The Kolob area is considered by some to be superior in beauty, and because it's isolated from the rest of the park, you aren't likely to run into any crowds here. Both sections hint at the extensive backcountry beyond, open for those with the stamina, time, and the courage to go off the beaten path.

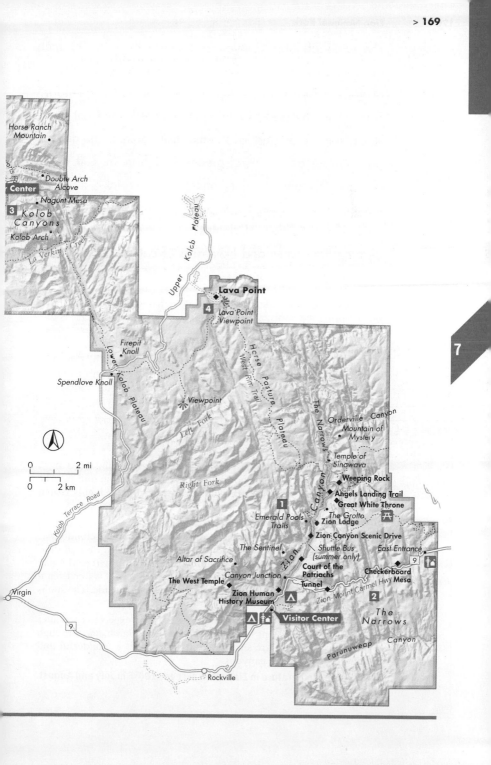

Horse Ranch
Mountain

Double Arch
Alcove

Center

3 *Kolob*
Canyons

Kolob Arch

La Verkin Creek

Nagunt Mesa

Upper Kolob Plateau

Lava Point

4 *Lava Point*
Viewpoint

Firepit
Knoll

Lower Kolob Plateau

Spendlove Knoll

Viewpoint

Left Fork

West Rim Trail

Horse Pasture Plateau

The Narrows

Orderville Canyon
Mountain of
Mystery

Temple of
Sinawava

Weeping Rock

Right Fork

Angels Landing Trail
Great White Throne

The Grotto
Zion Lodge

0   2 mi
0   2 km

Kolob Terrace Road

1

Emerald Pools
Trails

Zion Canyon Scenic Drive

Zion Canyon

The Sentinel

Shuttle Bus
(summer only)

East Entrance

Altar of Sacrifice

Zion

9

The West Temple

Canyon Junction

Court of the
Patriachs
Tunnel

Zion-Mount Carmel Hwy

Checkerboard
Mesa

2

Virgin

9

Zion Human
History Museum

Visitor Center

The
Narrows

Parunuweap Canyon

Rockville

7

Updated by
John Blodgett

The walls of Zion Canyon soar more than 2,000 feet above the valley below, but it's the character, not the size, of the sandstone forms that defines the park's splendor. Throughout the park, fantastically colored bands of limestone, sandstone, and lava in the strata point to the distant past. Stripes and spots of greenery high in the cliff walls create a "hanging garden" effect, and invariably indicate the presence of water seepage or a spring. Erosion has left behind a collection of domes, fins, and blocky massifs bearing the names and likenesses of cathedrals and temples, prophets and angels.

Trails lead deep into side canyons and up narrow ledges to waterfalls, serene spring-fed pools, and shaded spots of solitude. So diverse is this place that 85% of Utah's flora and fauna species are found here. Some, like the tiny Zion snail, appear nowhere else in the world.

The Colorado River helped create the Grand Canyon, while the Virgin River—the Colorado's muddy progeny—carved Zion's features. Because of the park's unique topography, distant storms and spring runoff can transform a tranquil slot canyon into a sluice.

ZION PLANNER

WHEN TO GO

Zion is the most heavily visited national park in Utah, receiving 3 million visitors each year. Locals used to call the spring and fall the shoulder seasons because traffic would drop off from the highly visited summer months. Not so much anymore. These days the park is busy from April through October.

Summer in the park is hot and dry, punctuated by sudden cloudbursts that can create flash flooding and spectacular waterfalls. Expect afternoon thunderstorms between July and September. Whether the day starts out sunny or not, wear sunscreen and drink lots of water, even if you aren't exerting yourself or spending much time outside. The sun is very powerful at this elevation.

Winters are mild at lower desert elevations. You can expect to encounter winter driving conditions from November to mid-March, and although most park programs are suspended in winter, it is a wonderful and solitary time to see the canyons.

■ TIP→ The temperature in Zion often exceeds 100°F in July and August.

AVG. HIGH/LOW TEMPS.

Jan.	Feb.	Mar.	Apr.	May	June
52/29	57/31	63/36	73/43	83/52	93/60
July	Aug.	Sept.	Oct.	Nov.	Dec.
100/68	97/66	91/60	78/49	63/37	53/30

FESTIVALS AND EVENTS

JANUARY

St. George Winter Bird Festival. Bird-watchers gather in St. George every January to peep at more than 100 feathered species. Join in three full days of field trips, exhibits, lectures, and activities. ⊠ *Tonaquint Park and Nature Center, 1851 S. Dixie Dr., St. George* ☎ *435/868–8756, 435/673–0996* ⊕ *www.sgcity.org* ✉ *$10.*

AUGUST

FAMILY **Western Legends Roundup.** For three days in late August, Kanab plays host to cowboy poets, musicians, and character actors from Old West TV series of yesteryear. A parade, tours to Western movie sites, a dutch-oven dinner, a quilt show, performances by Native American dancers, and a film festival draw visitors from all over the country. ☎ *435/644–3444* ⊕ *westernlegendsroundup.com.*

SEPTEMBER

Dixie Roundup. Dozens of professional rodeo cowboys from across the West take part in this three-day mid-September event held since the 1930s. Team roping, saddle-bronc riding, and bull riding are among the main attractions, along with the always entertaining mutton-busting competition for the kids and the rodeo parade. ⊠ *Sun Bowl Stadium, St. George* ☎ *435/703–4779* ⊕ *stgeorgelions.com* ✉ *$10.*

GETTING HERE AND AROUND

AIR TRAVEL

The nearest commercial airport is 46 miles away in St. George, Utah. McCarran International Airport (LAS) in Las Vegas, Nevada, 170 miles away, is the nearest large airport. Salt Lake City's airport is 310 miles away.

CAR TRAVEL

Zion National Park lies east of Interstate 15 in southwestern Utah. From the interstate, head east on Highway 9. After 21 miles you'll reach Springdale, which abuts the main entrance.

From mid-March through October, you can drive into the park only if you have reservations at the Zion Lodge. Otherwise, you must park your car in Springdale or at the Zion Canyon Visitor Center and take the shuttle. There are no car restrictions from November to mid-March.

The Zion Canyon Visitor Center parking lot fills up quickly. You can avoid parking heartburn by leaving your car in Springdale and riding the shuttle to the park entrance. Shuttles are accessible for people with disabilities and have plenty of room for gear. Consult the print park guide or check online at ⊕ *www.nps.gov/zion/planyourvisit/shuttle-system.htm* for the town shuttle schedule.

PARK ESSENTIALS

ACCESSIBILITY

Both visitor centers, all shuttle buses, and Zion Lodge are fully accessible to people in wheelchairs. Several campsites (sites A24 and A25 at Watchman Campground and sites 103, 114, and 115 at South Campground) are reserved for people with disabilities, and two trails—Riverside Walk and Pa'rus Trail—are accessible with some assistance.

PARK FEES AND PERMITS

Entrance to Zion National Park costs $30 per vehicle for a seven-day pass. People entering on foot or by bicycle pay $15 per person for a seven day pass; those on motorcycle pay $25.

Permits are required for backcountry camping and overnight hikes. Depending on which parts of the trails you intend to explore, you'll need a special permit for the Narrows and Kolob Creek or the Subway slot canyon. Climbing and canyoneering parties need a permit before using technical equipment.

Zion National Park limits the total number of overnight and canyoneering permits issued per day and has a reservation system with most of the permits now issued in an online lottery to apportion them fairly. Permits to the Subway, Mystery Canyon, the Narrows through-hikes, and West Rim are in short supply during high season. The maximum size of a group hiking into the backcountry is 12 people. Permits cost $15 for one or two people; $20 for three to seven; and $25 for eight or more. Permits are available at the visitor centers.

PARK HOURS

The park, open daily year-round, 24 hours a day, is in the Mountain time zone.

CELL-PHONE RECEPTION

Cell-phone reception is good in Springdale but spotty in Zion Canyon. Public telephones can be found at South Campground, Watchman Campground, Zion Canyon Visitor Center, Zion Lodge, and Zion Human History Museum.

EDUCATIONAL OFFERINGS

CLASSES AND SEMINARS

Zion Natl Park Forever Project. Formerly known as the Zion Natural History Association, the project conducts workshops about the park's natural and cultural history. Topics can include edible plants, bat biology, river geology, photography, and bird-watching. Most workshops include a hike. For a glimpse of Zion's inner workings, volunteer to assist with one of their ongoing projects. ⊠ *Zion National Park* ☎ *435/772–3264, 800/635–3959* ⊕ *www.zionpark.org* ⊠ *From $45.*

RANGER PROGRAMS

Evening Programs. Held each evening May through September in Watchman Campground and at Zion Lodge, these 45-minute ranger-led talks cover geology, biology, and history. You might learn about coyote calls, the night sky, animal hideouts, or observing nature with all your senses. Slide shows and audience participation are often part of the proceedings. Check the park guide and visitor center for

times, locations, and topics. ⊠ *Zion National Park* ☎ *435/772–3256* ⊕ *www.nps.gov/zion* 🎥 *Free.*

Fodor'sChoice
★
Expert Talks. Informal lectures take place on the Zion Human History Museum patio. Past topics have included wildlife, geology, and the stories of early settlers. Talks usually last from 20 to 30 minutes, though some run longer. Park bulletin boards and publications have schedules. ⊠ *Zion National Park* ☎ *435/772–3256* 🎥 *Free.*

FAMILY
Junior Ranger Program. Educational activities aimed at younger visitors include the chance to earn a Junior Ranger badge. Kids do so by attending at least one nature program and completing the free Junior Ranger Handbook, available at visitor centers and elsewhere. The ranger-led programs cover topics such as plants, animals, geology, and archaeology through hands-on activities, games, and hikes. ⊠ *Zion National Park* ☎ *435/772–3256* ⊕ *www.nps.gov/kids/jrRangers.cfm* 🎥 *Free.*

Ranger-Led Hike. A daily guided hike along the 2-mile Watchman Trail provides an overview of the park's geology and natural and other history. Groups meet at 8 am at Zion Canyon Visitor Center. Wear sturdy footgear and bring a hat, sunglasses, sunscreen, and water. ⊠ *Zion National Park* ⊕ *www.nps.gov/zion/planyourvisit/ranger-led-activities.htm* 🎥 *Free.*

FAMILY
Fodor'sChoice
★
Ride with a Ranger Shuttle Tours. Once a day, rangers conduct shuttle tours of points of interest along Zion Canyon Scenic Drive. In addition to learning about the canyon's geology, ecology, and history, you'll be treated to some great photo ops. The 90-minute tour takes place in the morning and departs from the Zion Canyon Visitor Center. Seating is limited to eight people. Make reservations in person at the visitor center up to three days in advance. ⊠ *Zion Canyon Visitor Center* ☎ *435/772–3256* ⊕ *www.nps.gov/zion* 🎥 *Free* ☉ *Closed Nov.–Mar.*

RESTAURANTS

Only one full-service restaurant operates within the park, but there are numerous choices just beyond it. Springdale is the best choice for family-friendly restaurants.

HOTELS

The Zion Lodge is rustic but clean and comfortable. Springdale has dozens of lodging options, from quaint bed-and-breakfasts to modest motels to chain hotels with riverside rooms. Panguitch and Hurricane have some good options for budget and last-minute travelers. *Hotel reviews have been shortened. For full information, visit Fodors.com.*

WHAT IT COSTS			
$	$$	$$$	$$$$
Restaurants	under $13	$13–$20	$21–$30	over $30
Hotels	under $100	$100–$150	$151–$200	over $200

Restaurant prices are the average cost of a main course at dinner, or if dinner is not served, at lunch. Hotel prices are the lowest cost of a standard double room in high season.

VISITOR INFORMATION

Park Contact Information Zion National Park. ⊠ *Hwy. 9, Springdale* ☎ *435/772–3256* ⊕ *nps.gov/zion.*

VISITOR CENTERS

Kolob Canyons Visitor Center. Make this your first stop as you enter this remote section of the park. There are books and maps, a small gift shop, and clean restrooms here, and rangers are on hand to answer questions about Kolob Canyons exploration. ⊠ *3752 E. Kolob Canyon Rd., Exit 40 off I–15* ☎ *435/586–9548* ⊕ *www.nps.gov/zion.*

Zion Canyon Visitor Center. Learn about the area's geology, flora, and fauna at an outdoor exhibit next to a gurgling stream. Inside, a large shop sells everything from field guides to souvenirs. Zion Canyon shuttle buses leave regularly from the center and make several stops along the canyon's beautiful scenic drive; ranger-guided shuttle tours depart once a day April to October. ⊠ *Zion Park Blvd. at south entrance, Springdale* ☎ *435/772–3256* ⊕ *www.nps.gov/zion.*

EXPLORING

SCENIC DRIVES

Driving is the only way to easily access Kolob Canyon, and from November through March it's the only way to access the Zion Canyon Scenic Drive.

Kolob Canyons Road. The beauty starts modestly at the junction with Interstate 15, but as you move along this 5-mile road the red walls of the Kolob finger canyons rise suddenly and spectacularly out of the earth. With the crowds left behind at Zion Canyon, this drive offers the chance to take in incredible vistas at your leisure. Trails include the short but rugged Middle Fork of Taylor Creek Trail, which passes two 1930s homestead cabins, culminating 2¾ miles later in the Double Arch Alcove. During heavy snowfall Kolob Canyons Road may be closed. ⊠ *I–15, Exit 40.*

Kolob Terrace Road. This 22-mile road begins 14 miles west of Springdale at Virgin and winds north to Kolob Reservoir. The drive meanders in and out of the park boundaries, crossing several important trailheads, all the while overlooking the cliffs of North Creek. A popular day-use trail (permit required) leads past fossilized dinosaur tracks to the Subway, a stretch of the stream where the walls of the slot canyon close in so tightly as to form a near tunnel. Farther along the road you reach the Wildcat Canyon trailhead, which connects to the path overlooking the North Guardian Angel. The road terminates at the reservoir, beneath 8,933-foot Kolob Peak. This narrow, twisting road is not recommended for RVs. Because of limited winter plowing, the road is closed from December through April or May. ⊠ *Zion National Park* ✛ *Drive begins at Hwy. 9 and Kolob Terrace Rd. in Virgin* ☉ *Closed Dec.–Apr. or May.*

Zion Canyon Scenic Drive. Vividly colored cliffs tower 2,000 feet above the road that meanders north from Springdale along the floor of Zion

Canyon. As you roll through the narrow, steep canyon you'll pass the Court of the Patriarchs, the Sentinel, and the Great White Throne, among other imposing rock formations. Unless you're staying at the lodge, Zion Canyon Scenic Drive is accessed only by park shuttle from mid-March through October. You can drive it yourself at other times. ⊠ *Zion Park Blvd./Hwy. 9.*

Zion–Mount Carmel Highway and Tunnels. Two narrow tunnels as old as the park itself lie between the east entrance and Zion Canyon on this breathtaking 24-mile (round-trip) stretch of Highway 9. One was once the longest man-made tunnel in the world. As you travel the (1.1-mile) passage through solid rock, five arched portals along one side provide fleeting glimpses of cliffs and canyons. When you emerge you'll find that the landscape has changed dramatically. Large vehicles require traffic control and a $15 permit, available at the park entrance, and have restricted hours of travel. This includes nearly all RVs, trailers, dual-wheel trucks, and campers. The Canyon Overlook Trail starts from a parking area between the tunnels. ⊠ *Hwy. 9, 5 miles east of Canyon Junction.*

HISTORIC SITES

Zion Human History Museum. This quaint museum tells the park's story from the perspective of its human inhabitants, among them Ancestral Puebloans and early Mormon settlers. Permanent exhibits illustrate how humans have dealt with wildlife, plants, and natural forces. Temporary exhibits include finds from recent archaeological excavations. Don't miss the incredible view of Towers of the Virgin from the back patio. ⊠ *Zion Canyon Scenic Dr., ½ mile north of south entrance* ☎ *435/772–3256* ⊕ *www.nps.gov/zion/historyculture/zion-human-history-museum.htm* ☒ *Free* ☺ *Closed after Thanksgiving–mid-Mar.*

Fodor'sChoice **Zion Lodge.** Architect Gilbert Stanley Underwood, responsible for many
★   noteworthy national park lodges, designed the original Zion Lodge, which opened in the 1920s but was destroyed by fire four decades later. In 1990, it was restored to its original rustic style, in some cases down to the very paint color. Natural beauty is on display inside and out, from the lobby's rock columns and exposed wood to the cottonwoods shading the sprawling lawn. The main building includes a gift shop, a fine-dining restaurant, and a snack bar. The lodge has received numerous awards for its eco-friendly practices. Recent amenities include bike rentals, open-air narrated tram rides, and an electric-vehicle charging station. ⊠ *Zion Canyon Scenic Dr.* ☎ *435/772–7700.*

SCENIC STOPS

The park comprises two distinct sections, Zion Canyon and the Kolob Plateau and Canyons. Most people restrict their visit to the better-known Zion Canyon, but the Kolob area has much to offer and should not be missed if time allows. Though there's little evidence of Kolob's beauty from the entrance point off Interstate 15, once you negotiate the first switchback on the park road, you are hit with a vision of red-rock cliffs shooting out of the earth. As you climb in elevation, you are treated first to a journey through these canyons, then to a view into the chasm. ■TIP→ **Because you must exit the park to get from Zion Canyon to Kolob Canyon, it is not easy to explore both sections in one day.**

Checkerboard Mesa. It's well worth stopping at the pull-out 1 mile west of Zion's east entrance to observe the distinctive waffle patterns on this huge white mound of sandstone. The stunning crosshatch effect visible today is the result of eons of freeze-and-thaw cycles that caused vertical fractures, combined with erosion that produced horizontal bedding planes. ⊠ *Zion–Mount Carmel Hwy.*

Court of the Patriarchs. This trio of peaks bears the names of, from left to right, Abraham, Isaac, and Jacob. Mount Moroni is the reddish peak on the far right that partially blocks the view of Jacob. Hike the trail that leaves from the Court of the Patriarchs Viewpoint, 1½ miles north of Canyon Junction, to get a much better view of the sandstone prophets; you may catch a glimpse of rock climbers camming their way up Isaac's sheer face. ⊠ *Zion Canyon Scenic Dr.*

Great White Throne. Dominating the Grotto picnic area near Zion Lodge, this massive Navajo sandstone peak juts 2,000 feet above the valley floor. The popular formation lies about 3 miles north of Canyon Junction. ⊠ *Zion Canyon Scenic Dr.*

Fodor's Choice **The Narrows.** This sinuous 16-mile crack in the earth where the Virgin
★ River flows over gravel and boulders is one of the world's most stunning gorges. If you hike through it, you'll find yourself surrounded—sometimes nearly boxed in—by smooth walls stretching high into the heavens. Plan to get wet. ⊠ *Zion National Park* ✛ *Begins at Riverside Walk.*

Weeping Rock. Surface water from the rim of Echo Canyon spends several thousand years seeping down through the porous sandstone before exiting at this picturesque alcove 4½ miles north of Canyon Junction. A paved walkway climbs ¼ mile to this flowing rock face where wildflowers and delicate ferns grow. In fall, the maples and cottonwoods burst with color, and lizards point the way down the path, which is not suitable for wheelchairs. ⊠ *Zion Canyon Scenic Dr.*

SPORTS AND THE OUTDOORS

Hiking is by far the most popular activity at Zion, with all sorts of trails leading to rewarding hinterland destinations: extreme slot canyons, gorgeous overlooks, verdant meadows, and dripping springs. Some sections of the Virgin River are ideal for canoeing (inner tubes are not allowed). In winter, hiking boots can be exchanged for snowshoes and cross-country skis, but check with a ranger to determine backcountry snow conditions.

BICYCLING

Zion National Park has something for every kind of biker. Mountain bikers can cake themselves with mud on the park's trails, and racers will find enough up and down to make their pulses race.

Zion has taken steps to become much more bicycle-friendly, including having bike racks at some of the facilities and on the shuttle buses themselves. If you are renting bikes by the hour from a Springdale outfitter, you can load your bike on the bus, have the shuttle take you to the last stop (Temple of Sinawava), and take an easy one-way pedal back to Springdale. ■ **TIP→ When you're on the park road, shuttle buses and cars have the right of way. You're expected to pull off to the side and let them pass.**

Within the park proper, bicycles are allowed only on established park roads and the 3½-mile Pa'rus Trail, which winds along the Virgin River in Zion Canyon. You cannot walk or ride your bicycle through the Zion–Mount Carmel tunnels; the only way to get your bike past this stretch of the highway is to transport it by motor vehicle. ⊕ *www.nps. gov/zion/planyourvisit/bicycling.htm*

TOURS AND OUTFITTERS

Bicycles Unlimited. A trusted southern Utah mountain-biking resource, this shop rents bikes and sells parts, accessories, and guidebooks. ⊠ *90 S. 100 E, St. George* ☎ *435/673–4492* ⊕ *bicyclesunlimited.com* ⊠ *From $25 for 4 hrs*

Zion Cycles. This shop rents bikes by the hour or longer, sells parts, and has a full-time mechanic on duty. You can pick up trail and other advice from the staff here. ⊠ *868 Zion Park Blvd., Springdale* ☎ *435/772– 0400* ⊕ *zioncycles.com* ⊠ *From $26 for 4 hrs.*

HIKING

The best way to experience Zion Canyon is to walk beneath, between and, if you can bear it (and have good balance!), along its towering cliffs. Trails vary, from paved and flat river strolls to precarious cliffside scrambles. Whether you're heading out for a day of rock hopping or an hour of meandering, pack and consume plenty of drinking water to counteract the effects of a high-altitude workout in the arid climate.

Keeping the sun at bay is a real challenge at Zion National Park. Put on sunscreen before you set out, and reapply at regular intervals. Because the park's hikes usually include uneven surfaces and elevation changes, wear sturdy shoes or hiking boots. Many veteran hikers carry good walking sticks, too, as they're invaluable along trails that ford or follow the Virgin River or its tributaries.

Zion is one of the most popular parks in the country, so it can be hard to envision just how alone you'll be on some of the less traveled trails. If you want to do a backcountry hike, make a reservation. Let park rangers know where you're going and when you plan to return.

■ **TIP→ Park rangers warn hikers to remain on alert for flash floods; these walls of water can appear out of nowhere, even when the sky above you is clear.** You can learn more about hiking safety and obtain a trail map at the visitor centers or online (⊕ *www.nps.gov/zion/plany-ourvisit/hiking-in-zion.htm*).

EASY

FAMILY **Emerald Pools Trail.** Multiple waterfalls cascade (or drip, in dry weather) into algae-filled pools along this trail, about 3 miles north of Canyon Junction. The path leading to the lower pool is paved and appropriate for strollers and wheelchairs. If you've got any energy left, keep going past the lower pool. The ¼ mile from there to the middle pool becomes rocky and steep but offers increasingly scenic views. A less crowded and exceptionally enjoyable return route follows the Kayenta Trail, connecting to the Grotto Trail. Allow 50 minutes for the 1¼-mile round-trip hike to the lower pool, and an hour more each round-trip to the middle (2 miles) and upper pools (3 miles). *Lower, easy. Upper, moderate.* ⊠ *Zion National Park* ✚ *Trailhead: at Zion Canyon Scenic Dr.*

FAMILY **Grotto Trail.** This flat trail takes you from Zion Lodge, about 3 miles north of Canyon Junction, to the Grotto picnic area, traveling for the most part along the park road. Allow 20 minutes or less for the walk along the ½-mile trail. If you are up for a longer hike and have two or three hours, connect with the Kayenta Trail after you cross the footbridge, and head for the Emerald Pools. You will begin gaining elevation, and it's a steady, steep climb to the pools, which you will begin to see after about 1 mile. *Easy.* ⊠ *Zion National Park* ✚ *Trailhead: at Zion Canyon Scenic Dr.*

Pa'rus Trail. An approximately 2-mile, relatively flat paved walking and biking path, Pa'rus parallels and occasionally crosses the Virgin River. Starting at South Campground, ½ mile north of the south entrance, the walk proceeds north along the river to the beginning of Zion Canyon Scenic Drive. Along the way you'll take in great views of the Watchman, the Sentinel, the East and West temples, and Towers of the Virgin. Leashed dogs are allowed on this trail. Wheelchair users may need assistance. *Easy.* ⊠ *Zion National Park* ✚ *Trailhead: at Canyon Junction.*

FAMILY **Riverside Walk.** This 2-mile round-trip hike shadows the Virgin River. In spring, wildflowers bloom on the opposite canyon wall in lovely hanging gardens. The trail, which begins 6½ miles north of Canyon Junction at the end of Zion Canyon Scenic Drive, is the park's most visited trail, so be prepared for crowds in high season. Riverside Walk is paved and suitable for strollers and wheelchairs, though some wheelchair users may need assistance. Round-trip it takes about 90 minutes. At the end, the Narrows Trail begins. *Easy.* ⊠ *Zion National Park* ✚ *Trailhead: at Temple of Sinawava shuttle stop, Zion Canyon Scenic Dr.*

MODERATE

FAMILY
Fodor's Choice
★
Canyon Overlook Trail. The parking area just east of Zion–Mount Carmel tunnel leads to this popular trail, which is about 1 mile round-trip and takes about an hour to finish. From the overlook at the trail's end you can see the West and East temples, the Towers of the Virgin, the Streaked Wall, and other Zion Canyon cliffs and peaks. The elevation change is 160 feet. *Moderate.* ⊠ *Zion National Park* ✚ *Trailhead: at Hwy. 9, east of Zion–Mount Carmel tunnel.*

Taylor Creek Trail. This trail in the Kolob Canyons area descends parallel to Taylor Creek, sometimes crossing it, sometimes shortcutting benches beside it. The historic Larsen Cabin precedes the entrance to the canyon of the Middle Fork, where the trail becomes rougher. After the old Fife Cabin, the canyon bends to the right into Double Arch Alcove, a large, colorful grotto with a high blind arch (or arch "embryo") towering above. To Double Arch it's 2¾ miles one-way—about four hours round-trip. The elevation change is 440 feet. *Moderate. ⊠ Zion National Park ✛ Trailhead: at Kolob Canyons Rd., about 1½ miles east of Kolob Canyons Visitor Center.*

Watchman Trail. For a view of Springdale and a look at lower Zion Creek Canyon and the Towers of the Virgin, this strenuous hike begins on a service road east of Watchman Campground. Some springs seep out of the sandstone, nourishing the hanging gardens and attracting wildlife. There are a few sheer cliff edges, so supervise children carefully. Plan on two hours for this 3-mile round-trip hike that has a 380-foot elevation change. *Moderate. ⊠ Zion National Park ✛ Trailhead: at Zion Canyon Visitor Center.*

DIFFICULT

Angels Landing Trail. As much a trial as a trail, this path beneath the Great White Throne is one of the park's most challenging hikes. Early on you work your way through Walter's Wiggles, a series of 21 switchbacks built out of sandstone blocks. From there you traverse sheer cliffs that have chains bolted into the rock face to serve as handrails in some (but not all) places. In spite of its hair-raising nature, this trail is popular. Allow 2½ hours round-trip if you stop at Scout's Lookout (2 miles), and four hours if you keep going to where the angels (and birds of prey) play. The trail is 5 miles round-trip and is not appropriate for children. *Difficult. ⊠ Zion National Park ✛ Trailhead: at Zion Canyon Scenic Dr., about 4½ miles north of Canyon Junction.*

Fodor's Choice ★ Narrows Trail. The hike on the Narrows Trail is a stunning and unique nature experience, but it's no picnic. After leaving the paved ease of the Gateway to the Narrows trail behind, the real fun begins. Rather than following a trail or path, you walk on the riverbed itself. In places you'll find a pebbly shingle or dry sandbar path, but when the walls of the canyon close in, you'll be forced into the chilly waters of the Virgin River, walking against the current—tack back and forth, don't fight it head-on. A walking stick and shoes with good tread and ankle support are highly recommended and will make hiking the riverbed much more enjoyable. Be prepared to swim, as chest-deep holes may occur even when water levels are low. Like any narrow desert canyon, this one is famous for sudden flash flooding, even when skies are clear. Before hiking into the Narrows, check with park rangers about the likelihood of flash floods. A day trip up the lower section of the Narrows is 6 miles one-way to the turnaround point. Allow at least five hours round-trip. *Difficult. ⊠ Zion National Park ✛ Trailhead: at end of Riverside Walk.*

HORSEBACK RIDING

TOURS AND OUTFITTERS

FAMILY **Canyon Trail Rides.** Grab your hat and boots and see Zion Canyon the way the pioneers did—on a horse or mule. Easygoing, one-hour and half-day guided rides are available (minimum age 7 and 10 years, respectively). Maximum weight is 220 pounds. These friendly folks have been around for years, and are the only outfitter for trail rides inside the park. Reservations are recommended and can be made online. ⊠ *Across from Zion Lodge* ☎ *435/772–3810* ⊕ *canyonrides.com* ⊠ *From $45.*

SWIMMING

Swimming is allowed in the Virgin River, but be careful of cold water, slippery rock bottoms, and the occasional flash floods when it rains. Swimming isn't permitted in the Emerald Pools. The use of inner tubes is prohibited within park boundaries, but some companies offer trips on a Virgin River tributary just outside the park.

WINTER SPORTS

Cross-country skiing and snowshoeing are best experienced in the park's higher elevations in winter, where snow stays on the ground longer. Inquire at the Zion Canyon Visitor Center for backcountry conditions. Snowmobiling is allowed only for residential access.

WHAT'S NEARBY

NEARBY ATTRACTIONS

Coral Pink Sand Dunes State Park. Visitors to this sweeping expanse of pink sand enjoy a slice of nature produced by eroding sandstone. Funneled through a notch in the rock, wind picks up speed and carries grains of sand into the area. Once the wind slows down, the sand is deposited, creating this giant playground for dune buggies, ATVs, and dirt bikes. A small area is fenced off for walking, but the sound of wheeled toys is always with you. Children love to play in the sand, but check the surface temperature; it can become very hot. Off-road vehicles must have current registration. ⊠ *Coral Sand Dunes Rd./Hwy. 43, 12 miles west of U.S. 89, off Hancock Rd., Kanab* ☎ *435/648–2800* ⊕ *stateparks.utah.gov* ⊠ *$8.*

Maynard Dixon Living History Museum. Two miles north of Mount Carmel Junction, this was the final residence of the famous painter of Western life and landscapes. The property and log cabin structure are now maintained by the nonprofit Thunderbird Foundation for the Arts. Tours are self-guided or, from mid-March to mid-November, you can call ahead to arrange a docent tour. ⊠ *U.S. 89, mile marker 84, Mount Carmel* ☎ *435/648–2653* ⊕ *thunderbirdfoundation.com* ⊠ *$10; $20 for docent tour.*

Snow Canyon State Park. Named not for winter weather but after a pair of pioneering Utahans named Snow, this gem of a state park is filled with natural wonders. Hiking trails lead to lava cones, sand dunes, cactus gardens, and high-contrast vistas. From the campground you can scramble up huge sandstone mounds and overlook the entire valley. Park staff lead occasional guided hikes. The park is about 10 miles northwest of St. George, and about an hour from Zion. ⊠ *1002 Snow Canyon Dr., Ivins* ☎ *435/628–2255* ⊕ *stateparks.utah. gov* ⊠ *$6 per vehicle.*

WHERE TO EAT

IN THE PARK

$ CAFÉ 🍴 **Castle Dome Café & Snack Bar.** Next to the shuttle stop at Zion Lodge, this small fast-food restaurant is all about convenience. You can grab a banana, burger, smoothie, or salad to go, or while away an hour with ice cream on the shaded patio. **Known for:** quick bites; bustling scene; family friendly. [$] *Average main: $6* ✉ *Zion Canyon Scenic Dr., 3¼ miles north of Canyon Junction* ☎ *435/772–7700* 🌐 *zionlodge.com/dining.*

$$ AMERICAN 🍴 **Red Rock Grill.** The fare at this restaurant at Zion Lodge includes steaks, seafood, and Western specialties such as trout and bison meat loaf headlining the dinner menu. Photos of the surrounding landscape adorn the walls of the spacious dining room, and the large patio has gorgeous views of the real thing. **Known for:** dinner reservations necessary in summer; outdoor seating; canyon setting. [$] *Average main: $18* ✉ *Zion Lodge, Zion Canyon Scenic Dr.* ☎ *435/772–7760* 🌐 *zionlodge.com/dining.*

PICNIC AREAS

FAMILY **The Grotto.** Get your food to go at the Zion Lodge, take a short walk to this lunch retreat, and dine beneath a shady oak. The amenities include drinking water, picnic tables, and restrooms, but there are no fire grates. A trail from here leads to the Emerald Pools. ✉ *Zion Canyon Scenic Dr.*

Kolob Canyons Viewpoint. Enjoy a shaded meal with a view at this picnic site 100 yards down the Timber Creek Trail, 5 miles from Kolob Canyons Visitor Center. ✉ *Zion National Park* ✥ *On Timber Creek Trail at end of Kolob Canyons Rd.*

FAMILY **Zion Nature Center.** On your way to or from the Junior Ranger Program you can feed your kids at the center's picnic area. When the center is closed, use the restrooms in South Campground. ✉ *Zion Canyon Scenic Dr.* ✥ *Near entrance to South Campground, ½ mile north of south entrance* ☎ *435/772–3256.*

OUTSIDE THE PARK

$$ SOUTHWESTERN 🍴 **Bit & Spur.** This laid-back Springdale institution has been serving locals and tourists for more than 30 years. The well-rounded menu includes fresh fish and pasta dishes, but the emphasis is on creative Southwestern fare such as roasted-sweet-potato tamales and chili-rubbed rib-eye steak. **Known for:** innovative margaritas; live music; signature rib eye. [$] *Average main: $20* ✉ *1212 Zion Park Blvd., Springdale* ☎ *435/772–3498* 🌐 *www.bitandspur.com* ⊘ *No lunch.*

$ DELI 🍴 **Sol Foods Supermarket.** Stop by the market's deli and check out the premade sandwiches and abundant salad bar, or order a quick sandwich, wrap, or vegetarian snack of your choice. The staff can also prepare a box lunch for your day in the park. **Known for:** box lunches; extensive menu; one-stop shop. [$] *Average main: $8* ✉ *995 Zion Park Blvd., Springdale* ☎ *435/772–3100* 🌐 *www.solfoods.com.*

7

CLOSE UP

Best Campgrounds in Zion

The two campgrounds within Zion National Park—South and Watchman—are family-friendly, convenient, and pleasant, but in high season they fill up fast. Outside Zion are the park-affiliated Lava Point campground and some private campgrounds.

South Campground. All the sites here are under big cottonwood trees that provide some relief from the summer sun. The campground operates on a first-come, first-served basis, and sites are usually filled before noon each day during high season. ✉ *Hwy. 9, ½ mile north of south entrance* ☎ *435/772–3256.*

Watchman Campground. This large campground on the Virgin River operates on a reservation system between April and October, but you do not get to choose your site. ✉ *Access road off Zion Canyon Visitor Center parking lot* ☎ *435/772–3256, 800/365–2267* 🌐 *www.recreation.gov.*

$$ ECLECTIC 🍴 **Spotted Dog Café.** This restaurant is more upscale than most in Springdale, but its staff makes patrons feel right at home even if they saunter in wearing hiking shoes. The exposed wood beams and large windows that frame the surrounding trees and rock cliffs set a Western mood, with tablecloths and original artworks supplying a dash of refinement. **Known for:** locally roasted coffee; sidewalk dining; breakfast buffet. [$] *Average main: $20* ✉ *Flanigan's Inn, 428 Zion Park Blvd., Springdale* ☎ *435/772–0700* 🌐 *www.flanigans.com/dining* 🕒 *Limited hrs Nov.–Mar. No lunch.*

$$$ AMERICAN 🍴 **The Switchback Grille.** Known for its USDA prime steaks and seafood flown in fresh daily, the high-ceilinged Switchback has walls of windows framing stunning views. Like all good steak houses, it serves comforting sides such as roasted potatoes and sautéed mushrooms. **Known for:** aged beef; casual elegance; seafood specials. [$] *Average main: $25* ✉ *Holiday Inn Express, 1149 S. Zion Park Blvd., Springdale* ☎ *435/772–3700* 🌐 *switchbackgrille.com* 🕒 *No lunch.*

WHERE TO STAY

IN THE PARK

$$$$ HOTEL 🏨 **Zion Lodge.** If location is your key concern, you'd be hard-pressed to improve on a stay at the historic Zion Lodge: the canyon's jaw-dropping beauty surrounds you, access to trailheads is easy, and guests can drive their cars in the park year-round. **Pros:** guests can drive their cars in the park year-round; incredible views; bike rentals on-site. **Cons:** pathways are dimly lit (bring a flashlight); Wi-Fi and cell reception can be spotty; sells out months ahead for summer. [$] *Rooms from: $227* ✉ *Zion Canyon Scenic Dr.* ☎ *888/297–2757 reservations only, 435/772–7700* 🌐 *zionlodge.com* 🛏 *82 rooms, 40 cabins* 🍽 *No meals.*

BRYCE CANYON
NATIONAL PARK

WELCOME TO
BRYCE CANYON NATIONAL PARK

TOP REASONS TO GO

★ **Hoodoo heaven:** The brashly colored, gravity-defying limestone tentacles reaching skyward—known locally as "hoodoos"—are the main attraction of Bryce Canyon.

★ **Famous fresh air:** With some of the clearest skies anywhere, the park offers views that, on a clear day, extend 200 miles and into three states.

★ **Spectacular sunrises and sunsets:** The deep orange and crimson hues of the park's hoodoos are intensified by the light of the sun at either end of the day.

★ **Dramatically different zones:** From the highest point of the rim to the canyon base, the park spans 2,000 feet, so you can explore three unique climatic zones: spruce-fir forest, ponderosa-pine forest, and pinyon pine-juniper forest.

★ **Snowy fun:** Bryce gets an average of 95 inches of snowfall a year, and is a popular destination for skiers and snowshoe enthusiasts.

1 Bryce Amphitheater. It's the heart of the park. From here you can access the historic Bryce Canyon Lodge as well as Sunrise, Sunset, and Inspiration points. Walk to Bryce Point at sunrise to view the mesmerizing collection of massive hoodoos known as Silent City.

2 Under-the-Rim Trail. This 23-mile trail is the best way to reach Bryce Canyon backcountry. It can be a challenging three-day adventure or a half day of fun via one of the four access points from the main road. A handful of primitive campgrounds lines the route.

3 Rainbow and Yovimpa Points. The end of the scenic road, but not of the scenery, here you can hike a trail to see some ancient bristlecone pines and look south into Grand Staircase–Escalante National Monument.

GETTING ORIENTED

Bryce Canyon National Park actually isn't a single canyon, but rather a series of natural amphitheaters on the eastern edge of the Paunsaugunt Plateau. The park's scenic drive runs along a formation known as the Pink Cliffs and offers more than a dozen amazing overlooks. Many visitors drive to the end of the 18-mile road and turn around before allowing their jaws to drop in wonder. (It's practical, too, as the scenic overlooks will then be on the right side of the road, making it easy to pull over.) The main park road leads to the most popular hiking trails, which wind their way down into the canyons. A handful of roads veers to the east of the scenic drive to access other points of interest. As relief from the frequent heavy (and slow) traffic during the high season of summer, consider riding in one of the park's shuttle buses.

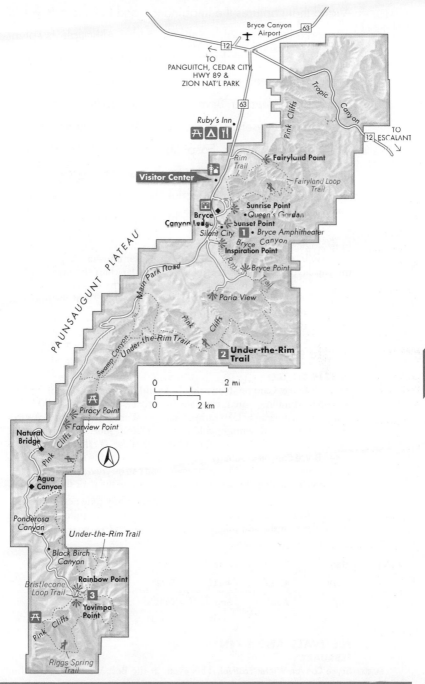

Updated by
John Blodgett

A land that captures the imagination and the heart, Bryce is a favorite among Utah's national parks. Although its splendor had been well known for decades, Bryce Canyon wasn't designated a national park until 1928. The park is named for Ebenezer Bryce, a pioneer cattleman and the first permanent settler in the area. His description of the landscape not being hospitable to cows has oft been repeated. Even more than his famous quote, however, Bryce Canyon is known for its fanciful "hoodoos," best viewed at sunrise or sunset, when the light plays off the red rock.

In geological terms, Bryce is actually an amphitheater, not a canyon. The hoodoos in the amphitheater took on their unusual shapes because the top layer of rock—"cap rock"—is harder than the layers below it. If erosion undercuts the soft rock beneath the cap too much, the hoodoo will tumble. Bryce continues to evolve today, but the hoodoos are a permanent feature; old ones may die, but new ones are constantly forming as the amphitheater rim recedes.

BRYCE CANYON PLANNER

WHEN TO GO

Around Bryce Canyon National Park and the nearby Cedar Breaks National Monument area, elevations approach and surpass 9,000 feet, making for temperamental weather, intermittent and seasonal road closures due to snow, and downright cold nights well into June. The air is cooler on the rim of the canyon than it is at lower altitudes. ■ TIP→ **If you choose to see Bryce Canyon in summer, you'll be visiting with the rest of the world. During these months, traffic on the main road can be crowded with cars following slow-moving RVs, so consider taking one of the park shuttle buses.**

If it's solitude you're looking for, come to Bryce any time between October and March. The park is open all year long, so if you come during the cooler months you might just have a trail all to yourself.

AVG. HIGH/LOW TEMPS.

Jan.	Feb.	Mar.	Apr.	May	June
39/8	41/13	48/17	56/25	68/31	75/38
July	Aug.	Sept.	Oct.	Nov.	Dec.
83/47	80/45	74/37	63/29	51/19	42/11

FESTIVALS AND EVENTS
FEBRUARY
FAMILY **Bryce Canyon Winter Festival.** This event at the Best Western Ruby's Inn features cross-country ski races, snow-sculpting contests, ski archery,

and ice-skating. Clinics to hone skills such as snowshoeing and photography also take place, and there's entertainment, too. ☎ *435/834–5341* ⊕ *www.rubysinn.com.*

Quilt Walk Festival. During the bitter winter of 1864, Panguitch residents set out over the mountains to fetch provisions from the town of Parowan, 40 miles away. Legend says the men, frustrated and ready to turn back, laid a quilt on the snow and knelt to pray. Soon they realized the quilt had kept them from sinking into the snow. Spreading quilts before them as they walked, leapfrog style, the men traveled to Parowan and back. This four-day event in June commemorates the event with quilting classes, a tour of pioneer homes, tractor pull, dinner-theater, and other events. ☎ *435/690–9228.*

Fodor's Choice   **Utah Shakespeare Festival.** For more than 50 years, Cedar City has gone
★   Bard-crazy, staging productions of Shakespeare's plays June through October in theaters both indoors and outdoors at Southern Utah University. The Tony award–winning regional theater offers literary seminars, backstage tours, cabarets featuring festival actors, and an outdoor preshow with Elizabethan performers. A new center for the arts, including the open-air Engelstad Shakespeare Theatre, made its debut during the 2016 season. It helps to reserve in advance as many performances sell out. ☎ *435/586–7878* ⊕ *www.bard.org.*

PLANNING YOUR TIME
BRYCE CANYON IN ONE DAY

Begin your day at the **visitor center** to get an overview of the park and to purchase books and maps. Watch the 20-minute film and peruse exhibits about the natural and cultural history of Bryce Canyon. Then, drive to the historic **Bryce Canyon Lodge.** From here, stroll along the relaxing **Rim Trail.** If you have the time and stamina to walk into the amphitheater, the portion of the Rim Trail near the lodge gets you to the starting point for either of the park's two essential hikes, the **Navajo Loop Trail** from **Sunset Point** or the **Queen's Garden Trail** that connects Sunset to **Sunrise Point.**

Afterward (or if you skip the hike), drive the 18-mile **main park road,** stopping at the overlooks along the way. Allowing for traffic, and if you stop at all 13 overlooks, this drive will take you between two and three hours.

If you have the time for more walking, a short, rolling hike along the **Bristlecone Loop Trail** at Rainbow Point rewards you with spectacular views and a cool walk through a forest of bristlecone pines. If you don't have time to drive the 18 miles to the end of the park, skip Bryce Canyon Lodge and drive 2 miles from the visitor center to **Inspiration Point** and then to the next overlook, **Bryce Point.**

End your day with sunset at Inspiration Point or dinner at Bryce Canyon Lodge. As you leave the park, stop at **Ruby's Inn** for American Indian jewelry, souvenirs for the kids, and groceries or snacks for the road.

GETTING HERE AND AROUND
AIR TRAVEL

The nearest commercial airport to Bryce Canyon is 80 miles west in Cedar City, Utah.

8

BUS TRAVEL

A shuttle bus system operates in Bryce Canyon from late April through September. Buses start at 8 am and run every 10 to 15 minutes, and are free with your admission fee. The route begins at Ruby's Inn and Ruby's Campground outside the park entrance and stops at the visitor center, lodge, campgrounds, and all the main overlooks and trailheads.

CAR TRAVEL

The closest major cities to Bryce Canyon are Salt Lake City and Las Vegas, each about 270 miles away. The park is reached via Route 63, just 3 miles south of the junction with Highway 12. You can see the park's highlights by driving along the well-maintained road running the length of the main scenic area. Bryce has no restrictions on automobiles on the main road, but in the summer you may encounter heavy traffic and full parking lots.

PARK ESSENTIALS

ACCESSIBILITY

Most park facilities were constructed between 1930 and 1960. Some have been upgraded for wheelchair accessibility, while others can be used with some assistance. The Sunset campground offers two sites with wheelchair access. Few of the trails, however, can be managed in a standard wheelchair due to the sandy, rocky, or uneven terrain. The section of the Rim Trail between Sunrise and Inspiration points is wheelchair accessible. The 1-mile Bristlecone Loop Trail at Rainbow Point has a hard surface and could be used with assistance, but several grades do not meet standards. Accessible parking is marked at all overlooks and public facilities.

PARK FEES

The entrance fee is $30 per vehicle for a seven-day pass and $15 for pedestrians or bicyclists, and includes unlimited use of the park shuttle. An annual Bryce Canyon park pass, good for one year from the date of purchase, costs $35. If you leave your private vehicle outside the park at the shuttle staging area or Ruby's Inn, the one-time entrance fee is $30 per party and includes transportation on the shuttle.

A $5 backcountry permit, available from the visitor center, is required for camping in the park's interior, allowed only on Under-the-Rim Trail and Rigg's Spring Loop, both south of Bryce Point. Campfires are not permitted.

PARK HOURS

The park is open 24/7, year-round. It's in the Mountain time zone.

AUTOMOBILE SERVICE STATIONS

Just outside the park you can fuel up, get your oil and tires changed, and have car repairs done.

CELL-PHONE RECEPTION

Cell-phone reception is hit-and-miss in the park, with the visitor center and lodge your best bet. If you're getting reception, take advantage of it and make your calls. Bryce Canyon Lodge, Bryce Canyon Pines General Store, Ruby's Inn, Sunset Campground, and the visitor center all have public telephones.

EDUCATIONAL OFFERINGS
RANGER PROGRAMS

Campfire and Auditorium Programs. Bryce Canyon's natural diversity comes alive in the park's North Campground amphitheater, the Visitor Center Theater, or in the Bryce Canyon Lodge Auditorium. Lectures, multimedia programs, and ranger walks introduce you to geology, astronomy, wildlife, history, and many other topics related to Bryce Canyon and the West. ⊠ *Bryce Canyon National Park* ☎ *435/834–5322.*

Full Moon Hike. Rangers lead guided hikes on the nights around each full moon (two per month May–October). You must wear heavy-traction shoes, and reserve a spot on the day of the hike. In peak season the tickets are distributed through a lottery system. ⊠ *Bryce Canyon National Park* ⊕ *www.nps.gov.*

Geology Talk. Rangers regularly host discussions about the long geological history of Bryce Canyon; they are nearly always held at Sunset Point. Talks are free and last 30 minutes. ⊠ *Bryce Canyon National Park.*

FAMILY **Junior Ranger Program.** Children ages three and over can sign up to be Junior Rangers at the Bryce Canyon Visitor Center. The park takes that title seriously, so kids have to complete several activities in their free Junior Ranger booklet, as well as collect some litter, and attend a ranger program. Allow three to six hours for all this. Ask a ranger about each day's schedules of events and topics, or look for postings at the visitor center, Bryce Canyon Lodge, and campground bulletin boards. ⊠ *Bryce Canyon National Park.*

Fodor'sChoice **Night Sky Program.** City folk are lucky to see 2,500 stars in their artifi-
★ cially illuminated skies, but out here among the hoodoos you see three times as many. The Night Sky Program includes low-key astronomy lectures and multimedia presentations, followed by telescope viewing (weather permitting). The program is typically offered on Tuesday, Thursday, and Saturday, May through September. Check with the visitor center for locations, times, and other details. ⊠ *Bryce Canyon National Park* ☎ *435/834–4747* ☎ *Free.*

Rim Walk. Join a park ranger for a ½-mile, hour-long stroll along the gorgeous rim of Bryce Canyon starting at the Sunset Point overlook. Reservations are not required for the walk, which is usually offered daily from May to September. Start time is usually 5 pm. Check with the visitor center for details. ⊠ *Bryce Canyon National Park* ☎ *Free.*

RESTAURANTS
Dining options in the park proper are limited to Bryce Canyon Lodge; the nearby Ruby's Inn complex is your best eating bet before you pay to enter the park. The restaurants in nearby locales tend to be of the meat-and-potatoes variety. Utah's drinking laws can be confusing, so ask your server what is available: beer is more common than wine or spirits.

HOTELS
Lodging options in and around Bryce Canyon include both rustic and modern amenities, but all fill up fast in summer. Bryce Canyon Lodge is the only hotel inside the park, but there are a number of options in Bryce Canyon City, just north of the park's entrance. Panguitch and

8

Plants and Wildlife in Bryce Canyon

Due to elevations approaching 9,000 feet, many of Bryce Canyon's 400 plant species are unlike those you'll see at less lofty places. Look at exposed slopes and you might catch a glimpse of the pygmy pinyon, or the gnarled, 1,000-year-old bristlecone pine. At lower altitudes are the Douglas fir, ponderosa pine, and the quaking aspen, sitting in groves of twinkling leaves. No fewer than three kinds of sagebrush—big, black, and fringed—grow here, as well as the blue columbine.

Mule deer and chipmunks are common companions on the trails and are used to human presence. You might also catch a glimpse of the endangered Utah prairie dog. Give them a wide berth; they may be cute, but they bite. Other animals include elk, black-tailed jackrabbits, and the desert cottontail. More than 170 species of bird live in the park or pass through as a migratory stop. Bird-watchers are often rewarded handsomely for their vigilance: eagles, peregrine falcons, and even the rare California condor have all been spotted in the park.

Tropic are small towns nearby with good options for budget and last-minute travelers. *Hotel reviews have been shortened. For full information, visit Fodors.com.*

WHAT IT COSTS			
$	$$	$$$	$$$$
Restaurants	under $13	$13–$20	$21–$30	over $30
Hotels	under $101	$101–$150	$151–$200	over $200

Restaurant prices are the average cost of a main course at dinner, or if dinner is not served, at lunch. Hotel prices are the average cost of a standard double room in high season, excluding taxes and service charges.

VISITOR INFORMATION
Park Contact Information Bryce Canyon National Park. ☎ *435/834–5322* ⊕ *www.nps.gov/brca.*

VISITOR CENTER
Bryce Canyon Visitor Center. Even if you're anxious to hit the hoodoos, the visitor center, just to your right after the park-entry pay station, is the best place to start if you want to know what you're looking at and how it got there. Rangers staff a counter where you can ask questions or let them map out an itinerary of "must-sees" based on your time and physical abilities. There are also multimedia exhibits, books, maps, and backcountry camping permits for sale. First aid, emergency, and lost-and-found services are offered here, along with free Wi-Fi. Do all your phone business here; it may be the last place in the park where you get cell reception. ⊠ *Hwy. 63* ☎ *435/834–5322* ⊕ *www.nps.gov/brca.*

EXPLORING

HISTORIC SITES

Bryce Canyon Lodge. The lodge's architect, Gilbert Stanley Underwood, was a national park specialist, having designed lodges at Zion and Grand Canyon before turning his T-square to Bryce in 1923. The results are worth a visit as this National Historic Landmark has been faithfully restored, right down to the lobby's huge limestone fireplace, and log and wrought-iron chandelier. Inside the historic building are a restaurant and gift shop, as well as plenty of information on park activities. The lodge operation includes several historic log cabins nearby on the wooded grounds, just a short walk from the rim trail. ⊠ *Hwy. 63* ☎ *435/834–8700.*

SCENIC DRIVES

Fodor'sChoice **Main Park Road.** Following miles of canyon rim, this thoroughfare gives
★ access to more than a dozen scenic overlooks between the park entrance and Rainbow Point. Major overlooks are rarely more than a few minutes' walk from the parking areas, and many let you see more than 100 miles on clear days. Remember that all overlooks lie east of the road. To keep things simple, proceed to the southern end of the park and stop at the overlooks on your northbound return; they will all be on the right side of the road. Allow two to three hours to travel the entire 36-mile round-trip. The road is open year-round, but may close temporarily after heavy snowfalls. Keep your eyes open for wildlife as you drive. Trailers are not allowed at Bryce Point and Paria View, but you can park them at the parking lot across the road from the visitor center. RVs can drive throughout the park, but vehicles longer than 25 feet are not allowed at Paria View. ⊠ *Bryce Canyon National Park.*

SCENIC STOPS

Agua Canyon. This overlook in the southern section of the park, 12 miles south of the park entrance, has a nice view of several standout hoodoos. Look for the top-heavy formation called the Hunter, which actually has a few small hardy trees growing on its cap. As the rock erodes, the park evolves; snap a picture because the Hunter may look different the next time you visit. ⊠ *Bryce Canyon National Park.*

Fairyland Point. Best seen as you exit the park, this scenic overlook adjacent to Boat Mesa, ½ mile north of the visitor center and a mile off the main park road, has splendid views of Fairyland Amphitheater and its delicate, fanciful forms. The Sinking Ship and other formations stand before the grand backdrop of the Aquarius Plateau and distant Navajo Mountain. Nearby is the Fairyland Loop trailhead; it's a stunning five-hour hike in summer and a favorite of snowshoers in winter. ⊠ *Off Hwy. 63.*

Inspiration Point. Not far (1½ miles) east along the Rim Trail from Bryce Point is Inspiration Point, site of a wonderful vista on the main amphitheater and one of the best places in the park to see the sunset. (You will have plenty of company and hear a variety of languages as the sun goes down.) ⊠ *Inspiration Point Rd.*

Natural Bridge. Formed over millions of years by wind, water, and chemical erosion, this 85-foot rusty-orange arch formation—one of several rock arches in the park—is an essential photo op. Beyond the parking lot lies a rare stand of aspen trees, their leaves twinkling in the wind. Watch out for distracted drivers at this stunning viewpoint. ⊠ *Off Hwy. 63, 11 miles south of park entrance.*

Rainbow and Yovimpa Points. Separated by less than half a mile, Rainbow and Yovimpa points offer two fine panoramas facing opposite directions. Rainbow Point's best view is to the north overlooking the southern rim of the amphitheater and giving a glimpse of Grand Staircase–Escalante National Monument; Yovimpa Point's vista spreads out to the south. On a clear day you can see all the way to Arizona, 100 miles away. Yovimpa Point also has a shady and quiet picnic area with tables and restrooms. You can hike between them on the easy Bristlecone Loop Trail or tackle the more strenuous 8¾-mile Riggs Spring Loop Trail, which passes the tallest point in the park. This is the outermost auto stop on the main road, so visitors often drive here first and make it their starting point, then work their way back to the main gate. ⊠ *Off Hwy. 63, 18 miles south of park entrance.*

Fodor's Choice ★ **Sunrise Point.** Named for its stunning views at dawn, this overlook is a short walk from Bryce Canyon Lodge, 2 miles south of the park entrance, and so one of the park's most popular stops. It's also the trailhead for the Queen's Garden Trail and the Fairyland Loop Trail. You have to descend the Queen's Garden Trail to get a glimpse of the regal **Queen Victoria,** a hoodoo that appears to sport a crown and glorious full skirt. The trail is popular and marked clearly, but moderately strenuous with 350 feet of elevation change. ⊠ *Off Hwy. 63.*

Sunset Point. Watch the late-day sun paint the hoodoos here. You can see **Thor's Hammer,** a delicate formation similar to a balanced rock, from the rim, but when you hike 550 feet down into the amphitheater on the Navajo Loop Trail you can walk through the famous and very popular Wall Street—a deep, shady "slot" canyon. The point is 2 miles south of the park entrance near Bryce Canyon Lodge. ⊠ *Bryce Canyon National Park.*

SPORTS AND THE OUTDOORS

Most visitors explore Bryce Canyon by car, but the hiking trails are far more rewarding. At these elevations, you'll have to stop to catch your breath more often than you're used to. It gets warm in summer but rarely uncomfortably hot, so hiking farther into the depths of the park is not difficult, so long as you don't pick a hike that is beyond your abilities.

AIR TOURS

OUTFITTERS

Bryce Canyon Airlines & Helicopters. For a bird's-eye view of Bryce Canyon National Park, take a dramatic helicopter ride or airplane tour over the fantastic sandstone formations. Longer full-canyon tours and added excursions to sites such as the Grand Canyon, Monument Valley, or Zion are also offered. Flight time can last anywhere from 35 minutes to four hours; family and group rates are available. ☎ *435/834–8060* ⊕ *www.rubysinn.com/scenic-flights* ✉ *From $110.*

BIRD-WATCHING

More than 170 bird species have been identified in Bryce. Violet-green swallows and white-throated swifts are common, as are Steller's jays, American coots, rufous hummingbirds, and mountain bluebirds. Lucky bird-watchers will see golden eagles floating across the skies above the pink rocks of the amphitheater, and experienced birders might spot an osprey nest high in the canyon wall. The best time in the park for avian variety is from May through July.

HIKING

To get up close and personal with the park's hoodoos, set aside a half day to hike into the amphitheater. There are no elevators, so remember that after you descend below the rim you'll have to get back up. The air gets warmer the lower you go, and the altitude will have you huffing and puffing unless you're a mountain native. The uneven terrain calls for lace-up shoes on even the well-trodden, high-traffic trails and sturdy hiking boots for the more challenging ones. No below-rim trails are paved. For trail maps, information, and ranger recommendations, stop at the visitor center. Bathrooms are at most trailheads but not down in the amphitheater.

EASY

Bristlecone Loop Trail. This 1-mile trail with a modest 200 feet of elevation gain lets you see the park from its highest points of more than 9,000 feet, alternating between spruce and fir forest and wide-open vistas across the Grand Staircase–Escalante National Monument and beyond. You might see yellow-bellied marmots and dusky grouse, critters not found at lower elevations in the park. The most challenging part of the hike is ungluing your eyes from the scenery long enough to read the signage at the many trail forks. Plan on 45 minutes to an hour. *Easy.* ✉ *Bryce Canyon National Park* ✛ *Trailhead: at Rainbow Point parking area, 18 miles south of park entrance.*

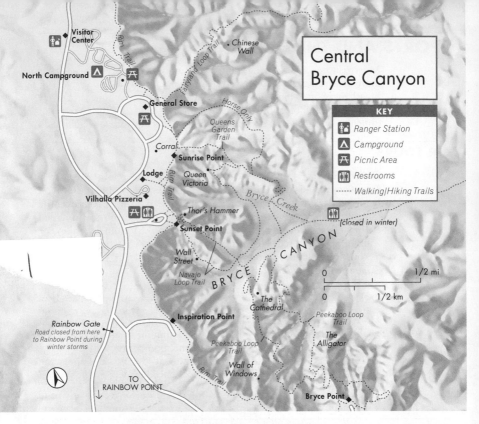

Map labels:

Visitor Center

North Campground

General Store

Chinese Wall

Fairyland Loop Trail

Rim Trail

Horse Only

Queens Garden Trail

Corral

Sunrise Point

Lodge

Queen Victoria

Vilhalla Pizzeria

Rim Trail

Thor's Hammer

Bryce Creek

Sunset Point

Wall Street

Navajo Loop Trail

BRYCE CANYON

(closed in winter)

The Cathedral

Inspiration Point

Peekaboo Loop Trail

The Alligator

Peekaboo Loop Trail

Rainbow Gate
Road closed from here
to Rainbow Point during
winter storms

Wall of Windows

Rim Trail

Bryce Point

TO RAINBOW POINT

**Central
Bryce Canyon**

KEY	
🧍	Ranger Station
⛺	Campground
🪵	Picnic Area
🚻	Restrooms
- - -	Walking/Hiking Trails

0   1/2 mi

0   1/2 km

FAMILY   **Queen's Garden Trail.** This hike is the easiest way down into the amphi-
Fodor's Choice theater, with 350 feet of elevation change leading to a short tunnel,
★   quirky hoodoos, and lots of like-minded hikers. It's the essential Bryce
"sampler." Allow two hours total to hike the 1½-mile trail plus the
½-mile rim-side path and back. *Easy.* ⊠ *Bryce Canyon National Park*
⊹ *Trailhead: at Sunrise Point, 2 miles south of park entrance.*

MODERATE

FAMILY   **Navajo Loop Trail.** One of Bryce's most popular and dramatic attractions
is this steep descent via a series of switchbacks leading to Wall Street, a
claustrophobic hallway of rock only 20 feet wide in places with walls 100
feet high. After a walk through the Silent City, the northern end of the
trail brings Thor's Hammer into view. A well-marked intersection offers
a shorter way back or continuing on the Queen's Garden Trail to Sunrise
Point. For the short version allow at least an hour on this 1½-mile trail
with 550 feet of elevation change. *Moderate.* ⊠ *Bryce Canyon National
Park* ⊹ *Trailhead: at Sunset Point, 2 miles south of park entrance.*

FAMILY   **Navajo/Queen's Garden Combination Loop.** By walking this extended
Fodor's Choice 3-mile loop, you can see some of the best of Bryce; it takes a little
★   more than two hours. The route passes fantastic formations and an
open forest of pine and juniper on the amphitheater floor. Descend into

the amphitheater from Sunrise Point on the Queen's Garden Trail and ascend via the Navajo Loop Trail; return to your starting point via the Rim Trail. *Moderate.* ⊠ *Bryce Canyon National Park* ⚓ *Trailheads: at Sunset and Sunrise points, 2 miles south of park entrance.*

DIFFICULT

Fairyland Loop Trail. Hike into whimsical Fairyland Canyon on this trail that gets more strenuous and less crowded as you progress along its 8 miles. It winds around hoodoos, across trickles of water, and finally to a natural window in the rock at Tower Bridge, 1½ miles from Sunrise Point and 4 miles from Fairyland Point. The pink-and-white badlands and hoodoos surround you the whole way. Don't feel like you have to go the whole distance to make it worthwhile. But if you do, allow at least five hours for the round-trip with 1,700 feet of elevation change. You can pick up the loop at Fairyland Point or Sunrise Point. *Difficult.* ⊠ *Bryce Canyon National Park* ⚓ *Trailheads: at Fairyland Point, 1 mile off main park road, 1 mile south of park entrance; Sunrise Point, 2 miles south of park entrance.*

Hat Shop Trail. The sedimentary haberdashery sits 2 miles from the trailhead. Hard gray caps balance precariously atop narrow pedestals of softer, rust-color rock. Allow three to four hours to travel this strenuous but rewarding 4-mile round-trip trail, the first part of the longer Under-the-Rim Trail. *Difficult.* ⊠ *Bryce Canyon National Park* ⚓ *Trailhead: at Bryce Point, 2 miles off main park road, 5½ miles south of park entrance.*

Peekaboo Loop. The reward of this steep trail is the Wall of Windows and the Three Wise Men. Horses use this trail in spring, summer, and fall and have the right-of-way. Start at Bryce, Sunrise, or Sunset Point and allow four to five hours to hike the 5-mile trail or 7-mile double-loop. *Difficult.* ⊠ *Bryce Canyon National Park* ⚓ *Trailheads: at Bryce Point, 2 miles off main park road, 5½ miles south of park entrance; Sunrise and Sunset points, 2 miles south of park entrance.*

Under-the-Rim Trail. Starting at Bryce Point, the trail travels 23 miles to Rainbow Point, passing through the Pink Cliffs, traversing Agua Canyon and Ponderosa Canyon, and taking you by several springs. Most of the hike is on the amphitheater floor, characterized by up-and-down terrain among stands of ponderosa pine; the elevation change totals about 1,500 feet. It's the park's longest trail, but four trailheads along the main park road allow you to connect to the Under-the-Rim Trail and cover its length as a series of day hikes. Allow at least two days to hike the route in its entirety, and although it's not a hoodoo-heavy hike there's plenty to see to make it a more leisurely three-day affair. *Difficult.* ⊠ *Bryce Canyon National Park* ⚓ *Trailheads: at Bryce Point, Swamp Canyon, Ponderosa Canyon, and Rainbow Point.*

HORSEBACK RIDING

Many of the park's hiking trails were first formed beneath the hooves of cattle wranglers. Today, hikers and riders share the trails. A number of outfitters can set you up with a gentle mount and lead you to the park's best sights. Not only can you cover more ground than you would walking, but equine traffic has the right-of-way at all times. Call ahead to the stables for reservations to find a trip that's right for you, from 90 minutes to all day. The biggest outfitters have more than 100 horses and mules to choose from. People under the age of seven or who weigh more than 220 pounds are prohibited from riding.

TOURS AND OUTFITTERS

Canyon Trail Rides. Descend to the floor of the Bryce Canyon amphitheater via horse or mule—most visitors have no riding experience so don't hesitate to join in. A two-hour ride ambles along the amphitheater floor through the Queen's Garden before returning to Sunrise Point. The half-day expedition follows Peekaboo Loop Trail, winds past the Fairy Castle, and passes the Wall of Windows before returning to Sunrise Point. Two rides a day of each type leave in the morning and early afternoon. Trips can now be booked online; there are no rides in winter. ☒ *Bryce Canyon Lodge, Off Hwy. 63* ☎ *435/679–8665* ⊕ *www. canyonrides.com* ☒ *$65 for 2 hrs; $90 for ½-day excursion.*

FAMILY **Ruby's Horseback Adventures.** Ride to the rim of Bryce Canyon, venture through narrow slot canyons in Grand Staircase–Escalante National Monument, or even retrace the trails taken by outlaw Butch Cassidy more than 100 years ago. Rides last from one hour to all day. Kids must be seven or older to ride, in some cases 10. Wagon rides to the rim of Bryce Canyon are available for all ages, as are sleigh rides in winter. ☒ *Bryce Canyon National Park* ☎ *866/782–0002* ⊕ *www.horserides.net* ☒ *From $55.*

WINTER SPORTS

Unlike Utah's other national parks, Bryce Canyon receives plenty of snow, making it a popular cross-country ski area. Rim Trail, Paria Loop, and other paths above the canyon are popular destinations. The visitor center sells shoe-traction devices, and some of the ranger-guided snowshoe activities include snowshoes and poles.

OUTFITTERS

FAMILY **Ruby's Winter Activities Center.** This facility grooms miles of private, no-cost trails that connect to the ungroomed trails inside the park. Rental snowshoes, ice skates, and cross-country ski equipment are available. ☒ *Hwy. 63, 1 mile north of park entrance* ☎ *435/834–5341* ⊕ *www. rubysinn.com/winter-activities.*

SHOPPING

Ruby's General Store. It may not be one of the area's geological wonders, but this giant mercantile center almost has to be seen to be believed. On a busy evening it is bustling with tourists plucking through souvenirs that range from sweatshirts to wind chimes. There is also Western wear, children's toys, a holiday-gift gallery, and groceries. Even the camping equipment is in ample supply. Need a folding stove, sleeping bag, or fishing gear? You will find it at Ruby's. You can also cross Main Street to where this ever-expanding complex has added a line of shops trimmed like an Old West town, complete with candy store and rock shop. ☒ *26 S. Main St.* ☎ *435/834–5484.*

WHAT'S NEARBY

Bryce Canyon is a bit off the beaten path, often a side trip for those who visit Zion National Park to the southwest, and far from major roads or large cities (both Las Vegas and Salt Lake City are approximately 270 miles away). The park is just one of a number of beautiful or unique natural areas in southern Utah worth exploring. Towns close to the park pulse with Western personality and are excellent bases for exploring the entire area. To the west, Red Canyon offers an array of activities not available inside the park, such as mountain biking. The expansive and remote Grand Staircase–Escalante National Monument is about an hour to the northeast. Nearby state parks Escalante Petrified Forest and Kodachrome Basin make for great side trips.

NEARBY TOWNS

Panguitch calls itself the "Center of Scenic Utah," and it's an accurate moniker. The small town 25 miles from Bryce Canyon has restaurants, motels, gas stations, and trinket shops. About 47 miles northeast of Bryce, **Escalante** has modern amenities and is a western gateway to the Grand Staircase–Escalante National Monument. If you're traveling through southwestern Utah on Interstate 15, **Cedar City** will be your exit to Bryce. The largest city you'll encounter in this part of Utah, it's 78 miles from Bryce Canyon. Southern Utah University is here, and the Utah Shakespeare Festival on its campus draws theater buffs from all over the country.

Visitor Information Cedar City/Brian Head Tourism Bureau. ✉ *581 N. Main St., Cedar City* ☎ *800/354-4849, 435/586-5124* ⊕ *www.scenicsouthernutah.com.* **Escalante Interagency Visitor Center.** ✉ *755 W. Main St., Escalante* ☎ *435/826-5499* ⊕ *www.blm.gov.* **Garfield County Travel Council (Panguitch).** ✉ *55 S. Main St., Panguitch* ☎ *800/444-6689* ⊕ *www.brycecanyoncountry.com.*

8

NEARBY ATTRACTIONS

Cedar Breaks National Monument. From the rim of Cedar Breaks, 23 miles east of Cedar City, a natural amphitheater plunges 2,000 feet into the Markagunt Plateau. Short hiking trails along the rim make this a wonderful summer stop, especially for Cedar City or Shakespeare festival visitors not planning to visit the Zion or Bryce park. ✉ *Hwy. 14, Brian Head* ☎ *435/586-9451* ⊕ *www.nps.gov/cebr* 🖭 *$6.*

Dixie National Forest. The forest's expansive natural area is divided into four noncontiguous swaths covering a total of nearly 2 million acres. Adjacent to three national parks, two national monuments, and several state parks, the forest has 26 campgrounds in a variety of backdrops lakeside, mountainside, and in the depths of pine and spruce forests. Recreational opportunities abound, including hiking, picnicking, horseback riding, and fishing. ✉ *Dixie National Forest Headquarters, 1789 N. Wedgewood La., Cedar City* ☎ *435/865-3700* ⊕ *www.fs.usda.gov/dixie* 🖭 *Free.*

FAMILY **Escalante Petrified Forest State Park.** This state park was created to protect a huge repository of petrified wood, easily spotted along two moderate-to-strenuous hiking trails. Of equal interest to area locals and visitors is the park's Wide Hollow Reservoir at the base of the hiking trails, which has a swimming beach and is good for boating, fishing, and birding. ⊠ *710 N. Reservoir Rd., Escalante* ☎ *435/826–4466* ⊕ *www. stateparks.utah.gov* ☜ *$8.*

FAMILY **Grand Staircase–Escalante National Monument.** In September 1996, President Bill Clinton designated 1.7 million acres in south-central Utah as Grand Staircase–Escalante National Monument. Its three distinct sections—the Grand Staircase, the Kaiparowits Plateau, and the Canyons of the Escalante—offer remote backcountry experiences hard to find elsewhere in the Lower 48. Waterfalls, shoulder-width slot canyons, and improbable colors all characterize this wilderness. Highway 12, which straddles the northern border of the monument, is one of the most scenic stretches in the Southwest. The small towns of Escalante and Boulder offer outfitters, lodging, and dining. ⊠ *Kanab* ☎ *435/644–1200* ⊕ *www.blm.gov* ☜ *Free.*

FAMILY **Kodachrome Basin State Park.** Yes, it is named after the old-fashioned color photo film; once you see it you'll understand why the National Geographic Society gave it the name. The stone spires known as "sand pipes" cannot be found anywhere else in the world. Hike any of the trails to spot some of the 67 pipes in and around the park. The short Angels Palace Trail takes you quickly into the park's interior, up, over, and around some of the badlands. ⊠ *Cottonwood Canyon Rd., Cannonville* ☎ *435/679–8562* ⊕ *www.stateparks.utah. gov* ☜ *$8.*

AREA ACTIVITIES

SPORTS AND THE OUTDOORS

BICYCLING

Hell's Backbone Road. For a scenic and challenging mountain-bike ride, follow the 44-mile Hell's Backbone Road from Panguitch to the Escalante region and beyond. The route, also known as Highway 12, gives riders stunning views and a half-dozen quaint townships as a reward for the steep grades. The road begins 7 miles south of Panguitch.

TOURS AND OUTFITTERS

Excursions of Escalante. Hiking, backpacking, photography, and canyoneering tours in the Escalante region are custom-fit to your needs and abilities by experienced guides. Canyoneers will be taken into the slot canyons to move through slot chutes or rappel down walls and other obstacles. All gear and provisions are provided whether it's a day hike or multiday adventure. ⊠ *125 E. Main St., Escalante* ☎ *800/839–7567* ⊕ *excursionsofescalante.com* ☜ *From $155.*

SCENIC DRIVES

FodorsChoice **Highway 12 Scenic Byway.** Keep your camera handy and steering wheel
★ steady along this route between Escalante and Loa, near Capitol Reef
National Park. Though the highway starts at the intersection of U.S.
89, west of Bryce Canyon National Park, the stretch that begins in
Escalante is one of the most spectacular. The road passes through Grand
Staircase–Escalante National Monument and on to Capitol Reef along
one of the most scenic stretches of highway in the United States. Be
sure to stop at the scenic overlooks; almost every one will give you an
eye-popping view, and information panels let you know what you're
looking at. Don't get distracted while driving, though; the paved road
is twisting and steep, and at times climbs over a hogback with sheer
drop-offs on both sides.

U.S. 89/Utah's Heritage Highway. Winding north from the Arizona border
all the way to Spanish Fork Canyon an hour south of Salt Lake City,
U.S. 89 is known as the Heritage Highway for its role in shaping Utah
history. At its southern end, Kanab is known as "Little Hollywood,"
having provided the backdrop for many famous Western movies and TV
commercials. The town has since grown considerably to accommodate
tourists who flock here to see where Ronald Reagan once slept and Clint
Eastwood drew his guns. Other towns north along this famous road
may not have the same notoriety in these parts, but they do provide a
quiet, uncrowded, and inexpensive place to stay near Zion and Bryce
Canyon National Parks. East of Kanab, U.S. 89 runs along the southern
edge of the Grand Staircase–Escalante National Monument.

WHERE TO EAT

IN THE PARK

$$$ ✕**Bryce Canyon Lodge.** Set among towering pines, this historic lodge, 2
AMERICAN miles south of the park entrance, is the featured place to dine within
the park. Designated as a certified Green Restaurant, the menu includes
organic, regional foods with choices ranging from Utah trout and prime
rib to creative vegetarian-friendly entrées. **Known for:** stone fireplace;
can accommodate special diets; rustic decor. $ *Average main: $27*
✉ *Hwy. 63* ☎ *435/834-8700* ⊕ *www.brycecanyonforever.com/dining*
☽ *Closed early Nov.–late Mar.*

$ ✕**Valhalla Pizzeria & Coffee Shop.** A former recreation room across the
ITALIAN parking lot from Bryce Canyon Lodge was converted into this 40-seat
FAMILY fast-casual pizzeria and coffee shop that offers breakfast and dinner.
Breakfast choices include homemade pastries and fresh fruit, or kick
back on the tranquil patio in the evening and enjoy fresh pizza made
from organic ingredients, along with your choice of beer or wine.
Known for: quick bites; friendly staff; pizza by the slice or whole.
$ *Average main: $10* ✉ *Off Hwy. 63* ✢ *2 miles south of park entrance*
☎ *435/834-8709* ⊕ *www.brycecanyonforever.com/pizza* ☽ *Closed mid-
Oct.–mid-May. No lunch.*

8

PICNIC AREAS

FAMILY **North Campground.** Across the road and slightly east of the Bryce Canyon visitor center, this campground includes several sites for tents and RVs, as well as access to scenic trails, a general store, and picnic area. ✉ *Bryce Canyon National Park* 🎫 *$30 per night.*

Yovimpa Point. At the southern end of the park, 18 miles south of the park entrance, this shady, quiet spot has tables and restrooms nearby. A short walk leads to the edge of the Paunsaugunt Plateau and offers long-distance, panoramic views. ✉ *Bryce Canyon National Park.*

OUTSIDE THE PARK

$$ AMERICAN 🍴 **Bryce Canyon Restaurant.** Part of the Bryce Canyon Pines motel, about 15 miles west of Tropic, this cozy eatery is only minutes from Bryce Canyon National Park and offers large portions of homemade fare, including soups and a famed selection of pies. **Known for:** homemade soups and pies; rustic charm; family-friendly. [$] *Average main: $15* ✉ *Hwy. 12, mile marker 10* ☎ *800/892–7923* 🌐 *www.brycecanyonmotel.com.*

$ ITALIAN Fodor's Choice ★ 🍴 **Centro Woodfired Pizzeria.** You can watch your handmade artisanal pizza being pulled from the fires of the brick oven, then sit back and enjoy a seasonal pie layered with ingredients such as house-made fennel sausage and wood-roasted cremini mushrooms. The creamy vanilla gelato layered with a balsamic reduction and sea salt is highly addictive. **Known for:** house-made sausage; thin crusts; creative desserts. [$] *Average main: $12* ✉ *50 W. Center St., Cedar City* ☎ *435/867–8123* 🕒 *Closed Sun.*

$$ AMERICAN 🍴 **Cowboy Blues.** This locals' favorite serves up bountiful American food in a rustic Old West setting and keeps it real by sourcing its Black Angus beef from Southern Utah ranches and plucking seasonal vegetables from a local garden. You can enjoy a cocktail or beer on the patio, along with a serving of the eatery's one-of-a-kind jalapeño poppers. **Known for:** outdoor dining; blue margaritas; BBQ ribs. [$] *Average main: $15* ✉ *530 W. Main St., Escalante* ☎ *435/826–4577* 🌐 *www.cowboyblues.net.*

$$ AMERICAN 🍴 **Cowboy's Smokehouse Café.** From the Western-style interior and creaky floors to the smoker out back, this rustic café has an aura of Texan authenticity with cowboy collectibles and game trophies lining the walls. No surprise that barbecue is the specialty here, with ample portions of favorites such as ribs, mesquite-flavored beef and pulled pork, and the restaurant's own house-made sauce. **Known for:** rustic charm; big steaks; sausage platter. [$] *Average main: $18* ✉ *95 N. Main St., Panguitch* ☎ *435/676–8030* 🌐 *www.thecowboysmokehouse.com* 💳 *No credit cards* 🕒 *Closed Sun.*

$$ CAFÉ 🍴 **Escalante Outfitters.** When you're spent after a day of exploration, this is a great place to sit back and relax. Try one of the build-your-own pizzas, known for fresh, local ingredients such as applewood bacon and slow-roasted tomatoes, and pair it with an icy Utah microbrew. **Known for:** hearty pizzas; casual space; delicious coffee. [$] *Average main: $17* ✉ *310 W. Main St., Escalante* ☎ *435/826–4266* 🌐 *www.escalanteoutfitters.com.*

$$ STEAKHOUSE 🍴 **Foster's Family Steakhouse.** This steak house is known for its prime rib and sautéed mushrooms, but you'll also find seafood on the menu. Whatever you choose, be sure to leave room for dessert—try the namesake mixed-berry pie that includes raspberries, rhubarb, and strawberries. **Known for:** prime rib; homemade pies; takeout bakery. [$] *Average main: $15* ✉ *1150 Hwy. 12* ☎ *435/834–5227* 🌐 *www.fostersmotel.com* 🕒 *Closed Dec. and Jan.*

$$$ STEAKHOUSE 🍴 **Milt's Stage Stop.** Locals and an increasing number of tourists have discovered the lodgelike surroundings, friendly service, and canyon views at this dinner spot a 10-minute drive from Cedar City. It's known for traditional, hearty steak house cuisine: rib-eye steaks, prime rib, seafood dishes, and a sizable salad bar, accompanied by loaded baked potatoes and other sides. **Known for:** steaks and seafood; salad bar; warm desserts. [$] *Average main: $25* ✉ *3560 E. Hwy. 14, Cedar City* ☎ *435/586–9344* 🌐 *www.miltsstagestop.com* 🕒 *No lunch.*

WHERE TO STAY

IN THE PARK

$$$$ HOTEL Fodor's Choice ★ 🏨 **Bryce Canyon Lodge.** This historic, rugged stone-and-wood lodge close to the amphitheater's rim offers motel-style rooms with semiprivate balconies or porches and cozy lodgepole pine cabins, some with cathedral ceilings and gas fireplaces. **Pros:** lodging close to canyon rim, trails; fine dining, pizzeria, and coffee shop on-site; cabins have fireplaces. **Cons:** closed in winter; books up fast; no TV. [$] *Rooms from: $202* ✉ *Off Hwy. 63* ☎ *435/834–8700, 877/386–4383* 🌐 *www.brycecanyonforever.com* 🕒 *Closed Jan. and Feb.* 🛏 *113 rooms* 🍽 *No meals.*

OUTSIDE THE PARK

$$ B&B/INN 🏨 **Bard's Inn Bed and Breakfast.** Rooms in this restored turn-of-the-20th-century house are named after famous characters from Shakespeare's plays and handcrafted quilts grace the beds. **Pros:** immaculate rooms; all rooms have private baths; close to historic downtown. **Cons:** thin walls and creaky floors; books up fast for festival season. [$] *Rooms from: $119* ✉ *150 S. 100 W, Cedar City* ☎ *435/586–6612* 🌐 *www.thebardsinn.com* 🕒 *Closed Sept.–May* 🛏 *8 rooms* 🍽 *Breakfast.*

$$$$ HOTEL 🏨 **Best Western Bryce Canyon Grand Hotel.** If you're into creature comforts but can do without charm, this four-story hotel is the place—rooms are relatively posh, with comfortable mattresses, pillows, and bedding, spacious bathrooms, and modern appliances. **Pros:** clean, spacious rooms; lots of indoor amenities. **Cons:** no pets allowed; breakfast can get crowded. [$] *Rooms from: $209* ✉ *30 N. 100 E* ☎ *866/866–6634, 435/834–5700* 🌐 *www.brycecanyongrand.com* 🛏 *164 rooms* 🍽 *Breakfast.*

$$ HOTEL 🏨 **Best Western Plus Ruby's Inn.** This bustling Southwestern-themed hotel has expanded over the years to include various wings with rooms that vary widely in terms of size and appeal. **Pros:** one-stop shopping for tours, amenities. **Cons:** can get very busy, especially when the big tour buses roll in; too big for charm or a quiet getaway. [$] *Rooms from: $150*

8

CLOSE UP

Best Campgrounds in Bryce Canyon

The two campgrounds in Bryce Canyon National Park fill up fast, especially in summer, and are family-friendly. All are drive-in, except for the handful of backcountry sites that only backpackers and gung-ho day hikers ever see. Both campgrounds completed a welcome renovation of their restrooms and shared facilities in 2012.

North Campground. A cool, shady retreat in a forest of ponderosa pines, this is a great home base for your exploration of Bryce Canyon. You're near the general store, trailheads, and the visitor center. ✉ *Main park road, ½ mile south of visitor center* ☎ *435/834–5322.*

Sunset Campground. This serene alpine campground is within walking distance of Bryce Canyon Lodge and many trailheads. All sites are filled on a first-come, first-served basis. ✉ *Main park road, 2 miles south of visitor center* ☎ *435/834–5322.*

✉ *26 S. Main St.* ☎ *435/834–5341, 866/866–6616* 🌐 *www.rubysinn.com* 🛏 *381 rooms* 🍴 *No meals.*

$$ HOTEL 🏨 **Bryce Canyon Pines.** Most rooms in this motel complex tucked into the woods 6 miles from the park entrance have excellent mountain views. **Pros:** guided horseback rides; close to park entrance. **Cons:** thin walls; room quality varies widely. [$] *Rooms from: $130* ✉ *Hwy. 12* ✣ *6 miles northwest of park entrance on Rte. 12* ☎ *800/892–7923* 🌐 *brycecanyonmotel.com* 🛏 *46 rooms.*

$$ HOTEL 🏨 **Bryce View Lodge.** Near the park entrance on Route 63, this motel is a practical, reasonably priced option, with clean rooms and access to the pool and other amenities across the way at the Best Western Plus Ruby's Inn, its sister property. **Pros:** good location for park access; less pricey than surrounding hotels; guided ATV and horseback riding available. **Cons:** a bit dated inside and out. [$] *Rooms from: $120* ✉ *105 E. Center St., Bryce Canyon City* ☎ *435/834–5180, 888/279–2304* 🌐 *www.bryceviewlodge.com* 🛏 *160 rooms* 🍴 *No meals.*

$$ B&B/INN 🏨 **Escalante's Grand Staircase Bed & Breakfast Inn.** Rooms are set apart from the main house, giving this property some motel-type privacy along with bed-and-breakfast amenities. **Pros:** spacious rooms; Wi-Fi. **Cons:** no pets. [$] *Rooms from: $142* ✉ *280 W. Main St., Escalante* ☎ *435/826–4890* 🌐 *www.escalantebnb.com* 🛏 *8 rooms* 🍴 *Breakfast.*

$ HOTEL 🏨 **Escalante Outfitters.** A good option if you want a one-stop place to plan and buy gear for your outdoor adventure, or if you're traveling on a budget and don't care about amenities. **Pros:** the food is a pleasant surprise; pet-friendly. **Cons:** right on the highway; you may have to wait in line for a shower. [$] *Rooms from: $55* ✉ *310 W. Main St., Escalante* ☎ *435/826–4266* 🌐 *www.escalanteoutfitters.com* 🛏 *8 cabins* 🍴 *No meals.*

SOUTHWESTERN UTAH

Updated by
Aly Capito

Just two hours of desert highway northbound from the glittering lights of Las Vegas is one of the most beautiful and unique regions of the United States. The area's brightest city, St. George, leads you far and wide across the amazing landscapes of Southwestern Utah. From Snow Canyon and its beautiful white and red Navajo sandstone with blackened blankets of lava, to Gunlock State Beach where camping, swimming, and hiking, adventure and sightseeing awaits.

Southwestern Utah has been dubbed "The Unexpected Southwest." It is a landscape of thrills and adrenaline, and a place to find relaxation and retreat at its renowned spas and luxury country clubs. This is the place where everyone in the family can find what they love to do. Rejuvenate yourself at a spa, or in the beauty of the wild red cliffs and history surrounding you. Take the mountain trails by bike or by foot. Entertainment and dining options bring worldly cultures and experiences to St. George, Utah's quaint summer paradise. Ruins, petroglyphs, pioneer graffiti, and ghost towns—monuments to what once was—continue to beckon explorers.

ORIENTATION AND PLANNING

GETTING ORIENTED

Southwestern Utah is remarkable in the range of activities and terrain it has to offer. On one summer day you can explore an arid desert canyon at Snow Canyon State Park (named for the settlers of the canyon, not actual snow). Next you can camp in a beautiful high-alpine aspen grove within Dixie National Forest; here snow is plenty, so be sure to bundle up. In winter you can try mountain biking at Gooseberry Mesa near Hurricane, and cut the slopes skiing at Brian Head Resort on the same trip.

Utah's Dixie. Many of southwestern Utah's Mormon settlers arrived from the American South and brought the name "Dixie" with them. St. George, the main population center in this area, is often the hottest place in the state—not just in temperature, but in culture, activities, and tourist attractions. Locals from the north migrate here during cold months, and the region has earned a second nickname: Utah's Miami.

Grand Staircase–Escalante National Monument. Three distinct sections define the 1.7 million acres of this region—the Grand Staircase, the Kaiparowits Plateau, and the Canyons of the Escalante. Here, among the waterfalls, Native American ruins and petroglyphs, and slot canyons, improbable colors abound.

TOP REASONS TO GO

Lava-capped mountains: As you hike along the lower trails of Snow Canyon State Park, look up to see ridges formed by lava from eruptions that may have happened as recently as 20,000 years ago.

Travel through history: Imagine travel in pioneer days in the one restored stagecoach that visitors can hop aboard at Iron Mission State Park Museum.

Drive the Scenic Byway: Highway 12 begins in Escalante and passes through Grand Staircase–Escalante National Monument. As it continues on to Capitol Reef National Park,

you can enjoy the spectacular views along with some hair-raising twists and turns.

Shakespeare and more: Watch productions such as *Othello* on a stage that replicates the old Globe Theatre during the Utah Shakespeare Festival.

Move in dinosaur herds: The St. George Dinosaur Discovery Site at Johnson Farm is a fantastic visit for anyone of any age. Fun Fact: This site would be developed land today if ancient footprints hadn't been accidentally unearthed by a backhoe in 2000.

PLANNING

WHEN TO GO

Year-round, far southwestern Utah is the warmest region in the state. St. George is usually the first city in Utah to break 100°F every summer, and even the winters remain mild at these lower desert elevations. Despite the summer's heat, most people visit SW Utah from June to September, making the off-season winter months pleasantly uncrowded. Utahns from the north tend to stay away from the southern parts of the state during peak months and tend to visit more often in the winter. But if you decide to brave the heat, wear sunscreen and drink lots of water, regardless of your activity level.

Do prepare for the increased elevation if you are from a region that is found below sea level. Elevation sickness can put a snag in anyone's travel plans. You may not think of it so much in St. George, but farther east around the Brian Head–Cedar Breaks National Monument, elevations can surpass 9,000 feet. At this altitude, the warm summer sun is perfect against the coolness of the alpine forests throughout the day. The resort here offers plenty to do throughout the year. Winter sports may still dominate this area, but summer recreation leaves you wanting for nothing; some of the finest hiking and mountain biking trails can be found here.

PLANNING YOUR TIME

No matter which part you visit or what adventure you're pursuing, driving time will take up a fair number of your hours. Be sure to leave time to take in the awe-inspiring scenery along your drive.

Find what you love here in the Southwest. Zion National Park and Grand Staircase–Escalante experiences are more outdoorsy and exhilarating for some, while others may prefer the St. Geroge

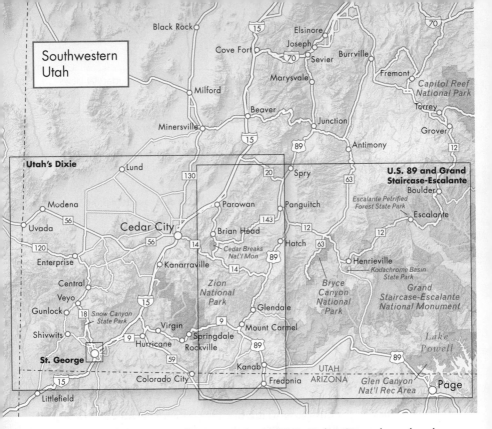

Southwestern Utah

Utah's Dixie

U.S. 89 and Grand Staircase-Escalante

downtown walking tour. Artsy? Visit Cedar City, where the playwright Shakespeare still holds the stage at The Professional Theatre at South Utah University.

Springdale or Hurricane are two smaller towns ideal for exploring Zion National Park; St. George and Cedar City offer great nightlife.

GETTING HERE AND AROUND
AIR TRAVEL
SkyWest flies to St. George Municipal Airport (SGU), and operates as a carrier for both United Express and Delta Connection flights. You can fly from just about any airport in the country straight to St. George.

Las Vegas's McCarran International Airport is 116 miles south of St. George. Drive, or take a shuttle so you can observe the open road free of distraction. The St. George Shuttle makes nine trips a day between the two cities.

Coming from up north? Aztec Shuttle provides round-trip service from Salt Lake City, with stops in St. George and Cedar City. Reservations are required, so be sure to plan ahead.

Airport Contacts McCarran International Airport (Las Vegas). ✉ 5757 Wayne Newton Blvd., Las Vegas ☎ 702/261 5211 General Information, 702/261–6100 McCarran Rent-A-Car Center ⊕ www.mccarran.com. **St. George**

Municipal Airport (SGU). ✉ *4550 S. Airport Way, St. George* ☎ *435/627–4080* ⊕ *www.flysgu.com.*

Airport Shuttle Aztec Shuttle. ☎ *435/656 9040* ⊕ *www.aztecshuttle.com.* **St. George Shuttle.** ✉ *1215 E. Redhills Pkwy., St. George* ☎ *435/628–8320,* *800/933–8320* ⊕ *www.stgshuttle.com.*

CAR TRAVEL

Interstate 15 is the main corridor through Utah. It reaches from St. George, through Salt Lake City, and on to Idaho, and traffic usually isn't an issue. If you're looking for the scenic tour, consider taking U.S. 89 just east of I–15. With access to Bryce Canyon National Park, the eastern side of Zion National Park, and the Kanab area, U.S. 89 travels a more natural north-south route.

When heading east or west, Highways 143 and 14 are both well-kept routes you can take.

Highway 9 is the primary access to Springdale and Zion National Park. ■**TIP→** If you need to travel between I-15 and U.S. 89 via Route 9 during the day, you must pay the $25 admission fee to Zion National Park even if you do not plan to stop and visit.

Access to the massive and remote Grand Staircase–Escalante National Monument is via Highway 12 to the north and U.S. 89 to the south.

In winter the primary access roads to Brian Head and Cedar Breaks National Monument may be closed for snow removal (Highway 143 from the north and east) or for the entirety of the season (Highway 148 from the south) from November 1 to March 1.

Utah Department of Transportation provides a free, up-to-the minute interactive state map for drivers. You can also download their app (⊕ *udottraffic.utah.gov*).

When traveling in states with extreme weather and terrain, always be sure to have a physical map with you. Mobile service and Wi-Fi will not always be available. The Utah Department of Tourism provides free state maps to anyone. Call ☎ *800/200–1160* to request yours, or purchase from any convenience store along the way.

RESTAURANTS

In the southwestern corner of the state, traditional and contemporary American cuisines are most common and reflect the pioneer heritage of the region. Mexican and American Southwest influences are also apparent throughout the region.

For the most diverse dining options, stops in St. George and Springdale are a must. You can even find freshly imported West Coast seafood in a number of St. George's more elite restaurants.

Utah has unique wine and liquor laws, but these days, most restaurants typically serve beer, wine, or cocktails. However, in smaller towns, you may want to check first if they have a drink menu.

LODGING

Most major hotel and motel chains can be found throughout this region of the state. Whether you're looking for chic, modern comfort or basic accommodations, you can find it all here. Just be sure to book early whenever possible. A popular destination in summer, lodging closest to major attractions and activities fill up early.

If chain hotels aren't your style, Southwestern Utah has plenty of options for you. Steeped in pioneer heritage, you'll find many older homes that have been refurbished as unique and cozy bed-and-breakfasts.

Experience true Southwestern Utah by staying in one of the many rentable cabins and lodges. These are private rentals, and should be booked as far in advance as possible. Be sure to discuss all amenities with your host prior to finalizing a stay.

The Utah Office of Tourism website has information on lodging and amenities in the southwestern part of the state. *Hotel reviews have been shortened. For full information, visit Fodors.com.*

WHAT IT COSTS				
	$	$$	$$$	$$$$
Restaurants	under $12	$12–$20	$21–$30	over $30
Hotels	under $100	$100–$150	$151–$200	over $200

Restaurant prices are the average cost of a main course at dinner or, if dinner is not served, at lunch. Hotel prices are the lowest cost of a standard double room in high season.

VISITOR INFORMATION
Contacts Utah Office of Tourism. ⌧ *300 N. State St., Salt Lake City* ☎ *800/200–1160* ⊕ *www.visitutah.com.*

UTAH'S DIXIE

Mormon pioneers from the American Southeast settled this part of Utah to grow cotton, and they brought the name Dixie with them. Some thought the move was a gamble, but the success of the settlement may be measured in the region's modern-day definition of risk: hopping the border to nearby Mesquite, Nevada, to roll the dice. St. George is often the hottest place in the state, but the Pine Valley Mountains and Brian Head offer alpine relief and summer recreation.

CEDAR CITY

250 miles southwest of Salt Lake City.

Rich iron-ore deposits here grabbed Mormon leader Brigham Young's attention, and he ordered a Church of Jesus Christ of Latter-day Saints (LDS) mission established. The first ironworks and foundry opened in 1851 and operated for only eight years; problems with the furnace, flooding, and hostility between settlers and regional Native Americans eventually put out the flame. Residents then turned to ranching and agriculture for their livelihood, and Cedar City has thrived ever since as an agricultural point of the state.

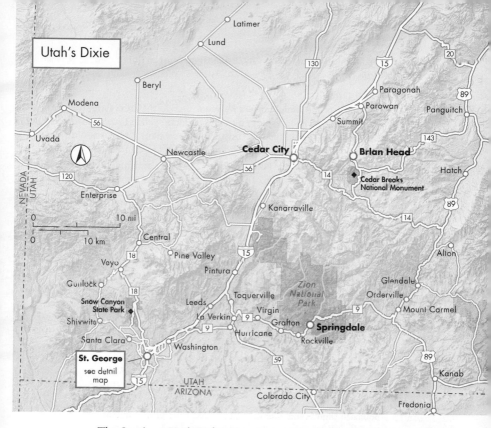

The Southern Utah University campus hosts the city's most popular event, the Utah Shakespeare Festival, with a season that gets longer as its reputation grows. Though better known for festivals than recreation, the city is well placed for exploring the Brian Head area.

GETTING HERE AND AROUND

Utah's I–15 cuts through Cedar City, providing it with easy access to fast travel for anyone in a hurry.

Travelers coming from the Brian Head area use the scenic Highway 14, winding from Cedar Canyon into downtown. Though town is walkable, you might want a car to get to major stores or conveniences.

FESTIVALS

Fodor's Choice ★ **Utah Shakespeare Festival.** For more than 50 years, Cedar City has gone Bard-crazy, staging productions of Shakespeare's plays June through October in theaters both indoors and outdoors at Southern Utah University. The Tony award–winning regional theater offers literary seminars, backstage tours, cabarets featuring festival actors, and an outdoor preshow with Elizabethan performers. A new center for the arts, including the open-air Engelstad Shakespeare Theatre, made its debut during the 2016 season. It helps to reserve in advance as many performances sell out. ☎ 435/586–7878 ⊕ www.bard.org.

ESSENTIALS

Visitor Information **Cedar City/Brian Head Tourism Bureau.** ✉ *581 N. Main St.* ☎ *800/354–4849, 435/586–5124* 🌐 *www.scenicsouthernutah.com.*

EXPLORING

Daughters of the Utah Pioneers Museum. Inside the Iron County Visitor Center, this museum displays pioneer artifacts such as an old treadle sewing machine, an antique four-poster bed, and photographs of old Cedar City and its inhabitants. ✉ *581 N. Main St.* ☎ *435/586–8269* 🎟 *Free.*

Frontier Homestead State Park Museum. Created as a memorial to the county's iron industry heritage, this local attraction allows visitors to explore western history, like the bullet-scarred stagecoach that ran in the days of Butch Cassidy. This state park even features the oldest standing home in all of southern Utah, built in 1851. Local artisans demonstrate pioneer crafts, and guests have the chance to see numerous mining artifacts and tools throughout their time in homestead history. ✉ *585 N. Main St.* ☎ *435/586–9290* 🌐 *www.frontierhomestead.org* 🎟 *$3* 🕒 *Closed Sun.*

SPORTS AND THE OUTDOORS

Dixie National Forest. The forest's expansive natural area is divided into four noncontiguous swaths covering a total of nearly 2 million acres. Adjacent to three national parks, two national monuments, and several state parks, the forest has 26 campgrounds in a variety of backdrops lakeside, mountainside, and in the depths of pine and spruce forests. Recreational opportunities abound, including hiking, picnicking, horseback riding, and fishing. ✉ *Dixie National Forest Headquarters, 1789 N. Wedgewood La.* ☎ *435/865–3700* 🌐 *www.fs.usda.gov/dixie* 🎟 *Free.*

HIKING

Southern Utah Scenic Tours. Experienced tour guides accompany visitors on all-day tours to some of Southern Utah's most popular destinations. Day trips include the ATV Slot Canyons Tour, a fun journey that combines riding ATVs and hiking through scenic terrain. Multiday trips like the Mighty Five take visitors to Utah's five national parks, with transportation, lodging, and some meals included. For shorter tours you can create your own custom itinerary or join a tour group. Day trips include hotel pickup and drop-off in St. George or Cedar City, park entrance fees, bottled water, and snacks. ☎ *435/656–1504, 888/404–8687* 🌐 *www.utahscenictours.com* 🎟 *ATV Slot Canyons Tour $310; Mighty Five $1595; call for prices of other tours.*

WHERE TO EAT

$ ITALIAN Fodor's Choice ★

🍴 **Centro Woodfired Pizzeria.** You can watch your handmade artisanal pizza being pulled from the fires of the brick oven, then sit back and enjoy a seasonal pie layered with ingredients such as house-made fennel sausage and wood-roasted cremini mushrooms. The creamy vanilla gelato layered with a balsamic reduction and sea salt is highly addictive. **Known for:** house-made sausage; thin crusts; creative desserts. [$] *Average main: $12* ✉ *50 W. Center St.* ☎ *435/867–8123* 🕒 *Closed Sun.*

$$ ITALIAN

🍴 **Chef Alfredo Italiano Ristorante.** With linen tablecloths, a decent wine list, and soft music playing in the background, this Sicilian-style restaurant tucked away in a strip mall may be the closest you'll get to fine dining in Cedar City. The menu features traditional antipasto appetizers and specials like butternut ravioli or eggplant Parmesan. **Known for:** quiet atmosphere; chicken parm. [$] *Average main: $20* ✉ *2313 W. Hwy. 56* ☎ *435/586–2693* 🌐 *www.chefalfredos.com* 🕑 *No lunch weekends.*

$$$ STEAKHOUSE 🍴 **Milt's Stage Stop.** Locals and an increasing number of tourists have discovered the lodgelike surroundings, friendly service, and canyon views at this dinner spot a 10-minute drive from Cedar City. It's known for traditional, hearty steak house cuisine: rib-eye steaks, prime rib, seafood dishes, and a sizable salad bar, accompanied by loaded baked potatoes and other sides. **Known for:** steaks and seafood; salad bar; warm desserts. [$] *Average main: $25* ✉ *3560 E. Hwy. 14* ☎ *435/586–9344* 🌐 *www.miltsstagestop.com* 🕑 *No lunch.*

$ CAFÉ FAMILY 🍴 **The Pastry Pub.** Don't be fooled by the name—coffee and tea are the only brews here, but pastries aren't the only thing on the menu. Build a sandwich of meat, egg, cheese, and more on a freshly baked bagel, croissant, artisan bread, or one of four flavors of wraps. **Known for:** walk from the Shakespeare Festival; espresso; seasonal soups. [$] *Average main: $8* ✉ *86 W. Center St.* ☎ *435/867–1400* 🌐 *www.cedarcitypastrypub.com* 🕑 *Closed Sun.*

WHERE TO STAY

$$$ B&B/INN Fodor's Choice ★ 🏨 **Amid Summer's Inn Bed & Breakfast.** This 1930s cottage is a gem on a tree-lined Cedar City street. **Pros:** incredible service; many repeat customers attest to quality; minutes from downtown. **Cons:** some rooms are accessible only by a narrow stairway; may be too intimate for some. [$] *Rooms from: $165* ✉ *140 S. 100 W* ☎ *435/586–2600, 888/586–2601* 🌐 *www.amidsummersinn.com* 🛏 *10 rooms* 🍽 *Breakfast.*

$$ B&B/INN 🏨 **Bard's Inn Bed and Breakfast.** Rooms in this restored turn-of-the-20th-century house are named after famous characters from Shakespeare's plays and handcrafted quilts grace the beds. **Pros:** immaculate rooms; all rooms have private baths; close to historic downtown. **Cons:** thin walls and creaky floors; books up fast for festival season. [$] *Rooms from: $119* ✉ *150 S. 100 W* ☎ *435/586–6612* 🌐 *www.thebardsinn.com* 🕑 *Closed Sept.–May* 🛏 *8 rooms* 🍽 *Breakfast.*

$$ HOTEL 🏨 **Best Western Town & Country Inn.** In downtown Cedar City, this renovated motel offers spacious rooms, complimentary breakfast, a fitness center, and two on-site eateries. **Pros:** convenient to shops and restaurants; great on-site pool. **Cons:** breakfast gets mixed reviews. [$] *Rooms from: $110* ✉ *189 N. Main St.* ☎ *435/586–9900* 🌐 *www.bestwestern.com* 🛏 *128 rooms, 17 suites* 🍽 *Breakfast.*

$$ HOTEL 🏨 **Springhill Suites by Marriott Cedar City.** Close to Brian Head ski resort, Bryce Canyon, and Zion, and convenient for downtown shops and eateries, this upscale hotel has spacious suites with contemporary style. **Pros:** close to parks; breakfast included. **Cons:** not within walking distance of downtown. [$] *Rooms from: $150* ✉ *1477 S. Old Hwy. 91* ☎ *435/586–1685* 🌐 *www.marriott.com/hotels/travel/cdcsh-springhill-suites-cedarcity* 🛏 *72 suites* 🍽 *Breakfast.*

BRIAN HEAD

29 miles northeast of Cedar City.

Brian Head Resort is Utah's southernmost and highest ski area at well over 9,000 feet, but the area's summer recreation, especially mountain biking, has been developed energetically. There are now more than 200 miles of trails for bikers, many of which are served by chairlift or shuttle services. The bright red-orange rock formations of Cedar Breaks Monument are several miles south of town.

The snow season is still the high season here, so book winter lodging in advance and expect high room rates. Food prices are high year-round. The fall "mud season" (October and November) and spring "slush season" (April and May) shut down some area businesses.

GETTING HERE AND AROUND

From Cedar City, take Highway 14 east to highways 143 and 148 north. Whichever way you arrive, the drive into Brian Head is scenic. The town isn't large, but the layout doesn't encourage walking.

During winter, snow closes highways 143 and 148 from the south. Be sure to check road conditions on the UDOT map online or on the app before heading out (⊕ *udottraffic.utah.gov).*

EXPLORING

Cedar Breaks National Monument. From the rim of Cedar Breaks, 23 miles east of Cedar City, a natural amphitheater plunges 2,000 feet into the Markagunt Plateau. Short hiking trails along the rim make this a wonderful summer stop, especially for Cedar City or Shakespeare festival visitors not planning to visit the Zion or Bryce park. ⊠ *Hwy. 14* ☎ *435/586–9451* ⊕ *www.nps.gov/cebr* 🎫 *$6.*

SPORTS AND THE OUTDOORS

BICYCLING

Brian Head is a great place to base mountain biking excursions. with your choice of terrain, difficulty, and views. The area's most popular ride is the 12-mile **Bunker Creek Trail,** which winds through forests and meadows to Panguitch Lake. Don't worry, you don't have to bike up in elevation if you'd rather not; Brian Head Resort runs its ski lift in summer, giving access to several mountain-bike trails. Brian Head Sports is one of many shuttles that takes riders to other trails at the resort.

Five miles south of Brian Head, road cyclists can explore Cedar Breaks National Monument and vicinity alongside traffic.

SKIING AND SNOWBOARDING

Brian Head Ski Resort. Eight lifts (including a new high-speed, detachable quad chairlift) transport skiers to runs covering more than 650 acres of terrain. Ski trails begin at a base elevation of 9,600 feet. Expert skiers head for the 11,300-foot summit of Brian Head Peak for access to more challenging runs. A half-pipe, trails, and a terrain park attract zealous snowboarders.

From the top of the resort's peak, you can see the red-rock cliffs of Cedar Breaks National Monument to the southwest.

During summer and fall, the resort is a favorite with mountain bikers. ✉ *329 S. Hwy. 143* ☎ *866/930–1010* ⊕ *www.brianhead.com* ⧉ *Lift tickets $59 weekend, $38 weekday.*

Brian Head Sports. As the largest outfitter in town, Brian Head Sports caters to cyclists, skiers, and snowboarders with equipment and accessories for rent or purchase. The store runs a mountain bike shuttle that's handy for riding area trails that end far from where they start. ✉ *269 S. Village Way* ☎ *435/677–2014* ⊕ *www.brianheadsports.com.*

Georg's Ski Shop and Bikes. Just down the road from Brian Head Resort, this popular ski shop has new and rental skis, snowboards, and bikes. The friendly staff is experienced at helping both beginning and advanced skiers find the perfect gear. ✉ *612 S. Hwy. 143* ☎ *435/677–2013* ⊕ *www.georgsskishop.com.*

WHERE TO EAT AND STAY

$$
AMERICAN

✕ **The Lift Bar and Grill.** Within the Grand Lodge Resort, this upscale bar and grill features expansive views of the mountains and an eclectic menu of contemporary entrées. With a rustic lodge feel, it features stone fireplaces and floor-to-ceiling windows to maximize the views, and the bar attracts a steady local clientele as well as resort guests. **Known for:** affordability; salads; outdoor fire pit. Ⓢ *Average main: $16* ✉ *314 Hunter Ridge Rd.* ☎ *435/677–9000* ⊕ *www.grandlodgeatbrianhead. com.*

$$
RESORT

⌂ **Cedar Breaks Lodge & Spa.** At an altitude of 9,600 feet, this lodge-style resort offers scenic views from its perch at the north end of town. **Pros:** scenic location with easy access to skiing, hiking, and mountain biking. **Cons:** early check-out; noisy parking lot; food gets mixed reviews. Ⓢ *Rooms from: $150* ✉ *223 Hunter Ridge Rd.* ☎ *435/677–3000, 888/282–3327* ⊕ *www.cedarbreakslodge.com* ⟿ *118 rooms* ⊙| *No meals*

$$$
RESORT

⌂ **Grand Lodge at Brian Head.** With its stunning scenery and prime location, this modern resort is the perfect stop for anyone looking for a bit of outdoor adventure during the day and luxury relaxation at night. **Pros:** modern comforts in a mountain setting; spa; every room has a view. **Cons:** a bit pricey; breakfast included only with certain packages; on-site restaurant gets mixed reviews. Ⓢ *Rooms from: $200* ✉ *314 Hunter Ridge Rd.* ☎ *435/677–9000* ⊕ *www.grandlodgebrianhead.com* ⟿ *88 rooms, 12 suites* ⊙| *No meals; Breakfast.*

9

ST. GEORGE

50 miles southwest of Cedar City.

Believing the mild year-round climate ideal for growing cotton, Brigham Young dispatched 309 LDS families in 1861 to found St. George. They were to raise cotton and silkworms and to establish a textile industry, to make up for textile shortages resulting from the Civil War. The area was subsequently dubbed "Utah's Dixie," a name that stuck even after the war ended and the "other" South could once again provide cotton to Utah.

The settlers—many of them originally from southern states—found the desert climate preferable to northern Utah's snow, and they remained as farmers and ranchers. Crops included fruit, molasses, and grapes for wine that the pioneers sold to nearby mining communities. St. Georgians now number approximately 75,000, many of whom are retirees attracted by the hot, dry climate and the numerous golf courses. But historic Ancestor Square, the city's many well-preserved original pioneer and Mormon structures, and a growing shopping district make St. George a popular destination for families as well. Walking tours are set up by the St. George Area Convention and Visitors Bureau.

GETTING HERE AND AROUND
This burgeoning city is easily reached via I–15 from north and south. Unless your hotel is downtown, it's best to get around by car.

FESTIVALS
St. George Arts Festival. Artisan booths, food, children's activities, and entertainment (including cowboy poets) are all part of this annual festival held at Town Square the Friday and Saturday of Easter weekend. ⊠ *St. George* ☎ *435/627–4500* ⊕ *www.sgcity.org.*

St. George Winter Bird Festival. Bird-watchers gather in St. George every January to peep at more than 100 feathered species. Join in three full days of field trips, exhibits, lectures, and activities. ⊠ *Tonaquint Park and Nature Center, 1851 S. Dixie Dr.* ☎ *435/868–8756, 435/673–0996* ⊕ *www.sgcity.org* ☒ *$10.*

ESSENTIALS
St. George Area Convention & Visitors Bureau. ⊠ *1835 Convention Center Dr.* ☎ *800/869–6635* ⊕ *www.visitstgeorge.com.*

EXPLORING
TOP ATTRACTIONS
Brigham Young Winter Home. Mormon leader Brigham Young spent the last five winters of his life in the warm, sunny climate of St. George. Built of adobe on a sandstone-and-basalt foundation, Young's winter home has been restored to its original condition and is open to the public. A portrait of Young hangs over one fireplace, and authentic furnishings from the late-19th-century time period have been donated by supporters. Guided tours are available. ⊠ *67 W. 200 N* ☎ *435/673–2517* ⊕ *www.lds.org/locations/brigham-young-winter-home* ☒ *Free.*

FAMILY **Rosenbruch World Wildlife Museum.** This 35,000-square-foot facility displays more than 300 species of wildlife created using fiberglass or foam forms with real skin and fur. Here you'll find species of animals from all over the planet; Africa, Asia, Australia, the Arctic, and more. Each display is made to represent the true feel of each species' natural habitat. Everyone can enjoy this beautiful museum's atmosphere, even beyond the amazing displays. Two waterfalls cascade from a two-story mountain, and hidden speakers provide ambient wildlife and nature sounds. Before your tour, check out the children's interactive area, and don't miss the art gallery and video theater. ⊠ *1835 Convention Center Dr.* ☎ *435/656–0033* ⊕ *www.rosenbruch.org* ☒ *$8.*

St. George Art Museum. Spend a few quiet hours out of the blazing sun in St. George's art museum. The permanent collection celebrates local potters, photographers, painters, and more. Special exhibits highlight local history and lore. Take in the beauty of this southwestern region with the comfort of air-conditioning and refreshments. ⊠ *47 E. 200 N* ☎ *435/627–4525* ⊕ *www.sgcity.org/artmuseum* ☞ *$3.*

St. George Temple. The red-sandstone temple, plastered over with white stucco, was completed in 1877 and was the first Mormon temple in Southwest Utah. It has served as a meeting place for both Mormons and other congregations over the decades. Today, only Mormons can enter the temple, but a visitor center next door offers guided tours. ⊠ *250 E. 400 S* ☎ *435/673–5181* ⊕ *www.lds.org* ☞ *Free.*

Snow Canyon State Park. Named not for winter weather but after a pair of pioneering Utahans named Snow, this gem of a state park is filled with natural wonders. Hiking trails lead to lava cones, sand dunes, cactus gardens, and high-contrast vistas. From the campground you can scramble up huge sandstone mounds and overlook the entire valley. Park staff lead occasional guided hikes. The park is about 10 miles northwest of St. George, and about an hour from Zion. ⊠ *1002 Snow Canyon Dr., Ivins* ☎ *435/628–2255* ⊕ *stateparks.utah.gov* ☞ *$6 per vehicle.*

WORTH NOTING

FAMILY **St. George Dinosaur Discovery Site at Johnson Farm.** Unearthed 20 years ago by property developers, this site allows visitors to view the ancient footprints left by dinosaurs from the Jurassic Period millions of years ago. Fossils unearthed at the site are also on display. Accurate replicas portray the creatures that left these tantalizing remains, and themed displays cover many details of the Jurassic era. There's an interactive area for children and a Dino Park outside the museum for play and fun. ⊠ *2180 E. Riverside Dr.* ☎ *435/574–3466* ⊕ *www.dinosite.org* ☞ *$6.*

St. George Tabernacle. This is one of the best-preserved pioneer buildings in the entire state, and it is still used for public meetings and programs for the community. Mormon settlers began work on the tabernacle just a few months after the city of St. George was established in June 1863. Upon completion of the sandstone building's 140-foot clock tower 13 years later, Brigham Young formally dedicated the site. Today, the heritage of the tabernacle still draws many visitors and locals alike. ⊠ *18 S. Main St.* ☎ *435/628–4072.*

SPORTS AND THE OUTDOORS

BICYCLING

Bicycles Unlimited. A trusted southern Utah mountain-biking resource, this shop rents bikes and sells parts, accessories, and guidebooks. ⊠ *90 S. 100 E* ☎ *435/673–4492* ⊕ *bicyclesunlimited.com* ☞ *From $25 for 4 hrs.*

HIKING

Snow Canyon State Park. Eight miles northwest of St. George off Highway 18, this park has several short trails and lots of small desert canyons to explore. While we recommend a map for all hikers, Snow Canyon is easy to navigate and explore on your own. ⊠ *St. George* ☎ *435/628–2255* ⊕ *www.stateparks.utah.gov.*

9

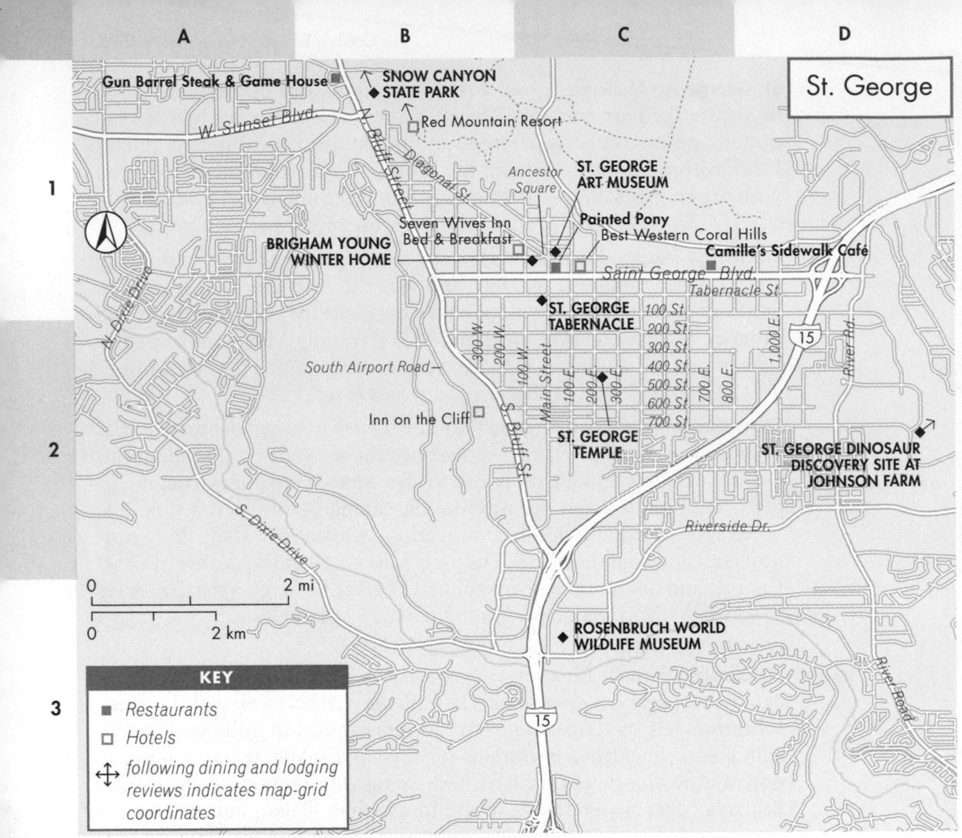
St. George
A
B
C
D
1
2
3
Gun Barrel Steak & Game House
SNOW CANYON STATE PARK
Red Mountain Resort
W. Sunset Blvd.
N. Bluff Street
Diagonal St.
Ancestor Square
ST. GEORGE ART MUSEUM
Painted Pony
Seven Wives Inn Bed & Breakfast
Best Western Coral Hills
Camille's Sidewalk Café
BRIGHAM YOUNG WINTER HOME
Saint George Blvd.
Tabernacle St.
ST. GEORGE TABERNACLE
100 St.
200 St.
300 St.
400 St.
500 St.
600 St.
700 St.
300 W.
200 W.
100 W.
Main Street
100 E.
200 E.
300 E.
700 E.
800 E.
1,000 E.
River Rd.
15
N. Dixie Drive
South Airport Road
Inn on the Cliff
S. Bluff St.
ST. GEORGE TEMPLE
ST. GEORGE DINOSAUR DISCOVERY SITE AT JOHNSON FARM
Riverside Dr.
S. Dixie Drive
0
2 mi
0
2 km
ROSENBRUCH WORLD WILDLIFE MUSEUM
River Road
KEY
Restaurants
Hotels
following dining and lodging reviews indicates map-grid coordinates

HORSE RACING AND RODEO

Dixie Roundup. Dozens of professional rodeo cowboys from across the West take part in this three-day mid-September event held since the 1930s. Team roping, saddle-bronc riding, and bull riding are among the main attractions, along with the always entertaining mutton-busting competition for the kids and the rodeo parade. ✉ *Sun Bowl Stadium* ☎ *435/703–4779* 🌐 *stgeorgelions.com* 🎟 *$10.*

WHERE TO EAT

Use the coordinates (✥ A1) at the end of each listing to locate a site on the corresponding map.

$ CAFÉ FAMILY 🍴 **Camille's Sidewalk Café.** This charming café offers a variety of healthy breakfast and lunch choices. Enjoy artisan flatbread pizzas, breakfast sandwiches, gourmet wraps, and other favorites at the cozy tables inside or on the covered patio. **Known for:** grilled pretzel roll; flatbread pizzas; healthy options. [$] *Average main: $8* ✉ *661 E. St. George Blvd.* ☎ *435/767–9727* 🌐 *camillescafe.com* 🕘 *Closed Sun.* ✥ *C1.*

$$$ AMERICAN 🍴 **Gun Barrel Steak & Game House.** Inspired by the Wyoming Wildlife and Taxidermy Museum and dotted with unique artifacts, you'll feel like you're dining in the Old West at this family-owned restaurant. Serving hearty steaks and wild game, you're invited to try specialties like buffalo or elk steaks. **Known for:** rib-eye steak; Prime Rib Special

Night (Monday); great service. $ *Average main: $25* ✉ *1091 N. Bluff St.* ☎ *435/652–0550* ⊕ *www.gunbarrelutah.com* ⊙ *Closed Sun. No lunch* ✛ *B1.*

$$$

AMERICAN

Fodor'sChoice

★

✕ **Painted Pony.** Shaded patio dining and contemporary Southwestern art on the walls provide a romantic setting in which to savor the creative meals found here. The focus at Painted Pony is on fresh ingredients, many from the owners' private organic garden. **Known for:** upscale atmosphere; French onion soup; huge rib eye. $ *Average main: $28* ✉ *2 W. St. George Blvd.* ☎ *435/634 1700* ⊕ *www.painted-pony.com* ⊙ *No lunch Sun.* ✛ *C1.*

WHERE TO STAY

Use the coordinates (✛ A1) at the end of each listing to locate a site on the corresponding map.

$$

HOTEL

Best Western Coral Hills. If you're looking for a downtown location, this attractive two-story hotel gets you close to the Convention Center, Dixie State University, the Tuacahn Amphitheater, and several restaurants. **Pros:** large suites with sunken tubs; breakfast included; 19 restaurants nearby. **Cons:** rooms near the road and the indoor pool can suffer some noise. $ *Rooms from: $100* ✉ *125 E. St. George Blvd.* ☎ *435/673–4844, 800/542–7733* ⊕ *www.coralhills.com* ⇗ *95 rooms, 3 suites* ⏀ *Breakfast* ✛ *C1.*

$$

HOTEL

Inn on the Cliff. This modern boutique hotel features panoramic views of St. George, spacious accommodations, and attentive service. **Pros:** high quality at an affordable price; stunning views; luxury toiletries in rooms. **Cons:** premade continental breakfast; can't walk to downtown. $ *Rooms from: $138* ✉ *511 S. Airport Rd.* ☎ *435/216–5864* ⊕ *www. innonthecliff.com* ⇗ *27 rooms* ⏀ *Breakfast* ✛ *B2.*

$$$$

RESORT

Fodor'sChoice

★

Red Mountain Resort. This luxury retreat, with its stunning surroundings near the mouth of Snow Canyon, offers a range of outdoor adventures and fitness packages for the body and mind. **Pros:** down-to-earth spa experience with activities suited to all levels of fitness; packages are among the least expensive among fitness resorts; rate includes meals and spa/fitness facilities. **Cons:** caters more to activity-seekers than those looking to relax. $ *Rooms from: $215* ✉ *1275 E. Red Mountain Circle, Ivins* ✛ *7 miles northwest of St. George* ☎ *435/673–4905, 877/246–4453* ⊕ *www.redmountainresort.com* ⇗ *82 rooms, 24 villa suites* ⏀ *All meals* ✛ *B1.*

$$$

B&B/INN

Seven Wives Inn Bed & Breakfast. Named for an ancestor of the owner who indeed had seven wives, this quaint bed-and-breakfast occupies two Victorian homes and is full of historic charm. **Pros:** near Ancestor Square and other downtown attractions; antique furnishings; historic charm. **Cons:** rooms fill quickly in summer; setting too quiet for some travelers. $ *Rooms from: $189* ✉ *217 N. 100 W* ☎ *435/628–3737* ⊕ *www.sevenwivesinn.com* ⇗ *13 rooms* ⏀ *Breakfast* ✛ *C1.*

PERFORMING ARTS

Tuacahn. A rotating series of musicals such as *Beauty and the Beast, Sister Act* , and *The Wizard of Oz* entertain at this outdoor amphitheater nestled in a natural sandstone cove. The venue is also used for big name rock concerts and movies! Be sure to check their line-up

9

online, or ask locally. ✉ *1100 Tuacahn Dr., Ivins* ☎ *800/746–9882, 435/652–3300* ⊕ *www.tuacahn.org.*

SHOPPING

Ancestor Square. The centerpiece shopping area of downtown St. George is a great place to browse stores and art galleries. Nearby restaurants and cafés offer plenty of options to grab lunch or dinner while out and about. Check out the numerous history-fact plaques throughout this downtown hot spot. ✉ *St. George Blvd. and Main St.* ☎ *435/656–8238* ⊕ *www.ancestorsquare.com.*

Red Cliffs Mall. Serving the needs of both residents and visitors, this popular mall has a variety of specialty shops and sporting goods stores. Visitors can easily find weather-appropriate clothing or gear here before heading back out to the parks and attractions. ✉ *1750 E. Red Cliffs Dr.* ☎ *435/673–0099* ⊕ *www.redcliffsmall.com.*

The Shoppes at Zion. Southern Utah's popular factory-outlet center has more than 30 stores, including Eddie Bauer, Pendleton, Levi, and Downeast Outfitters. Located off of Exit 8 on I-15, you won't regret stopping at this outlet mall. Amazing prices and plenty of variety in stores make it a place to keep everyone happy. ✉ *250 N. Red Cliffs Dr.* ☎ *435/674–0133* ⊕ *www.theoutletsatzion.com.*

SPRINGDALE

40 miles east of St. George.

Springdale's growth has followed that of its next-door neighbor, Hurricane. Main attraction Zion National Park, the most popular park destination in Utah and one of the most popular in the United States, keeps this small town lively. Hotels, restaurants, and shops continue to pop up, yet the town still manages to maintain its small-town charm.

GETTING HERE AND AROUND

You'll need a car to get to Springdale, via Highway 9, but getting around once you're there is easy. The canyon-road shuttle bus—from April through October—makes getting from one end of Springdale to the other stress-free, with bus stops throughout town. It's also a pleasant town to wander through, with shops, galleries, and restaurants all in a central district.

EXPLORING

FAMILY **Grafton.** A stone school, dusty cemetery, and a few wooden structures are all that remain of the nearby town of Grafton. This ghost town has been featured in films such as *Butch Cassidy and the Sundance Kid.* Attacks by Native Americans drove the original settlers from the site, and their haunting presence can still be felt today. ✉ *Bridge La., 2 miles west of Rockville.*

WHERE TO EAT

$$ ✕ **Bit & Spur.** This laid-back Springdale institution has been serving locals
SOUTHWESTERN   and tourists for more than 30 years. The well-rounded menu includes fresh fish and pasta dishes, but the emphasis is on creative Southwestern fare such as roasted-sweet-potato tamales and chili-rubbed rib-eye steak. **Known for:** innovative margaritas; live music; signature rib

eye. $ *Average main: $20* ✉ *1212 Zion Park Blvd.* ☎ *435/772–3498* ⊕ *www.bitandspur.com* ⊙ *No lunch.*

$$
CAFÉ
FAMILY
✗ **Oscar's Café.** A popular destination for hikers and tourists with hearty appetites, this café has a surprisingly extensive menu. Prepare for an active day with their filling breakfast menu, which includes omelets, pancakes, and French toast. **Known for:** mucho nachos; heated patio; unique side dishes. $ *Average main: $15* ✉ *948 Zion Park Blvd.* ☎ *435/772–3232* ⊕ *www.cafeoscars.com.*

$
DELI
✗ **Sol Foods Supermarket.** Stop by the market's deli and check out the premade sandwiches and abundant salad bar, or order a quick sandwich, wrap, or vegetarian snack of your choice. The staff can also prepare a box lunch for your day in the park. **Known for:** box lunches; extensive menu; one-stop shop. $ *Average main: $8* ✉ *995 Zion Park Blvd.* ☎ *435/772–3100* ⊕ *www.solfoods.com*

$$
ECLECTIC
✗ **Spotted Dog Café.** This restaurant is more upscale than most in Springdale, but its staff makes patrons feel right at home even if they saunter in wearing hiking shoes. The exposed wood beams and large windows that frame the surrounding trees and rock cliffs set a Western mood, with tablecloths and original artworks supplying a dash of refinement. **Known for:** locally roasted coffee; sidewalk dining; breakfast buffet. $ *Average main: $20* ✉ *Flanigan's Inn, 428 Zion Park Blvd.* ☎ *435/772–0700* ⊕ *www.flanigans.com/dining* ⊙ *Limited hrs Nov.–Mar. No lunch.*

$$$
AMERICAN
✗ **The Switchback Grille.** Known for its USDA prime steaks and seafood flown in fresh daily, the high-ceilinged Switchback has walls of windows framing stunning views. Like all good steak houses, it serves comforting sides such as roasted potatoes and sautéed mushrooms. **Known for:** aged beef; casual elegance; seafood specials. $ *Average main: $25* ✉ *Holiday Inn Express, 1149 S. Zion Park Blvd.* ☎ *435/772–3700* ⊕ *switchbackgrille.com* ⊙ *No lunch.*

WHERE TO STAY

$$$$
HOTEL
🏨 **Holiday Inn Express.** A recent addition to the Holiday Inn Express chain, this property has smartly renovated guest rooms, but what hasn't changed is a location with amazing views and the convenience of being on the park's shuttle route. **Pros:** on shuttle route; beautiful views; room rate includes breakfast. **Cons:** breakfast area fills up fast. $ *Rooms from: $259* ✉ *1215 Zion Park Blvd.* ☎ *435/772–3200, 800/465–4329 reservations only* ⊕ *holidayinnexpress.com* 🛏 *117 rooms, 6 suites* ⫿⊙⫿ *Breakfast.*

SHOPPING

Bumbleberry Gifts. Next to the Bumbleberry Inn, this quaint gift shop is best known for its fresh-baked bumbleberry pies and locally produced bumbleberry jams. You'll also find a wide array of gifts and souvenirs, plus an extensive selection of outdoor apparel and footwear. ✉ *897 Zion Park Blvd.* ☎ *435/772–3224* ⊕ *www.bumbleberrygifts.com.*

Fodor's Choice
★
Worthington Gallery. The emphasis at this superb gallery is on regional art, including pottery, works in glass, jewelry, beguiling copper wind sculptures by Lyman Whitaker, and paintings that capture the dramatic beauty of Southern Utah. ✉ *789 Zion Park Blvd.* ☎ *435/772–3446* ⊕ *worthingtongallery.com.*

9

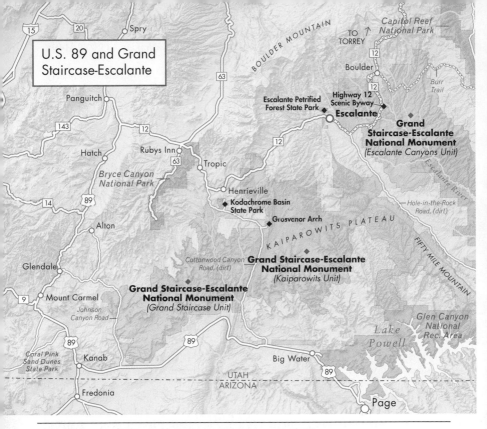

U.S. 89 and Grand Staircase-Escalante

GRAND STAIRCASE–ESCALANTE NATIONAL MONUMENT

In September 1996, 1.9 million acres in south-central Utah were designated as the Grand Staircase–Escalante National Monument. Its three distinct sections—the Grand Staircase, the Kaiparowits Plateau, and the Canyons of the Escalante—offer remote backcountry experiences that are hard to find elsewhere in the Lower 48. Waterfalls, Native American ruins and petroglyphs, shoulder-width slot canyons, and dramatic colors all characterize this wilderness. Straddling the northern border of the monument, the small towns of Escalante and Boulder offer access, information, outfitters, lodging, and dining to adventurers. The highway that connects them, Highway 12, is one of the most scenic stretches of road in the Southwest.

Visitor centers in Big Water, Kanab, Cannonville, and Escalante provide current information on road conditions and self-guided tours. Each center has a different theme, with exhibits on archaeology, geology, paleontology, and biology.

Popular day trips include Lower Calf Creek Falls, Spooky Canyon, Devil's Garden, and Grosvenor Arch. Other worthwhile destinations include Johnson Canyon/Skutumpah Road, Cottonwood Canyon Road, and nearby Kodachrome Basin State Park.

A good way to plan your visit is to hire one of the many experienced outfitters and guides who offer options ranging from narrated tours in air-conditioned vehicles to hiking and backpacking adventures. Most tours feature areas with colorful sandstone rock formations, slot canyons, dramatic cliffs, waterfalls, and scenic back roads.

ESCALANTE

47 miles east of Bryce Canyon National Park entrance.

Though the Dominguez and Escalante expedition of 1776 came nowhere near this area, the town's name does honor the Spanish explorer. It was bestowed nearly a century later by a member of a survey party led by John Wesley Powell, charged with mapping this remote area. Today, it has modern amenities and is a gateway to the national monument.

GETTING HERE AND AROUND

Escalante is only accessible via Highway 12 from the north and south. Fortunately, it's a drive not to be missed. The tiny downtown is where most amenities are found.

ESSENTIALS

Visitor Information Big Water Visitor Center. ⊠ *100 Upper Revolution Way, Big Water* ☎ *435/675–3200* ⊕ *www.blm.gov/visit/big-water-visitor-center.* **Cannonville Visitor Center.** ⊠ *10 Center St., Cannonville* ☎ *435/826–5640* ⊕ *www.blm.gov/visit/cannonville-visitor-center.* **Escalante Interagency Visitor Center.** ⊠ *755 W. Main St.* ☎ *435/826–5499* ⊕ *www.blm.gov.*

TOURS

Opportunities for exploring this fascinating area abound; a good way to start is in the company of an expert tour guide. Activity-based tours include hiking, canyoneering, and horseback riding. Special interest tours cover such subjects as photography, geology, and the area's flora and fauna.

Escape Goats. Providing guided tours of the slot canyons and other Southwest Utah destinations for more than 15 years, this family-owned operation offers a variety of day and evening hikes, multiday backpacking trips, and photo and artist tours. The company provides shuttle services and personalized attention, and can customize tours for families with children and travelers with limited mobility. ⊠ *Boulder* ☎ *435/826–4652* ⊕ *www.escalantecanyonguides.com* 🖃 *From $90.*

Excursions of Escalante. Hiking, backpacking, photography, and canyoneering tours in the Escalante region are custom-fit to your needs and abilities by experienced guides. Canyoneers will be taken into the slot canyons to move through slot chutes or rappel down walls and other obstacles. All gear and provisions are provided whether it's a day hike or multiday adventure. ⊠ *125 E. Main St.* ☎ *800/839–7567* ⊕ *excursionsofescalante.com* 🖃 *From $155.*

Grand Staircase Discovery Tours. This outfitter has a little bit of everything to offer, from half-day and full-day hikes, to hiking/camping gear, shuttle

9

service, photography, and customized trips. Tours take visitors to ghost towns, slot canyons, rock formations, and more. ✉ *Big Water* ☎ *928/614–4099* ⊕ *www.grandstaircasediscoverytours.com* ✉ *From $125.*

Hondoo Rivers & Trails. This tour company has been providing high-quality backcountry trips into Capitol Reef National Park, Escalante Canyons, and the High Plateaus for 40 years. From April to October, they'll take you on hiking, horseback-riding, and Jeep day tours. Trips are designed to explore the geologic landforms in the area, seek out wildflowers in season, and to encounter free-roaming mustangs, bison, and bighorn sheep when possible. Multiday trips can also be arranged. ✉ *90 E. Main St., Torrey* ☎ *435/425–3519* ⊕ *www.hondoo.com* ✉ *From $120.*

Southwest Adventure Tours. This experienced tour operator partners with Paria Outpost and Outfitters to offer hikes that wind past the most incredible scenery, including the Wahwaep hoodoos (sandstone rock formations), Sidestep Canyon, the Rimrocks, Deer Range Point, and the Cockscomb area. Hikes range from 1½ to 8 miles round-trip with some moderate climbing. Multiday backpacking and camping trips are available, along with advice about self-guided driving tours and visits to other Utah parks. ✉ *382 E. 650 S, Cedar City* ☎ *435/590–5864, 800/970–5864* ⊕ *www.southwestadventuretours.com* ✉ *$125 half-day hike, $175 full-day hike.*

EXPLORING

FAMILY **Escalante Petrified Forest State Park.** This state park was created to protect a huge repository of petrified wood, easily spotted along two moderate-to-strenuous hiking trails. Of equal interest to area locals and visitors is the park's Wide Hollow Reservoir at the base of the hiking trails, which has a swimming beach and is good for boating, fishing, and birding. ✉ *710 N. Reservoir Rd.* ☎ *435/826–4466* ⊕ *www.stateparks. utah.gov* ✉ *$8.*

NEED A BREAK

✕ **Kiva Koffeehouse.** A fun place to stop along the way for the spectacular view and a quick bite, this unusual coffeehouse at mile marker 73.86, 13 miles east of Escalante, was constructed by the late artist and inventor Bradshaw Bowman. He began building it when he was in his eighties and spent two years finding and transporting the 13 Douglas-fir logs surrounding the structure. ✉ *7144 S. Hwy. 12* ☎ *435/826–4550* ⊕ *www.kivakoffeehouse.com.*

Fodor$Choice **Highway 12 Scenic Byway.** Keep your camera handy and steering wheel
★ steady along this route between Escalante and Loa, near Capitol Reef National Park. Though the highway starts at the intersection of U.S. 89, west of Bryce Canyon National Park, the stretch that begins in Escalante is one of the most spectacular. The road passes through Grand Staircase–Escalante National Monument and on to Capitol Reef along one of the most scenic stretches of highway in the United States. Be sure to stop at the scenic overlooks; almost every one will give you an eye-popping view, and information panels let you know what you're looking at. Don't get distracted while driving, though; the paved road is twisting and steep, and at times climbs over a hogback with sheer drop-offs on both sides.

OFF THE BEATEN PATH

Kodachrome Basin State Park. Yes, it is named after the old-fashioned color photo film; once you see it you'll understand why the National Geographic Society gave it the name. The stone spires known as "sand pipes" cannot be found anywhere else in the world. Hike any of the trails to spot some of the 67 pipes in and around the park. The short Angels Palace Trail takes you quickly into the park's interior, up, over, and around some of the badlands. ✉ *Cottonwood Canyon Rd., Cannonville* ☎ *435/679–8562* 🌐 *www.stateparks.utah.gov* 🎫 *$8.*

SPORTS AND THE OUTDOORS

Larger than most national parks at 1.7 million acres, the Grand Staircase–Escalante National Monument is popular with backpackers and hard-core mountain-bike enthusiasts. You can explore the rocky landscape, which represents some of America's last wilderness, via dirt roads with a four-wheel-drive vehicle; most roads depart from Highway 12. Roadside views into the monument are most impressive from Highway 12 between Escalante and Boulder. It costs nothing to enter the park, but fees apply for camping and backcountry permits.

BICYCLING

Hell's Backbone Road. For a scenic and challenging mountain-bike ride, follow the 44-mile Hell's Backbone Road from Panguitch to the Escalante region and beyond. The route, also known as Highway 12, gives riders stunning views and a half-dozen quaint townships as a reward for the steep grades. The road begins 7 miles south of Panguitch.

HIKING

Lower Escalante River. Some of the best backcountry hiking in the area lies 15 miles east of Escalante on Route 12, where the Lower Escalante River carves through striking sandstone canyons and gulches. You can camp at numerous sites along the river for extended trips, or spend a little time in the small park where the highway crosses the river.

Utah Canyon Outdoor Store. This outfitter is a great source for local information and offers guided trips into the canyons of Grand Staircase–Escalante and the surrounding area, as well as interpretive nature hikes. The on-site store includes a wide selection of camping and hiking necessities, clothing, and locally handcrafted gifts, jewelry, and art. Be sure to try the freshly made espresso and whole-fruit smoothies. ✉ *325 W. Main St.* ☎ *435/826–4967* 🌐 *utahcanyonoutdoors.com* 🎫 *Guided hikes from $120.*

WHERE TO EAT AND STAY

$$ AMERICAN

🍴 **Cowboy Blues.** This locals' favorite serves up bountiful American food in a rustic Old West setting and keeps it real by sourcing its Black Angus beef from Southern Utah ranches and plucking seasonal vegetables from a local garden. You can enjoy a cocktail or beer on the patio, along with a serving of the eatery's one-of-a-kind jalapeño poppers. **Known for:** outdoor dining; blue margaritas; BBQ ribs. [$] *Average main: $15* ✉ *530 W. Main St.* ☎ *435/826–4577* 🌐 *www.cowboyblues.net.*

$$ CAFÉ

🍴 **Escalante Outfitters.** When you're spent after a day of exploration, this is a great place to sit back and relax. Try one of the build-your-own pizzas, known for fresh, local ingredients such as applewood bacon and slow-roasted tomatoes, and pair it with an icy Utah microbrew. **Known**

for: hearty pizzas; casual space; delicious coffee. $ *Average main: $17* ✉ *310 W. Main St.* ☎ *435/826–4266* 🌐 *www.escalanteoutfitters.com.*

$$ B&B/INN 🏨 **Escalante's Grand Staircase Bed & Breakfast Inn.** Rooms are set apart from the main house, giving this property some motel-type privacy along with bed-and-breakfast amenities. **Pros:** spacious rooms; Wi-Fi. **Cons:** no pets. $ *Rooms from: $142* ✉ *280 W. Main St.* ☎ *435/826–4890* 🌐 *www.escalantebnb.com* 🛏 *8 rooms* 🍴 *Breakfast.*

$ HOTEL 🏨 **Escalante Outfitters.** A good option if you want a one-stop place to plan and buy gear for your outdoor adventure, or if you're traveling on a budget and don't care about amenities. **Pros:** the food is a pleasant surprise; pet-friendly. **Cons:** right on the highway; you may have to wait in line for a shower. $ *Rooms from: $55* ✉ *310 W. Main St.* ☎ *435/826–4266* 🌐 *www.escalanteoutfitters.com* 🛏 *8 cabins* 🍴 *No meals.*

SHOPPING

Sculptured Furniture, Art and Ceramics. A husband-and-wife team opened Sculptured Furniture, Art and Ceramics, a gallery offering beautiful clay, ceramic, and wood artistic and functional pieces in their workshop and garden. Three-day workshops focus on creating pottery using traditional methods. ✉ *1540 W. Hwy. 12* ☎ *435/826–4631* 🌐 *sculpturedfurnitureartandceramics.com.*

Serenidad Gallery. The Priskas have owned this gallery/shop for more than two decades, seven rooms of eclectic artwork and crafts ranging from paintings inspired by the local landscape and American Indian pottery to Turkish rugs and bronze sculptures. ✉ *170 S. 100 West* ☎ *435/826–4720* 🌐 *www.serenidadgallery.com.*

ARCHES
NATIONAL PARK

WELCOME TO ARCHES NATIONAL PARK

TOP REASONS TO GO

★ **Arch appeal:** Nowhere in the world has as large an array or quantity of natural arches.

★ **Legendary landscape:** A photographer's dream— no wonder it's been the chosen backdrop for many Hollywood films.

★ **Treasures hanging in the balance:** Landscape Arch and Balanced Rock look like they might topple any day—and they could. Come quick as the features in this park erode and evolve constantly.

★ **Fins and needles:** Fins are parallel vertical shafts of eroding rock that slowly disintegrate into tower-like "needles." The spaces around and between them will carve their way into your memories like the wind and water that formed them.

★ **Moab:** Known as Utah's "adventure capital," this small town is a great base from which to explore by foot, bicycle, balloon, watercraft, and four-wheeler.

1 Devils Garden. 18 miles from the visitor center, this is the end of the paved road in Arches. The park's only campground, a picnic area, and access to drinking water can be found here. Trails in Devils Garden lead to formations like the Landscape Arch.

2 Fiery Furnace. About 14 miles from the visitor center this area is so labeled because its orange spires of rock look much like tongues of flame. Reservations are required weeks in advance to join the twice-daily ranger-guided treks. To visit the Fiery Furnace on your own you'll need a permit and canyoneering savvy.

3 Delicate Arch/Wolfe Ranch. A spur road about 11.7 miles from the visitor center leads to the trail and viewpoint for the park's most famous feature— Delicate Arch. To see it from below, follow the road to the viewpoint, then walk to one or both easily accessible viewing areas.

4 The Windows. Reached on a spur 9.2 miles from the visitor center, here you can see many of the park's natural arches from your car or on an easy rolling trail.

5 Balanced Rock. This giant rock teeters atop a pedestal, creating a 128-foot formation of red rock grandeur right along the roadside, about 9 miles from the visitor center.

6 Petrified Dunes. Just a tiny pull-out about 5 miles from the visitor center, stop here for pictures of acres and acres of petrified sand dunes.

7 Courthouse Towers. The Three Gossips, Sheep Rock, and Tower of Babel are all here. Enter this section of the park 3 miles past the visitor center. The Park Avenue Trail winds through the area.

8 Moab. A river-running, mountain-biking, canyoneering hub, Moab—about 5 miles south of the park—is the can't-miss base for all your adventures.

GETTING ORIENTED

Southeastern Utah's Arches National Park boasts some of the most unimaginable rock formations in the world. Off U.S. 191, Arches is 236 miles southeast of Salt Lake City, 27 miles south of I–70, and 5 miles north of Moab.

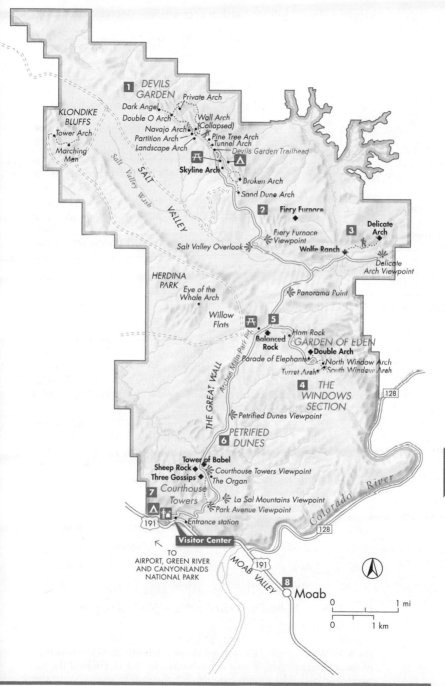

1 DEVILS GARDEN

Private Arch

Dark Angel

Double O Arch

Wall Arch (Collapsed)

KLONDIKE BLUFFS

Navajo Arch

Pine Tree Arch

Tower Arch

Partition Arch

Tunnel Arch

Landscape Arch

Devils Garden Trailhead

Marching Men

Skyline Arch

Broken Arch

SALT VALLEY

Sand Dune Arch

Salt Valley Wash

2 Fiery Furnace

3 Delicate Arch

Fiery Furnace Viewpoint

Salt Valley Overlook

Wolfe Ranch

Delicate Arch Viewpoint

HERDINA PARK

Eye of the Whale Arch

Panorama Point

Willow Flats

5

Ham Rock

GARDEN OF EDEN

Balanced Rock

Double Arch

Parade of Elephants

North Window Arch

South Window Arch

Turret Arch

4 THE WINDOWS SECTION

THE GREAT WALL

Arches Main Park Rd

128

Petrified Dunes Viewpoint

PETRIFIED DUNES

6

Tower of Babel

Sheep Rock

Courthouse Towers Viewpoint

Three Gossips

The Organ

7 Courthouse Towers

La Sal Mountains Viewpoint

Park Avenue Viewpoint

Entrance station

191

Visitor Center

Colorado River

128

10

TO AIRPORT, GREEN RIVER AND CANYONLANDS NATIONAL PARK

MOAB VALLEY

191

8 Moab

0 ___ 1 mi

0 ___ 1 km

Updated by
John Blodgett

More than 1 million visitors come to Arches annually, drawn by the red rock landscape and its teasing wind- and water-carved rock formations. The park is named for the 2,000-plus sandstone arches that frame horizons, cast precious shade, and nobly withstand the withering forces of nature and time. Fancifully named attractions like Three Penguins, Queen Nefertiti, and Tower of Babel stir the curiosity, beckoning even the most delicate of travelers from roadside locales. Immerse yourself in this immense park, but don't lose yourself entirely—summer temperatures frequently crack 100°F, and water is hard to come by inside the park boundaries.

ARCHES PLANNER

WHEN TO GO

The busiest times of year are spring and fall. In the spring blooming wildflowers herald the end of winter, and temperatures in the 70s bring the year's largest crowds. The crowds remain steady in summer as the thermostat approaches 100°F and above in July and August. Sudden dramatic cloudbursts create rainfalls over red rock walls in late-summer "monsoon" season.

Fall weather is perfect—clear, warm days and crisp, cool nights. The park is much quieter in winter, and from December through February you can hike many of the trails in relative solitude. Snow seldom falls in the valley beneath the La Sal Mountains, and when it does, Arches is a photographer's paradise, as snow drapes slickrock mounds and natural rock windows.

AVG. HIGH/LOW TEMPS.

Jan.	Feb.	Mar.	Apr.	May	June
44/19	53/25	64/33	76/39	84/49	98/58

July	Aug.	Sept.	Oct.	Nov.	Dec.
100/62	99/61	86/50	77/40	58/32	48/21

Note: Extreme highs often exceed 100°F in July and August.

FESTIVALS AND EVENTS
SPRING
Moab Art Walk. Moab galleries and shops celebrate the perfect weather of spring and fall with a series of exhibits. Art Walks are held the second Saturday of the month from March through June and September

through November. Stroll the streets (5–9 pm) to see and purchase original works by Moab and regional artists. ⊠ *Moab* ☏ *435/259–6272* ⊕ *www.moabartwalk.com.*

FAMILY
Fodor'sChoice
★

Moab Arts Festival. Every Memorial Day weekend, artists from across the West gather at Moab's Swanny City Park to show their wares, including pottery, photography, and paintings. This fun festival is small enough to be manageable, charges no admission, and sells a variety of affordable artworks. Soundtracked by live music, they also have activities for kids and lots of food. The arts festival partners with local libation producers to bring a wine and beer festival to the park as part of the event. ⊠ *Moab* ☏ *435/259–2742 Moab Arts Council* ⊕ *www. moabartsfestival.org.*

SUMMER

FAMILY
Fodor'sChoice
★

Canyonlands PRCA Rodeo. Cowboys come to the Old Spanish Trail Arena (just south of Moab) for three days in late May or early June to try their luck on thrashing bulls and broncs at this annual Western tradition. ⊠ *3641 S. Hwy. 191, Moab* ☏ *435/259–4852* ⊕ *www.moabcanyonlandsrodeo.com.*

FALL

FAMILY

Green River Melon Days. The town claims its melon festival, dating to 1906, is the world's oldest. All the watermelon you can eat, an old-fashioned parade, a 5k run, and other small-town-America activities await on the third Saturday of September. ⊠ *Green River* ☏ *435/564–3427* ⊕ *melon-days.com.*

Moab Music Festival. Moab's red rocks resonate with world-class music—classical, jazz, and traditional—during this annual festival that takes place at indoor and outdoor venues including the city park, local auditoriums, private homes, and a natural stone grotto along the Colorado River. Musicians from all over the globe perform, and it's one of the West's top music showcases. The festival starts the Thursday before Labor Day and runs about two weeks. ⊠ *Moab* ☏ *435/259–7003* ⊕ *www.moabmusicfest.org.*

PLANNING YOUR TIME

10

There's no food service within the park, so you'll need to pack snacks, lunch, and plenty of water each day before you head into Arches. You'll also need to plan ahead to get tickets to the daily Fiery Furnace walk with a ranger. It's a highlight for those who are adventurous and in good shape, but during most of the year you must reserve your spot in advance at ⊕ *www.recreation.gov*. If you don't have a reservation, you can check for spots at the visitor center (make that your very first stop). The one-day itinerary *(below)* is based on what to do if you can't take the walk or what to do on a different day. On the day of your Fiery Furnace walk, you can fill your spare time with a walk on the Park Avenue trail. If you have a third day, take a rafting trip on the Colorado River, which runs along the park's boundary.

ARCHES IN ONE DAY

Start as early as sunrise for cool temperatures and some of the best natural light, and head out on the 3-mile round-trip hike on the **Delicate Arch Trail.** The route is strenuous but quite rewarding. Pause for a healthy snack before heading to **Devils Garden,** another great spot for morning photography, where you'll also find the easy, primarily flat trail to **Landscape Arch,** the second of the park's two must-see arches. If you're accustomed to hiking, continue on to **Double O,** but be aware that this portion of the trail is strenuous. Along the way, picnic in the shade of a juniper or in a rock alcove. By the time you return you'll be ready to see the rest of the park by car, with some short strolls on easy paths.

In the mid- to late afternoon, drive to **Balanced Rock** for photos, then on to the **Windows.** Wander around on the easy gravel paths for more great photo ops. Depending on what time the sun is due to set, go into town for dinner before or after you drive out to Delicate Arch or the **Fiery Furnace,** and watch the sun set the rocks on fire.

GETTING HERE AND AROUND

AIR TRAVEL

The nearest large airport to southeastern Utah is Walker Field Airport in Grand Junction, Colorado, 110 miles from Moab. Rental cars are available at the Moab Airport, 18 miles north of town, although advance reservations are recommended (☎ 970/244–9100).

CAR TRAVEL

Interstate 70 is the highway that gets you across Utah from Denver. To dip southeast toward Moab, exit the interstate onto U.S. 191, a main artery running all the way south to the Arizona border, skirting Arches' western border, Moab, and the Manti–La Sal National Forest along the way. Alternatively, you can take Route 128, the Colorado River Scenic Byway, traveling just east of Arches. On either road, services can be far apart.

Branching off the main, 18-mile park road are two spurs, one 2½ miles to the Windows section and one 1.6 miles to the Delicate Arch trailhead and viewpoint. There are several four-wheel-drive roads in the park; always check at the visitor center for conditions before attempting to drive them. U.S. 191 tends to back up midmorning to early afternoon. There's likely to be less traffic at 8 am or sunset.

TRAIN TRAVEL

The *California Zephyr,* operated by Amtrak (☎ 800/872–7245), stops daily in Green River, about 50 miles northwest of Moab.

PARK ESSENTIALS

ACCESSIBILITY

Not all park facilities meet federally mandated accessibility standards, but as visitation to Arches climbs, the park is making efforts to increase accessibility. Visitors with mobility impairments can access the visitor center, all restrooms throughout the park, and one campsite (#7) at the Devils Garden Campground. The Park Avenue Viewpoint is a paved path with a slight decline near the end, and both Delicate Arch and Balanced Rock viewpoints are partially hard-surfaced.

PARK FEES AND PERMITS

Admission to the park is $25 per vehicle, $15 per motorcycle, and $10 per person entering on foot or bicycle, good for seven days. To encourage visitation to the park during less busy times, Arches also offers an off-peak admission fee of $10 for vehicles and motorcycles; check the Arches website (⊕ *www.nps.gov/arch*) and at the Moab Information Center in town for updated information. You must pay admission to Canyonlands separately. A $50 local park pass grants you admission to both Arches and Canyonlands parks as well as Natural Bridges and Hovenweep national monuments for one year.

Fees are required for the Fiery Furnace ranger-led hike ($16 per adult, $8 per child ages 7–12) and for a permit to hike without a park ranger in the Fiery Furnace ($6 per adult, $3 per child).

PARK HOURS

Arches National Park is open year-round, seven days a week, around the clock. It's in the Mountain time zone.

CELL-PHONE RECEPTION

Cell-phone reception is available intermittently in the park. You can find a public telephone at the park's visitor center.

EDUCATIONAL OFFERINGS

RANGER PROGRAMS

As you explore Arches, look for sandwich boards announcing "Ranger Sightings" and stop for a 3- to 10-minute program led by park staff. Topics range from geology and desert plants to mountain lions and the Colorado River. Most nights, spring through fall, more in-depth campfire programs are available at Devils Garden Campground amphitheater. You may also find guided walks (in addition to the beloved Fiery Furnace walk) during your visit. For information on current schedules and locations of park programs, contact the visitor center (☎ 435/719–2299) or check the bulletin boards throughout the park.

FAMILY

Fodor's Choice

★

Fiery Furnace Walk. Join a park ranger on a two- or three-hour walk through a labyrinth of rock fins and narrow sandstone canyons. You'll see arches that can't be viewed from the park road and spend time listening to the desert. You should be relatively fit and not afraid of heights if you plan to take this moderately strenuous walk. Wear sturdy hiking shoes, sunscreen, and a hat, and bring at least a liter of water. Walks into the Fiery Furnace are usually offered twice a day (hours vary) and leave from Fiery Furnace Viewpoint, off the main road, about 15 miles from the park visitor center. Tickets for the morning walks must be reserved up to six months in advance (at ⊕ *www.recreation.gov*) mid-March through October, or purchased at the visitor center November through February. Tickets for afternoon Fiery Furnace ranger-led walks must be purchased in advance at the park visitor center, ideally as soon as you arrive in Moab and at least a day or two ahead. Children ages 7–12 pay half price; the walk is not recommended for children under 5. Book early as the program usually fills months prior to each walk. ⊠ *Arches National Park ⊹ Trailhead: on Arches Scenic Dr.* ⊕ *www.nps.gov/arch* ☑ *$16.*

FAMILY

Junior Ranger Program. Kids 2–12 can pick up a Junior Ranger booklet at the visitor center. It's full of activities, word games, drawings, and thought-provoking material about the park and the wildlife. To earn your Junior Ranger badge, you must complete several activities in the booklet,

10

attend a ranger program, or watch the park film and pick up some trash in the park. ✉ *Arches National Park* ☎ *435/719–2299* 🖳 *Free.*

LEARNING RESOURCES

FAMILY **Red Rock Explorer Pack.** Families can check out a youth backpack filled with tools for learning about both Arches and Canyonlands national parks. A guide for naturalists, a three-ring binder of activities, hand lens magnifier, and binoculars are just some of the loaner items. Backpacks can be returned to either Arches or Island in the Sky visitor centers. Use of the backpack is free with a credit-card imprint in case of loss or damage to the pack or enclosed items. ✉ *Arches National Park* ☎ *435/719–2299* 🖳 *Free.*

RESTAURANTS

Whether you select an award-winning Continental restaurant in Moab, a nearby resort, or the tavern in Green River, you can dress comfortably in shorts or jeans. But don't let the relaxed attire fool you: culinary surprises await, with spectacular views as a bonus.

In the park itself, there are no dining facilities and no snack bars. Supermarkets, bakeries, and delis in downtown Moab will be happy to make you food to go. If you bring a packed lunch, there are several picnic areas from which to choose.

HOTELS

Though there are no hotels or cabins in the park itself, in the surrounding area every type of lodging is available, from economy chain motels to B&Bs and high-end, high-adventure resorts. It's important to know when popular events are held, however, as accommodations can, and do, fill up weeks ahead of time. *Hotel reviews have been shortened. For full information, visit Fodors.com.*

WHAT IT COSTS			
$	$$	$$$	$$$$
Restaurants under $13	$13–$20	$21–$30	over $30
Hotels under $101	$101–$150	$151–$200	over $200

Restaurant prices are the average cost of a main course at dinner, or if dinner is not served, at lunch. Hotel prices are the lowest cost of a standard double room in high season.

VISITOR INFORMATION

Park Contact Information Arches National Park. ✉ *N. U.S. 191* ☎ *435/719–2299* ⊕ *www.nps.gov/arch.*

VISITOR CENTER

FAMILY **Arches Visitor Center.** With hands-on exhibits that provide information
Fodor's Choice about the park's geology, wildlife, and history; helpful rangers; and
★ a bookstore; the center is a great way to start any visit to the park. Newcomers will find it especially helpful, but even those who have traveled to the park before often discover something new. ✉ *N. U.S. 191* ☎ *435/719–2299* ⊕ *nps.gov/arch.*

CLOSE UP

Plants and Wildlife in Arches

As in any desert environment, the best time to see wildlife in Arches is early morning or evening. Summer temperatures keep most animals tucked away in cool places, though ravens and lizards are exceptions. If you happen to be in the right place at the right time, you may spot one of the beautiful turquoise-necklace-collared lizards. It's more likely you'll see the western whiptail. Mule deer, jackrabbits, and small rodents are usually active in cool morning hours or near dusk. You may spot a lone

coyote foraging day or night. The park protects a small herd of desert bighorns, and some of their tribe are sometimes seen early in the morning grazing beside U.S. 191 south of the Arches entrance. If you encounter bighorn sheep, do not approach them. They have been known to charge people who attempt to get too close. The park's ravens, mule deer, and small mammals such as chipmunks are very used to seeing people and may allow you to get close—but don't feed them.

EXPLORING

SCENIC DRIVES

Arches Main Park Road. Although they are not formally designated as such, the main park road and its two short spurs are scenic and allow you to enjoy many park sights from your car. The main road leads through Courthouse Towers, where you can see Sheep Rock and the Three Gossips, then alongside the Great Wall, the Petrified Dunes, and Balanced Rock. A drive to the Windows section takes you to attractions like Double Arch, and you can see Skyline Arch along the roadside as you approach the Devils Garden campground. The road to Delicate Arch is not particularly scenic, but it allows hiking access to one of the park's main features. Allow about two hours to drive the 45-mile round-trip, more if you explore the spurs and their features and stop at viewpoints along the way. ⊠ *Arches National Park* ⊕ *www.nps.gov/arch.*

10

HISTORIC SITES

Wolfe Ranch. Civil War veteran John Wesley Wolfe and his son started a small ranch here in 1888. He added a cabin in 1906 when his daughter Esther and her family came west to live. Built out of Fremont cottonwoods, the rustic one-room cabin still stands on the site, listed on the National Register of Historic Places. Look for remains of a root cellar and a corral as well. Even older than these structures is the nearby Ute rock-art panel by the Delicate Arch trailhead. About 150 feet past the footbridge and before the trail starts to climb, you can see images of bighorn sheep and figures on horseback, as well as some smaller images believed to be dogs. To reach the panel, follow the narrow dirt trail along the rock escarpment until you see the interpretive sign. The cabin is 12.9 miles from park entrance, 1.2 miles off main road. ⊠ *Off Delicate Arch Rd.*

SCENIC STOPS

It's easy to spot some of the arches from your car, but you should really take the time to step outside and walk beneath the spans and giant walls of orange rock. This gives you a much better idea of their proportion. No doubt you will feel as writer Edward Abbey did when he awoke on his first day as a park ranger in Arches: that you're walking in the most beautiful place on Earth.

Visit as the sun goes down. At sunset, the rock formations in Arches glow like fire, and you'll often find photographers behind their tripods waiting for magnificent rays to descend on Delicate Arch or other popular park sites. The Fiery Furnace earns its name as its narrow fins glow red just before the sun dips below the horizon. Full-moon nights are particularly dramatic in Arches as the creamy white Navajo sandstone reflects light, and eerie silhouettes are created by towering fins and formations.

Balanced Rock. One of the park's favorite sights, 9¼ miles from the park entrance, this rock is visible for several minutes as you approach—and just gets more impressive and mysterious as you get closer. The formation's total height is 128 feet, with the huge balanced rock rising 55 feet above the pedestal. Be sure to hop out of the car and walk the short (530-yard) loop around the base. ⊠ *Arches Scenic Dr.*

Fodor's Choice ★ **Delicate Arch.** The iconic symbol of the park and the state (it appears on many of Utah's license plates), the Delicate Arch is frankly tall and muscular compared to many of the spans in the park—and it's big enough to shelter a four-story building. The arch is a remnant of an Entrada Sandstone fin; the rest of the rock has eroded and now frames the La Sal Mountains in the background. Drive 2.2 miles off the main road to the viewpoint to see the arch from a distance, or hike right up to it from the trailhead that starts near Wolfe Ranch. The trail, 13 miles from the park entrance and 1.2 miles off the main road, is a moderately strenuous 3-mile round-trip hike. ⊠ *Delicate Arch Rd.*

Double Arch. In the Windows section of the park, 11¾ miles from the park entrance, Double Arch has appeared in several Hollywood movies, including *Indiana Jones and the Last Crusade.* The northern arch is visible from the parking lot, but walk the short trail to see the southern one, as well as Turret Arch. ⊠ *The Windows Rd.*

Fiery Furnace. Fewer than 10% of the park's visitors ever descend into the chasms and washes of Fiery Furnace (a permit or a ranger-led hike is the only way to go), but you can gain an appreciation for this twisted, unyielding landscape from the Overlook, 14 miles from the park entrance. At sunset, the rocks glow a vibrant flamelike red, which gives the formation its daunting moniker. ⊠ *Off Arches Scenic Dr.*

Skyline Arch. A quick walk from the parking lot at Skyline Arch, 16½ miles from the park entrance, gives you closer views and better photos. The short trail is less than a half mile round-trip and only takes a few minutes to travel. ⊠ *Devil's Garden Rd.*

FAMILY **The Windows.** As you head north from the park entrance, turn right at Balanced Rock to find this concentration of natural windows, caves, and needles 11¾ miles from the park entrance. Stretch your legs on

---

GOOD READS

Arches Visitor Center Bookstore. Operated by Canyonlands Natural History Association, this bookstore at the park entrance is the place in the park to buy maps, guidebooks, driving tours on CD, and material about the natural and cultural history of Arches National Park. Park souvenirs are also sold here. ⊠ *Off Hwy. 191* ☎ *435/259–6003.*

■ *127 Hours: Between a Rock and a Hard Place* by Aron Ralston. This true story—made into a movie of the same name starring James Franco—took place southeast of Arches and is a modern-day survivor story of solitary man in nature.

■ *A Naturalist's Guide to Canyon Country,* by David Williams and Gloria Brown, is an excellent, compact field guide for both Arches and Canyonlands national parks.

■ *Desert Solitaire.* Eminent naturalist Edward Abbey's first ranger assignment was Arches; this classic is a must-read.

■ *Road Guide to Arches National Park,* by Peter Anderson, has basic information about the geology and natural history in the park.

■ *Moab Classic Hikes,* by Damian Fagan, succinctly gives the skinny on 40 area hikes and includes maps and photos.

---

the easy paths that wind between the arches and soak in a variety of geological formations. ⊠ *The Windows Rd.*

SPORTS AND THE OUTDOORS

Arches National Park lies in the middle of one of the adventure capitals of the United States. Deep canyons and towering walls are everywhere you look. Slick sandstone surfaces, known as slickrock, make for some of the world's best mountain biking. Thousand-foot sandstone walls draw rock climbers from across the globe. Hikers can choose from shady canyons or red rock ridges that put you in the company of the West's big sky. The Colorado River forms the southeast boundary of the park and can give you every grade of white-water adventure.

10

Moab-based outfitters can set you up for any sport you may have a desire to try: mountain biking, ATVs, dirt bikes, four wheel-drive vehicles, kayaking, climbing, stand-up paddleboarding, and even skydiving. Within the park, it's best to stick with basics such as hiking, sightseeing, and photography. Climbers and other adventure seekers should always inquire at the visitor center about restrictions.

MULTISPORT OUTFITTERS

FAMILY **Adrift Adventures.** This outfitter takes pride in well-trained guides who can take you via foot, raft, kayak, 4X4, jet boat, stand-up paddleboard, and more, all over the Moab area, including the Colorado and Green rivers. They also offer history, movie, and rock-art tours. They've been in business since 1977 and have a great reputation around town. ⊠ *378 N. Main St., Moab* ☎ *435/259–8594, 800/874–4483* ⊕ *www.adrift.net* ☎ *From $52.*

Dual Sport Utah. If you're into dirt biking, this is the only outfitter in Moab specializing in street-legal, off-road dirt-bike tours and rentals. Follow the Klondike Bluffs trail to Arches, or negotiate the White Rim Trail in Canyonlands in a fraction of the time you would spend on a mountain bike. You can also rent jet skis here. ⊠ *197 W. Center. St., Moab* ☎ *435/260–2724* ⊕ *www.dualsportutah.com* 🖾 *From $225.*

Moab Adventure Center. At the prominent storefront on Main Street you can schedule most any type of local adventure experience you want, including rafting, 4X4 tours, scenic flights, hikes, balloon rides, and much, much more. You can also purchase clothing and outdoor gear for your visit. ⊠ *225 S. Main St., Moab* ☎ *435/259–7019, 866/904–1163* ⊕ *www.moabadventurecenter.com* 🖾 *From $62.*

NAVTEC. Doc Williams was the first doctor in Moab in 1896, and some of his descendants never left, sharing his love for the area through this rafting, canyoneering, and 4X4 company. Whether you want to explore by boat, boots, or wheels, you'll find a multitude of one-day and multiday options here. ⊠ *321 N. Main St., Moab* ☎ *435/259–7983, 800/833–1278* ⊕ *www.navtec.com.*

BICYCLING

There's world-class biking all around Arches National Park, but the park proper is not the best place to explore on two wheels. Bicycles are allowed only on established roads, and because there are no shoulders cyclists share the roadway with drivers and pedestrians gawking at the scenery. If you do want to take a spin in the park, try the dirt-and-gravel Willow Flats Road, the old entrance to the park. The road is about 6½ miles long one-way and starts directly across from the Balanced Rock parking lot. It's a pretty mountain-bike ride on dirt and sand through slickrock, pinyon, and juniper country. You must stay on the road with your bicycle or chance steep fines.

TOURS AND OUTFITTERS

Fodor's Choice ★ **Poison Spider Bicycles.** In a town of great bike shops, this fully loaded shop is considered one of the best. Poison Spider serves the thriving road-cycling community as well as mountain bikers. Rent, buy, or service your bike here. You can also arrange for shuttle and guide services and purchase merchandise. Want to ship your bike to Moab for your adventure? Poison Spider will store it until you arrive and the staff will reassemble it for you and make sure everything is in perfect working order. ⊠ *497 N. Main St., Moab* ☎ *435/259–7882, 800/635–1792* ⊕ *www.poisonspiderbicycles.com.*

Rim Tours. Reliable, friendly, and professional, Rim Tours has been taking guests on guided one-day or multiday mountain-bike tours, including Klondike Bluffs (which enters Arches) and the White Rim Trail (inside Canyonlands) since 1985. Road-bike tours as well as bike rentals are also available. Bike skills a little rusty? Rim Tours also offers mountain-bike instructional tours and skill clinics. ⊠ *1233 S. U.S. 191, Moab* ☎ *435/259–5223, 800/626–7335* ⊕ *www.rimtours.com* 🖾 *Day tours from $145; multiday from $825.*

Western Spirit Cycling Adventures. Head here for fully supported, go-at-your-own-pace, multiday mountain-bike and road-bike tours throughout the western states, including trips to Canyonlands, Trail of the Ancients, and the 140-mile Kokopelli Trail, which runs from Grand Junction, Colorado, to Moab. Guides versed in the geologic wonders of the area cook up meals worthy of the scenery each night. Ask about family rides, and road bike trips, too. There's also the option to combine a Green River kayak trip with the three-night White Rim Trail ride. ✉ *478 Mill Creek Dr., Moab* ☎ *435/259–8732, 800/845–2453* ⊕ *www.westernspirit.com* 💲 *From $950.*

BIRD-WATCHING

Within the park you'll definitely see plenty of the big, black, beautiful raven. Look for them perched on top of a picturesque juniper branch or balancing on the bald knob of a rock. The noisy black-billed magpie populates the park, as do the more melodic canyon and rock wrens. Lucky visitors will spot a red-tailed hawk and hear its distinctive call.

Serious birders will have more fun visiting the **Scott M. Matheson Wetlands Preserve,** 5 miles south of the park. The wetlands is home to more than 225 species of birds including the wood duck, western screech owl, indigo bunting, and plumbeous vireo.

BOATING AND RIVER EXPEDITIONS

Although the Colorado River runs along the border of the park, there is no boating within the park proper. You can, however, enjoy a splashy ride nearby on the Fisher Towers stretch of the river north of Moab, and there are plenty of fine outfitters in Moab that can set you up for expeditions.

TOURS AND OUTFITTERS

FAMILY
Fodor'sChoice
★

Canyon Voyages Adventure Co. This is an excellent choice for rafting or kayaking adventures on the Colorado or Green River. Don and Denise Oblak run a friendly, professional company with a retail store and rental shop that's open year round. Most of their customers take one-day trips, but they also offer multiday itineraries, guided tours, and rentals. It's also the only company that operates a kayak school for those who want to learn how to run the rapids on their own. Ask about stand-up paddleboarding, biking, and horseback riding, too. ✉ *211 N. Main St., Moab* ☎ *435/363–3794, 866/484–4506* ⊕ *www.canyonvoyages.com* 💲 *From $58.*

Holiday River Expeditions. Since 1966, this outfitter has offered one- to eight-day adventures on the San Juan, Green, and Colorado rivers, including inside Canyonlands National Park. They also offer multisport trips, women's retreats, and bike adventures, including the White Rim Trail. ✉ *2075 E. Main St., Green River* ☎ *435/564–3273, 800/624–6323* ⊕ *www.bikeraft.com* 💲 *From $190.*

10

FISHING

There is no fishing in Arches National Park, and the Colorado River is too silty to offer good fishing. The nearby La Sal Mountains are dotted with small lakes that are stocked with small trout, but finding good native trout fishing in the area will take some effort.

FOUR-WHEELING

With thousands of acres of nearby Bureau of Land Management lands to enjoy, it's hardly necessary to use the park's limited trails for four-wheel adventures. You can, however, go backcountry in Arches on the Willow Flats Road and the Salt Valley Road—just don't set out for this expedition without first stopping at the visitor center to learn of current conditions. Salt Valley Road is very sandy and requires experience to drive on it.

TAKING DOGS TO THE PARK

Dogs aren't allowed on national park trails and must be on leash in the Devils Garden Campground. However, canines can join you on Bureau of Land Management trails. The heat can be stifling, so remember to bring enough water for you and your four-legged friend and hit the trails in the early morning hours.

TOURS AND OUTFITTERS

Coyote Land Tours. Imposing Mercedes Benz Unimog trucks (which dwarf Hummers) take you to parts of the backcountry where you could never wander on your own. Technical tours challenge drivers with imposing rock formations, washes, and assorted obstacles, and there are tamer sunset excursions and camp-style ride-and-dine trips. They stand by their money-back "great time" guarantee. ⊠ *Moab* ☎ *435/260–6056* ⊕ *www.coyotelandtours.com* ⊠ *From $59.*

High Point Hummer & ATV. You can rent vehicles, including ATVs, UTVs, and Jeeps, or get a guided tour of the backcountry in open-air Hummer vehicles or ATVs, or dune buggy–like "side-by-sides" that seat up to six people. The enthusiastic owners love families and small, intimate groups, and offer hiking and canyoneering as well. ⊠ *281 N. Main St., Moab* ☎ *435/259–2972, 877/486–6833* ⊕ *www.highpointhummer.com* ⊠ *Guided tours from $69.*

HIKING

Getting out on any one of the park trails will surely cause you to fall in love with this Mars-like landscape. But remember, you are hiking in a desert environment and approximately 1 mile above sea level. Many people succumb to heat and dehydration because they do not drink enough water. Park rangers recommend a gallon of water per day per person.

EASY

FAMILY **Balanced Rock Trail.** You'll want to stop at Balanced Rock for photo ops, so you may as well walk the easy, partially paved trail around the famous landmark. This is one of the most accessible trails in the park and is suitable for small children and folks who may have difficulty walking. The trail is only about 530 yards round-trip; you should allow 15 minutes for the walk. *Easy.* ⊠ *Arches National Park* ✛ *Trailhead: approximately 9¼ miles from park entrance,*

Broken Arch Trail. An easy walk across open grassland, this loop trail passes Broken Arch, which is also visible from the road. The arch gets its name because it appears to be cracked in the middle, but it's not really broken. The trail is 1¼ miles round-trip; allow about an hour for the walk. *Easy.* ⊠ *Arches National Park* ✛ *Trailhead: at end of Sand Dune Arch trail, off Devil's Garden Rd., 16½ miles from park entrance.*

Double Arch Trail. If it's not too hot, anyone can walk here from Windows Trail. This relatively flat trail leads to two massive arches that make for great photo opportunities. The ¾-mile round-trip gives you a good taste of desert flora and fauna. *Easy.* ⊠ *Arches National Park* ✛ *Trailhead: 2½ miles from main road, on Windows Section spur road, 9¼ miles from main entrance.*

Landscape Arch. This natural rock opening competes with Kolob Arch at Zion for the title of largest geologic span in the world. Measuring 306 feet from base to base, it appears as a delicate ribbon of rock bending over the horizon. In 1991, a slab of rock about 60 feet long, 11 feet wide, and 4 feet thick fell from the underside, leaving it even thinner. You can reach it by walking a rolling, gravel, 1.6-mile-long trail. *Easy.* ⊠ *Arches National Park* ✛ *Trailhead: at Devil's Garden Rd., 18 miles north of park entrance off main road.*

FAMILY **Sand Dune Arch Trail.** Your kids will return to the car with shoes full of bright red sand from this giant sandbox in the desert and will love exploring in and around the rock. Do not climb or jump off the arch, as doing so has frequently resulted in injuries. Set aside five minutes for this shady, 330-yard walk and as much time as your children's imaginations allow for play. The trail intersects with the Broken Arch Trail, so if you visit both arches it's a 1½-mile round-trip. *Easy.* ⊠ *Arches National Park* ✛ *Trailhead: off Arches Scenic Dr., about 16½ miles from park entrance.*

FAMILY **Windows Trail.** The first stop for many visitors to the park, Windows Trail gives you an opportunity to get out and enjoy the desert air. Here you'll see three giant openings in the rock and walk on a trail that leads right through the holes. Allow about an hour on this gently inclined, 1-mile round-trip hike. As 90% of visitors won't follow the "primitive" trail around the backside of the two windows, take advantage if you want some desert solitude. The primitive trail adds an extra half hour to the trip. *Easy.* ⊠ *Arches National Park* ✛ *Trailhead: on the Windows Rd., off Arches Scenic Dr., 12 miles from park entrance.*

MODERATE

Fodor's Choice ★ **Delicate Arch Trail.** To see the park's most famous freestanding arch up close takes effort and won't offer you much solitude—but it's worth every step. The 3-mile round-trip trail ascends via steep slickrock, sandy paths, and along one narrow ledge (at the very end) that might give pause to anyone afraid of heights. Plus, there's almost no shade. First-timers should start early to avoid the midday heat in summer. Still, at sunrise, sunset, and every hour in between, it's the park's most popular

and busy trail. Heat mixed with lack of shade makes this a strenuous hike in the summer. Bring plenty of water as heatstroke is a very real possibility. Allow two to three hours for this hike, depending on your fitness level and how long you plan to linger at the arch. If you go at sunset or sunrise, bring a headlamp or flashlight. Don't miss Wolfe Ranch and some ancient rock art near the trailhead. *Moderate.* ⊠ *Arches National Park* ⊹ *Trailhead: on Delicate Arch Rd., 13 miles from park entrance, 2¼ miles off main road.*

Fodor's Choice
★

Devils Garden Trail. Landscape Arch is the highlight of this trail but is just one of several arches within reach, depending on your ambitions and the temperature. It's an easy ¾-mile one-way trip (mostly gravel, relatively flat) to Landscape Arch, one of the longest stone spans in the world at 306 feet and one of the most fragile-looking. In fact, you can see where a 60-foot-long piece fell off the underside in 1991, leading to the closure of the trail that used to go under the span. This serves as a reminder of the impermanence of the features in the park. Beyond Landscape Arch the scenery changes dramatically and the hike becomes more strenuous, as you must climb and straddle slickrock fins and negotiate some short, steep inclines. Finally, the stacked spans that compose Double O Arch come into view around a sharp bend. Allow up to three hours for this round-trip hike of just over 4 miles. For a still longer hike, venture on to see a formation called Dark Angel and then return to the trailhead on the primitive loop. The hike to Dark Angel is a difficult route through fins with a short side trip to Private Arch. If you hike all the way to Dark Angel and return on the primitive loop, the trail is about 6 miles round-trip, not including possible (and worthwhile) detours to Navajo Arch, Partition Arch, Tunnel Arch, and Pine Tree Arch. Allow about five hours for this adventure, take plenty of water, and watch your route carefully. Pick up the park's useful guide to Devils Garden, or download it from the website before you go. *Moderate.* ⊠ *Arches National Park* ⊹ *Trailhead: on Devils Garden Rd., off main road, 18 miles from park entrance.*

Park Avenue Trail. The first named trail that park visitors encounter, this is an easy, 2-mile round-trip walk (with only one small hill but a somewhat steep descent into the canyon) amid walls and towers that resemble a New York City skyline. You'll walk under the gaze of Queen Nefertiti, a giant rock formation that some observers think has Egyptian-looking features. If you are traveling with companions, make it a one-way, 1-mile downhill trek by having them pick you up at the Courthouse Towers Viewpoint. Allow about 45 minutes for the one-way journey. *Easy.* ⊠ *Arches National Park* ✛ *Trailhead: on Arches Scenic Drive, 2 miles from park entrance.*

Tower Arch Trail. Check with park rangers before attempting the dirt road to Klondike Bluffs parking area. If rains haven't washed out the road, a trip to this seldom-visited area provides a solitude-filled hike culminating in a giant rock opening. Allow from two to three hours for this 3½-mile round-trip hike, not including the drive. *Moderate.* ⊠ *Arches National Park* ✛ *Trailhead: at Klondike Bluffs parking area, 24½ miles from park entrance, 7¾ miles off main road.*

DIFFICULT

Fiery Furnace. This area of the park has taken on a near-mythical lure for park visitors, who are drawn to the forbidden nature of Fiery Furnace. Rangers strongly discourage inexperienced hikers from entering here—in fact, you can't enter without watching a safety video and getting a permit ($6). As a result, up to one month's advance reservations are now required to get a spot on the 2-mile round-trip ranger-led hikes ($16) through this unique formation. A hike here is a challenging but fascinating trip amid rugged rocks and sandy washes into the heart of Arches. The trek may require the use of hands and feet to scramble up and through narrow cracks and along vertigo-inducing ledges above drop-offs, and there are no trail markings. If you're not familiar with the Furnace you can easily get lost and cause resource damage, so watch your step and use great caution. Call or visit the website (⊕ *recreation. gov*) for reservations, which are a must. The less intrepid should look into Fiery Furnace from the Overlook off the main road. *Difficult.* ⊠ *Arches National Park* ✛ *Trailhead: off main road, about 15 miles from visitor center.*

ROCK CLIMBING AND CANYONEERING

Rock climbers travel from across the country to scale the sheer red rock walls of Arches National Park and surrounding areas. Most climbing routes in the park require advanced techniques. Permits are not required, but climbers are encouraged to register for a free permit, either online or at a kiosk outside the visitor center. Climbers are responsible for knowing park regulations, temporary route closures, and restricted routes. Two popular routes ascend Owl Rock in the Garden of Eden (about 10 miles from the visitor center); the well-worn route has a difficulty of 5.8, while a more challenging option is 5.11 on a scale that goes up to 5.13-plus. Many climbing routes are available in the Park Avenue area, about 2.2 miles from the visitor center. These routes are also extremely difficult climbs. No commercial outfitters are allowed to lead rock-climbing excursions in the park, but guided canyoneering (which involves ropes, rappelling, and some basic climbing) is permitted. Before climbing, it's imperative that you stop at the visitor center and check with a ranger about climbing regulations.

10

TOURS AND OUTFITTERS

Desert Highlights. This guide company takes adventurous types on descents and ascents through canyons (with the help of ropes), including those found in the Fiery Furnace at Arches National Park. Full-day and multiday canyoneering treks are available to destinations both inside and outside the national parks. Desert Highlights does not offer guided rock climbing. ⊠ *50 E. Center St., Moab* ☎ *435/259–4433, 800/747–1342* ⊕ *www.deserthighlights.com* ⊠ *From $120.*

Moab Cliffs & Canyons. In a town where everyone seems to offer rafting and 4X4 expeditions, Moab Cliffs & Canyons focuses exclusively on canyoneering, climbing, and rappelling—for novice and veteran adventurers. Prices vary according to how many people sign up. This is the outfitter that provided technical assistance to the crew on the movie *127 Hours.* ⊠ *253 N. Main St., Moab* ☎ *435/259–3317, 877/641–5271* ⊕ *www.cliffsandcanyons.com* ⊠ *From $72.*

WHAT'S NEARBY

NEARBY TOWNS

Moab is the primary gateway to both Arches and Canyonlands national parks. Don't let its outsize image and status as Grand County seat fool you: only about 5,000 people live here year-round—compared with the 1 million who visit annually. Near the Colorado River in a beautiful valley between red rock cliffs, Moab is an interesting, eclectic place to visit, especially if you would welcome a variety of restaurants, Southwestern-inspired souvenirs, art galleries, and a plethora of lodging options. Also, here you'll find an array of sports outfitters to help you enjoy the parks. For those who want civilization and a sprinkling of culture with their outdoor itineraries, Moab is the place to be.

The next-closest town to Arches, about 47 miles to the northwest, is **Green River.** Unlike hip Moab, this dusty highway outpost is off the tourists' radar screen, except for boaters headed Moab's way on the Green. It's worth a visit for Ray's Tavern. Also, each September the fragrance of fresh cantaloupe, watermelon, and honeydew fills the air, especially during Melon Days, a family-fun event celebrating the harvest on the third weekend of September.

VISITOR INFORMATION

Green River Information Center. ⊠ *John Wesley Powell River History Museum, 1765 E. Main St., Green River* ☎ *435/564–3427* ⊕ *destinationgreenriver.com.* **Moab Information Center.** ⊠ *25 E. Center St., Moab* ☎ *435/259–8825* ⊕ *www.discovermoab.com/visitorcenter.htm.*

NEARBY ATTRACTIONS

Canyonlands by Night & Day. For more than 50 years, this outfitter was best known for its two-hour, after-dark boat ride on the Colorado River (March–October). While illuminating the canyon walls with 40,000 watts, the trip includes music and narration highlighting Moab's history,

Native American legends, and geologic formations along the river. You can also combine the boat trip with a Dutch-oven dinner. Daytime jet boat tours are offered, too, as well as tours by Hummer, airplane, and helicopter (land and air tours are offered year-round). ⊠ *1861 Hwy. 191, Moab* ☎ *435/259–5261, 800/394–9978* ⊕ *www.canyonlandsbynight.com.*

Courthouse Wash. Although this rock-art panel fell victim to an unusual case of vandalism in 1980, when someone scoured the petroglyphs and pictographs that had been left by four cultures, you can still see ancient images if you take a short walk from the parking area on the left-hand side of the road, heading south. ⊠ *Hwy. 191, about 2 miles south of park entrance.*

FAMILY
Fodor's Choice
★

John Wesley Powell River History Museum. Learn what it was like to travel down the Green and Colorado rivers in the 1800s in wooden boats. A series of displays tracks the Powell Party's arduous, dangerous 1869 journey, and visitors can watch the award-winning film *Journey Into the Unknown* for a cinematic taste of the white-water adventure. The center also houses the River Runner's Hall of Fame, a tribute to those who have followed in Powell's wake. River-themed art occupies a gallery and there's a dinosaur exhibit on the lower level. ⊠ *1765 E. Main St., Green River* ☎ *435/564–3427* ⊕ *www.jwprhm.com* 🎟 *$6.*

FAMILY

Museum of Moab. Exhibits on the history, geology, and paleontology of the Moab area include settler-era antiques, and ancient and historic Native Americans are remembered in displays of baskets, pottery, sandals, and other artifacts. Displays also chronicle early Spanish expeditions into the area, regional dinosaur finds, and the history of uranium discovery. ⊠ *118 E. Center St., Moab* ☎ *435/259–7985* ⊕ *www.moab-museum.org* 🎟 *$5.*

NIGHTLIFE AND PERFORMING ARTS

Moab Arts and Recreation Center. Offering a slice of Moab's arts scene, from "Quick Draw Sales" where artists have three hours to create pieces during the annual Plein Air Festival, to dance, crafts, and fitness classes, this has been the spirited hub of arts activities in Moab since 1997. ⊠ *111 E. 100 N, Moab* ☎ *435/259–6272* ⊕ *www.moabrecreation.com.*

10

SHOPPING

ART GALLERIES

Lema's Kokopelli Gallery. The Lema family has built a reputation for fair prices on a large selection of Native American and Southwest-themed jewelry, art, pottery, rugs, and more. Everything sold here is authentic. ⊠ *70 N. Main St., Moab* ☎ *435/259–5055* ⊕ *www.kokopellioutlet.com.*

BOOKS

FAMILY

Back of Beyond Books. A Main Street treasure, this comprehensive bookstore features the American West, environmental studies, Native American cultures, water issues, and Western history, as well as rare antiquarian books on the Southwest. There's also a nice nook for kids. ⊠ *83 N. Main St., Moab* ☎ *435/259–5154, 800/700–2859* ⊕ *www.backofbeyondbooks.com* ☉ *Daily 9–6 (to 9 pm Mar.–Nov.).*

SCENIC DRIVES

Fodor's Choice ★ **Colorado River Scenic Byway—Highway 128.** One of the most scenic drives in the country, Highway 128 intersects U.S. 191 3 miles south of Arches. The 44-mile highway runs along the Colorado River with 2,000-foot red rock cliffs rising on both sides. This gorgeous river corridor is home to a winery, orchards, and a couple of luxury lodging options. It also offers a spectacular view of world-class climbing destination Fisher Towers before winding north to Interstate 70. The drive from Moab to I–70 takes at least an hour. ✉ *Hwy. 128, Moab.*

WHERE TO EAT

IN THE PARK

PICNIC AREAS

Balanced Rock. The view is the best part of this picnic spot opposite the Balanced Rock parking area. There are no cooking facilities or water, but there are tables. If you sit just right you might find some shade under a small juniper; otherwise, this is an exposed site. Pit toilets are nearby. ✉ *Arches Scenic Dr., 9¼ miles from park entrance on main road.*

Devils Garden. There are grills, water, picnic tables, and restrooms here and, depending on the time of day, some shade from junipers and rock walls. It's a good place for lunch before or after a hike. ✉ *On main road, 18 miles from park entrance.*

OUTSIDE THE PARK

GREEN RIVER

$$ MEXICAN 🍴 **La Veracruzana.** The Polito family continues the long tradition of good food in this older, unassuming building on Green River's main drag. Couples and families should try the *molcajete*, a two-person entrée with meat, chicken, shrimp, and nopal (cactus) served on a volcanic-rock stone mortar. **Known for:** street tacos; molcajete; chile verde. [$] *Average main: $15* ✉ *125 W. Main St., Green River* ☎ *435/564–3257.*

$ AMERICAN 🍴 **Ray's Tavern.** Ray's is something of a Western legend and a favorite hangout for river runners. The bar that runs the length of the restaurant reminds you this is still a tavern and a serious watering hole—but all the photos and rafting memorabilia make it comfortable for families as well. **Known for:** legendary burgers; mixed clientele; homemade pie. [$] *Average main: $10* ✉ *25 S. Broadway, Green River* ☎ *435/564–3511* 🌐 *www.raystavern.com.*

MOAB

$ ECLECTIC Fodor's Choice ★ 🍴 **Eklecticafe.** The funky font on the sign makes this place easy to miss but worth finding for one of the more creative, healthy menus in Moab. Breakfast and lunch items include a variety of burritos and wraps, scrambled tofu, salmon cakes, Indonesian satay kebabs, and many fresh, organic salads. **Known for:** rich coffee; creative menu; artistic setting. [$] *Average main: $9* ✉ *352 N. Main St., Moab* ☎ *435/259–6896* ⏲ *No dinner.*

$$$$ STEAKHOUSE 🍴 **Jeffrey's Steakhouse.** Melt-in-your-mouth tender wagyu beef is this restaurant's specialty. Jeffrey's offers plenty of salads and side dishes, but remember—this is a steak house, so there's a separate charge for everything, and that can quickly make for a pricey meal. The menu also features lamb and pork chops, chicken and salmon, and a few other entrée options. **Known for:** wagyu beef; hearty menu; historic setting. [$] *Average main: $32* ✉ *218 N. 100 W, Moab* ☎ *435/259–3588* 🌐 *www.jeffreyssteakhouse.com* 🕒 *No lunch.*

$ AMERICAN FAMILY 🍴 **Moab Brewery.** Southern Utah's award-winning brewery is known for its Scorpion Pale Ale, Dead Horse Amber Ale, and an assortment of other brews from light to dark. Their on-site restaurant is spacious and comfortable and decorated with kayaks, bikes, and other adventure paraphernalia. **Known for:** spacious setting; made gelato; outdoorsy clientele. [$] *Average main: $12* ✉ *686 S. Main St., Moab* ☎ *435/259–6333* 🌐 *www.themoabbrewery.com.*

$ AMERICAN FAMILY 🍴 **Moab Diner.** For breakfast, lunch, and dinner, this is the place where old-time Moabites go. Try the dishes smothered in green chili (burritos, burgers, omelets, and more), which they claim is Utah's best. **Known for:** all-day breakfast; local's favorite; green chili. [$] *Average main: $10* ✉ *189 S. Main St., Moab* ☎ *435/259–4006* 🌐 *www.moabdiner.com* 🕒 *Closed Sun.*

$$ ITALIAN FAMILY 🍴 **Pasta Jay's.** Mountain bikers, families, and couples pack this downtown restaurant's patio from noon until well into the evening. This bustling spot's friendly servers rapidly dish up a dozen kinds of pasta in an equal number of preparations, perfect for hungry adventurers. **Known for:** American Italian vibe; extensive menu; patio dining. [$] *Average main: $15* ✉ *4 S. Main St., Moab* ☎ *435/259–3900* 🌐 *www.pastajays.com.*

$$ CAFÉ 🍴 **Peace Tree Juice Café.** Start with your choice of a dozen smoothies, then select from a menu that ranges from wraps to sandwiches to full entrées prepared primarily from local, natural, and organic ingredients for a healthy, filling meal. Try the quinoa-stuffed red pepper or sweet-and-salty beet salad for interesting new flavor combinations. **Known for:** healthy bites; bright setting; outdoor dining. [$] *Average main: $15* ✉ *20 S. Main St., Moab* ☎ *435/259–0101* 🌐 *www.peacetreejuicecafe.com.*

$$$ AMERICAN 🍴 **River Grill Restaurant.** The most scenic dining experience in the area is 17 miles upstream from Moab at the Sorrel River Ranch, beside the Colorado River, with views of La Sal Mountains, and the red-rock spires and towers surrounding the ranch. This fine-dining restaurant follows a farm-to-table ethic and its seasonal menu changes regularly; look for local options like buffalo, pheasant, lamb, and trout as well as vegetarian entrées. **Known for:** innovative dining; stunning setting; wine list. [$] *Average main: $28* ✉ *Sorrel River Ranch, Hwy. 128, mile marker 17.5, Moab* ☎ *435/259–4642* 🌐 *www.sorrelriver.com* 🕒 *Lunch for takeout only, Nov.–Mar.*

$$ MODERN ASIAN Fodor's Choice ★ 🍴 **Sabaku Sushi.** Sushi in the desert may seem surprising, but the chefs here know what they're doing. The fish is flown in fresh several times a week, the veggies are crisp, and the sauces are spicy—locals particularly love the spicy tuna roll with cucumber and avocado served with sriracha and eel sauce. **Known for:** accommodating menu; friendly service; sake

10

list. $ *Average main: $15* ⊠ *90 E. Center St., Moab* ☎ *435/259–4455* ⊕ *www.sabakusushi.com* ◔ *Closed Mon. No lunch.*

$ ✕**Sweet Cravings Bakery + Bistro.** Cinda Culton has created a sensation
BAKERY in Moab with some of the largest and most delicious cookies and cin-
FAMILY namon rolls you've ever seen. The secret here, though, is an amazing
roster of breakfast and lunch panini, wraps, and sandwiches, and daily
comfort foods like potpies and soups. **Known for:** cinnamon rolls; many
gluten-free options; local produce. $ *Average main: $10* ⊠ *397 N. Main
St., Moab* ☎ *435/259–8983* ⊕ *www.cravemoab.com* ◔ *No dinner.*

$$ ✕**Zax.** Wood-fired pizza ovens are the focal point of this downtown
AMERICAN eatery and sports bar, where baseball bats double as door handles. For
FAMILY $15 you can try the pizza-salad-soup buffet (a popular choice, so the
pies are constantly coming out of the oven). **Known for:** take-n-bake
pizza; sports fans; broad menu. $ *Average main: $15* ⊠ *96 S. Main St.,
Moab* ☎ *435/259–6555* ⊕ *www.zaxmoab.com.*

WHERE TO STAY

OUTSIDE THE PARK

Some of the best nightly lodging values in the area are rental con-
dominiums and homes. Accommodations Unlimited is a great place
to start, with units ranging from in-town studios to private homes.
☎ *435/259–6575* ⊕ *www.moabcondorentals.com.*

GREEN RIVER

$$ ▦**Green River Comfort Inn.** This clean, updated motel is convenient if
HOTEL you're staying only one night, as many do on family rafting outings
(Holiday River Expeditions is behind the hotel). **Pros:** clean and comfortable; close to town's premier rafting outfitter; kids under 18 stay
for free. **Cons:** remote, barren town; no elevator to second floor; Green
River's two best restaurants are not in walking distance. $ *Rooms from:
$139* ⊠ *1975 E. Main St., Green River* ☎ *435/564–3300* ⊕ *www.com-
fortinngreenriver.com* ⤳ *57 rooms* ◍*Breakfast.*

MOAB

$$$ ▦**Adobe Abode.** A lovely B&B near the nature preserve, this single-story
B&B/INN inn offers solitude. **Pros:** beautifully decorated common area; continen-
tal breakfast included; peace and quiet. **Cons:** too far to walk to town
(but close enough to bike); no children under 16 permitted. $ *Rooms
from: $179* ⊠ *778 W. Kane Creek Blvd., Moab* ☎ *435/259–7716*
⊕ *www.adobeabodemoab.com* ⤳ *6 rooms* ◍*Breakfast.*

$$$$ ▦**Best Western Canyonlands Inn.** The confluence of Main and Center
HOTEL streets is the epicenter of Moab, and this comfortable, contemporary,
FAMILY impeccably clean hotel anchors the intersection, providing a perfect
Fodor's Choice base for families. **Pros:** downtown location; updated, sparkling rooms;
★ breakfast alfresco on outdoor patio. **Cons:** pricey due to location; better
for families than solo travelers. $ *Rooms from: $287* ⊠ *16 S. Main St.,
Moab* ☎ *435/259–2300, 800/649–5191* ⊕ *www.canyonlandsinn.com*
⤳ *80 rooms* ◍*Breakfast.*

CLOSE UP

Best Campgrounds In and Around Arches

Campgrounds in and around Moab range from sprawling RV parks with myriad amenities to quaint, shady retreats near a babbling brook. The Devils Garden Campground in the park is a wonderful spot to call home for a few days, though it is often full and does not provide an RV dump station. More than 350 campsites are operated in the vicinity by the Bureau of Land Management—their sites on the Colorado River and near the Slickrock Trail are some of the nicest (and most affordable) in the area. The most centrally located campgrounds in Moab will generally provide services needed by RV travelers.

IN THE PARK

Devils Garden Campground. This campground is one of the most unusual—and gorgeous—in the West, and in the national park system, for that matter. ⊠ *Off main road, 18 miles from park entrance* ☎ *435/719-2299, 435/259-4351 for group reservations, 877/444-6777 for NRRS reservations* ⊕ *www.recreation.gov.*

OUTSIDE THE PARK

Bureau of Land Management Campgrounds. Most of the 350 sites at 25 different BLM campgrounds are in the Moab area, including some stunning sites along the Colorado River (Route 120 and Route 279), Sand Flats Recreation Area (near

the Slickrock Trail), and Canyon Flats Recreation Area (outside Needles District of Canyonlands). ☎ *435/259-2100* ⊕ *www.blm.gov/utah/moab.*

Canyonlands RV Resort and Campground. Although this camping park is in downtown Moab, the campground is astride Pack Creek and has many shade trees. ⊠ *555 S. Main St., Moab* ☎ *435/259-6848 or 888/522-6848* ⊕ *www.canyonlandsrv.com.*

Moab Valley RV Resort and Campground. Near the Colorado River, this campground with an expansive view feels more like a mall than a campground with its abundant space, activities, and services. ⊠ *1773 N. U.S. 191, Moab* ☎ *435/259-4469* ⊕ *www.moabvalleyrv.com.*

Slickrock Campground. At one of Moab's older campgrounds you find lots of mature shade trees and all the basic amenities—plus three hot tubs where adults have priority. ⊠ *1301½ N. U.S. 191, Moab* ☎ *435/259-7660 or 800/448-8873* ⊕ *www.slickrockcampground.com.*

Up the Creek Campground. Perhaps the quietest of the in-town campgrounds, Up the Creek lies under big cottonwoods on the banks of Mill Creek. ⊠ *210 E. 300 S, Moab* ☎ *435/260-1888* ⊕ *www.moabupthecreek.com.*

10

$$$
B&B/INN
Fodor's Choice
★

⌖ Cali Cochitta Bed & Breakfast. One of the first homes built in Moab, this 19th-century Victorian in the heart of town, two blocks from Main Street shops and restaurants, has been restored to its classic style by owners David and Kim Boger. **Pros:** gracious owners pay attention to the details; easy walk to the hub of town; breakfast in the garden from accomplished chef. **Cons:** historic construction, some quarters feel small. $ *Rooms from: $175* ⊠ *110 S. 200 E, Moab* ☎ *435/259-4961* ⊕ *www.moabdreaminn.com* ⇥ *6 rooms* ⌾ *Breakfast.*

$$$$ HOTEL 🏨 **Fairfield Inn and Suites.** Views of the Colorado River are sure to wow guests at this hotel. **Pros:** warm, inviting, and very clean; views of river and red rocks; buffet, continental, or hot breakfast included. **Cons:** 4 miles from downtown Moab; pricey. [$] *Rooms from: $224* ✉ *1863 N. Hwy. 191, Moab* ☎ *435/259–5350, 888/236–2427* 🌐 *www.marriott.com* 🛏 *89 rooms* 🍴 *Breakfast.*

$$$ HOTEL 🏨 **Gonzo Inn.** This eclectic inn stands out for its design, color, art, and varnished adobe construction. **Pros:** unique, spotless, and hip; steps to Main Street; pool and hot tub. **Cons:** interior hallways can be dark; no elevator; not all rooms have a good view. [$] *Rooms from: $199* ✉ *100 W. 200 S, Moab* ☎ *435/259–2515, 800/791–4044* 🌐 *www.gonzoinn.com* 🛏 *43 rooms* 🍴 *Breakfast.*

$$$$ RENTAL 🏨 **Moab Springs Ranch.** First developed by William Granstaff in the late 19th century, this 18-acre property about 3 miles from Arches and 2 miles from downtown Moab features comfortable hotel rooms and condos set by a meandering spring and decades-old sycamores, mulberries, and cottonwoods. **Pros:** scenic setting; along bike path to town. **Cons:** remote location; some Highway 191 traffic noise. [$] *Rooms from: $210* ✉ *1266 N. Main St., Moab* ☎ *435/259–7891* 🌐 *www.moabspringsranch.com* 🛏 *19 condos, from studios to larger rentals* 🍴 *No meals.*

$$ HOTEL 🏨 **Moab Red Stone Inn.** One of the best bargains in town, this timber-frame motel offers small, clean rooms at the south end of the Moab strip near restaurants and shops. **Pros:** walking distance to Moab restaurants and shops; the price is right. **Cons:** pool is at sister property across busy Main Street; no frills. [$] *Rooms from: $130* ✉ *535 S. Main St., Moab* ☎ *435/259–3500, 800/772–1972* 🌐 *www.moabredstone.com* 🛏 *52 rooms* 🍴 *No meals.*

$$ HOTEL 🏨 **River Terrace Hotel.** The peaceful setting, on the bank of the Green River, is conducive to a good night's rest, and the hotel is conveniently less than 2 miles off I–70. **Pros:** shady riverside location (be sure to request a river-view room); discounts often available; on-site restaurant; convenient for the passing traveler. **Cons:** remote, barren town; Green River's best two restaurants are not in walking distance. [$] *Rooms from: $141* ✉ *1740 E. Main St., Green River* ☎ *435/564–3401, 877/564–3401* 🌐 *www.river-terrace.com* 🛏 *50 rooms* 🍴 *Breakfast.*

CANYONLANDS
NATIONAL PARK

WELCOME TO CANYONLANDS NATIONAL PARK

TOP REASONS TO GO

★ **Endless vistas:** The view from the Island in the Sky stretches for miles as you look out over millennia of sculpting by wind and rain.

★ **Seeking solitude:** Needles, the most interesting part of the park to explore on foot, sees very few visitors, so you'll have it all to yourself.

★ **Radical rides:** The Cataract Canyon rapids and the White Rim Trail are world-class adventures by boat or bike.

★ **American Indian artifacts:** View rock art and Ancestral Puebloan dwellings in the park.

★ **Wonderful wilderness:** Some of the country's most untouched landscapes are within the park's boundaries, and they're worth the extra effort needed to get there.

★ **The night skies:** Far away from city lights, Canyonlands is ideal for stargazing.

1 Island in the Sky. From any of the overlooks here you can see for miles and look down thousands of feet to canyon floors. Chocolate-brown canyons are capped by white rock, and deep-red monuments rise nearby.

2 Needles. Pink, orange, and red rock is layered with white rock and stands in spires and pinnacles around grassy meadows. Extravagantly red mesas and buttes interrupt the horizon as in a picture postcard of the Old West.

3 The Maze. Only the most intrepid adventurers explore this incredibly remote mosaic of rock formations. There's a reason Butch Cassidy hid out here.

4 Rivers. For many, rafting through the waterways is the best way to see the park. The Green and Colorado are as wild as when John Wesley Powell explored them in the mid-1800s.

5 Horseshoe Canyon. Plan on several hours of dirt-road driving to get here, but the famous rock-art panel "Great Gallery" is a grand reward at the end of a long hike.

GETTING ORIENTED

Canyonlands National Park, in southeastern Utah, is divided into three distinct land districts and the river district, so it can be a little daunting to visit. It's exhausting, but not impossible, to explore the Island in the Sky and Needles in the same day.

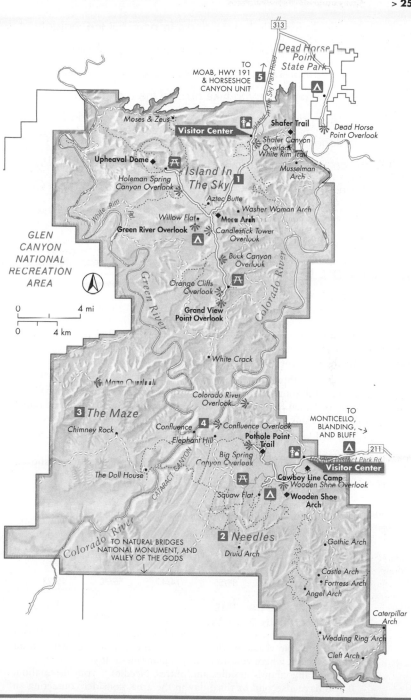

313

TO
MOAB, HWY 191
& HORSESHOE
CANYON UNIT

5

*Dead Horse
Point
State Park*

Road on the Sky Park Road

Moses & Zeus

Visitor Center

Shafer Trail

*Shafer Canyon
Overlook*

*Dead Horse
Point Overlook*

White Rim Trail

Upheaval Dome

*Island In
The Sky*

1

*Musselman
Arch*

*Holeman Spring
Canyon Overlook*

White Rim Rd.

Aztec Butte

Washer Woman Arch

Willow Flat

Mesa Arch

Green River Overlook

*Candlestick Tower
Overlook*

GLEN
CANYON
NATIONAL
RECREATION
AREA

*Buck Canyon
Overlook*

Green River

Colorado River

*Orange Cliffs
Overlook*

**Grand View
Point Overlook**

0   4 mi

0   4 km

White Crack

Maze Overlook

*Colorado River
Overlook*

3 *The Maze*

TO
MONTICELLO,
BLANDING,
AND BLUFF

Chimney Rock

Confluence

4

Confluence Overlook

Elephant Hill

**Pothole Point
Trail**

211

Needles District Park Rd.

*Big Spring
Canyon Overlook*

Visitor Center

The Doll House

CATARACT CANYON

Cowboy Line Camp

Wooden Shoe Overlook

Squaw Flat

**Wooden Shoe
Arch**

Colorado River

TO NATURAL BRIDGES
NATIONAL MONUMENT, AND
VALLEY OF THE GODS

2 *Needles*

Druid Arch

Gothic Arch

Castle Arch

Fortress Arch

Angel Arch

*Caterpillar
Arch*

Wedding Ring Arch

Cleft Arch

Updated by
John Blodgett

Canyonlands is truly four parks in one, but the majority of visitors drive through the panoramic vistas of Island in the Sky and barely venture anywhere else. If you've come this far, plan a half day to hike around the Needles district and see the park from the bottom up. To truly experience Canyonlands you should also float down the Green and Colorado rivers on a family-friendly rafting trip. (Rapids-lovers can take on the white water in the legendary Cataract Canyon.) The Maze is so remote that its river beds, slot canyons, and stark rock formations are only for the truly hardy.

CANYONLANDS PLANNER

WHEN TO GO

Gorgeous weather means that spring and fall are most popular for visitors. Canyonlands is seldom crowded, but in the spring backpackers and four-wheelers populate the trails and roads. During Easter week, some of the four-wheel-drive trails in the park are used for Jeep Safari, an annual event drawing thousands of visitors to town.

The crowds thin out by July as the thermostat approaches 100°F and beyond for about four weeks. It's a great time to get out on the Colorado or Green River winding through the park. October can be rainy, but the region receives only 8 inches of rain annually.

The well-kept secret is that winter is the best time in the park. Crowds are gone, roads are good, and snowcapped mountains stand in the background. Winter here is one of nature's most memorable shows, with red rock dusted white and low-floating clouds partially obscuring canyons and towers.

AVG. HIGH/LOW TEMPS.

Jan.	Feb.	Mar.	Apr.	May	June
44/22	52/28	64/35	71/42	82/51	93/60
July	Aug.	Sept.	Oct.	Nov.	Dec.
100/67	97/66	88/55	74/42	56/30	45/23

PLANNING YOUR TIME
CANYONLANDS IN ONE DAY

Your day begins with a choice: Island in the Sky or Needles. If you want expansive vistas looking across southeast Utah's canyons, head for the island, where you stand atop a giant mesa. If you want to walk among Canyonlands' needles and buttes, Needles is your destination. If you have a second or third day in the area, consider contacting an outfitter to take you on a rafting or 4X4 trip. ■TIP→ Before venturing into the park, top off your gas tank, pack a picnic lunch, and stock up on plenty of water.

ISLAND IN THE SKY — Make your first stop along the main park road at **Shafer Canyon Overlook**. A short walk takes you out on a finger of land with views of the canyon over both sides. From here you can see Shafer Trail's treacherous descent as it hugs the canyon walls below.

Stop at the visitor center to learn about ranger talks or special programs, then drive to **Mesa Arch**. Grab your camera and water bottle for the short hike out to the arch perched on the cliff's edge. After your excursion, take the spur road to Upheaval Dome, with its picnic spot in the parking lot. A short walk takes you to the first viewpoint of this crater. If you still have energy, 30 more minutes and a little sense of adventure, continue to the second overlook.

Retrace your drive to the main park road and continue to **Grand View Point**. Stroll along the edge of the rim, and see how many landmarks you can spot in the distance. White Rim Overlook is the best of the scenic spots, particularly if you're not afraid of heights and venture all the way out to the end of the rocky cliffs (no guardrail here). On the way back to dinner in Moab, spend an hour in Dead Horse Point State Park.

NEEDLES — If you can stay overnight as well, then begin today by setting up camp at Squaw Flat or one of the other wonderful campgrounds in Needles. Then hit the **Joint Trail**, or any of the trails that begin from Squaw Flat, and spend the day hiking in the backcountry of the park. Save an hour for the brief but terrific little hike to **Cave Springs**. Sleep under more stars than you've seen in a long time.

GETTING HERE AND AROUND
AIR TRAVEL
The nearest mid-sized airport to southeastern Utah is Grand Junction Regional Airport in Grand Junction, Colorado, approximately 110 miles from Moab.

CAR TRAVEL
Off U.S. 191, Canyonlands' Island in the Sky visitor center is 21 miles from Arches National Park and 32 miles from Moab on Route 313 west of U.S. 191; the Needles District is reached via Route 211, west of U.S. 191.

Before starting a journey to any of Canyonlands' three districts, make sure your gas tank is topped off, as there are no services inside the large park. Island in the Sky is 32 miles from Moab, Needles District is 80 miles from Moab, and the Maze is more than 100 miles from Moab. The Island in the Sky road from the district entrance to Grand View Point is 12 miles, with one 5-mile spur to Upheaval Dome. The Needles scenic drive is 10 miles with two spurs, about 3 miles each. Roads in the Maze, suitable only for rugged, high-clearance, four-wheel-drive vehicles, wind for hundreds of miles through the canyons. Within the parks, safety and courtesy mandate that you always park only in designated pull-outs or parking areas.

TRAIN TRAVEL

The nearest train "station" is a solitary Amtrak stop in Green River, about 50 miles northwest of Moab.

PARK ESSENTIALS

ACCESSIBILITY

There are currently no trails in Canyonlands that are accessible to people in wheelchairs, but Grand View Point and Buck Canyon Overlook at Island in the Sky are wheelchair accessible. In Needles, the visitor center, restrooms, Squaw Flat Campground, and Wooden Shoe Overlook are wheelchair accessible. The visitor centers at the Island in the Sky and Needles districts are also accessible, and the park's pit toilets are accessible with some assistance.

PARK FEES AND PERMITS

Admission is $25 per vehicle, $10 per person on foot or bicycle, and $15 per motorcycle, good for seven days. Your Canyonlands pass is good for all the park's districts. There's no entrance fee to the Maze District of Canyonlands. A $50 local park pass grants you admission to both Arches and Canyonlands as well as Natural Bridges and Hovenweep national monuments for one year.

You need a permit for overnight backpacking, four-wheel-drive camping, mountain-bike camping, four-wheel-drive day use in Horse and Lavender canyons, and river trips. Day-use permits are also now required for all motorized vehicles and bicycles on the Elephant Hill and White Rim trails and group sizes are limited. Reservations need to be made at least two weeks in advance.

PARK HOURS

Canyonlands National Park is open 24 hours a day, seven days a week, year-round. It is in the Mountain time zone.

CELL-PHONE RECEPTION

Cell-phone reception may be available in some parts of the park, but not reliably so. Public telephones are at the park's visitor centers.

EDUCATIONAL OFFERINGS

For more information on current schedules and locations of park programs, contact the visitor centers or check the bulletin boards throughout the park. Note that programs change periodically and may sometimes be canceled because of limited staffing.

FAMILY **Explorer Pack.** Just like borrowing a book from a library, kids can check out a backpack filled with tools for learning. The sturdy backpack includes binoculars, a magnifying glass, and a three-ring binder full of activities. It can be cumbersome to carry everything on a hike, but the backpack is great for around the campfire or back in your hotel room. Explorer packs are available in Canyonlands National Park at the Needles and the Island in the Sky visitor centers. ⊠ *Canyonlands National Park* ☎ *435/719–2313* ☜ *Free.*

RANGER PROGRAMS

Grand View Point Overlook Talk. Between April and October, rangers lead short presentations at Grand View Point about the geology that created Utah's Canyonlands. ⊠ *Grand View Point, 12 miles from park entrance off main park road, Island in the Sky* ☜ *Free* ☉ *Closed Oct.–Mar.*

FAMILY **Junior Ranger Program.** Kids ages five to 12 can pick up a Junior Ranger booklet at the visitor centers. It's full of puzzles, word games, and fun facts about the park and its wildlife. To earn the Junior Ranger badge, they must complete several activities in the booklet, attend a ranger program, watch the park film, and/or gather a bag of litter. ⊠ *Canyonlands National Park* ☎ *435/719–2313* ☜ *Free.*

RESTAURANTS

There are no dining facilities in the park itself. Restaurants in Monticello and Blanding offer simple meals; most are closed on Sunday and do not serve alcohol. Moab has a multitude of dining options.

HOTELS

There is no lodging inside Canyonlands. Most visitors use Moab as a base to explore the park. The towns of Monticello and Blanding offer basic motels, both family-owned and national chains. Bluff also has motels and bed-and-breakfasts and offers a quiet place to stay. *Hotel reviews have been shortened. For full information, visit Fodors.com.*

WHAT IT COSTS			
$	$$	$$$	$$$$
Restaurants	under $13	$13–$20	$21–$30	over $30
Hotels	under $101	$101–$150	$151–$200	over $200

Restaurant prices are the average cost of a main course at dinner, or if dinner is not served, at lunch. Hotel prices are the lowest cost of a standard double room in high season.

VISITOR INFORMATION

Park Contact Information Canyonlands National Park. ⊠ *2282 S.W. Resource Blvd., Moab* ☎ *435/719–2313* ⊕ *www.nps.gov/cany.*

VISITOR CENTERS

Hans Flat Ranger Station. This remote outpost—46 miles east of Route 24; 21 miles south and east of the Y junction and Horseshoe Canyon kiosk on a dirt road—is a treasure trove of books, maps, and other documents about the unforgiving Maze District of Canyonlands. The slot canyons, pictographs, and myriad rock formations are tempting, but having experience is key. The rangers will be direct with you—inexperienced off-road drivers and backpackers can get themselves into serious trouble in the Maze. Just to get here you must drive 46 miles on a dirt road that is sometimes impassable even to 4X4 vehicles. There's a pit toilet, but no water, food, or services of any kind. If you're headed for the backcountry, permits cost $30 per group for up to seven days. Rangers offer guided hikes in Horseshoe Canyon on most weekends during the spring and fall. ⊠ *Recreation Rds. 777 and 633, Maze* ☎ *435/259–2652.*

Island in the Sky Visitor Center. The gateway to the world-famous White Rim Trail, this visitor center 21 miles from U.S. 191, past the park entrance off the main park road, is often filled with a mix of mountain bikers, hikers, and tourists. Enjoy the orientation film, then browse the bookstore for information about the Canyonlands region. Exhibits help explain animal adaptations as well as some of the history of the park. Rangers give short talks twice a day. ⊠ *Grand View Point Rd., Island in the Sky* ☏ *435/259–4712.*

Needles District Visitor Center. This gorgeous building is 34 miles from U.S. 191 and less than 1 mile from the park entrance, off the main park road. Needles is remote, so it's worth stopping to inquire about road, weather, and park conditions. You can also watch the interesting orientation film and get books, trail maps, and other information. ⊠ *Hwy. 211, Needles* ☏ *435/259–4711.*

EXPLORING

SCENIC DRIVES

Island in the Sky Park Road. This 12-mile-long main road inside the park is bisected by a 5-mile side road to the Upheaval Dome area. To enjoy dramatic views, including the Green and Colorado rivers, stop at the overlooks and take the short walks. Once you get to the park, allow at least two hours to explore. ⊠ *Island in the Sky.*

Needles District Park Road. You'll feel like you've driven into a Hollywood Western as you roll along the park road in the Needles District. Red mesas and buttes rise against the horizon, blue mountain ranges interrupt the rangelands, and the colorful red-and-white needles stand like soldiers on the far side of grassy meadows. You should get out of the car at a few of the marked roadside stops, including both overlooks at Pothole Point. Allow at least 90 minutes in this less-traveled section of the park. ⊠ *Needles.*

HISTORIC SITES

ISLAND IN THE SKY
Shafer Trail. This road was probably first established by ancient Native Americans, but in the early 1900s ranchers used it to drive cattle into the canyon. Originally narrow and rugged, it was upgraded during the uranium boom, when miners hauled ore by truck from the canyon floor. Check out the road's winding route down canyon walls from Shafer Canyon Overlook before you drive it to see why it's mostly used by daring four-wheelers and energetic mountain bikers. Off the main road, less than 1 mile from the park entrance, it descends 1,400 feet to the White Rim. Check with the visitor center about road conditions before driving the Shafer Trail. It's often impassable after rains or snow. ⊠ *Island in the Sky.*

CLOSE UP

Plants and Wildlife in Canyonlands

11

Wildlife is not the attraction in Canyonlands, as many of the creatures sleep during the heat of the day. On the bright side, there are fewer people and less traffic to scare the animals away. Cool mornings and evenings are the best time to spot them, especially in summer when the heat keeps them in cool, shady areas. Mule deer are nearly always seen along the roadway as you enter the Needles District, and you'll no doubt see jackrabbits and small rodents darting across the roadway. Approximately 250 bighorn sheep populate the park in the Island in the Sky District, and the Maze shelters about 100 more. If you happen upon one of these regal animals, do not approach it even if it is alone, as bighorn sheep are skittish by nature and easily stressed. Also, report your sighting to a ranger.

NEEDLES

FAMILY **Cowboy Line Camp.** This fascinating stop on the **Cave Springs Trail** is an authentic example of cowboy life more than a century ago. You do not need to complete the entire trail (which includes two short ladders and some rocky hiking) to see the 19th-century artifacts at the Cowboy Camp. ⊠ *Off Cave Springs Rd., 2.3 miles from visitor center, Needles.*

SCENIC STOPS

ISLAND IN THE SKY

Fodor'sChoice **Grand View Point.** This 360-degree view is the main event for many
★ visitors to Island in the Sky. Look down on the Colorado and Green rivers and contemplate the power and persistence of water and the vast canyons carved over the millennia. Stretch your legs on the trails along the canyon edge. ⊠ *Off main road, 12 miles from park entrance, Island in the Sky.*

Green River Overlook. From the road it's just 100 yards to this stunning view of the Green River Canyon to the south and west. It's not far from Island in the Sky campground. ⊠ *About 1 mile off Upheaval Dome Rd., 8 miles from park entrance, Island in the Sky.*

Fodor'sChoice **Mesa Arch.** If you don't have time for the 2,000 arches in nearby Arches
★ National Park, you should take the easy, half-mile walk to Mesa Arch. The arch is above a cliff that drops 800 feet to the canyon bottom. Through the arch, views of Washerwoman Arch and surrounding buttes, spires, and canyons make this a favorite photo opportunity. ⊠ *Off main road, 7 miles from park entrance, Island in the Sky.*

Upheaval Dome. This mysterious crater is one of the wonders of Island in the Sky. Some geologists believe it's an eroded salt dome, but others think it was made by a meteorite. The trip to the first overlook is about a half-mile; energetic visitors can continue to the second overlook as well for a better perspective. ⊠ *Upheaval Dome Rd., 12 miles from park entrance, Island in the Sky.*

NEEDLES

Pothole Point Trail. Microscopic creatures lie dormant in pools that fill only after rare rainstorms. When the rains do come, some eggs hatch within hours and life becomes visible. If you're lucky, you'll hit Pothole Point after a storm. The dramatic views of the Needles and Six Shooter Peak make this easy, 0.6-mile round-trip worthwhile. Plan for about 45 minutes. There's no shade, so wear a hat and take plenty of water. ⊠ *Off main road, about 10 miles from Needles district park entrance, Needles.*

Wooden Shoe Arch. Kids will enjoy looking for the tiny window in the rock that looks like a wooden shoe with a turned-up toe. If you can't find it on your own, there's a marker to help you. ⊠ *Off main road, about 6 miles from Needles entrance to park, Needles.*

> ### MEET ME AT SUNSET
>
> Sunset is one of the picture-perfect times in Canyonlands, as the slanting sun shines over the vast network of canyons that stretch out below Island in the Sky. A moonlight drive to Grand View Point can also give you lasting memories as the moon drenches the white sandstone in light. Likewise, late-afternoon color in the spires and towers at the Needles District is a humbling, awe-inspiring scene.

SPORTS AND THE OUTDOORS

Canyonlands is one of the world's best destinations for adrenaline junkies. You can rock climb, mountain bike treacherous terrain, tackle world-class white-water rapids, and make your 4X4 crawl over steep cliffs along precipitous drops. Compared with other national parks, Canyonlands allows you to enjoy an amazing amount of solitude while having the adventure of a lifetime.

MULTISPORT OPERATORS

Holiday River Expeditions. Since 1966, this outfitter has offered one- to eight-day adventures on the San Juan, Green, and Colorado rivers, including inside Canyonlands National Park. They also offer multisport trips, women's retreats, and bike adventures, including the White Rim Trail. ⊠ *2075 E. Main St., Green River* ☎ *435/564–3273, 800/624–6323* ⊕ *www.bikeraft.com* ⊠ *From $190.*

NAVTEC. Doc Williams was the first physician in Moab in 1896, and some of his descendants never left, sharing his love for the area through this rafting, canyoneering, and 4X4 company. Whether you want to explore by boat, boots, or wheels, you'll find a multitude of one-day and multiday options here. ⊠ *321 N. Main St., Moab* ☎ *435/259–7983, 800/833–1278* ⊕ *www.navtec.com.*

Sheri Griffith Expeditions. In addition to trips through the white water of Cataract, Westwater, and Desolation canyons, on the Colorado and Green rivers, this company also offers specialty expeditions for women, writers, and families. One of their more luxurious expeditions features dinners cooked by a professional chef and served on linen-covered tables. Cots and other sleeping amenities also make roughing it a little more comfortable. ⊠ *2231 S. U.S. 191, Moab* ☎ *435/259–8229, 800/332–2439* ⊕ *www.griffithexp.com* ⊠ *From $85.*

AIR TOURS

TOURS

Redtail Aviation. This company's daily, regional tours give you an eagle's-eye view of the park, and you'll walk away with new respect and understanding of the word "wilderness." The Canyonlands Tour, one of several flightseeing options, lasts for one hour. A two-person minimum applies. ⊠ *Canyonlands Field Airport, N. Hwy. 191, 94 W. Aviation Way, Moab* ☎ *435/259–7421* ⊕ *www.redtailaviation.com* ⊠ *From $99 per person.*

BICYCLING

TOURS AND OUTFITTERS

Magpie Cycling. Professional guides and mountain biking instructors lead groups (or lone riders) on daylong and multiday bike trips exploring the Moab region's most memorable terrain, including the White Rim, Needles, and the Maze. If you need to rent a bike, Magpie will meet you at its preferred shop, Poison Spider Bicycles (☎ *435/259–7882 or 800/635–7882* ⊕ *poisonspiderbicycles.com*). ⊠ *497 N. Main St., Moab* ☎ *435/259–4464, 800/546–4245* ⊕ *www.magpieadventures.com.*

Rim Tours. Reliable, friendly, and professional, Rim Tours has been taking guests on guided one-day or multiday mountain-bike tours, including Klondike Bluffs (which enters Arches) and the White Rim Trail (inside Canyonlands) since 1985. Bike rentals are also available. Bike skills a little rusty? Rim Tours also offers mountain-bike instructional tours and skill clinics. ⊠ *1233 S. U.S. 191, Moab* ☎ *435/259–5223* ⊕ *www.rimtours.com* ⊠ *Day tours from $145; multiday from $825.*

Western Spirit Cycling Adventures. Head here for fully supported, go-at-your-own-pace, multiday mountain-bike and road-bike tours throughout the western states, including trips to Canyonlands, Trail of the Ancients, and the 140-mile Kokopelli Trail, which runs from Grand Junction, Colorado, to Moab. Guides versed in the geologic wonders of the area cook up meals worthy of the scenery each night. Ask about family rides, too. There's also the option to combine a Green River kayak trip with the three-night White Rim Trail ride. ⊠ *478 Mill Creek Dr., Moab* ☎ *435/259–8732, 800/845–2453* ⊕ *www.westernspirit.com* ⊠ *From $950.*

TRAILS

White Rim Road. Mountain bikers from all over the world like to brag that they've conquered this 100-mile ride. The trail's fame is well deserved: it traverses steep roads, broken rock, and dramatic ledges, as well as long stretches that wind through the canyons and look down onto others. If you're biking White Rim without an outfitter, you'll need careful planning, vehicle support, and much sought-after backcountry reservations. Permits are available no more than four months, and no less than two days, prior to permit start date. There is a 15-person, three-vehicle limit for groups. Day-use permits are also now required and can be obtained at the Island in the Sky visitor center or reserved 24 hours in advance through the park's website. Fifty bicycle permits are available each day. ⊠ *Off main park road about 1 mile from entrance, then about 11 miles on Shafer Trail, Island in the Sky* ☎ *435/259–4351* ⊕ *www.nps.gov/cany.*

BOATING AND RAFTING

In Labyrinth Canyon, north of the park boundary, and in Stillwater Canyon, in the Island in the Sky District, the river is quiet and calm and there's plenty of shoreside camping. The Island in the Sky leg of the Colorado River, from Moab to its confluence with the Green River and downstream a few more miles to Spanish Bottom, is ideal for both canoeing and for rides with an outfitter in a large, stable jet boat. If you want to take a self-guided flat-water float trip in the park you must obtain a $30 permit, which you have to request by mail or fax. Make your upstream travel arrangements with a shuttle company before you request a permit. For permits, contact the reservation office at park headquarters (☎ *435/259–4351*).

Below Spanish Bottom, about 64 miles downstream from Moab, 49 miles from the Potash Road ramp, and 4 miles south of the confluence, the Colorado churns into the first rapids of legendary Cataract Canyon. Home of some of the best white water in the United States, this piece of river between the Maze and the Needles districts rivals the Grand Canyon stretch of the Colorado River for adventure. During spring melt-off these rapids can rise to staggering heights and deliver heart-stopping excitement. The canyon cuts through the very heart of Canyonlands, where you can see this amazing wilderness area in its most pristine form. The water calms down a bit in summer. Outfitters will take you for the ride of your life in this wild canyon, where the river drops more steeply than anywhere else on the Colorado River (in ¾ mile, the river drops 39 feet). You can join an expedition lasting anywhere from one to six days, or you can purchase a $30 permit for a self-guided trip from park headquarters.

TOURS

Oars. This well-regarded outfitter can take you for several days of rafting and/or hiking on the Colorado and Green rivers. Hiking/interpretive trips are available in Canyonlands and Arches national parks, and for those not into white water, they also offer calm-water trips. ⊠ *2540 S. Hwy. 191, Moab* ☎ *435/259–5865, 800/342–5938* ⊕ *www.oarsutah.com* ⌨ *From $119.*

Tag-A-Long Expeditions. This outfitter, more than 50 years in business, has been taking people into the white water of Cataract Canyon and Canyonlands for longer than any other outfitter in Moab. They also run 4X4 expeditions into the backcountry and calm-water excursions on the Colorado and Green rivers. Half-day to six-day trips are available for groups of three to 11 people. ⊠ *452 N. Main St., Moab* ☎ *435/259–8946, 800/453–3292* ⊕ *www.tagalong.com* ⌨ *From $185.*

FOUR-WHEELING

11

Nearly 200 miles of challenging backcountry roads lead to campsites, trailheads, and natural and cultural features in Canyonlands. All of the roads require high-clearance, four-wheel-drive vehicles, and many are inappropriate for inexperienced drivers. The 100-mile White Rim Trail, for example, can be extremely challenging, so make sure that your four-wheel-drive skills are well-honed and that you are capable of making basic road and vehicle repairs. Carry at least one full-size spare tire, extra gas, extra water, a shovel, a high-lift jack, and—October through April—chains for all four tires. Double-check to see that your vehicle is in top-notch condition, for you definitely don't want to break down in the interior of the park: towing expenses can exceed $1,000.

Day-use permits, available at the park visitor centers or 24 hours in advance through the park website, are required for motorized and bicycle trips on the Elephant Hill and White Rim trails. For overnight four-wheeling trips you must purchase a $30 permit, which you can reserve no more than four months and no fewer than two days in advance by contacting the Backcountry Reservations Office (☎ 435/259–4351). Cyclists share all roads, so be aware and cautious of their presence. Vehicular traffic traveling uphill has the right-of-way. It's best to check at the visitor center for current road conditions before taking off into the backcountry. You must carry a washable, reusable toilet with you in the Maze District and carry out all waste.

ISLAND IN THE SKY

White Rim Road. Winding around and below the Island in the Sky mesa top, the dramatic, 100-mile White Rim Road offers a once-in-a-lifetime driving experience. As you tackle Murphy's Hogback, Hardscrabble Hill, and more formidable obstacles, you will get some fantastic views of the park. A trip around the loop can be done in one long day, or you can camp overnight with advance reservations. Campsite reservations open in July for the subsequent year, and popular spring and fall weekends fill up immediately. Day-use permits, which are available at the park visitor center or 24 hours in advance through the park website, are required for motorized and bicycle trips on White Rim Road. Fifty permits are available each day for vehicles, and 50 for bicycles. Bring plenty of water, a spare tire, and a jack, as no services are available on the road. White Rim Road starts at the end of Shafer Trail. ⊠ *Off main park road about 1 mile from entrance, then about 11 miles on Shafer Trail, Island in the Sky* ☎ *435/259–4351* ⊕ *www.nps.gov/cany.*

THE MAZE

Flint Trail. This remote, rugged road is the most popular in the Maze District, but it's not an easy ride. It has 2 miles of switchbacks that drop down the side of a cliff face. You reach Flint Trail from the Hans Flat Ranger Station, 46 miles from the closest paved road. From Hans Flat to the end of the road at the Doll House it's 41 miles, a drive that takes at least six hours one-way. The Maze is not generally a destination for a day trip, so you'll have to purchase an overnight backcountry permit for $30. Despite its remoteness, the Maze District can fill to capacity

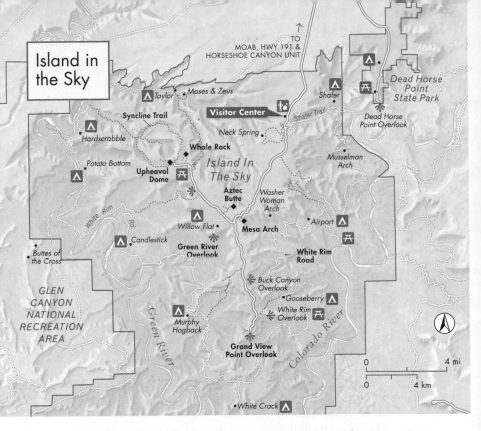

Island in the Sky

TO
MOAB, HWY 191 &
HORSESHOE CANYON UNIT

Taylor · Moses & Zeus

Syncline Trail

Visitor Center

Hardscrabble

Neck Spring

Shafer

Shafer Trail

Dead Horse
Point
State Park

Dead Horse
Point Overlook

Potato Bottom

Upheaval
Dome

Whale Rock

Island In
The Sky

Musselman
Arch

White Rim Rd.

Aztec
Butte

Washer
Woman
Arch

Willow Flat

Mesa Arch

Airport

Candlestick

Green River
Overlook

Buttes of
the Cross

White Rim
Road

Buck Canyon
Overlook

GLEN
CANYON
NATIONAL
RECREATION
AREA

Green River

Murphy
Hogback

Gooseberry

White Rim
Overlook

Grand View
Point Overlook

Colorado River

White Crack

0   4 mi

0   4 km

during spring and fall, so plan ahead. ⊠ *Hans Flat Ranger Station, National Park Rd. 777, 46 miles east of Rte. 24, Maze.*

NEEDLES

Elephant Hill. The first 3 miles of this route are designated as passable by all vehicles, but don't venture out without asking about road conditions. For the rest of the trail, only 4X4 vehicles are allowed. The route is so difficult that many people get out and walk—it's faster than you can drive it in some cases. The trek from Elephant Hill Trailhead to Devil's Kitchen is 3½ miles; from the trailhead to the Confluence Overlook, it's a 14½-mile round-trip and requires at least eight hours. Don't attempt this without a well-maintained 4X4 vehicle and spare gas, tires, and off-road knowledge. A day-use permit, which is available at the park visitor center or 24 hours in advance through the park website, is required for motorized and bicycle trips on the Elephant Hill Trail. ⊠ *Off main park road, 7 miles from park entrance, Needles.*

HIKING

At Canyonlands National Park you can immerse yourself in the intoxicating colors, smells, and textures of the desert. Many of the trails are long, rolling routes over slickrock and sand in landscapes dotted with juniper, pinyon, and sagebrush. Interconnecting trails in the Needles District provide excellent opportunities for weeklong backpacking excursions. The Maze trails are primarily accessed via four-wheel-drive vehicle. In the separate Horseshoe Canyon area, Horseshoe Canyon Trail takes a considerable amount of effort to reach, as it is more than 100 miles from Moab, 32 miles of which are a bumpy, and often sandy, dirt road.

ISLAND IN THE SKY
EASY

Aztec Butte Trail. The highlight of the 2-mile round-trip hike is the chance to see Ancestral Puebloan granaries. The view into Taylor Canyon is also nice. *Easy.* ⊠ *Island in the Sky* ⊹ *Trailhead: on Upheaval Dome Rd., about 6 miles from park entrance.*

Grand View Point Trail. If you're looking for a level walk with some of the best scenery in the West, stop at Grand View Point and wander this 2-mile round-trip trail along the cliff edge. Many people just stop at the paved overlook and drive on, but you'll gain breathtaking perspective by strolling along this flat cliffside trail. On a clear day you can see up to 100 miles to the Maze and Needles districts of the park, the confluence of the Green and Colorado rivers, and each of Utah's major laccolithic mountain ranges: the Henrys, Abajos, and La Sals. *Easy.* ⊠ *Island in the Sky* ⊹ *Trailhead: on main park road, 12 miles from visitor center.*

FAMILY

Fodor's Choice

★

Mesa Arch Trail. After the overlooks, this is the most popular trail in the park, a ½-mile loop that acquaints you with desert plants and terrain and offers vistas of the La Sal Mountains. The highlight of this hike is a natural arch window perched over an 800-foot drop, giving a rare downward glimpse through the arch rather than the usual upward view of the sky. Park rangers say this is one of the best spots to enjoy the sunrise. *Easy.* ⊠ *Island in the Sky* ⊹ *Trailhead: 6 miles from visitor center.*

FAMILY

Whale Rock Trail. If you've been hankering to walk across some of that pavement-smooth stuff they call slickrock, the hike to Whale Rock will make your feet happy. This 1-mile round-trip adventure, complete with handrails to help you make the tough final 100-foot climb, takes you to the very top of the whale's back. Once you get there, you are rewarded with great views of Upheaval Dome and Trail Canyon. *Easy.* ⊠ *Island in the Sky* ⊹ *Trailhead: on Upheaval Dome Rd., 11 miles from park entrance.*

MODERATE

Upheaval Dome Trail. It's fun to imagine that a giant meteorite crashed to earth here, sending shockwaves around the planet. But some people believe that salt, collecting and expanding upward, formed a dome and then exploded, causing the crater. Either way, it's worth the steep hike to see it and decide for yourself. You reach the main overlook after just 0.8 mile, but you can double your pleasure by going on to a second overlook for a better view. The trail is steeper and rougher after the first overlook. Round-trip to the second overlook is 2 miles. *Moderate.* ⊠ *Island in the Sky* ⊹ *Trailhead: on Upheaval Dome Rd., 12 miles from park entrance.*

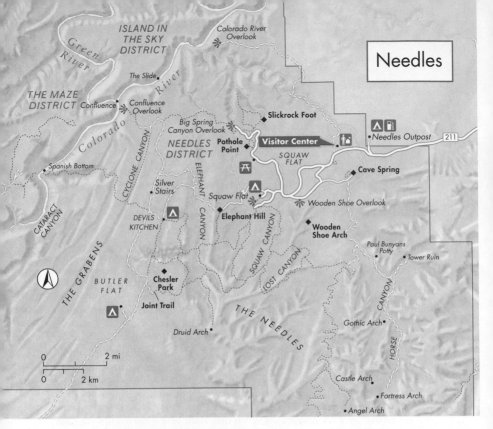

DIFFICULT

Syncline Loop Trail. If you're up for a strenuous day of hiking, try this 8-mile trail that circles Upheaval Dome. You get limited views of the dome itself as you actually make a complete loop around the outside of the crater. Stretches of the trail are rocky, rugged, and steep. *Difficult.* ⊠ *Island in the Sky* ✢ *Trailhead: on Upheaval Dome Rd., 12 miles from park entrance.*

THE MAZE
DIFFICULT

Horseshoe Canyon Trail. This remote region of Canyonlands National Park is accessible by dirt road, and then only in good weather. Park at the lip of the canyon and hike 6½ miles round-trip to the Great Gallery, considered by some to be the most significant rock-art panel in North America. Ghostly life-size figures in the Barrier Canyon style populate the amazing panel. The hike is moderately strenuous, with a 750-foot descent. Allow at least six hours for the trip and take a gallon of water per person. There's no camping allowed in the canyon, although you can camp on top near the parking lot. *Difficult.* ⊠ *Maze* ✢ *Trailhead: 32 miles east of Rte. 24.*

NEEDLES

EASY

Slickrock Trail. Wear a hat and carry plenty of water. If you're on this trail in summer—you won't find any shade along the 2.4-mile round-trip trek. This is the rare frontcountry site where you might spot one of the few remaining native herds of bighorn sheep in the national park system. Nice panoramic views. *Easy.* ⊠ *Needles* ⊹ *Trailhead: on main park road, about 10 miles from park entrance.*

MODERATE

FAMILY **Cave Spring Trail.** One of the best, most interesting trails in the park takes you past a historic cowboy camp, prehistoric pictographs, and great views. Two wooden ladders and one short, steep stretch may make this a little daunting for the extremely young or old, but it's also a short hike (0.6 mile), features some shade, and has many features packed into half a mile. Allow about 45 minutes. *Moderate.* ⊠ *Needles* ⊹ *Trailhead: off main park road on Cave Springs Rd., 2.3 miles from visitor center.*

DIFFICULT

Chesler Park Loop. Chesler Park is a grassy meadow dotted with spires and enclosed by a circular wall of colorful "needles." One of Canyonlands' more popular trails leads through the area to the famous Joint Trail. The trail is 6 miles round-trip to the viewpoint. The entire loop is 11 miles. *Difficult.* ⊠ *Needles* ⊹ *Trailhead: accessed via Elephant Hill Trailhead, off main park road, about 7 miles from park entrance.*

Fodor'sChoice **Joint Trail.** Part of the Chesler Park Loop, this well-loved trail follows a
★ series of deep, narrow fractures in the rock. A shady spot in summer, it will give you good views of the Needles formations for which the district is named. The loop travels briefly along a four-wheel-drive road and is 11 miles round-trip; allow at least five hours to complete the hike. *Difficult.* ⊠ *Needles* ⊹ *Trailhead: accessed by Elephant Hill Trailhead, off main park road, 7 miles from park entrance.*

ROCK CLIMBING

Fodor'sChoice Canyonlands and many of the surrounding areas draw climbers from
★ all over the world. Permits are not required, but because of the sensitive archaeological nature of the park it's imperative that you stop at the visitor center to pick up regulations pertaining to the park's cultural resources. Popular climbing routes include Moses and Zeus towers in Taylor Canyon, and Monster Tower and Washerwoman Tower on the White Rim Road. Like most routes in Canyonlands, these climbs are for experienced climbers only. Just outside the Needles District, in Indian Creek, is one of the country's best traditional climbing areas.

WHAT'S NEARBY

NEARBY TOWNS

Moab is the major gateway to both Arches and Canyonlands national parks, with the most outfitters, shops, and lodging options of the area. A handful of communities that are much smaller and have fewer amenities is scattered around the Needles and Island in the Sky districts along U.S. 191.

Roughly 55 miles south of Moab is **Monticello.** Convenient to the Needles District, it lies at an elevation of 7,000 feet, making it a cool summer refuge from the desert heat. In winter, it gets downright cold and sees deep snow; the Abajo Mountains, whose highest point is 11,360 feet, rise to the west of town. Monticello motels serve the steady stream of tourists who venture south of Moab, but the town offers few dining or shopping opportunities. **Blanding,** 21 miles south of Monticello, prides itself on old-fashioned conservative values. By popular vote there's a ban on the sale of liquor, beer, and wine, so the town has no state liquor store and its restaurants do not serve alcoholic beverages. Blanding is a good resting point if you're traveling south from Canyonlands to Natural Bridges Natural Monument, Grand Gulch, Lake Powell, or the Navajo Nation. About 25 miles south of Blanding, tiny **Bluff** is doing its best to stay that way. It's a great place to stop if you aren't looking for many amenities but value beautiful scenery, silence, and starry nights. Bluff is the most common starting point for trips on the San Juan River, which serves as the northern boundary for the Navajo Reservation; it's also a wonderful place to overnight if you're planning a visit to Hovenweep National Monument about 30 miles away.

Visitor Information Blanding Visitor Center. ⊠ *12 N. Grayson Pkwy., Blanding* ☎ *435/678–3662* ⊕ *www.blanding-ut.gov.* **Southeastern Utah Welcome Center.** ⊠ *216 S. Main St., Monticello* ☎ *435/587–3401* ⊕ *www.monticelloutah.org.*

UP, UP, AND AWAY

Bluff International Balloon Festival. Colorful hot-air balloons—some from as far away as England—take to the skies over Valley of the Gods and the town of Bluff during this mid-January festival. It's always a friendly crowd, and the balloon pilots often will trade a free ride if you help as part of their chase crew. Attend the "glow in" if weather doesn't prohibit, and see balloons illuminated against the night sky by the flame from the propane heaters that fill them with hot air. Bring warm clothing and expect crisp, clear weather. ⊠ *Bluff Community Center, 3rd East St. at Mulberry Ave., Bluff* ☎ *435/672–2290* ⊕ *bluffutah. org/bluffballoonfestival.*

NEARBY ATTRACTIONS

Fodor'sChoice ★ **Dead Horse Point State Park.** One of the gems of Utah's state park system, 34 miles southwest from Moab, this park overlooks a sweeping oxbow of the Colorado River some 2,000 feet below. Dead Horse Point itself is a small peninsula connected to the main mesa by a narrow neck of land. As the story goes, cowboys used to drive wild mustangs onto the point and pen them there with a brush fence. There's a modern visitor center with a coffee shop (March–October) and museum. The park's Intrepid Trail System has become popular with mountain bikers and hikers alike. Be sure to walk the 4-mile rim trail loop and drive to the park's eponymous point if it's a nice day. ⊠ *Hwy. 313* ☎ *435/259–2614, 800/322–3770 camping reservations* ⊕ *www.stateparks.utah.gov* ⌨ *$15 per vehicle.*

FAMILY
Fodor'sChoice
★

Edge of the Cedars State Park Museum. Possibly the most interesting state park in Utah, Edge of the Cedars is one of the nation's foremost museums dedicated to the Ancestral Puebloan culture. Behind the museum, an interpretive trail leads to an ancient village that they once inhabited. Portions of the village have been partially excavated and visitors can climb down a ladder into a 1,000-year-old ceremonial room called a kiva. The museum displays a variety of pots, baskets, spear points, and rare artifacts—even a pair of sandals said to date back 1,500 years. ⊠ *660 W. 400 N, Blanding* ☎ *435/678–2238* ⊕ *stateparks.utah.gov* ⌨ *$5* ⊘ *Closed Sun. in Nov.–Mar.*

Natural Bridges National Monument. Stunning natural bridges, ancient Native American ruins, and magnificent scenery throughout make Natural Bridges National Monument a must-see if you have time to make the trip. Sipapu is one of the largest natural bridges in the world, spanning 225 feet and standing more than 140 feet tall. You can take in the Sipapu, Owachomo, and Kachina bridges via an 8.6-mile round-trip hike that meanders around and under them. A 13-site primitive campground is an optimal spot for stargazing. The national monument is about 120 miles southwest of the Needles District of Canyonlands National Park and approximately 45 miles from Blanding. ⊠ *Hwy. 275, off Hwy. 95, Natural Bridges National Monument* ☎ *435/692–1234* ⊕ *www.nps.gov/nabr* ⌨ *$10 per vehicle, $5 for those entering park on foot, bicycle, or motorcycle.*

EN
ROUTE

Valley of the Gods. A red fairyland of slender spires and buttes, the Valley of the Gods is a smaller version of Monument Valley. Approximately 12 miles west of Bluff, you can take a pretty, private drive through this relatively unvisited area on the 17-mile-long Valley of the Gods Road, which begins on Route 163 and ends on Route 261. ⊠ *Mexican Hat* ☎ *435/587–1500.*

SHOPPING

Thin Bear Indian Arts. The Hosler family has operated this tiny little trading post in the same location since 1973. Authentic jewelry, rugs, baskets, and pottery are for sale at this friendly spot. ⊠ *1944 S. Main St., Blanding* ☎ *435/678–2940* ⊘ *Closed Sun.*

CLOSE UP

Best Campgrounds in Canyonlands

Canyonlands campgrounds are some of the most beautiful in the national park system. At the Needles District, campers will enjoy fairly private campsites tucked against red rock walls and dotted with pinyon and juniper trees. At Island in the Sky, starry nights and spectacular vistas make the small campground an intimate treasure. Hookups are not available in either of the park's campgrounds; however, the sites are long enough to accommodate units up to 28 feet long.

Squaw Flat Campground. The defining features of the camp sites at Squaw Flat are house-size red rock formations, which provide some shade, offer privacy from adjacent campers, and make this one of the more unique campgrounds in the national park system. ✉ *Off main road, about 5 miles from park entrance, Needles* ☎ *435/259–4711.*

Willow Flat Campground. From this little campground on a mesa top, you can walk to spectacular views of the Green River. Most sites have a bit of shade from juniper trees. ✉ *Off main park road, about 9 miles from park entrance, Island in the Sky* ☎ *435/259–4712.*

WHERE TO STAY

OUTSIDE THE PARK

$$$ HOTEL **Desert Rose Inn and Cabins.** Bluff's largest hotel is an attractive, wood-sided lodge with a huge two-story front porch. **Pros:** clean, comfortable rooms; friendly staff; pool, Jacuzzi, and fitness room. **Cons:** no historic charm; town not a culinary hub. $ *Rooms from: $160* ✉ *701 W. Main St., Bluff* ☎ *435/672–2303, 888/475–7673* 🌐 *www.desertroseinn.com* *46 rooms, 7 cabins* 🍴 *No meals.*

$ HOTEL **Recapture Lodge.** The knowledgeable owners for 30 years of this family-owned and -operated inn have detailed tips for exploring the surrounding canyon country. **Pros:** set on shady grounds with riverside walking trails; owner is a wildlife biologist and naturalist happy to share his knowledge; pets and horses welcome. **Cons:** older property; small rooms and basic amenities; no phones in rooms. $ *Rooms from: $98* ✉ *220 E. Main St. (U.S. 191), Bluff* ☎ *435/672–2281* 🌐 *www.recapturelodge.com* *26 rooms, 2 houses* 🍴 *Breakfast.*

MOAB AND SOUTHEASTERN UTAH

Updated by
Aly Capito

Southeastern Utah—especially Moab—is full of converts, and not so much in a religious sense. These are people formerly from suburbs or cities who came here long ago for vacation and never truly left. They may have spent just a few days surrounded by the vast desert and the clean, welcoming rivers, but in that short time, the land became a part of them. Moab has a certain kind of magic to it, as anyone who has ever visited will tell you, and many stay for the empty beauty of the region.

Although the towns tend to be visually simple in this part of the state, the beauty that surrounds them is awe-inspiring. You can hear about the canyons, arches, and natural bridges, but no words come close to their enormous presence.

ORIENTATION AND PLANNING

GETTING ORIENTED

Interstate 70 is the speedway that gets you across Utah, but to dip into southeastern Utah you'll need to use the main artery, U.S. 191, which runs south toward the Arizona border. The only road that stretches any distance westward across the region is Highway 95, which dead-ends at Lake Powell. No matter which of the state roads you use to explore the area, you're in for a treat. Here, the earth is red, purple, and orange. The Manti–La Sal Mountains rise out of the desert like ships. Mesas, buttes, and pinnacles interrupt the horizon in a most surprising way. But this is some of the most remote country in the United States, so services are sometimes far apart.

Moab. Small but unbelievably busy in spring, summer, and fall, Moab is on the Colorado River, south of I–70 on U.S. 191. More than 100 miles from any large town, it's close to nothing, and its residents are just fine with that.

Southeastern Utah. From Green River to Mexican Hat, this large swath of desert has a very small population. The most easily reached destinations are the small towns right on U.S. 191 or I–70, but some of the most beautiful stops require substantial but worthwhile detours off these main roads. Lake Powell, about three hours southwest of Moab, remains a favorite among visitors and locals alike.

TOP REASONS TO GO

Beauty from another world: The terra-cotta expanse of moonlike and open desert here is unparalleled.

Get out and play: Mountain and road biking, rafting, rock climbing, hiking, four-wheeling, and cross-country skiing are all wildly popular.

Creature comforts: Remote, southeastern Utah—and Moab, in particular—has an array of lodging and dining options, including elegant bistros, fancy hotels, and quaint bed-and-breakfasts.

Catch a festival: Especially in the spring and summer months, this area is chock-full of gatherings focused on art, music, and recreation.

Another state of being: The openness of this desert creates a friendly culture in which time and money aren't the main focus. Once that red sand gets in your blood, you might never leave.

12

PLANNING

WHEN TO GO

The most enjoyable times to be in this part of Utah are the beginning and end of high season, March and October, respectively. April and May have the best weather, but also the most visitors. May to September is the best time to hit the river, but is also when the towns and national parks are filled with people, and the temperatures can be downright fiery. From the beginning of November through the end of February some restaurants and stores shut down, and things can get eerily quiet. To compensate, almost all hotels offer steep discounts (sometimes as much as 40% off high-season prices), which can make visiting in the off-season a steal.

PLANNING YOUR TIME

With its variety of restaurants and lodgings, Moab is a great place to base your southeastern Utah adventures. From here, it's an easy drive to both **Arches** and **Canyonlands** national parks, each of which require at least a day to take in. At Arches, hike to the famous **Delicate Arch.** At Canyonlands, the **Island in the Sky District** is a stunning area to visit, with its crow's-nest views of deep canyons, thin spires, and the Colorado River. After a few days surrounded by rock and dust, you can spend one or several more days on the **Green, San Juan,** or **Colorado** river. Outfitters also offer half-day, one-day, or multiday trips on mountain bikes and jeeps, if either of those are more your speed. Many side trips from Moab can be taken in a day, some worthwhile treks being to the **La Sal Mountains, Goblin Valley State Park,** and the little town of **Bluff.** More southern locales, like **Natural Bridges National Monument, Lake Powell,** and **Monument Valley,** will be much more enjoyable with an overnight stay.

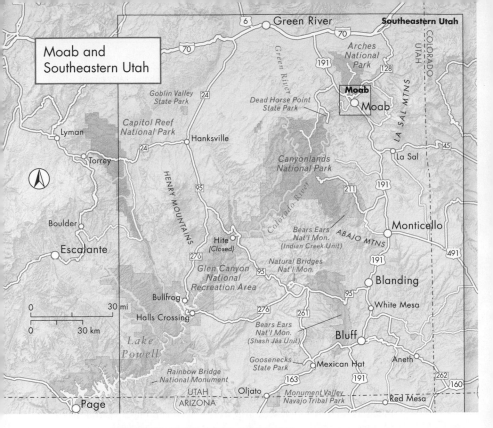

GETTING HERE AND AROUND

AIR TRAVEL

The nearest large airport to southeastern Utah is Walker Field Airport in Grand Junction, Colorado, 110 miles from Moab, but you can catch a regional flight directly to Moab. Rental cars are now available at the Moab Airport; advanced reservations are highly recommended.

Air Contacts Grand Junction Regional Airport. ⊠ *2828 Walker Field Dr., Grand Junction* ☎ *970/244–9100* ⊕ *www.gjairport.com.*

CAR TRAVEL

To reach southeastern Utah from Salt Lake City, take I–15 to U.S. 6 and then U.S. 191 south. From Colorado or more eastern locations, use I–70 or U.S. 491. Take U.S. 191 from either Wyoming or Arizona. Most roads are well-maintained two-lane highways, though snow can be a factor during winter travel. Be sure your car is in good working order and keep the gas tank topped off, as there are long stretches of empty road between towns.

Information Utah State Road Conditions. ☎ *511 toll-free within Utah, 866/511 8824 toll-free outside Utah* ⊕ *www.udot.utah.gov.*

RESTAURANTS

Including a few surprising twists, Moab-area restaurants have anything you might crave. The other smaller towns in southeastern Utah don't have quite the culinary kaleidoscope, and focus on all-American cuisine. Though not the best destination for vegetarians or those with a restricted diet, the comfort food will satisfy after a day of activity.

HOTELS

Every type of lodging is available in southeastern Utah, from economy chain motels, to B&Bs and high-end, high-adventure resorts. Some of the best values in Moab are condominiums available for rent. Start with the Moab Travel Council for listings and suggestions of accommodations to suit your group size and budget. *Hotel reviews have been shortened. For full information, visit Fodors.com.*

Contacts Moab Property Management. ☎ 435/259-5955, 800/505-5343, 435/514-7281 ⊕ www.moabutahlodging.com.

WHAT IT COSTS				
	$	$$	$$$	$$$$
Restaurants	under $12	$12–$20	$21–$30	over $30
Hotels	under $100	$100–$150	$151–$200	over $200

Restaurant prices are the average cost of a main course at dinner or, if dinner is not served, at lunch. Hotel prices are the lowest cost of a standard double room in high season.

MOAB

When you first drive down Main Street (Moab's commercial, downtown strip), you might not get the town's appeal right away. The wide thoroughfare is lined with T-shirt shops and touristy restaurants. But don't let Moab's impersonal exterior fool you; take a few walks, visit some of the town's shops, and talk to some of the residents, and you'll realize this is a town centered on community. Local theater, local radio, and local art rule. At its core, this is a frontier outpost, where people have had to create their own livelihoods for more than 100 years. In the late 1880s, it was settled as a farming and ranching community. By the 1950s it became a center for uranium mining after Charlie Steen found a huge deposit of the stuff outside town. After about a decade of unbelievable monetary success, there was a massive downturn in the mining industry, and Moab plunged into an economic free fall. Then came tourism. Moab was able to rebuild itself with the dollars of sightseers, four-wheelers, bikers, and boaters. Today the town is dealing with environmental and development issues while becoming more and more popular with tourists and second-homeowners from around the world. No matter how it changes, though, one thing simply doesn't: this town has a different flavor from any other found in the state.

GETTING HERE AND AROUND

Although Moab is friendly to bikes and pedestrians, the only practical way to reach it is by car. If you're coming from the south, U.S. 191 runs straight into Moab. If you're arriving from Salt Lake City, travel 50 miles via I–15, then go 150 miles southeast via U.S. 6, and finally 30 miles south via U.S. 191. Signs for Moab will be obvious past Green River. ■ TIP→ **If you are approaching from the east on U.S. 70, take Exit 214 into the ghost town of Cisco, and then drive down Colorado River Scenic Byway—Route 128 into Moab. The views of the river, rocks, and mesas are second to none.**

FESTIVALS

As much as Moab is a place for the outdoors, it's also a spot to experience extremely popular festivals and events in a small-town setting. For the most part, these are time-honored institutions that draw quite a crowd of both locals and visitors.

Easter Jeep Safari. Each year during the weeklong Easter Jeep Safari, thousands of 4X4 vehicles descend on Moab to tackle some of the toughest backcountry roads in America. ⊠ *Moab* ☎ *435/259–7625* ⊕ *www.rr4w.com.*

FAMILY
Fodor'sChoice
★

Moab Arts Festival. Every Memorial Day weekend, artists from across the West gather at Moab's Swanny City Park to show their wares, including pottery, photography, and paintings. This fun festival is small enough to be manageable, charges no admission, and sells a variety of affordable artworks. Soundtracked by live music, they also have activities for kids and lots of food. The arts festival partners with local libation producers to bring a wine and beer festival to the park as part of the event. ⊠ *Moab* ☎ *435/259–2742 Moab Arts Council* ⊕ *www.moabartsfestival.org.*

Moab Music Festival. Moab's red rocks resonate with world-class music—classical, jazz, and traditional—during this annual festival that takes place at indoor and outdoor venues including the city park, local auditoriums, private homes, and a natural stone grotto along the Colorado River. Musicians from all over the globe perform, and it's one of the West's top music showcases. The festival starts the Thursday before Labor Day and runs about two weeks. ⊠ *Moab* ☎ *435/259–7003* ⊕ *www.moabmusicfest.org.*

Pumpkin Chuckin' Festival. This unique event brings together the diverse Moab community on the last Saturday of October. This festival may not be like any other you've attended; here, people from all over the Southwest build contraptions—catapults, trebuchets, and slingshots—that send pumpkins across the sky. Live music, about 25 vendor booths, and typically beautiful weather make this a popular event. Proceeds go toward the Youth Garden Project. ⊠ *Grand County High School, 400 E. and Red Devil Dr.* ☎ *435/259–2326* ⊠ *$10.*

TOURS

Canyonlands by Night & Day. For more than 50 years, this outfitter was best known for its two-hour, after-dark boat ride on the Colorado River (March–October). While illuminating the canyon walls with 40,000 watts, the trip includes music and narration highlighting Moab's history,

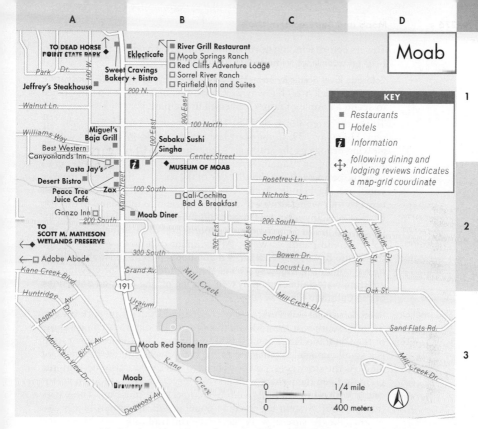

Native American legends, and geologic formations along the river. You can also combine the boat trip with a Dutch-oven dinner. Daytime jet boat tours are offered, too, as well as tours by Hummer, airplane, and helicopter (land and air tours are offered year round). ⊠ *1861 Hwy. 191* ☎ *435/259–5261, 800/394–9978* ⊕ *www.canyonlandsbynight.com.*

ESSENTIALS

The Moab Information Center is right in the heart of town and it's the best place to find information on Arches and Canyonlands national parks. Hours vary, but in the peak tourist season it's open until at least 7 pm, and for a few hours each morning and afternoon in winter.

Visitor Information Moab Information Center. ⊠ *25 E. Center St.* ☎ *435/259–8825* ⊕ *www.discovermoab.com/visitorcenter.htm.*

EXPLORING

Fodor's Choice ★ **Colorado River Scenic Byway—Highway 128.** One of the most scenic drives in the country, Highway 128 intersects U.S. 191 3 miles south of Arches. The 44-mile highway runs along the Colorado River with 2,000-foot red rock cliffs rising on both sides. This gorgeous river corridor is home to a winery, orchards, and a couple of luxury lodging options. It also offers a spectacular view of world-class climbing destination Fisher

Towers before winding north to Interstate 70. The drive from Moab to I–70 takes at least an hour. ✉ *Hwy. 128.*

Colorado River Scenic Byway—Highway 279. If you're interested in Native American rock art, Highway 279 northwest of Moab is a perfect place to spend a couple of hours immersed in the past.

To get there, go north on U.S. 191 for about 3½ miles and turn left onto Highway 279. If you start late in the afternoon, the cliffs will be glowing orange as the sun sets. Along the first part of the route you'll see signs reading "Indian Writings." Park only in designated areas to view the petroglyphs on the cliff side of the road. At the 18-mile marker you'll see Jug Handle Arch. A few miles beyond this point the road turns to four-wheel-drive only, and takes you into the Island in the Sky District of Canyonlands. Do not continue onto the Island in the Sky unless you are in a high-clearance four-wheel-drive vehicle with a full gas tank and plenty of water. Allow about two hours round-trip for the Scenic Byway drive. ■TIP➔ **If you happen to be in Moab during a heavy rainstorm, Highway 279 is also a good option for viewing the amazing waterfalls caused by rain pouring off the cliffs on both sides of the Colorado River.** ✉ *Hwy. 279.*

Fodor's Choice ★   **Dead Horse Point State Park.** One of the gems of Utah's state park system, 34 miles southwest from Moab, this park overlooks a sweeping oxbow of the Colorado River some 2,000 feet below. Dead Horse Point itself is a small peninsula connected to the main mesa by a narrow neck of land. As the story goes, cowboys used to drive wild mustangs onto the point and pen them there with a brush fence. There's a modern visitor center with a coffee shop (March–October) and museum. The park's Intrepid Trail System has become popular with mountain bikers and hikers alike. Be sure to walk the 4-mile rim trail loop and drive to the park's eponymous point if it's a nice day. ✉ *Hwy. 313, Canyonlands National Park* 🕾 *435/259–2614, 800/322–3770 camping reservations* ⊕ *www.stateparks.utah.gov* 💲 *$15 per vehicle.*

FAMILY   **Museum of Moab.** Exhibits on the history, geology, and paleontology of the Moab area include settler-era antiques, and ancient and historic Native Americans are remembered in displays of baskets, pottery, sandals, and other artifacts. Displays also chronicle early Spanish expeditions into the area, regional dinosaur finds, and the history of uranium discovery. ✉ *118 E. Center St.* 🕾 *435/259–7985* ⊕ *www.moabmuseum.org* 💲 *$5.*

Scott M. Matheson Wetlands Preserve. Owned and operated by the Nature Conservancy, this is the best place in the Moab area for bird-watching. The 894-acre oasis is home to more than 200 species, including such treasures as the pied-billed grebe, the cinnamon teal, and the northern flicker. It's also a great place to spot beavers and muskrats playing in the water. Hear a big "Slap!" on the water? That's a beaver warning you that you're too close. Always remember to respect the wildlife preserved in these areas, and enjoy the nature you find here. An information kiosk greets visitors just inside the preserve and a boardwalk winds through the property to a viewing shelter. To reach the preserve, turn northwest off U.S. 191 at Kane Creek Boulevard and continue northwest approximately 2 miles. ✉ *934 W. Kane Creek Blvd.* ☎ *435/259–4629* ⊕ *www.nature.org* ✉ *Free.*

SPORTS AND THE OUTDOORS

Moab's towering cliffs and deep canyons can be intimidating, and some are unreachable without the help of a guide. Fortunately, guide services are abundant in Moab. Whether you are interested in a 4x4 expedition into the rugged backcountry, a river-rafting trip, a jet-boat tour on calm water, bicycle tours, rock-art tours, or a scenic flight, you can find the pro to help you on your way. It's always best to make reservations. Book the Fiery Furnace tour in Arches National Park at least one month in advance.

SHUTTLES

If you need a ride to or from your trailhead or river trip put-in point, a couple of Moab companies provide the service (and also provide airport shuttle service by reservation), with vehicles large enough to handle most groups. Coyote's website is worth checking out for trail and river conditions and other information. Inquiries for Roadrunner are handled by Dual Sport, under the same ownership.

FOUR-WHEELING

There are thousands of miles of four-wheel-drive roads in and around Moab suitable for all levels of drivers. Seasoned 4x4 drivers might tackle the daunting Moab Rim, Elephant Hill, or Poison Spider Mesa. Novices will be happier touring Long Canyon, Hurrah Pass. If you're not afraid of precipitous cliff edges, the famous Shafer Trail may be a good option for you. Expect to pay around $75 for a half-day tour and $120 for a full day; multiday safaris usually start at around $600. Almost all of Moab's river-running companies also offer four-wheeling excursions.

OUTFITTERS AND EXPEDITIONS

Coyote Land Tours. Imposing Mercedes Benz Unimog trucks (which dwarf Hummers) take you to parts of the backcountry where you could never wander on your own. Technical tours challenge drivers with imposing rock formations, washes, and assorted obstacles, and there are tamer sunset excursions and camp-style ride-and-dine trips. They stand by their money-back "great time" guarantee. ✉ *Moab* ☎ *435/260–6056* ⊕ *www.coyotelandtours.com* ✉ *From $59.*

Dual Sport Utah. If you're into dirt biking, this is the only outfitter in Moab specializing in street-legal, off-road dirt-bike tours and rentals. Follow the Klondike Bluffs trail to Arches, or negotiate the White Rim Trail in Canyonlands in a fraction of the time you would spend on a mountain bike. You can also rent jet skis here. ✉ *197 W. Center. St.* ☎ *435/260–2724* ⊕ *www.dualsportutah.com* ✉ *From $225.*

High Point Hummer & ATV. You can rent vehicles, including ATVs, UTVs, and Jeeps, or get a guided tour of the backcountry in open-air Hummer vehicles or ATVs, or dune buggy–like "side-by-sides" that seat up to six people. The enthusiastic owners love families and small, intimate groups, and offer hiking and canyoneering as well. ✉ *281 N. Main St.*

☎ *435/259–2972, 877/486–6833*
⊕ *www.highpointhummer.com*
✉ *Guided tours from $69.*

HIKING

For a great view of the Moab Valley and surrounding red-rock country, hike up the steep **Moab Rim Trail.** For something a little less taxing, hike the shady, cool path of **Grandstaff Canyon,** which is off Route Highway 129. At the end of the trail you'll find giant Morning Glory Arch towering over a serene pool created by a natural spring. If you want to take a stroll through the heart of Moab, hop on the **Mill Creek Parkway,** which winds along the creek from one side of town to the other. It's paved and perfect for bicycles, strollers, or joggers. For a taste of slickrock hiking that feels like the backcountry but is easy to access, try the **Corona Arch Trail** off Highway 279. You'll be rewarded with two large arches hidden from view of the highway. The Moab Information Center carries a free hiking trail guide.

MOUNTAIN BIKING

Mountain biking originated in Moab, and the region has earned the well-deserved reputation as the mountain-biking capital of the world. Riders of all ages and skill levels are drawn to the many rugged roads and trails found here. One of the most popular routes is the **Slickrock Trail,** a stunning area of steep Navajo Sandstone dunes a few miles east of Moab. ■ **TIP→ Beginners should master the 2⅓-mile practice loop before attempting the longer, and very challenging, 10-mile loop.** More moderate rides can be found on the **Gemini Bridges** or **Monitor and Merrimac** trails, both found off U.S. 191 north of Moab. **Klondike Bluffs,** north of Moab, is an excellent novice ride, as are sections of the newer trails in the Klonzo trail system. The Moab Information Center carries a free biking trail guide. Mountain-bike rentals range from $40 for a good bike to $75 for a top-of-the-line workhorse. If you want to go on a guided ride, expect to pay between $120 and $135 per person for a half-day, and $155 to $190 for a full day, including the cost of the bike rental. You can save money by joining a larger group to keep the per-person rates down; even a party of two will save drastically over a single rider. Several companies offer shuttles to and from the trailheads.

OUTFITTERS AND EXPEDITIONS

Fodor'sChoice **Poison Spider Bicycles.** In a town of great bike shops, this fully loaded
★ shop is considered one of the best. Poison Spider serves the thriving road-cycling community as well as mountain bikers. Rent, buy, or service your bike here. You can also arrange for shuttle and guide services and purchase merchandise. Want to ship your bike to Moab for your adventure? Poison Spider will store it until you arrive and the staff will reassemble it for you and make sure everything is in perfect working

order. ✉ *497 N. Main St.* ☎ *435/259–7882, 800/635–1792* ⊕ *www. poisonspiderbicycles.com.*

Rim Tours. Reliable, friendly, and professional, Rim Tours has been taking guests on guided one-day or multiday mountain-bike tours, including Klondike Bluffs (which enters Arches) and the White Rim Trail (inside Canyonlands) since 1985. Road-bike tours as well as bike rentals are also available. Bike skills a little rusty? Rim Tours also offers mountain-bike instructional tours and skill clinics. ✉ *1233 S. U.S. 191* ☎ *435/259–5223, 800/626–7335* ⊕ *www.rimtours.com* ✑ *Day tours from $145; multiday from $825.*

Western Spirit Cycling Adventures. Head here for fully supported, go-at-your-own-pace, multiday mountain-bike and road-bike tours throughout the western states, including trips to Canyonlands, Trail of the Ancients, and the 140-mile Kokopelli Trail, which runs from Grand Junction, Colorado, to Moab. Guides versed in the geologic wonders of the area cook up meals worthy of the scenery each night. Ask about family rides, and road bike trips, too. There's also the option to combine a Green River kayak trip with the three-night White Rim Trail ride. ✉ *478 Mill Creek Dr.* ☎ *435/259–8732, 800/845–2453* ⊕ *www. westernspirit.com* ✑ *From $950.*

MULTISPORT

Outdoor lovers wear many hats in Moab: boaters, bikers, and even Jeep-drivers. Here are a few companies that cater to a range of adventure seekers.

OUTFITTERS AND EXPEDITIONS

FAMILY **Adrift Adventures.** This outfitter takes pride in well-trained guides who can take you via foot, raft, kayak, 4X4, jet boat, stand-up paddleboard, and more, all over the Moab area, including the Colorado and Green rivers. They also offer history, movie, and rock-art tours. They've been in business since 1977 and have a great reputation around town. ✉ *378 N. Main St.* ☎ *435/259–8594, 800/874–4483* ⊕ *www.adrift. net* ✑ *From $52.*

Moab Adventure Center. At the prominent storefront on Main Street you can schedule most any type of local adventure experience you want, including rafting, 4X4 tours, scenic flights, hikes, balloon rides, and much, much more. You can also purchase clothing and outdoor gear for your visit. ✉ *225 S. Main St.* ☎ *435/259–7019, 866/904–1163* ⊕ *www. moabadventurecenter.com* ✑ *From $62.*

NAVTEC. Doc Williams was the first doctor in Moab in 1896, and some of his descendants never left, sharing his love for the area through this rafting, canyoneering, and 4X4 company. Whether you want to explore by boat, boots, or wheels, you'll find a multitude of one-day and multiday options here. ✉ *321 N. Main St.* ☎ *435/259–7983, 800/833–1278* ⊕ *www.navtec.com.*

Oars. This well-regarded outfitter can take you for several days of rafting and/or hiking on the Colorado and Green rivers. Hiking/interpretive trips are available in Canyonlands and Arches national parks, and for those not into white water, they also offer calm-water trips. ✉ *2540*

S. Hwy. 191 ☎ *435/259–5865, 800/342–5938* ⊕ *www.oarsutah.com* 🍴 *From $119.*

Tag-A-Long Expeditions. This outfitter has been taking people into the white water of Cataract Canyon and Canyonlands for more than 50 years, longer than any other outfitter in Moab. They also run 4X4 expeditions into the backcountry and calm-water excursions on the Colorado and Green rivers. Trips, for 3 to 11 people, run from a half-day to five days. ✉ *452 N. Main St.* ☎ *435/259–8946, 800/453–3292* ⊕ *www.tagalong.com* 🍴 *From $55.*

RIVER EXPEDITIONS

On the Colorado River northeast of Arches and very near Moab, you can take one of America's most scenic—but not intimidating—river-raft rides. The river rolls by the red Fisher Towers as they rise into the sky in front of the La Sal Mountains. A day trip on this stretch of the river will take you about 15 miles. Outfitters offer full, half, or multiday adventures here. Upriver, in narrow, winding Westwater Canyon near the Utah–Colorado border, the Colorado River cuts through the oldest exposed geologic layer on Earth. Most outfitters offer this trip as a one-day getaway, but you may also take as long as three days to complete the journey. A permit is required from the Bureau of Land Management (BLM) in Moab to run Westwater Canyon.

OUTFITTERS AND EXPEDITIONS

FAMILY **Canyon Voyages Adventure Co.** This is an excellent choice for rafting or
Fodor's Choice kayaking adventures on the Colorado or Green River. Don and Denise
★ Oblak run a friendly, professional company with a retail store and rental shop that's open year-round. Most of their customers take one-day trips, but they also offer multiday itineraries, guided tours, and rentals. It's also the only company that operates a kayak school for those who want to learn how to run the rapids on their own. Ask about stand-up paddleboarding, biking, and horseback riding, too. ✉ *211 N. Main St.* ☎ *435/363–3794, 866/484–4506* ⊕ *www.canyonvoyages. com* 🍴 *From $58.*

Holiday River Expeditions. Since 1966, this outfitter has offered one- to eight-day adventures on the San Juan, Green, and Colorado rivers, including inside Canyonlands National Park. They also offer multisport trips, women's retreats, and bike adventures, including the White Rim Trail. ✉ *2075 E. Main St., Green River* ☎ *435/564–3273, 800/624–6323* ⊕ *www.bikeraft.com* 🍴 *From $190.*

Sheri Griffith Expeditions. In addition to trips through the white water of Cataract, Westwater, and Desolation canyons, on the Colorado and Green rivers, this company also offers specialty expeditions for women, writers, and families. One of their more luxurious expeditions features dinners cooked by a professional chef and served at linen-covered tables. Cots and other sleeping amenities also make roughing it a little more comfortable. ✉ *2231 S. U.S. 191* ☎ *435/259–8229, 800/332–2439* ⊕ *www.griffithexp.com* 🍴 *From $85.*

ROCK CLIMBING

Rock climbing is an integral part of Moab culture. The area's rock walls and towers bring climbers from around the world, and a surprising number end up sticking around. Moab offers some of the best climbing challenges in the country, and any enthusiast will find bliss here.

OUTFITTERS AND EXPEDITIONS

Desert Highlights. This guide company takes adventurous types on descents and ascents through canyons (with the help of ropes), including those found in the Fiery Furnace at Arches National Park. Full-day and multiday canyoneering treks are available to destinations both inside and outside the national parks. Desert Highlights does not offer guided rock climbing. ✉ *50 E. Center St.* ☎ *435/259–4433, 800/747–1342* 🌐 *www.deserthighlights.com* 🎫 *From $120.*

Moab Cliffs & Canyons. In a town where everyone seems to offer rafting and 4X4 expeditions, Moab Cliffs & Canyons focuses exclusively on canyoneering, climbing, and rappelling—for novice and veteran adventurers. Prices vary according to how many people sign up. This is the outfitter that provided technical assistance to the crew on the movie *127 Hours.* ✉ *253 N. Main St.* ☎ *435/259–3317, 877/641–5271* 🌐 *www.cliffsandcanyons.com* 🎫 *From $72.*

Pagan Mountaineering. Climbers in need of gear and advice on local terrain should speak with the knowledgeable staff here, who can help plot your adventure. ✉ *59 S. Main St., No. 2* ☎ *435/259–1117* 🌐 *paganclimber.com.*

SKYDIVING

Because the area gets only a few days of rain, the skydiving season is long, lasting from March 1 to November 15.

OUTFITTERS AND EXPEDITIONS

Skydive Moab. Find the best view of Moab and the surrounding landscape with something you can check off your bucket list. You're in good hands at Skydive Moab. All flights take off from Moab's Canyonlands Field, 16 miles north of town. They also host the annual Mother of All Boogies Skydiving Festival each year in September. ✉ *Canyonlands Field/Moab Airport, Hwy. 191 N* ☎ *435/259–5867* 🌐 *www.skydivemoab.com* 🎫 *From $199 for a tandem skydive.*

WHERE TO EAT

From juicy steaks and fresh sushi to rich Mexican and savory Thai, there are enough menu options in Moab to keep you satiated.

Use the coordinates (✣ A1) at the end of each listing to locate a site on the corresponding map.

$$$$ MODERN AMERICAN Fodor's Choice ★

🍴 **Desert Bistro.** Moab's finest dining experience is found in a small adobe house just off Main Street. Whether you dine inside or on either of the peaceful patios, anticipate thoughtful flavor combinations in artful salads, locally sourced beef, and delicious vegetables. **Known for:** excellent service; wine selection; bison entrées. [$] *Average main: $32* ✉ *36 S. 100 W* ☎ *435/259–0756* 🌐 *www.desertbistro.com* ⏲ *Closed Dec.–Feb., Mon. in Sept. and Oct., and Mon. and Tues. in Nov. No lunch* ✣ *A2.*

$ ✗**Eklecticafe.** The funky font on the sign makes this place easy to miss
ECLECTIC but worth finding for one of the more creative, healthy menus in Moab.
Fodor's Choice Breakfast and lunch items include a variety of burritos and wraps,
★ scrambled tofu, salmon cakes, Indonesian satay kebabs, and many
fresh, organic salads. **Known for:** rich coffee; creative menu; artistic
setting. $ *Average main: $9* ⊠ *352 N. Main St.* ☎ *435/259–6896* ⊙ *No
dinner* ✛ *B1.*

$$$$ ✗**Jeffrey's Steakhouse.** Melt-in-your-mouth tender wagyu beef is this
STEAKHOUSE restaurant's specialty. Jeffrey's offers plenty of salads and side dishes,
but remember—this is a steak house, so there's a separate charge for
everything, and that can quickly make for a pricey meal. The menu also
features lamb and pork chops, chicken and salmon, and a few other
entrée options. **Known for:** wagyu beef; hearty menu; historic setting.
$ *Average main: $32* ⊠ *218 N. 100 W* ☎ *435/259–3588* ⊕ *www.jef-
freyssteakhouse.com* ⊙ *No lunch* ✛ *A1.*

$$ ✗**Miguel's Baja Grill.** This isn't the cheapest Mexican menu around, but
MEXICAN it's definitely the best. Not your standard south-of-the-border fare, the
food here comes from the culinary spirit of Baja, California, which
means some excellent fish dishes like ceviche, a tangy blend of raw
fish, onions, tomatoes, and spices. **Known for:** house-made margaritas;
convenient location on Main Street; fresh ingredients. $ *Average main:
$15* ⊠ *51 N. Main St.* ☎ *435/259–6546* ⊕ *www.miguelsbajagrill.com*
⊙ *Closed Dec.–Feb. No lunch* ✛ *A1.*

$ ✗**Moab Brewery.** Southern Utah's award-winning brewery is known
AMERICAN for its Scorpion Pale Ale, Dead Horse Amber Ale, and an assortment
FAMILY of other brews from light to dark. Their on-site restaurant is spacious
and comfortable and decorated with kayaks, bikes, and other adventure
paraphernalia. **Known for:** spacious setting; made gelato; outdoorsy
clientele. $ *Average main: $12* ⊠ *686 S. Main St.* ☎ *435/259–6333*
⊕ *www.themoabbrewery.com* ✛ *B3.*

$ ✗**Moab Diner.** For breakfast, lunch, and dinner, this is the place where
AMERICAN old-time Moabites go. Try the dishes smothered in green chili (burritos,
FAMILY burgers, omelets, and more), which they claim is Utah's best. **Known
for:** all-day breakfast; local's favorite; green chili. $ *Average main: $10*
⊠ *189 S. Main St.* ☎ *435/259–4006* ⊕ *www.moabdiner.com* ⊙ *Closed
Sun.* ✛ *B2.*

$$ ✗**Pasta Jay's.** Mountain bikers, families, and couples pack this down-
ITALIAN town restaurant's patio from noon until well into the evening. This
FAMILY bustling spot's friendly servers rapidly dish up a dozen kinds of pasta
in an equal number of preparations, perfect for hungry adventurers.
Known for: American Italian vibe; extensive menu; patio dining. $ *Av-
erage main: $15* ⊠ *4 S. Main St.* ☎ *435/259–2900* ⊕ *www.pastajays.
com* ✛ *A1.*

$$ ✗**Peace Tree Juice Café.** Start with your choice of a dozen smoothies, then
CAFÉ select from a menu that ranges from wraps to sandwiches to full entrées
prepared primarily from local, natural, and organic ingredients for a
healthy, filling meal. Try the quinoa-stuffed red pepper or sweet-and-
salty beet salad for interesting new flavor combinations. **Known for:**
healthy bites; bright setting; outdoor dining. $ *Average main: $15* ⊠ *20
S. Main St.* ☎ *435/259–0101* ⊕ *www.peacetreejuicecafe.com* ✛ *A2.*

12

$$$ ✕**River Grill Restaurant.** The most scenic dining experience in the area
AMERICAN is 17 miles upstream from Moab at the Sorrel River Ranch, beside the
Colorado River, with views of La Sal Mountains, and the red-rock
spires and towers surrounding the ranch. This fine-dining restaurant
follows a farm-to-table ethic and its seasonal menu changes regularly;
look for local options like buffalo, pheasant, lamb, and trout as well
as vegetarian entrées. **Known for:** innovative dining; stunning setting;
wine list. $ *Average main: $28* ⊠ *Sorrel River Ranch, Hwy. 128, mile
marker 17.5* ☎ *435/259–4642* ⊕ *www.sorrelriver.com* ☽ *Lunch for
takeout only, Nov.–Mar.* ✛ *B1.*

$$ ✕**Sabaku Sushi.** Sushi in the desert may seem surprising, but the chefs
MODERN ASIAN here know what they're doing. The fish is flown in fresh several times a
Fodor'sChoice week, the veggies are crisp, and the sauces are spicy—locals particularly
★ love the spicy tuna roll with cucumber and avocado served with sriracha
and eel sauce. **Known for:** accommodating menu; friendly service; sake
list. $ *Average main: $15* ⊠ *90 E. Center St.* ☎ *435/259–4455* ⊕ *www.
sabakusushi.com* ☽ *Closed Mon. No lunch* ✛ *B1.*

$$ ✕**Singha.** Authentic Thai food may not be what you expect to find in
THAI the middle of the desert, and that's exactly why this cozy, central place
so highly recommended by locals. Some of the tastiest dishes here are
the noodle options, such as the tangy pad Thai or the spicy, pan-fried
drunken noodles. **Known for:** affordability; friendly service; takeout
menu. $ *Average main: $15* ⊠ *92 E. Center St.* ☎ *435/259–0039*
☽ *Closed Sun.* ✛ *B1.*

$ ✕**Sweet Cravings Bakery + Bistro.** Cinda Culton has created a sensation
BAKERY in Moab with some of the largest and most delicious cookies and cin-
FAMILY namon rolls you've ever seen. The secret here, though, is an amazing
roster of breakfast and lunch panini, wraps, and sandwiches, and daily
comfort foods like potpies and soups. **Known for:** cinnamon rolls; many
gluten-free options; local produce. $ *Average main: $10* ⊠ *397 N. Main
St.* ☎ *435/259–8983* ⊕ *www.cravemoab.com* ☽ *No dinner* ✛ *A1.*

$$ ✕**Zax.** Wood-fired pizza ovens are the focal point of this downtown
AMERICAN eatery and sports bar, where baseball bats double as door handles. For
FAMILY $15 you can try the pizza-salad-soup buffet (a popular choice, so the
pies are constantly coming out of the oven). **Known for:** take-n-bake
pizza; sports fans; broad menu. $ *Average main: $15* ⊠ *96 S. Main St.*
☎ *435/259–6555* ⊕ *www.zaxmoab.com* ✛ *A2.*

WHERE TO STAY

*Use the coordinates (✛ A1) at the end of each listing to locate a site on
the corresponding map.*

$$$ ⊡**Adobe Abode.** A lovely B&B near the nature preserve, this single-story
B&B/INN inn offers solitude. **Pros:** beautifully decorated common area; continen-
tal breakfast included; peace and quiet. **Cons:** too far to walk to town
(but close enough to bike); no children under 16 permitted. $ *Rooms
from: $179* ⊠ *778 W. Kane Creek Blvd.* ☎ *435/259–7716* ⊕ *www.ado-
beabodemoab.com* ⊸ *6 rooms* ⦿⦵ *Breakfast* ✛ *A2.*

$$$$ HOTEL FAMILY Fodor's Choice ★ [🏨] **Best Western Canyonlands Inn.** The confluence of Main and Center streets is the epicenter of Moab, and this comfortable, contemporary, impeccably clean hotel anchors the intersection, providing a perfect base for families. **Pros:** downtown location; updated, sparkling rooms; breakfast alfresco on outdoor patio. **Cons:** pricey due to location; better for families than solo travelers. [$] *Rooms from: $287* ✉ *16 S. Main St.* ☎ *435/259–2300, 800/649–5191* 🌐 *www.canyonlandsinn.com* 🛏 *80 rooms* 🍴 *Breakfast* ✥ *A1.*

FRIENDLY FOLK DANCING

Community Contra Dance. During the Community Contra Dance locals from every clique come together for a night of folk dancing with live tunes provided by the Moab Community Dance Band. Even if you've never tried this all-American dance form, it's less intimidating than it looks; an emcee announces the moves, and fellow participants will be happy to show you the ropes. You don't need rhythm or a partner, just a $5 donation, which goes to a different charity each month. The dances spring into action the third Saturday of most months at the Moab Arts and Recreation Center. ✉ *111 E. 100 N* ☎ *435/259–6272.*

$$$ B&B/INN Fodor's Choice ★ [🏨] **Cali Cochitta Bed & Breakfast.** One of the first homes built in Moab, this 19th-century Victorian in the heart of town, two blocks from Main Street shops and restaurants, has been restored to its classic style by owners David and Kim Boger. **Pros:** gracious owners pay attention to the details; easy walk to the hub of town; breakfast in the garden from accomplished chef. **Cons:** historic construction, some quarters feel small. [$] *Rooms from: $175* ✉ *110 S. 200 E* ☎ *435/259–4961* 🌐 *www.moabdreaminn.com* 🛏 *6 rooms* 🍴 *Breakfast* ✥ *B2.*

$$$$ HOTEL [🏨] **Fairfield Inn and Suites.** Views of the Colorado River are sure to wow guests at this hotel. **Pros:** warm, inviting, and very clean; views of river and red rocks; buffet, continental, or hot breakfast included. **Cons:** 4 miles from downtown Moab; pricey. [$] *Rooms from: $224* ✉ *1863 N. Hwy. 191* ☎ *435/259–5350, 888/236–2427* 🌐 *www.marriott.com* 🛏 *89 rooms* 🍴 *Breakfast* ✥ *B1.*

$$$ HOTEL [🏨] **Gonzo Inn.** This eclectic inn stands out for its design, color, art, and varnished adobe construction. **Pros:** unique, spotless, and hip; steps to Main Street; pool and hot tub. **Cons:** interior hallways can be dark; no elevator; not all rooms have a good view. [$] *Rooms from: $199* ✉ *100 W. 200 S* ☎ *435/259–2515, 800/791–4044* 🌐 *www.gonzoinn.com* 🛏 *43 rooms* 🍴 *Breakfast* ✥ *A2.*

$$$$ RENTAL [🏨] **Moab Springs Ranch.** First developed by William Granstaff in the late 19th century, this 18-acre property about 3 miles from Arches and 2 miles from downtown Moab features comfortable hotel rooms and condos set by a meandering spring and decades-old sycamores, mulberries, and cottonwoods. **Pros:** scenic setting; along bike path to town. **Cons:** remote location; some Highway 191 traffic noise. [$] *Rooms from: $210* ✉ *1266 N. Main St.* ☎ *435/259–7891* 🌐 *www.moabspringsranch.com* 🛏 *19 condos, from studios to larger rentals* 🍴 *No meals* ✥ *B1.*

$$$$ RESORT [🏨] **Red Cliffs Adventure Lodge.** Discovered in the late 1940s by director John Ford, this former ranch was the setting for several 1950s Westerns.

Pros: great riverfront views; private cabins are woodsy but modern; the movie museum chronicles local filmmaking history. Cons: far from town; spotty cell service. $ *Rooms from: $239* ⊠ *Hwy. 128, mile marker 14* 🕾 *435/259–2002, 866/812–2002* ⊕ *www.redcliffslodge. com* ⤳ *79 rooms, 30 cabins, 1 suite* ☉ *No meals* ✛ *B1.*

$$
HOTEL

⛑ **Moab Red Stone Inn.** One of the best bargains in town, this timber-frame motel offers small, clean rooms at the south end of the Moab strip near restaurants and shops. **Pros:** walking distance to Moab restaurants and shops; the price is right. **Cons:** pool is at sister property across busy Main Street; no frills. $ *Rooms from: $130* ⊠ *535 S. Main St.* 🕾 *435/259–3500, 800/772–1972* ⊕ *www.moabredstone.com* ⤳ *52 rooms* ☉ *No meals* ✛ *A3.*

$$$$
RESORT
Fodor's Choice
★

⛑ **Sorrel River Ranch.** This lavish ranch resort is the biggest splurge around—and it's worth absolutely every penny. **Pros:** the most luxurious hotel in the area; very attentive staff; guided hikes and yoga at additional cost. **Cons:** 30 minutes from Moab; resort fee of 9% is added to your bill. $ *Rooms from: $479* ⊠ *Hwy. 128, mile marker 17* 🕾 *435/259–4642, 877/359–2715* ⊕ *www.sorrelriver.com* ⤳ *39 rooms, 16 suites* ☉ *No meals* ✛ *B1.*

NIGHTLIFE AND PERFORMING ARTS

Moab Happenings is a great resource for visitors to the area. It includes a calendar of events and options for activities, shopping, restaurants, and other necessities for travelers.

NIGHTLIFE

Moab's nightlife can be pretty quiet, especially in winter. In high season, live bands perform every weekend.

Club Rio. At this local hangout and sports bar, decent bar food and cold beer make a perfect pairing for watching a weekend game on TV. Live music, DJs, karaoke, comedy, and lots of local flair make it worth a visit, game-time or not. There's a cover charge for some events, but in most cases entrance is free. ⊠ *2 S. 100 W* 🕾 *435/259–2654* ⊕ *riomoab.com.*

World Famous Woody's Tavern. An old-school style tavern that's a favorite hangout for locals, this Main Street standby offers beer, bands, and a little bit of ruckus. The front porch still looks like a perfect place to ride up and secure a horse, and there is a great patio. ⊠ *221 S. Main St.* 🕾 *435/259–3550* ⊕ *www.worldfamouswoodystavern.com.*

PERFORMING ARTS

Moab Arts and Recreation Center. Offering a slice of Moab's arts scene, from "Quick Draw Sales" where artists have three hours to create pieces during the annual Plein Air Festival, to dance, crafts, and fitness classes, this has been the spirited hub of arts activities in Moab since 1997. ⊠ *111 E. 100 N* 🕾 *435/259–6272* ⊕ *www.moabrecreation.com.*

SHOPPING

Shopping opportunities are plentiful in Moab, with art galleries, jewelry stores, and shops carrying T-shirts and souvenirs throughout Main Street.

ART GALLERIES

Lema's Kokopelli Gallery. The Lema family has built a reputation for fair prices on a large selection of Native American and Southwest-themed jewelry, art, pottery, rugs, and more. Everything sold here is authentic. ⊠ *70 N. Main St.* ☎ *435/259–5055* ⊕ *www.kokopellioutlet.com.*

Moab Art Walk. Moab galleries and shops celebrate the perfect weather of spring and fall with a series of exhibits. Art Walks are held the second Saturday of the month from March through June and September through November. Stroll the streets (5–9 pm) to see and purchase original works by Moab and regional artists. ⊠ *Moab* ☎ *435/259–6272* ⊕ *www.moabartwalk.com.*

BOOKS

FAMILY **Back of Beyond Books.** A Main Street treasure, this comprehensive bookstore features the American West, environmental studies, Native American cultures, water issues, and Western history, as well as rare antiquarian books on the Southwest. There's also a nice nook for kids. ⊠ *83 N. Main St.* ☎ *435/259–5154, 800/700–2859* ⊕ *www.backofbeyondbooks.com* ☉ *Daily 9–6 (to 9 pm Mar.–Nov.).*

SUPPLIES

Dave's Corner Market. You can get most anything you may need here for your travels, including some of the best cappuccino and Colombian coffee in town. The store is also the heartbeat of the local community, where everyone gossips, discusses local politics, and swaps info on the best hiking and adventure spots. ⊠ *401 Mill Creek Dr.* ☎ *435/259–6999.*

GearHeads. If you forget anything for your camping, climbing, hiking, or other outdoor adventure, you can get a replacement here. GearHeads is packed with essentials, and fun extras like booties and packs for your dog, water filtration straws, and cool souvenirs. The store's owners invented a high-end LED flashlight that has become very popular with the U.S. military, available at the store. ⊠ *471 S. Main St.* ☎ *435/259–4327* ⊕ *www.moabgear.com.*

Walker Drug Co. A Moab landmark since the 1950s, this is as close as you'll get to a department store for more than 100 miles. Besides pharmacy and drugstore items, you can buy all the essentials, including camping supplies, swimsuits, hats, sunglasses, and souvenirs. The pharmacy section is closed on weekends. ⊠ *290 S. Main St.* ☎ *435/259–5959.*

SOUTHEASTERN UTAH

Utah scenery is dramatic, from the wide span of water at Lake Powell to the huge, sandstone formations (called "mittens") in Monument Valley. Around Green River you'll encounter a world of agriculture and boating, with melon stands popping up in the late summer and fall. Farther south you'll see the influence of Native American culture including ancient rock-art and dwellings. Along the way to Mexican Hat, you'll enjoy Navajo tacos and handmade jewelry.

GREEN RIVER

70 miles west of the Colorado state line.

Named for the river that runs through town, Green River, Utah, and its namesake are historically important. Early Native Americans used the river for centuries; the Old Spanish Trail crossed it, and the Denver and Rio Grande Railroad bridged it in 1883. Some say the "green" refers to the color of the water; others claim it's named for the plants along the riverbank. And yet another story gives the credit to a mysterious trapper named Green. Whatever the etymology, Green River remains a sleepy little town, and a nice break from some of the more "hip" tourist towns in southern Utah.

12

GETTING HERE AND AROUND

Reaching Green River is as easy as finding I–70. The town is 180 miles southeast of Salt Lake City, 100 miles west of Grand Junction, Colorado, and 50 miles northwest of Moab.

ESSENTIALS

Green River Information Center. ⊠ *John Wesley Powell River History Museum, 1765 E. Main St.* ☎ *435/564–3427* ⊕ *destinationgreenriver. com.*

EXPLORING

Green River State Park. A shady respite on the banks of the Green River, this park is best known for its golf course. It's also the starting point for boaters drifting along the river through Labyrinth and Stillwater canyons. Fishing and bird-watching are favorite pastimes here. ⊠ *450 S. Green River Rd.* ☎ *435/561 3633, 800/322–3770 for campground reservations* ⊕ *www.stateparks.utah.gov* ⊠ *$5 per vehicle.*

FAMILY

Fodor's Choice

★

John Wesley Powell River History Museum. Learn what it was like to travel down the Green and Colorado rivers in the 1800s in wooden boats. A series of displays tracks the Powell Party's arduous, dangerous 1869 journey, and visitors can watch the award-winning film *Journey Into the Unknown* for a cinematic taste of the white-water adventure. The center also houses the River Runner's Hall of Fame, a tribute to those who have followed in Powell's wake. River-themed art occupies a gallery and there's a dinosaur exhibit on the lower level. ⊠ *1765 E. Main St.* ☎ *435/564–3427* ⊕ *www.jwprhm.com* ⊠ *$6.*

Sego Canyon Rock Art Panels. Sego is one of the most dramatic and mystifying rock-art sites in the entire state. Large, ghostlike rock-art figures painted and etched by Native Americans approximately 4,000 years ago cover these canyon walls. There's also art left by the Ute from the 19th-century. Distinctive for their large anthropomorphic figures, and for horses, buffalo, and shields painted with red-and-white pigment, these rare drawings are a must-see. ⊠ *I–70, Exit 187, Thompson Springs* ✛ *25 miles east of Green River on I–70, at Exit 187 go north onto Hwy. 94 through Thompson Springs* ☎ *435/259–2100 Bureau of Land Management Office in Moab* ⊕ *www.blm.gov.*

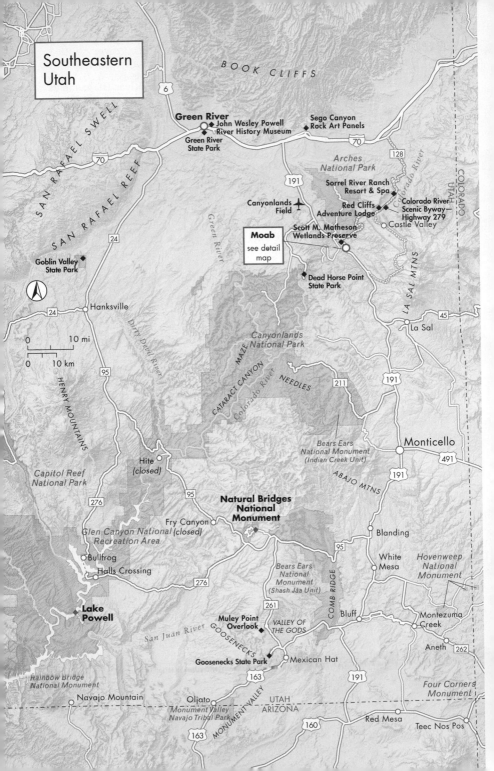

12

Goblin Valley State Park. Strange-looking "hoodoos" rise up from the desert landscape 12 miles north of Hanksville, making Goblin Valley home to hundreds of strange goblin-like rock formations with a dramatic orange hue. Short, easy trails wind through the goblins making it a fun walk for kids and adults. ⊠ *Hwy. 24* ☎ *435/275–4584* ⊕ *stateparks. utah.gov* ⊠ *$13 per vehicle.*

SPORTS AND THE OUTDOORS

RIVER FLOAT TRIPS

Bearing little resemblance to its name, Desolation Canyon acquaints those who venture down the Green River with some of the last true American wilderness: a lush, verdant canyon, where the rapids promise more laughter than fear. It's a favorite destination of canoe paddlers, kayakers, and novice rafters. May through September, raft trips can be arranged by outfitters in Green River or Moab. South of town the river drifts at a lazier pace through Labyrinth and Stillwater canyons, and the stretch south to Mineral Bottom in Canyonlands is best suited to canoes and motor boats.

For river-trip outfitters, see the Moab Sports and the Outdoors section.

WHERE TO EAT AND STAY

$$

MEXICAN

✕ **La Veracruzana.** The Polito family continues the long tradition of good food in this older, unassuming building on Green River's main drag. Couples and families should try the *molcajete,* a two-person entrée with meat, chicken, shrimp, and nopal (cactus) served on a volcanic-rock stone mortar. **Known for:** street tacos; molcajete; chile verde. Ⓢ *Average main: $15* ⊠ *125 W. Main St.* ☎ *435/564–3257.*

$

AMERICAN

✕ **Ray's Tavern.** Ray's is something of a Western legend and a favorite hangout for river runners. The bar that runs the length of the restaurant reminds you this is still a tavern and a serious watering hole—but all the photos and rafting memorabilia make it comfortable for families as well. **Known for:** legendary burgers; mixed clientele; homemade pie. Ⓢ *Average main: $10* ⊠ *25 S. Broadway* ☎ *435/564–3511* ⊕ *www.ray-stavern.com.*

$

AMERICAN

✕ **Tamarisk Restaurant.** Views of the Green River make this no-frills restaurant a nice stop after a long drive. Breakfasts and lunches are traditional American diner fare. **Known for:** the view; fish tacos; buffalo burger. Ⓢ *Average main: $10* ⊠ *1710 E. Main St.* ⊕ *www.tama-riskrestaurant.com.*

$$

HOTEL

🏨 **Green River Comfort Inn.** This clean, updated motel is convenient if you're staying only one night, as many do on family rafting outings (Holiday River Expeditions is behind the hotel). **Pros:** clean and comfortable; close to town's premier rafting outfitter; kids under 18 stay for free. **Cons:** remote, barren town; no elevator to second floor; Green River's two best restaurants are not in walking distance. Ⓢ *Rooms from: $139* ⊠ *1975 E. Main St.* ☎ *435/564–3300* ⊕ *www.comfortinngreen-river.com* ⤳ *57 rooms* ⦿⌾ *Breakfast.*

$$

HOTEL

🏨 **River Terrace Hotel.** The peaceful setting, on the bank of the Green River, is conducive to a good night's rest, and the hotel is conveniently less than 2 miles off I–70. **Pros:** shady riverside location (be sure to request a river-view room); discounts often available; on-site restaurant;

convenient for the passing traveler. **Cons:** remote, barren town; Green River's best two restaurants are not in walking distance. $ *Rooms from: $141* ⊠ *1740 E. Main St.* ☎ *435/564–3401, 877/564–3401* ⊕ *www. river-terrace.com* ⌨ *50 rooms* ⫧ *Breakfast.*

NATURAL BRIDGES NATIONAL MONUMENT

The scenery and rock formations found in this national monument must be seen to be believed.

Natural Bridges National Monument. Stunning natural bridges, ancient Native American ruins, and magnificent scenery throughout make Natural Bridges National Monument a must-see if you have time to make the trip. Sipapu is one of the largest natural bridges in the world, spanning 225 feet and standing more than 140 feet tall. You can take in the Sipapu, Owachomo, and Kachina bridges via an 8.6-mile round-trip hike that meanders around and under them. A 13-site primitive campground is an optimal spot for stargazing. The national monument is about 120 miles southwest of the Needles District of Canyonlands National Park and approximately 45 miles from Blanding. ⊠ *Hwy. 275, off Hwy. 95* ☎ *435/692–1234* ⊕ *www.nps.gov/nabr* ⫧ *$10 per vehicle, $5 for those entering park on foot, bicycle, or motorcycle.*

LAKE POWELL

The placid waters of Lake Powell allow you to depart the landed lifestyle and float away on your own houseboat. With 96 major side canyons spread across 186 miles, you can spend months exploring more than 2,000 miles of shoreline. Every water sport imaginable awaits, from waterskiing to fishing. Small communities around marinas in Page (Arizona), Bullfrog, Wahweap, Hite, and Hall's Crossing have hotels, restaurants, and shops where you can restock vital supplies.

GETTING HERE AND AROUND

AIR TRAVEL   Getting here can be your biggest challenge, so it's best to plan ahead whenever possible. Great Lakes Airlines serves Page, Arizona, from Phoenix. To get to Bullfrog, Utah, it's a three-and-a-half-hour drive from Canyonlands Airport in Moab (served by Delta) and five hours from Walker Field Airport in Grand Junction, Colorado.

CAR TRAVEL   Many people visit Lake Powell as part of grand drives across the southwestern United States. Bullfrog, Utah, is about 300 miles from Salt Lake City via I–15 to I–70 to U.S. 95 south. Take I–70 from Colorado and the east. Take U.S. 191 from either Wyoming or Arizona. Most roads are well-maintained two-lane highways, though snow can be a factor in winter. Be sure your car is in good working order, as there are long stretches of empty road, and top off the gas tank whenever possible.

FERRY TRAVEL   Hall's Crossing Marina is the eastern terminus of the ferry. You and your vehicle can float across a 3-mile stretch of the lake to the Bullfrog Basin Marina in 25 minutes; from there it is an hour's drive north to rejoin Highway 95. Ferries run several times each day (less frequently during the off-season). Call ahead for departures information.

Lake Powell Ferry. ✉ *Hall's Crossing Marina, Hwy. 276* ☎ *435/684–3088* ⊕ *www.lakepowell.com* ✍ *$25 per car.*

Information Utah State Road Conditions. ☎ *511 toll-free within Utah, 866/511–8824 toll-free outside Utah* ⊕ *www.udot.utah.gov.*

EXPLORING

Lake Powell. With a shoreline longer than America's Pacific coast, Lake Powell is the heart of the huge 1,255,400-acre **Glen Canyon National Recreation Area.** Created by the Glen Canyon Dam—a 710-foot wall of concrete in the Colorado River—Lake Powell took 17 years to fill. The second-largest man-made lake in the nation, it extends through terrain so rugged that it was the last major area of the country to be mapped. Red cliffs ring the lake and twist off into 96 major canyons and countless inlets with huge, red-sandstone buttes randomly jutting from the sapphire waters.

The most popular thing to do at Lake Powell is to rent a houseboat and chugg leisurely across the lake, exploring coves and inlets at leisure. You'll have plenty of company, though, since more than 2 million people visit the lake each year. Fast motorboats, Jet Skis, and sailboats all share the lake. Unless you love crowds and parties, it's best to avoid visiting during Memorial Day or Labor Day weekends. It's also important to check with the National Park Service for current water levels, closures, and other weather-related conditions.

Guided day-tours are available for those who don't want to rent a boat of their own. A popular full-day or half-day excursion sets out from the Bullfrog and Hall's Crossing marinas to **Rainbow Bridge National Monument.** This is the largest natural bridge in the world, and its 290-foot-high, 275-foot-wide span is a breathtaking sight. The main National Park Service visitor center is at Bullfrog Marina; a gas station, campground, general store, and boat docks are there for supplies, snacks, and chit-chat with locals. ✉ *Bullfrog visitor center, Hwy. 276* ☎ *435/684–7420* ⊕ *www.nps.gov/glca* ✍ *$15 per vehicle.*

SPORTS AND THE OUTDOORS

Lake Powell Resorts & Marinas. Boating and fishing are the major sports at Lake Powell. Conveniently, all powerboat rentals and tours are conducted by this company. Daylong tours (departing from Wahweap Marina near Page, Arizona) go to Rainbow Bridge or Antelope Canyon. There's also a tour that goes into some of the more interesting canyons and a dinner cruise. The company rents houseboats for anyone looking to make their stay here last. ✉ *Bullfrog Marina, Rte. 276* ☎ *800/528–6154* ⊕ *www.lakepowell.com* ✍ *Tours $45–$120.*

WHERE TO STAY

$$$$
RESORT
Fodor's Choice
★

Amangiri. One of just two U.S. properties operated by the famously luxurious Aman resort company, this ultraplush and ultraexpensive 34-suite compound lies just a few miles north of Lake Powell on a 600-acre plot of rugged high desert, soaring red-rock cliffs, and jagged mesas. **Pros:** stunning accommodations inside and out; exceedingly gracious and professional staff; world-class restaurant and spa. **Cons:** many times more expensive than most accommodations in the area; extremely remote. $ *Rooms from: $1900* ⊠ *1 Kayenta Rd., Canyon Point* ✛ *15 miles northwest of Page, off U.S. 89* ☎ *435/675–3999, 877/695–3999* ⊕ *www.amanresorts.com* ↬ *34 suites* ⦿ *All meals.*

$$$
HOTEL ▦ **Defiance House Lodge.** At the Bullfrog Marina, this cliff-top lodge has comfortable and clean rooms anyone can appreciate, but the real draw is the view. **Pros:** beautiful lakefront setting; adjacent restaurant. **Cons:** very remote; no general store for miles. $ *Rooms from: $160* ☎ *435/684–2233, 888/896–3829* ⊕ *www.lakepowell.com* ↬ *48 rooms* ⦿ *No meals.*

$$$
B&B/INN ▦ **Dreamkatchers' B&B.** This sleek, contemporary Southwestern-style home sits on a bluff just a few miles northwest of Lake Powell and 15 miles from Page. **Pros:** peaceful and secluded location perfect for stargazing; delicious breakfasts; laid-back, friendly hosts. **Cons:** often booked months in advance; two-night minimum stay. $ *Rooms from: $175* ⊠ *1055 S. American Way, Big Water* ☎ *435/675–5828* ⊕ *www. dreamkatcherslakepowell.com* ☾ *Closed mid-Nov.–mid-Mar.* ↬ *3 rooms* ⦿ *Breakfast.*

TRAVEL SMART UTAH

GETTING HERE AND AROUND

Salt Lake City is Utah's major air gateway, although if southern Utah is your primary destination, traveling there from Las Vegas is a convenient and often less expensive alternative. Once on the ground, a car is your best bet for getting around. Outside of the urban corridor from Provo to Ogden (including Salt Lake City), much of the state's interest lies in natural attractions, including five national parks and terrain that ranges from sunbaked desert to mountain peaks that soar above 10,000 feet. Be prepared for wide open vistas, extreme temperature variations and long stretches of asphalt.

▌AIR TRAVEL

Salt Lake City has a reputation for having one of the nation's easiest airports for travelers—with a low rate of delayed or canceled flights. Plus, it's a western hub for Delta, so your Utah explorations should get off to a timely start. Nonstop flights are available from larger U.S. cities as well as Europe, Mexico, and Canada.

Salt Lake City is about 12 hours from London, 5 hours from New York, 4 hours from Chicago and D.C., 3 hours from Dallas, 2 hours from Los Angeles, and an hour from Las Vegas.

If you're traveling during snow season, allow extra time to get to the airport, as weather conditions can slow you down. If you'll be checking skis, arrive even earlier.

Airlines and Airports Airline and Airport Links.com. ⊕ *www.airlineandairportlinks.com.*

Airline Security Issues Transportation Security Administration. ⊕ *www.tsa.gov.*

AIRPORTS

The major gateway to Utah is Salt Lake City International Airport. If you're staying in Salt Lake City, you'll appreciate that it's one of the closest airports to downtown of any American city, and security wait times are minimal. Be advised that

the first phase of major airport construction, including the building of a new terminal and parking garage, is ongoing through at least 2020. The second phase is due to be completed in 2024.

Flights to smaller, regional, or resort-town airports generally connect through Salt Lake. Provo, Cedar City, Logan, Ogden, and Moab all have small airports. A convenient gateway to southern Utah, particularly Zion and Bryce Canyon national parks, is McCarran International Airport in Las Vegas. More and more visitors to southern Utah are using St. George Regional Airport, which has daily flights to Salt Lake City and Denver. There are limited services, but you can rent cars here and it's less than an hour's drive to Zion National Park once you're on the road.

Airport Information McCarran International Airport (LAS). ⊠ *5757 Wayne Newton Blvd., Las Vegas* ☎ *702/261–5211* ⊕ *www. mccarran.com.* **Salt Lake City International Airport (SLC).** ⊠ *776 N. Terminal Dr., Salt Lake City* ☎ *801/575–2400* ⊕ *www.slcairport.com.* **St. George Regional Airport (SGU).** ⊠ *4550 S. Airport Pkwy., St. George* ☎ *435/627–4080* ⊕ *www.flysgu.com.*

GROUND TRANSPORTATION

You can get to and from the Salt Lake City Airport by light-rail, taxi, bus, or hotel shuttle. A light-rail line called TRAX connects you in less than 30 minutes (and for just $2.50) from Terminal 1 to downtown Salt Lake City and the rest of the rapid-transit network. It runs every 15 minutes on weekdays and every 20 minutes on weekends. Taxis, though, are faster (15 minutes); the trip to downtown costs $20–$25. If you're in downtown Salt Lake City, your best bet is to call ahead for a taxi rather than hope to flag one down. Shared-ride shuttle services from the airport are similarly priced to taxis, but can take longer. Lyft and Uber also pick up at the Salt Lake City airport and can cost less than half the price of a taxi.

Contacts City Cab Company. ☎ *801/363–5550.* **Utah Transit Authority (UTA).** ☎ *801/743–3882, 888/743–3882* ⊕ *www.rideuta.com.* **Ute Cab Company.** ☎ *801/359–7788.* **Yellow Cab.** ☎ *801/521–2100* ⊕ *yellowcabutah.com.*

FLIGHTS

Salt Lake City has a large international airport, so you'll be able to fly here from anywhere, though you may have to connect somewhere else first. The airport is a major hub for Delta Airlines. Delta and its affiliates offer almost 250 daily departures to destinations around the country. Southwest ranks second in terms of daily flights, with roughly 30 daily departures. Alaska, American, jetBlue, United, and Frontier also have flights each day.

If you're flying in from somewhere other than the United States, you'll likely connect in Los Angeles or San Francisco if you're coming from Asia, or a major airport in the East, such as Detroit, Atlanta, or New York, if you're traveling from Europe. Occasionally you may be delayed by a major snowstorm, but these generally affect the mountain areas, not the airport.

If you're heading to southern Utah, it may be more convenient to fly into Las Vegas, which has more flights and is often cheaper. Be advised that the 120-mile drive from Las Vegas to St. George passes through extremely remote country, and the Virgin River Canyon near the Arizona/Utah border can make for treacherous driving, especially at night.

Airline Contacts Alaska Airlines. ☎ ⊕ *www.alaskaair.com.* **American Airlines.** ☎ *800/433–7300* ⊕ *www.aa.com.* **Delta Airlines.** ☎ *800/221–1212 for U.S. reservations, 800/241–4141 for international reservations* ⊕ *www.delta.com.* **Frontier.** ☎ *801/401–9000* ⊕ *www.flyfrontier.com.* **jetBlue.** ☎ *800/538–2583* ⊕ *www.jetblue.com.* **Southwest Airlines.** ☎ *800/435–9792* ⊕ *www.southwest.com.* **United Airlines.** ☎ *800/864–8331 for U.S. reservations, 800/538–2929 for international reservations* ⊕ *www.united.com.*

▮ CAR TRAVEL

You'll need a car in Utah. Public transportation is available primarily along the Wasatch Front (Ogden to Salt Lake City to Provo), but caters to commuters, not tourists. Scenery ranges from snowcapped mountains to endless stretches of desert with strange rock formations and intense color. There are more national parks here than in any other state except Alaska and California, although their interiors are not always accessible by car.

Outside of the Salt Lake City and Park City areas, much of what draws most people to Utah is in the southern part of the state. I–15 is the main north–south thoroughfare, branching off to U.S. 6 toward Moab and to Arches and Canyonlands National Parks in the southeast, passing west of Capitol Reef National Park in the south–central region, and continuing all the way to the St. George area for Zion and Bryce National Parks in the southwest. Many visitors approach the southern Utah parks by way of I–70, which runs west from Denver through Moab. Highway 89 parallels I–15 for much of the state, offering a slower, back roads alternative and includes Main Street in many small towns. Highway 12 is a nationally recognized Scenic Byway in the Grand Staircase–Escalante National Monument and is also worth incorporating into your itinerary.

TRAVEL TIMES FROM SALT LAKE CITY BY CAR	
TO	**HOURS**
Park City	40 min
Zion National Park	4½ hours
Bryce National Park	4 hours
Arches National Park and Moab	3¾ hours
Canyonlands National Park	4 hours
Capitol Reef National Park	3½ hours

GASOLINE

In cities throughout Utah, gas prices are similar to those in the rest of the continental United States; in rural and resort towns prices are considerably higher. In urban areas stations are plentiful, and most stay open late (some are open 24 hours). In rural areas stations are less numerous, and hours are more limited, particularly on Sunday; you can sometimes drive more than 100 miles on back roads without finding a gas station. It's best to always keep your tank at least half full.

PARKING

Parking is generally easy to find, even in Salt Lake City. Many parking garages offer free visitor parking for one or two hours. Meters are usually free for two hours at a stretch on Saturday and all day on Sunday.

ROAD CONDITIONS

Utah has some of the most spectacular vistas in the world. Roads range from multilane divided blacktop to narrow dirt roads; from twisting switchbacks to primitive backcountry paths. Scenic routes and lookout points are clearly marked, enabling you to slow down and pull over to take in the views. You'll find highways and the national parks crowded in summer, and almost deserted (and occasionally impassable) in winter.

In many locations, particularly in the Salt Lake Valley and St. George areas, there always seems to be road construction. Check road conditions before you set out.

Unpleasant sights along the highway are road kills. Exercise caution, not only to save an animal's life, but also to avoid possible extensive damage to your car.

Road Conditions In Utah. ☎ 511
⊕ commuterlink.utah.gov.

RULES OF THE ROAD

Utah law requires seat belts for drivers and all passengers in vehicles so equipped. Always strap children under age 8 into approved child-safety seats. Helmets are required for motorcyclists and passengers under the age of 18.

You may turn right at a red light after stopping if there is no sign stating otherwise and no oncoming traffic. When in doubt, wait for the green.

The speed limit on U.S. interstates is 75–80 mph in rural areas and 65–70 mph in urban zones. Increased speeds are allowed only where clearly posted. Transition zones from one speed limit to the next are indicated with pavement markings and signs. Fines are doubled for speeding in work zones and school zones.

It is illegal in Utah to send, read, or write text messages while driving. Drivers under the age of 18 may not use hands-free or hand-held cell phones while driving.

Beginning on December 30, 2018, Utah will have the strictest drunk driving law in the nation, lowering the maximum blood alcohol limit for drivers from .08% (the threshold elsewhere in the U.S.) to .05%.

WINTER AND DESERT DRIVING

It is best to have a complete tune-up before setting out on the road. For emergencies, take along a spare tire, flares or reflector triangles, jumper cables, an empty gas can, a flashlight, a plastic tarp, blankets, water, and coins or a calling card for phone calls (cell phones don't always work in high mountain areas).

Although winter driving can occasionally present some real challenges, road maintenance is good and plowing is prompt. However, severe winter storms occasionally close I–80 between Salt Lake City and Park City and I–15 near Cedar City. Tire chains and/or all-wheel drive or four-wheel-drive vehicles are often required in the canyons surrounding the Wasatch Front during storms, including Parley's Canyon between Salt Lake City and Park City and Big and Little Cottonwood canyons. Also, Highway 6 between Provo and Green River is considered the most dangerous road in the state. Its windy stretches and dramatic elevation changes cause slide-offs and mishaps, particularly in winter. If you're planning to drive into high elevations (and even Salt Lake City is at 4,000-plus feet above sea level), be sure to check the weather forecast and call for road conditions beforehand. Even main highways can close, and winter weather isn't confined to winter in the high country (it's been known to snow on July 4). If you do get stalled by deep snow, do not leave your car. Wait for help, running the engine only if needed.

Desert driving can be dangerous in winter or summer. You may encounter drifting snow, blowing sand, and flash floods, with little chance of anyone driving by to help. Never leave children or pets in a car— summer temperatures climb quickly above 100°F.

CAR RENTAL

You can rent an economy car with air-conditioning, automatic transmission, and unlimited mileage in Salt Lake City for about $30 a day and $150 a week. This does not include tax on car rentals, which is 16.35% in Salt Lake City. If you're planning to do any skiing, biking, four-wheeling, or towing, check into renting an SUV, van, or pickup from a local company like Rugged Rentals, which specializes in outdoor vehicles and provides supplemental insurance as part of the rental charge. You can rent a relatively new SUV or van with bike rack, ski rack, or towing equipment included. Call for rates (☎ 801/977–9111).

Renting a car in Las Vegas can be less expensive than renting one in Salt Lake City, especially if you're visiting southern Utah. The driving time between Las Vegas and Salt Lake City is seven to nine hours, but it's only a three hour trip from Las Vegas to Zion National Park.

In Utah you must be 21 or over and have a valid driver's license to rent a car; most companies also require a major credit card. If you're over 65, check the rental company's policy on overage drivers. You may pay extra for child seats (but shop around; some companies don't charge

extra for them), which are compulsory for children under eight, and for additional drivers. Non-U.S. residents will need a reservation voucher, a passport, a driver's license, and a travel policy that covers each driver to pick up a car.

Local Agencies Rugged Rental. ☎ 801/977–9111 ⊕ www.ruggedrental.com.

Major Rental Agencies Advantage. ☎ 800/777–5500 ⊕ www.advantage.com. **Alamo.** ☎ 844/354–6962 ⊕ www.alamo. com. **Avis.** ☎ 800/633–3469 ⊕ www.avis.com. **Budget.** ☎ 800/218–7992 ⊕ www.budget. com. **Hertz.** ☎ 800/654–3131 ⊕ www.hertz. com. **National Car Rental.** ☎ 877/222–9058 ⊕ www.nationalcar.com.

❚ TRAIN TRAVEL

Amtrak connects Utah to Chicago and the San Francisco Bay Area daily via the *California Zephyr*, which stops in Salt Lake City, Provo, Helper, and Green River. However, trains are notorious for delays.

Information Amtrak. ☎ 800/872–7245 ⊕ www.amtrak.com.

SCENIC TRAIN TRIPS

On the Heber Valley Historic Railroad you can catch the *Heber Creeper,* a turn-of-the-20th-century steam-locomotive train that runs from Heber City across Heber Valley, alongside Deer Creek Reservoir, and down Provo Canyon to Vivian Park. Depending on the time of year, you can catch the Polar Express, the Cowboy Train, or an Adventure Train that includes a stop for rafting or zip-lining.

Information Heber Valley Historic Railroad. ✉ 450 S. 600 W, Heber ☎ 435/654–5601 ⊕ www.hebervalleyrr.org.

ESSENTIALS

▋ ACCOMMODATIONS

Utah is home to the founders of the Marriott chain of hotels, and its accommodations are plentiful, varied, and reasonably priced throughout the state. Chain motels are everywhere. The ski resorts along the Wasatch Front—especially in Park City—cater to the wealthy jet set, and there are posh resorts such as Deer Valley and the Waldorf Astoria Park City, and pampering at Red Mountain Resort. Salt Lake City has hotels in every price range. National chains like Holiday Inn, Marriott, Hilton, Best Western, Super 8, and Motel 6 are dependable in Utah, and are occasionally the best beds in town. The gateway towns to the national parks usually have a large range of accommodations. There are also more bed-and-breakfasts, as international tourists often prefer to meet the locals at such places. Independent motels can also be found all over the state. Look for guest ranches if you're trying to find an authentic Western experience. They often require a one-week stay, and the cost is all-inclusive. During the busy summer season, from Memorial Day to Labor Day, it's a good idea to book hotels and bed-and-breakfasts in advance. Most motels and resorts have off-season rates. Take advantage of these, because hiking is best in the south in cool weather, and the mountains are beautiful even without snow.

▋ TIP→ **Assume that hotels do not include any meals in their room rates, unless we specify otherwise.**

General Information Utah Hotel & Lodging Association. ☎ 801/593-2213 ⊕ www.uhla. org.

APARTMENT AND HOUSE RENTALS

Increasingly, condos and private homes are available for rent, with more and more options on websites such as Airbnb and Vacation Rentals By Owner. Rentals range from one-night to month-long stays. Enjoy slope-side accommodations with all the amenities of home such as multiple bathrooms and full kitchens at most ski resorts. Condo and home rentals are also available outside Zion, Bryce, Arches, and Canyonlands national parks.

Rental Information Airbnb. ⊕ www.airbnb. com. **Vacation Rentals By Owner.** ⊕ www. vrbo.com.

HOTELS

Most Salt Lake City hotels cater to business travelers with such facilities as restaurants, cocktail lounges, Internet, swimming pools, exercise equipment, and meeting rooms. Most other Utah towns and cities have less expensive hotels that are clean and comfortable but have fewer facilities.

Many properties have special weekend rates, sometimes up to 50% off regular prices. However, these deals are usually not extended during peak months (summer near the national parks and winter in the ski resorts), when hotels are normally full. Salt Lake City hotels are generally full only during major conventions.

All hotels listed have private bath unless otherwise noted.

RESORTS

Ski towns throughout Utah such as Park City, Sundance, and Brian Head, are home to resorts in all price ranges (but primarily high-end); any activities lacking in any individual property are usually available in the town itself—in summer as well as winter. Off the slopes, there are both wonderful rustic and luxurious resorts in the southern part of the state: Red Mountain Resort in St. George, Zion Ponderosa Ranch Resort near Zion, Sorrel River Ranch near Arches, and Amangiri near Lake Powell and Four Corners.

▌DINING OUT

Dining in Utah is generally casual. Menus are becoming more varied, but you can nearly always order a hamburger or a steak. There is a growing number of fine restaurants in Salt Lake City and Park City, and good places are cropping up in various other areas. Also look for good dining in Springdale, Moab, and Torrey. Seek out colorful diners along the secondary highways like U.S. 89; they usually serve up meat and potatoes along with the local flavor of each community. Authentic ethnic food is easy to find in Salt Lake City, but generally not available elsewhere. The restaurants we list are the cream of the crop in each price category.

MEALS AND MEALTIMES

Although you can find all types of cuisine in the major cities and resort towns of Utah, be sure to try native dishes like trout, elk, and buffalo (the latter two have less fat than beef and are just as tasty); organic fruits and vegetables are also readily available, especially in finer establishments in Salt Lake City and Park City. Southwestern food is popular, and you'll find several restaurants that specialize in it or show Southwestern influences in menu selections. Asian and Latin American cuisines are both gaining in popularity (and quality) in the Salt Lake area.

Unless otherwise noted, the restaurants listed in this guide are open daily for lunch and dinner. Dinner hours are usually from 6 to 9 pm. Outside of the large cities and resort towns in the high seasons, many restaurants close by 10 and are closed on Sunday.

RESERVATIONS AND DRESS

Reservations are relatively rare outside of the top restaurants in the urban and resort areas. It's a good idea to call ahead if you can. We only mention them specifically when reservations are essential (there's no other way you'll ever get a table) or when they are not accepted. Large parties should always call ahead to check the reservations policy. We mention dress only when men are required to wear a jacket or a jacket and tie—which is almost never in casual Utah. Even at nice resorts dress is usually casual, and in summer you're welcome nearly everywhere in your shorts, T-shirt, and hiking shoes.

WINES, BEER, AND SPIRITS

Despite what you've heard, it's not hard to get a drink in Utah, though you must be 21 to purchase or consume alcohol. The state overhauled liquor laws in 2009 to bring it more in line with the rest of the United States. The state abolished the "private club" system, which required each patron have an annual or short-term membership in order to enter the premises. Many restaurants have licenses, which allow them to serve you wine and beer—and occasionally liquor—with a meal. At restaurants, you will have to order food in addition to alcohol. Some restaurants—generally those that cater to families—opt not to carry a liquor license. If you're set on having a drink with your meal, check before you go. Some restaurants will allow you to bring your own wine, but may charge a corkage fee. Call ahead if you want to take your own wine or other liquor to a restaurant—lots of regulations cover brown bagging.

Utah has a thriving microbrewery scene, with local lagers produced in Salt Lake City, Park City, Moab, Springdale, Vernal, Ogden, and beyond. There are several brewpubs with their own beers on tap—try Latter Day Stout and Polygamy Porter to get a taste of the local drinking culture. Some brewpubs also have a liquor license that allows the sale of wine and spirits.

Most hotel restaurants carry a liquor license, and you'll be able to get your own drinks from the minibar in your room.

Beer with 3.2% alcohol is available in grocery stores and some convenience stores. For anything else, you'll have to go to a state liquor store. There are 17 liquor stores throughout Salt Lake City and others throughout the state. They are closed on Sunday, Election Day, and holidays.

Note that Utah recently lowered the maximum legal blood alcohol level in drivers from .08% to .05%, giving it the lowest and strictest DUI threshold in the country.

HEALTH

Salt Lake City and Logan are surrounded by mountains, which can trap pollution and create some of the worst air quality in the nation, particularly in winter. Red Alert action days happen several times a year (often for more than a week at a time) when strenuous activity, particularly by young and elderly people, is discouraged. Visit the Utah Department of Environmental Quality website to find out about air quality if you have asthma, allergies, or other breathing sensitivities.

Information Utah Department of Environmental Quality. ⊕ *www.airquality.utah.gov.*

MONEY

Hotel prices in Salt Lake City run the gamut, but on average the prices are a bit lower than in most major cities. You can pay $100–$350 a night for a room in a major business hotel, though some "value" hotel rooms go for $50–$75, and budget motels are also readily available. Weekend packages at city hotels can cut prices in half (but may not be available in peak winter or summer seasons). As a rule, costs outside cities are lower, except in the deluxe resorts, where costs can be at least double those anywhere else in the state. Look for senior and kids' discounts at many attractions.

Prices throughout this guide are given for adults. Substantially reduced fees are almost always available for children, students, and senior citizens.

CREDIT CARDS

Some small-town restaurants may not accept credit cards, but otherwise plastic is readily accepted at dining, lodging, shopping, and other facilities throughout the state. Minimum purchase amounts may apply.

Throughout this guide, we only mention credit cards when they are not accepted.

PACKING

Informality reigns here; jeans, sport shirts, and T-shirts fit in almost everywhere. The few restaurants and performing-arts events where dressier outfits are required, usually in resorts and larger cities, are the exception.

If you plan to spend much time outdoors, and certainly if you go in winter, choose clothing appropriate for cold and wet weather. Cotton clothing, including denim—although fine on warm, dry days—can be uncomfortable and even dangerous when it gets wet and when the weather's cold. A better choice is clothing made of wool or any of a number of new synthetics that provide warmth without bulk and maintain their insulating properties even when wet.

In summer you'll want shorts during the day. But because early morning and night can be cold, and high passes windy, pack a sweater and a light jacket, and perhaps also a wool cap and gloves. Try layering—a T-shirt under another shirt under a jacket—and peel off layers as you go. For walks and hikes, you'll need sturdy footwear. To take you into the wilds, boots should have thick soles and plenty of ankle support; if your shoes are new and you plan to spend much time on the trail, break them in at home. Bring a day pack for short hikes, along with a canteen or water bottle, and don't forget rain gear, a hat, sunscreen, and insect repellent.

In winter, prepare for subfreezing temperatures with good boots, warm socks and liners, thermal underwear, a well-insulated jacket, and a warm hat and mittens. Dress in layers so you can add or remove clothes as the temperatures fluctuate.

If you attend dances and other events at Native American reservations, dress conservatively—skirts or long pants—or you may be asked to leave.

When traveling to mountain areas, remember that sunglasses and a sun hat are essential at high altitudes, even in winter; the thinner atmosphere requires sunscreen with a greater SPF than you might need at lower elevations. Bring moisturizer even if you don't normally use it. Utah's dry climate can be hard on your skin.

■ SAFETY

It's always best to tell someone—the hotel desk clerk, the ski-rental person—where you're going. Cell phones don't always work in the backcountry, and even a general idea of where you are can help rescuers find you quickly. Know your limits.

Many trails are at high altitudes, where oxygen is thinner. They're also frequently desolate. Hikers and bikers should carry a flashlight, a compass, waterproof matches, a first-aid kit, a knife, and a light plastic tarp for shelter. Backcountry skiers should add a repair kit, a blanket, an avalanche beacon, and a lightweight shovel to their lists. Always bring extra food and a canteen of water. Never drink from streams or lakes, unless you boil the water first or purify it with tablets. Giardia, an intestinal parasite, may be present.

Always check the condition of roads and trails, and get the latest weather reports before setting out. In summer take precautions against heat stroke or exhaustion by resting frequently in shaded areas; in winter take precautions against hypothermia by layering clothing.

You may feel dizzy and weak and find yourself breathing heavily—signs that the thin mountain air isn't giving you your accustomed dose of oxygen. Take it easy and rest often for a few days until you're acclimatized. Throughout your stay, drink plenty of water and watch your alcohol consumption, as dehydration is a common occurrence at high altitudes. If you experience severe headaches and nausea, see a doctor. It is easy to go too high too fast. The remedy for altitude-related discomfort is to go down quickly into heavier air.

Flash floods can strike at any time and any place with little or no warning. The danger in mountainous terrain intensifies when distant rains are channeled into gullies and ravines, turning a quiet streamside campsite or wash into a rampaging torrent in seconds; similarly, desert terrain can become dangerous when heavy rains fall on land that is unable to absorb the water and thus floods quickly. Check weather reports before heading into the backcountry, and be prepared to head for higher ground if the weather turns severe.

One of the most wonderful features of Utah is its abundant wildlife. To avoid an unpleasant situation while hiking, make plenty of noise and keep dogs on a leash and small children between adults. While camping, be sure to store all food, utensils, and clothing with food odors far away from your tent, preferably high in a tree or in a bear box. If you do come across a bear or big cat, do not run. For bears or moose, back away while talking calmly; for mountain lions, make yourself look as big as possible. In either case, be prepared to fend off the animal with loud noises, rocks, sticks, and so on. And, as the saying goes, do not feed the bears—or any wild animals, whether they're dangerous or not.

When in any park, give all animals their space. If you want to take a photograph, use a long lens and keep your distance. This is particularly important for winter visitors. Approaching an animal can cause stress and affect its ability to survive the sometimes-brutal climate. In all cases, remember that the animals have the right-of-way; this is their home, and you are the visitor.

■ SPECIAL INTEREST TOURS

BICYCLING
Utah offers a wide range of topography and scenery to satisfy cyclists of all styles. Moab has been heralded for years as a mecca for mountain bikers, but fat-tire lovers pedal all corners and all elevations of the state; bike shops in St. George, Salt

Lake City, Parky City, and Ogden can also help you find an itinerary. Excellent multiday (and multisport) tours crisscross the desert including the incomparable White Rim Trail in Canyonlands National Park. Hard-core road cyclists, including pros in training, challenge themselves by climbing the grueling canyons to the east of Salt Lake City. But there are plenty of roads for the less gonzo rider to explore, and biking is an excellent way for a family to bond while getting some exercise.

■ TIP→ **Most airlines accommodate bikes as luggage for an extra fee, provided they're dismantled and boxed.**

Contacts Bicycle Adventures. ☎ 800/443–6060 ⊕ www.bicycleadventures.com. **Escape Adventures.** ☎ 800/596–2953 ⊕ www.escapeadventures.com. **Rim Tours.** ☎ 435/259–5223, 800/626–7335 ⊕ www.rimtours.com. **Western Spirit.** ☎ 800/845–2453 ⊕ www.westernspirit.com.

FISHING

Close to Salt Lake City, the Provo and Logan rivers are world-class trout-fishing rivers that attract anglers from around the globe. In some parts of the Provo, it is said that there are upward of 7,500 trout per square mile.

Contacts Fish Heads Fly Shop. ⊕ www.fishheadsflyshop.com.

GOLF

From a dozen public courses in the Salt Lake Valley, to world-class courses in Park City, to the sunny southern Utah courses set against red-rock backdrops, Utah offers a proliferation of golf courses, many of which are highlighted on the Utah tourism website (⊕ utah.com/golf-courses). You will find variety in terrain, scenery, and level of difficulty.

HORSEBACK RIDING

You can still throw on some jeans and boots and head out on a multiday horseback trek. Several Utah operators will match you with your steed, give you as much or as little instruction as you need, and get you out on the trail. Excursions

range from day trips to week-long adventures. Find guides and rides on the Utah tourism website (⊕ utah.com/horseback-riding).

RAFTING

For an instant respite from summer heat that ranges from toasty to torrid, book a one-to-five-day river-rafting adventure. Itineraries exist for families with adventurers as young as three years old and range from leisurely multiday floats to days that culminate in unforgettable rapids. Utah's river guides have been at it for decades, and will gladly share river-bottom views of red rock cliffs, petroglyphs, and wildlife. The Utah tourism website (⊕ www.utah.com/raft) is a useful resource.

SKIING

If ever an outdoor activity was synonymous with Utah tourism, skiing is it. The bulk of the state's resorts, known for the fluffy powder that falls on average 400 to 600 inches or more a year, are within a one-hour drive from the Salt Lake City Airport. Ski the same runs that Olympians traversed in 2002: the downhill and slaloms were held at Snowbasin near Ogden, while aerials, slalom, and snowboarding took place at Park City or Deer Valley. Finally, challenge yourself on the Nordic competition trails at Heber Valley's Soldier Hollow Olympic venue. Every ski resort and many private travel agents can assist you with your ski planning. Ski Utah is the state's official and very useful website for ski information; it should be your starting point for any ski activity in the state.

Information SkiUtah. ☎ 800/754–8824 ⊕ www.skiutah.com.

▌ TAXES

State sales tax is 4.7% in Utah. Most areas have additional local sales and lodging taxes, which can be quite significant. For example, in Salt Lake City the combined sales tax is 6.85%, plus a 1% tax on all restaurant checks. Utah sales tax is reduced for some items, such as groceries.

▌ TIME

Utah is in the mountain time zone. In summer Utah observes Daylight Savings Time.

▌ TIPPING

It is customary to tip at least 15% at restaurants; 18%–20% in resort towns is increasingly the norm. For coat checks and bellhops, $1 per coat or bag is the minimum. Taxi drivers expect 15% to 20%, depending on where you are. In resort towns, ski technicians, sandwich makers, coffee baristas, and the like also appreciate tips. For ski instructors, a 10%–15% tip is standard.

TIPPING GUIDELINES FOR UTAH	
Bartender	$1 to $5 per round of drinks, depending on the number of drinks
Bellhop	$1 to $5 per bag, depending on the level of the hotel
Hotel Concierge	$5 or more, if he or she performs a service for you
Hotel Doorman	$1–$2 if he helps you get a cab
Hotel Maid	$1–$3 a day (either daily or at the end of your stay, in cash)
Hotel Room-Service Waiter	$1 to $2 per delivery, even if a service charge has been added
Porter at Airport or Train Station	$1 per bag
Skycap at Airport	$1 to $3 per bag checked
Taxi Driver	15%–20%, but round up the fare to the next dollar amount
Tour Guide	10% of the cost of the tour
Valet Parking Attendant	$1–$2, but only when you get your car
Waiter	15%–20%, with 20% being the norm at high-end restaurants; nothing additional if a service charge is added to the bill

▌ TRIP INSURANCE

Comprehensive trip insurance is valuable if you're booking a very expensive or complicated trip (particularly to an isolated region) or if you're booking far in advance. Comprehensive policies typically cover trip cancellation and interruption, letting you cancel or cut your trip short because of illness, or, in some cases, acts of terrorism in your destination. Such policies might also cover evacuation and medical care. Some also cover you for trip delays because of bad weather or mechanical problems as well as for lost or delayed luggage.

Another type of coverage to consider is financial default—that is, when your trip is disrupted because a tour operator or airline goes out of business. Generally you must buy this when you book your trip or shortly thereafter, and it's available to you only if your operator isn't on a list of excluded companies.

Always read the fine print of your policy to make sure that you're covered for the risks that most concern you. Compare several policies to be sure you're getting the best price and range of coverage available.

Comprehensive Insurers AIG Travel Guard. ☎ *800/826–5248* ⊕ *www.travelguard.com.* **Allianz Global Assistance.** ☎ *866/884–3556* ⊕ *www.allianztravelinsurance.com.* **Generali Global Assistance.** ☎ *800/874–2442* ⊕ *www. generalitravelinsurance.com.* **Travelex Insurance.** ☎ *800/228–9792* ⊕ *www.travelexinsurance.com.* **Travel Insured International.** ☎ *800/243–3174* ⊕ *www.travelinsured.com.*

Insurance Comparison Information Insure My Trip. ☎ *800/487–4722* ⊕ *www.insuremytrip.com.* **Square Mouth.** ☎ *800/240–0369* ⊕ *www.squaremouth.com.*

▮ VISITOR INFORMATION

Utah Office of Tourism has an excellent website, and its office (across the street from the state capitol) is open weekdays.

Contacts Utah Office of Tourism. ✉ *Council Hall, Capitol Hill, 300 N. State St., Salt Lake City* ☎ *801/538–1900, 800/200–1160* ⊕ *www. visitutah.com.*

INSPIRATION: BOOKS AND MOVIES

The desert environment has been explored by a host of writers: Everett Reuss (*A Vagabond for Beauty*); Terry Tempest Williams (*Refuge: An Unnatural History of Family and Place*); Edward Abbey (*Desert Solitaire*); Wallace Stegner (*Mormon Country*); Jon Krakauer (*Under the Banner of Heaven*).

Utah's famous desert landscape makes it a top destination for filmmakers as well: *How the West Was Won* (1963); *2001: A Space Odyssey* (1968); *Butch Cassidy and the Sundance Kid* (1969); *Thelma and Louise* (1991); *High School Musical* (2006); *The Tree of Life* (2008); *127 Hours* (2011); and many more.

INDEX

A

Abravanel Hall, 65
Accommodations, 298
Agua Canyon, 191
Ailulia (shop), 124
Air tours, 144, 193, 259
Air travel, 18, 294–295
Arches National Park, 230
Bryce Canyon National Park, 187
Canyonlands National Park, 253
Capitol Reef National Park, 156
Dinosaurland and Eastern Utah, 136
Moab and Southeastern Utah, 272, 290
North of Salt Lake City, 117
Park City and the Southern Wasatch, 84
Salt Lake City, 38
Southwestern Utah, 206–207
Zion National Park, 171
Alpine Loop Scenic Byway, 80
Alta Ski Resort, 72, 74
Amangiri ⊞, 291–292
Amid Summer's Inn Bed & Breakfast ⊞, 211
Anasazi State Park, 163
Antelope Island State Park, 77–78
Apartment and house rentals, 298
Arches Main Park Road, 233
Arches National Park, 17, 225–248
camping, 247
festivals, 228–229
itineraries, 229–230
lodging, 232, 246–248
nightlife and the arts, 243
permits, 230–231
plants and wildlife, 233
restaurants, 232, 244–246
scenic drives, 233, 244
shopping, 243
sports and the outdoors, 235–242
transportation, 230
visitor information, 232, 242
Art galleries. ⇨See Museums and art galleries

B

Balanced Rock, 226, 230, 234
Banks. ⇨See Money matters
Baseball, 50
Basketball, 51
Bear Lake, 115
Bear Lake Country, 115, 129–132
Bear Lake State Park, 129–130
Beehive House, 40
Behunin Cabin, 158
Best Western Canyonlands Inn ⊞, 246, 284
Bicknell, 162
Bicycling, 19
Arches National Park, 236–237
Bryce Canyon National Park, 198
Canyonlands National Park, 259–260
Capitol Reef National Park, 159–160
Dinosaurland and Eastern Utah, 135, 140, 144, 148
Moab and Southeastern Utah, 278–279
North of Salt Lake City, 121, 130
Park City and the Southern Wasatch, 92–93, 110
Salt Lake City and environs, 51, 63, 73–74, 78
Southwestern Utah, 212, 215, 223
tours, 177, 198, 301–302
Zion National Park, 176–177
Big Cottonwood Canyon, 69, 71–72
Bird-watching, 48, 190, 193, 214, 237
Blanding, 266
Blanding Visitor Center, 266
Bluff, 266
Buff International Balloon Festival, 266
Boating, 130, 148–149, 237, 260, 291
Books, 160, 192, 235, 243, 286
Boulder, 163
Brian Head, 212–213
Brigham Young's Winter Home, 214
Browns Park, 143
Bryce Amphitheater, 184
Bryce Canyon Lodge ⊞, 191, 201

B (continued)

Bryce Canyon National Park, 16, 183–202
campgrounds, 202
festivals, 186–187
itineraries, 187
lodging, 189–190, 201–202
permits, 188
plants and wildlife, 190
restaurants, 189, 199–201
scenic drives, 191, 199
shopping, 196
sports and the outdoors, 193–196, 198
tours, 193, 196, 198
transportation, 187–188
visitor information, 190, 197
Bryce Canyon Visitor Center, 191
Bus travel, 38–39, 85, 156, 188, 277

C

Cafe Diablo ✕, 165
Cali Cochitta Bed & Breakfast ⊞, 247, 284
Camping
Arches National Park, 247
Bryce Canyon National Park, 202
Canyonlands National Park, 268
Capitol Reef National Park, 166
Dinosaurland and Eastern Utah, 136, 150
Park City and the Southern Wasatch, 85–86
Canyon Overlook Trail, 178
Canyon Voyages Adventure Company, 237
Canyonlands National Park, 17, 249–268
camping, 268
itineraries, 252–253
lodging, 255, 268
permits, 254
plants and wildlife, 257
restaurants, 255
scenic drives, 256
shopping, 267
sports and the outdoors, 258–265
tours, 259
transportation, 253–254
visitor information, 255–256
Canyonlands PRCA Rodeo, 229
Capitol Dome, 158

Capitol Gorge, 158
Capitol Reef National Park, 15, 151–166
camping, 166
festivals, 155
itineraries, 155–156
lodging, 157, 166
nightlife and the arts, 164
permits, 156
restaurants, 157, 165
scenic drives, 158, 164
shopping, 164–165
sports and outdoors, 159–162, 163
transportation, 156
visitor information, 157
Car travel and rentals, 18, 295–297
Arches National Park, 230
Bryce Canyon National Park, 188
Canyonlands National Park, 253
Capitol Reef National Park, 156
Dinosaurland and Eastern Utah, 136–137
Moab and Southeastern Utah, 272, 290
North of Salt Lake City, 117
Park City and the Southern Wasatch, 84–85
Salt Lake City, 24
Southwestern Utah, 207
Zion National Park, 171
Castle Country, 137–141
Cathedral of the Madeleine, 44
Cathedral Valley, 160
Cedar Breaks National Monument, 197, 212
Cedar City, 197, 208–211
Centro Woodfired Pizzeria ✕, 200, 210
Checkerboard Mesa, 176
Children, attractions for, 30
Arches National Park, 229, 231, 232, 234–235, 237, 239, 243, 245, 246
Bryce Canyon National Park, 186–187, 189, 194–195, 196, 198, 199, 200
Canyonlands National Park, 254, 255, 257, 263, 265, 267
Capitol Reef National Park, 155, 156–157, 158–159, 161, 163
Dinosaurland and Eastern Utah, 139, 140, 141, 143, 145, 146, 149

Moab and Southeastern Utah, 274, 276, 279, 280, 282, 283, 284, 286, 287
North of Salt Lake City, 119, 120, 123, 124, 125–126, 130, 131, 132
Park City and the Southern Wasatch, 87–88, 89, 91, 95–96, 100, 102, 103, 106, 107
Salt Lake City and environs, 38, 41–42, 43, 47–48, 49, 50, 51, 52, 54, 58, 59, 61–62, 67, 68, 79
Southwestern Utah, 211, 214, 215, 216, 218, 219, 222
Zion National Park, 171, 173, 178, 179–180, 181
Chimney Rock, 158
Church of Jesus Christ of Latter-day Saints Conference Center, 40–41
City and County Building, 42–43
City Creek Canyon, 51
Clark Planetarium, 43
Cleveland-Lloyd Dinosaur Quarry, 139
Colorado River Scenic Byway - Route 128, 244, 275–276
Colorado River Scenic Byway - Route 279, 276
Community Contra Dance, 284
Condo rentals, 105
Contender Bicycles, 51
Copper Onion ✕, 53
Coral Pink Sand Dunes Park, 180
Court of the Patriarchs, 176
Courthouse Towers, 226
Cowboy Line Camp, 257
Credit cards, 11

D
Daughters of the Utah Pioneers Museum (Cedar City), 210
Dead Horse Point State Park, 266–267, 276
Deer Valley Resort, 95
Deer Valley Snow Park Amphitheater, 87
Delicate Arch, 226, 234
Delicate Arch Trail, 229, 239–240
Desert Bistro ✕, 281
Devils Garden, 226, 230
Devils Garden Trail, 240
Dining. ⇨See Restaurants

Dinosaur National Monument, 145–147
Dinosaur National Monument Quarry Exhibit Hall, 146
Dinosaur sites, 24
Dinosaurland and Eastern Utah, 135, 139, 140, 142, 143, 144, 145, 146
North of Salt Lake City, 119
Southwestern Utah, 205, 215
Dinosaurland and Eastern Utah, 15, 133–150
campgrounds, 136, 150
festivals, 139, 142, 143
lodging, 137, 141, 145, 149
nightlife and the arts, 141
restaurants, 137, 140–141, 144–145
sports and the outdoors, 140, 144, 146–147, 148–149, 150
tours, 144, 147
transportation, 136–137, 142
visitor information, 137, 142
Discovery Gateway Children's Museum, 41
Dixie National Forest, 197, 210
Double Arch, 230, 234
Dry Fork Canyon, 143

E
Eastern Utah. ⇨See Dinosaurland and Eastern Utah
Eccles Community Art Center, 120
Edge of the Cedars State Park Museum, 267
Eklecticafe ✕, 244, 282
El Chubasco ✕, 99
Escalante, 197, 221–224
Escalante Petrified Forest State Park, 198, 222

F
Fairyland Point, 191
Farm, The ✕, 99
Ferry travel, 290–291
Festivals and seasonal events, 18
Arches National Park, 228–229
Bryce Canyon National Park, 186–187
Capitol Reef National Park, 155
Dinosaurland and Eastern Utah, 139, 142, 143
Moab and Southeastern Utah, 229, 271, 274
North of Salt Lake City, 130
Park City and the Southern Wasatch, 87–89, 112

Salt Lake City, 35, 38
Southwestern Utah, 209, 214
Fiery Furnace, 226, 231, 234, 241
Firewood ✕, 99
Fishing, 19–20, 93, 109, 131, 148–149, 163, 238, 291
tours, 302
Flaming Gorge Dam Visitor Center, 147
Flaming Gorge National Recreation Area, 147–149
Fly fishing, 20, 93, 109
Fort Buenaventura Park, 120
Foundry Grill ✕, 110
Four-wheeling, 160, 235, 236, 238, 261, 277–278
Fremont Petroglyphs, 158
Freshies Lobster Co. ✕, 99
Frontier Homestead State Park Museum, 210
Fruita Historic District, 158–159

G

Gallivan Center, 43
Gateway Mall, 41
Geology, 111
George S. Eccles Dinosaur Park, 119
Goblin Valley State Park, 163, 289
Golden Spike Empire, 114, 127–129
Golden Spike National Historic Site, 128–129
Golf, 131
tours, 302
Grafton, 218
Grand America Hotel, The 🏨, 61
Grand Staircase-Escalante National Monument, 198, 204, 220–224
Grand View Point, 257
Great Salt Lake, 49, 50
Great Salt Lake State Park, 49
Great White Throne, 176
Green River, 242, 287
Green River Overlook, 257
Green River State Park, 287

H

Hampton Inn and Suites 🏨, 122
Handle ✕, 100
Hanksville, 163
Hatch Family Chocolates ✕, 45
Health concerns, 300
Hell's Backbone Grill ✕, 165

High West Distillery ✕, 100
Highway 12 Scenic Byway, 199, 222
Hiking, 20–21
Arches National Park, 238–241
Bryce Canyon National Park, 193–195
Canyonlands National Park, 262–265
Capitol Reef National Park, 161–162
Dinosaurland and Eastern Utah, 140, 144, 146, 149
Moab and Southeastern Utah, 278
North of Salt Lake City, 121, 125, 131
Park City and the Southern Wasatch, 93–94, 109
Salt Lake City environs, 69, 73, 74
Southwestern Utah, 210, 215, 223
Zion National Park, 177–179
Hill Aerospace Museum, 115, 119
Hire's Big H ✕, 59
Historic 25th Street District, 115, 119
Hogle Zoo, 47
Horse racing, 216
Horseback riding, 21–22, 94, 125, 179–180, 195–196
tours, 302
Horseshoe Canyon Trail, 250
Hot-air ballooning, 94, 266
Hotels, 11, 298. ⇨See also Lodging

I

Ice-skating, 51–52, 94, 120
Inspiration Point, 191–192
Island in the Sky Park Road (Canyonlands National Park), 250, 256
Itineraries, 26–29. ⇨See also under specific cities and areas

J

John Jarvie Ranch, 143
John Wesley Powell River History Museum, 243, 287
Joint Trail, 265

K

Kayaking, 121, 235
Kearns Mansion, 44
Kimball Art Center, 91

Kimpton Hotel Monaco Salt Lake City 🏨, 61
Kodachrome Basin State Park, 198, 223
Kolob Canyon Road, 174

L

Lake Powell, 290–292
Lake Powell Ferry, 291
Landscape Arch, 230
Layla Grill and Mezze ✕, 59–60
Leonardo, The, 41–42
Liberty Park, 48, 52
Little Cottonwood Canyon, 72–77
Lodging, 11. ⇨See also Hotels
Logan Canyon Drive, 129
Logan Canyon National Scenic Byway, 115, 129
Log Haven ✕, 60
Lucky 13 Bar and Grill ✕, 59

M

Main Park Road (Bryce Canyon National Park), 191
Maynard Dixon Living History Museum, 180
Maze, The, 250
Memory Grove Park, 45
Mesa Arch, 257
Mesa Arch Trail, 263
Mirror Lake, 150
Mirror Lake Scenic Byway, 149–150
Moab and Southeastern Utah, 17, 226, 242, 266, 269–292
festivals, 229, 271, 274
itineraries, 271
lodging, 273, 283–285, 289–290, 291–292
nightlife and the arts, 284, 285
restaurants, 273, 281–283, 289
shopping, 285–286
sports and the outdoors, 271, 277–281, 289, 291
tours, 274–275
transportation, 272, 287, 290–291
visitor information, 275, 287, 291
Moab Arts Festival, 229, 274
Moab Information Center, 275
Moab Music Festival, 274
Money matters, 300
Montage Deer Valley 🏨, 103
Monticello, 266
Mormon Tabernacle, 40

Mountain biking. ⇨*See*
  Bicycling
Mountain Town Music, *106*
Museum of Church History and
  Art, *41*
Museum of Moab, *243, 276*
Museums and art galleries
  Arches National Park, 243
  Canyonlands National Park,
    267
  Capitol Reef National Park,
    158–159
  Dinosaurland and Eastern Utah,
    140, 143, 146, 147, 148
  Moab and Southeastern Utah,
    243, 276, 287
  North of Salt Lake City, 115,
    119, 120, 124
  Park City and the Southern
    Wasatch, 91, 107
  Salt Lake City, 38, 40, 41–42,
    43, 44, 45, 47, 49, 68
  Southwestern Utah, 210, 214,
    215, 219, 224
  Zion National Park, 175, 180

N

Narrows, The, *176*
Narrows Trail, *179*
Natural Bridge, *192*
Natural Bridges National Mon-
  ument, *267, 290*
Natural History Museum of
  Utah, *47*
Needles District Park Road
  (Canyonlands National Park),
    250, 256
Night Sky Program, *189*
Nine Mile Canyon, *139*
No Name Saloon, *105–106*
North of Salt Lake City, *14–15,*
    113–132
  festivals, 130
  itineraries, 116
  lodging, 118, 122, 127, 132
  nightlife and the arts, 123
  restaurants, 118, 121–122,
    127, 132
  shopping, 123–124
  sports and the outdoors, 121,
    125–127, 130–131
  transportation, 117, 119, 125,
    129–130
  visitor information, 118
Northeast-Central Utah,
    137–141

O

Ogden, *118–124*
Ogden City & Valley, *114,*
    118–127
Ogden Nature Center, *120*
Ogden's Own Distillery, *124*
Old Town Guest House 🖫, *104*
Olympic Cauldron Park, *47*

P

Packing, *300–301*
Painted Pony ✕, *217*
Panguitch, *197*
Park City and the Southern
  Wasatch, *14, 81–112*
  camping, 85–86
  exploring, 89–92
  festivals, 87–89, 112
  lodging, 85, 102–105, 110
  nightlife and arts, 105–106,
    110–112
  restaurants, 85, 98–102, 110
  shopping, 107, 112
  South of Salt Lake City, 82,
    108–112
  sports and the outdoors, 92–98,
    109–110
  transportation, 84–85
  visitor information, 86, 87
Park City Kimball Arts Festival,
    88
Park City Mountain Resort, *89,*
    91, 95–96
Park City Museum, *91*
Park Silly Sunday Market, *91*
Peery's Egyptian Theater, *123*
Permits, *156, 172, 188,*
    230–231, 254
Petrified Dunes, *226*
Pets, *238*
Phillips Gallery, *38*
Picnic areas, *181, 244*
Pineview Reservoir, *125*
Pioneer Day, *18*
Pioneer Memorial Museum, *45*
Pioneer Register, *159*
Plan-B Theater, *67*
Poison Spider Bicycles, *236,*
    278–279
Pony Express Trail, *70*
Pothole Point Trail, *258*
Powder Mountain, *126*
Prehistoric Museum USU East-
  ern, *140*
Price, *138–141*
Price categories, *11*
  dining, 53, 86, 137, 157, 173,
    190, 208, 232, 255, 273

lodging, 60, 86, 137, 157, 173,
    190, 208, 232, 255, 273

Q

Queen's Garden Trail, *194*

R

Rafting, *22, 94–95, 121,*
    146–147, 149, 235, 236, 250,
    260, 280
  tours, 302
Rainbow Point, *184, 192*
Ranger programs, *156–157,*
    172–173, 189, 231, 254–255
Red Butte Garden and Arbore-
  tum, *47–48*
Red Canyon Lodge 🖫, *149*
Red Canyon Visitor Center,
    147–148
Red Iguana ✕, *55*
Red Mountain Resort 🖫, *217*
Red Rock Grill ✕, *127*
Religion, *18*
Restaurants, *11, 24–25, 52–60,*
    299–300
River expeditions, *280, 289*
Riverhorse on Main ✕, *101*
Rock climbing, *95, 241–242,*
    265, 281
Rodeos, *216, 229*
Rosenbruch Wildlife Museum,
    214
Ruth's Diner ✕, *59*

S

Sabaku Sushi ✕, *245–246, 283*
Safety concerns, *20, 301*
St. George, *213–218*
St. George Art Museum, *215*
St. George Dinosaur Discovery
  Site at Johnson Farm, *215*
St. George Tabernacle, *215*
St. George Temple, *215*
St. Regis Deer Valley 🖫, *104*
Saloman Center, *120*
Salt Lake City, *14, 31–80*
  Capitol Hill and the Avenues,
    34, 43–45, 58, 62
  downtown, 34, 41–43, 53–55,
    58, 61–62
  East Side and University of
    Utah, 34, 45–49, 58–59, 63
  exploring, 39–49, 73, 77–78,
    79–80
  festivals, 35, 38
  Great Salt Lake, 34–35, 49, 50
  lodging, 60–64, 71–72, 76
  nightlife and the arts, 64–67,
    72, 77

North of, 14–15
restaurants, 45, 52–60, 75–76, 78
shopping, 67–69, 79
side trips, 69–80
sports and the outdoors, 49–52, 69–71, 73, 78
Temple Square, 34, 40–41
timing the visit, 35, 38
tours, 39
transportation, 38–39, 69, 73, 79
visitor information, 39, 73
Wasatch Front, 35
Salt Lake City Public Library, 42
Salt Lake City Sports Complex, 51–52
Salt Lake Temple, 40
San Rafael Swell, 140, 163
Scott M. Matheson Wetlands Preserve, 237, 276–277
Sego Canyon Rock Art Panels, 287
Shafer Trail, 256
Sheep Creek Canyon Geological Area, 148
Sherald's ✕, 141
Shooting Star Saloon ✕, 127
Shopping
Arches National Park, 243
Bryce Canyon National Park, 196
Canyonlands National Park, 267
Capitol Reef National Park, 164–165
Moab and Southeastern Utah, 285–286
North of Salt Lake City, 123–124
Park City and the Southern Wasatch, 107, 112
Salt Lake City, 67–69, 79
Southwestern Utah, 218, 219, 224
Skiing, 18, 22–23
Bryce Canyon National Park, 196
North of Salt Lake City, 115, 125–126, 131
Park City and the Southern Wasatch, 95–97, 110
Salt Lake City, 52, 71, 74–75
Southwestern Utah, 212–213
tours, 75, 97, 302
Zion National Park, 180
Skydiving, 281
Skyline Arch, 234

Snow Canyon State Park, 180, 215
Snow tubing, 98
Snowbird Ski and Summer Resort, 72, 73–74, 75, 77
Snowboarding, 22–23, 95–97, 212–213
Snowmobiling, 126–127
Snowshoeing, 180, 196
Soccer, 52
Sorrel River Ranch ⌸, 285
South of Salt Lake City, 82, 108–112
Southeastern Utah. ⇨See Moab and Southeastern Utah
Southern Wasatch. ⇨See Park City and the Southern Wasatch
Southwestern Utah, 203–224
festivals, 209, 214
lodging, 207–208, 211, 213, 217, 219, 224
nightlife and the arts, 217–218
restaurants, 207, 210–211, 213, 216–217, 218–219, 222, 223–224
shopping, 218, 219, 224
sports and the outdoors, 210, 212–213, 215–216, 223
timing the visit, 205
tours, 210, 214, 215, 221–222
transportation, 206–207, 209, 212, 221
visitor information, 208, 210, 214, 221
Spirit Lake Scenic Backway, 148
Spiral Jetty, 129
Sports and outdoor activities, 19–23
Arches National Park, 235–242
Bryce Canyon National Park, 193–196, 198
Canyonlands National Park, 258–265
Capitol Reef National Park, 159–162, 163
Dinosaurland and Eastern Utah, 140, 144, 146–147, 148–149, 150
Moab and Southeastern Utah, 271, 277–281, 289, 291
North of Salt Lake City, 121, 125–127, 130–131
Park City and the Southern Wasatch, 92–98, 109–110
Salt Lake City and environs, 48, 49–52, 69–71, 73–75, 77, 78, 79–80

Southwestern Utah, 210, 212–213, 215–216, 223
Zion National Park, 176–180
Springdale, 218–219
Stein Erikson Lodge ⌸, 104
Sugar House Business District, 48
Sugar House Park, 48, 52
Sundance Film Festival, 18, 38, 89, 112
Sundance Resort, 83, 108–112
Sundance Resort ⌸, 110
Sunrise Point, 192
Sunset Point, 192
Swaner Preserve & EcoCenter, 91–92
Swett Ranch, 148
Swimming, 180
Symbols, 11

T

Taxes, 302
Taxis, 39
Teasdale, 162
Temple Square, 34, 40–41
Thanksgiving Point, 79
This Is the Place Heritage Park, 48
Time, 303
Timing the visit, 18
Timpanogos Cave National Monument, 79–80
Tipping, 303
Tona Sushi Bar and Grill ✕, 122
Tony Caputo's Market and Deli ✕, 58
Torrey, 162
Tour operators
Bryce Canyon National Park, 193, 196, 198
Canyonlands National Park, 259
Dinosaurland and Eastern Utah, 144, 147
Moab and Southeastern Utah, 274–275
Park City and the Southern Wasatch, 93, 94, 97
Salt Lake City, 39
Southwestern Utah, 210, 214, 215, 221–222
Zion National Park, 173, 177, 179–180
Tracy Aviary, 48
Train travel, 38–39, 117, 230, 254, 297
Tree Room ✕, 110
Treehouse Museum, 120

Trip insurance, *303*
Trolley Square, *48–49*

U

U.S. 89/Utah's Heritage Highway, *199*
Uinta Basin (Dinosaurland), *142–150*
Uintah County Heritage Museum, *143*
Under-the-Rim Trail, *184*
Union Pacific Building, *43*
Union Station (Ogden), *120*
Upheaval Dome, *257*
Upper Provo Falls, *150*
Utah Arts Festival, *38*
Utah Field House of Natural History State Park, *143*
Utah Museum of Fine Arts, *49*
Utah Olympic Oval, *52*
Utah Olympic Park, *91*
Utah Shakespearean Festival, *187, 209*
Utah State Capitol, *45*
Utah's Dixie, *204, 208–219*

V

Valley of the Gods, *267*
Vernal, *142–145*
Vernal Brewing Company ✕, *145*
Visitor information, *304.* ⇨*See also* under specific cities and areas

W

Wahso ✕, *102*
Waldorf Astoria Park City 🏨, *104*
Washington School House 🏨, *105*
Waterpocket Fold, *159*
Weather, *18, 35, 83, 115, 136, 154–155, 170–171, 186, 205, 228, 252, 271*
Weeping Rock, *176*
White Pine Touring, *97*
Wildlife preserves
  Scott M. Matheson Wetlands Preserve, *237, 276–277*
Windows, The, *226, 230, 234–235*
Winter sports, *180, 196*
Wolfe Ranch, *226, 233*
Wooden Shoe Arch, *258*
Worthington Gallery, *219*

Y

Yovimpa Point, *184, 192*

Z

Zion Human History Museum, *175*
Zion Lodge, *175*
Zion-Mount Carmel Highway and Tunnels, *175*
Zion National Park, *16, 167–182*
  camping, *182*
  festivals, *171*
  itineraries, *170–171*
  lodging, *173, 182*
  permits, *172*
  plants and wildlife, *168*
  restaurants, *173, 181, 182*
  scenic drives, *174–175*
  sports and the outdoors, *176–180*
  tours, *173*
  transportation, *171*
  visitor information, *174*
Zoos, *47*

Fodor's UTAH

Editorial: Douglas Stallings, *Editorial Director*; Margaret Kelly, Jacinta O'Halloran, *Senior Editors*; Kayla Becker, Alexis Kelly, Amanda Sadlowski, *Editors*; Teddy Minford, *Content Editor*; Rachael Roth, *Content Manager*

Design: Tina Malaney, *Design and Production Director*; Jessica Gonzalez, *Production Designer*

Photography: Jennifer Arnow, *Senior Photo Editor*

Maps: Rebecca Baer, *Senior Map Editor*; David Lindroth, Inc., Ed Jacobus, and Mark Stroud (Moon Street Cartography), *Cartographers*

Production: Jennifer DePrima, *Editorial Production Manager*; Carrie Parker, *Senior Production Editor*; Elyse Rozelle, *Production Editor*

Business & Operations: Chuck Hoover, *Chief Marketing Officer*; Joy Lai, *Vice President and General Manager*; Stephen Horowitz, *Director of Business Development and Revenue Operations*; Tara McCrillis, *Director of Publishing Operations*; Eliza D. Aceves, *Content Operations Manager and Strategist*

Public Relations and Marketing: Joe Ewaskiw, *Manager*; Esther Su, *Marketing Manager*

Writers: John Blodgett, Aly Capito, Johanna Droubay, Kwynn Gonzalez-Pons, Caitlin Martz Streams

Editor: Rachael Roth

Production Editor: Carrie Parker

6th Edition

ISBN 978-1-64097-034-2

ISSN 1547–870X

SPECIAL SALES

This book is available at special discounts for bulk purchases for sales promotions or premiums. For more information, e-mail SpecialMarkets@fodors.com.

PRINTED IN THE UNITED STATES OF AMERICA

10 9 8 7 6 5 4 3 2 1

ABOUT OUR WRITERS

Writer **John Blodgett** moved to Utah three times in 16 years and still visits often. He's explored almost every corner of the Beehive State, but has a particular passion for the south's silent canyons and wide-open lands. He also became a better skier schussing Utah's famous powder. Currently based in Libby, Montana, he has written for *Utah Business, Salt Lake Magazine, Utah Homes & Garden, Salt Lake City Weekly,* and *Catalyst*; and is now an editor, reporter, and photojournalist at The Western News. He updated the chapters on Capitol Reef, Zion, Bryce Canyon, Arches, and Canyonlands national parks.

Aly Capito updated our Moab and Southeastern Utah, Dinosaurland and Eastern Utah, and Southwestern Utah chapters.

Johanna Droubay was raised in the beautiful Ogden Valley and recently relocated from Virginia to live there with her family. She is a freelance writer and editor, and a communications consultant for schools. Her work has been published by *Potomac Review, The American Scholar, Willamette Week*, and multiple alumni magazines. She is writing a memoir about returning to Utah. She updated the North of Salt Lake City, Experience, and Travel Smart chapters.

Kwynn Gonzalez-Pons is currently pursuing a PhD in social work, while also contributing to publications including *Crixeo, Rewire,* and the *Foster Care Roundup* as a freelance writer. She is a full-time resident of Salt Lake City. She updated the Salt Lake City chapter.

Caitlin Martz Streams is a Denver-based mountain enthusiast who spent 6 years living the dream in Park City, Utah. By day she is a tourism and hospitality public relations professional, and by night/weekends/every available spare hour she can be found in the mountains skiing, camping, hiking, or mountain biking with her husband, Ryan. Her second-greatest passion—travel—means she takes every opportunity to explore new places around the world, and of course, travel back to where her heart will always be: Utah. She updated the Park City chapter.